Industrial-Strength Denial

EIGHT STORIES OF CORPORATIONS
DEFENDING THE INDEFENSIBLE,
FROM THE SLAVE TRADE
TO CLIMATE CHANGE

Barbara Freese

UNIVERSITY OF CALIFORNIA PRESS

The publisher and the University of California Press Foundation gratefully acknowledge the generous support of the Anne G. Lipow Endowment Fund in Social Justice and Human Rights.

University of California Press
Oakland, California

© 2020 by Barbara Freese

Cataloging-in-Publication Data is on file at the Library of Congress.

ISBN 9780520296282 (cloth)
ISBN 9780520968851 (ebook)

Manufactured in the United States of America

29 28 27 26 25 24 23 22 21 20
10 9 8 7 6 5 4 3 2 1

Industrial-Strength Denial

Contents

Introduction

A DANGEROUS PHENOMENON

The head of the biggest American tobacco company said to a journalist in 1998, "Do I feel badly about selling cigarettes? No I do not, and I don't know why I should." He explained, "Nobody knows what you'd turn to if you didn't smoke. Maybe you'd beat your wife. Maybe you'd drive cars fast. Who knows what the hell you'd do?" Two years later, this CEO told a newspaper that he had quit smoking on the advice of his doctor. There was no mention in the article of whether he then turned to domestic abuse or reckless driving.

This book tells the stories of eight major campaigns of corporate denial—a term I use to broadly include the lies, delusions, and rationalizations that emerge when people working in competitive, profit-driven group enterprises are faced with powerful evidence that they are causing harm. Tobacco is the poster-child of this phenomenon, but we have seen it from people selling many other risky products, creating workplace hazards, or releasing dangerous pollutants. Previous generations even saw it from people in the business of selling and owning their fellow human beings.

In almost every case, the story begins with an exciting discovery—of, for example, a New World, a new element or chemical, a new means of mass production, or a new way of packaging financial risk. An industry races to exploit that discovery and succeeds, sometimes changing society along the way. And in each case this commercial activity causes a grave harm to other people or the planet. Those outside the industry find evidence of this harm, raise the alarm, and a public debate ensues. Corporate representatives offer a flurry of denials, perpetuating the harm by blocking policies that would reduce it. The specific denials—which are the focus of this book—vary, but the themes echo from campaign to campaign.

Each chapter also describes how other people challenge the industry's denials and eventually reduce the harm, usually through a mix of evidence gathering, media attention, lawsuits, social activism, political movements, and new laws. While it was not my intent when I began, these chapters stand as a handy reminder of just why so many types of corporate activity need to be monitored, challenged, and regulated.

It is no surprise that those working for corporations accused of causing harm would deny it; many of us would be surprised by the lack of such denials. Some people just shrug, viewing the denials with a kind of boys-will-be-boys and corporations-will-be-corporations acceptance. Others shake their heads in condemnation, chalking the denials up to greed. What such resigned acceptance and blanket moral judgment have in common is a failure to take a closer look at this dangerous phenomenon. But corporate denial is worth some serious attention.

For one thing, this rich realm of reality distortion offers a revealing window into the human mind. The struggle to understand reality may be interesting, but the struggle to *avoid* unwelcome realities is fascinating, demanding far more mental acrobatics. When this struggle plays out within a group dynamic—with inventive and motivated groups urging others to accept a skewed view of the facts, sometimes with life and death consequences—you have an epic human drama. The body of denials proffered by industry after industry can be seen as both its own genre of fiction and its own subfield of psychology.

Moreover, we should study corporate denial because corporations dominate our economy and shape our democracy, and for a huge proportion of Americans, corporate incentives, pressures, norms, and culture govern our work lives. In America, about seven of every ten members of the labor force work in for-profit corporations (and about half of these in businesses of over five hundred employees). Picture the output of the nation's workforce as great river of human effort, skill, and creativity and then realize that most of this river flows through a corporate setting. Surely, we need to better understand how this dominant but artificial form of human organization affects our mental processes and moral behavior, including the extremes of denial it can foster.

It is also worth looking at corporate denial for the light it sheds on two defining controversies of our own moment in history. The first is the growing dispute over what is actually, factually true, and how society should determine that—a sort of metadispute that includes everything from the reality of climate change to the size of inauguration crowds. We live in a highly polarized political era many call "post-truth," where the perception of objective reality that was once widely shared across society has been fractured. This is usually seen as a result of social media and cable news, which let people live in partisan information bubbles that confirm what they believe, dismissing unwelcome information as "fake news" or hopelessly biased. Certainly the new information landscape has fueled this trend, but corporate denial helped usher in the current era with decades of skewing facts, eroding social trust, and inviting people to embrace the reality they prefer rather than the one the evidence supports.

The second controversy is over corporate power and social responsibility. Every few decades this issue rises from the background hum of social controversies to command broader attention, and this is one of those times. In the United States, the libertarian right—promoting a faith in unregulated capitalism that was till recently considered extreme—largely dominates the Republican Party. While the Trump administration deviates from this market fundamentalism in some ways (like its taste for tariffs), it is indeed unraveling many environmental, financial, and other limits on corporate behavior, while stocking the federal judiciary with judges who appear inclined to continue the unraveling for years to come.

Meanwhile, a growing segment of society, on the political left and in the middle, is calling for a far more activist government to rein in corporate power and address grave social problems linked to unregulated capitalism, including income inequality and climate change. This push for a more muscular government response could reshape the Democratic Party just as the libertarian right has reshaped the Republican Party, and could usher in major policy shifts in the years ahead. As we consider how to handle the social harms caused by corporate activity, it helps to remember how some of yesterday's harms—and the denials associated with them—were handled.

PUTTING AN ONGOING DANGER INTO HISTORICAL CONTEXT

While corporate denial is nothing new, our era may be looked back upon as a golden age of it, thanks to the world-threatening example of climate denial. A strong scientific consensus about the threat of climate change began emerging decades ago. By 1992 it was compelling enough to spur adoption of a global treaty aimed at preventing dangerous warming—a treaty the US Senate ratified and a Republican president signed. Since then thousands of scientists have been gathering and assessing the data, tracking the melting ice sheets and growing storms, and projecting severe and irreversible changes ahead. A rare joint statement by the national scientific academies of the United States and twelve other major nations bluntly warned in 2009 that "the need for urgent action to address climate change is now indisputable." Since then, the need for action, including dramatically cutting our heat-trapping emissions, has only grown more urgent. We now face the daunting challenge of replacing much of today's global fossil fuel infrastructure with a new energy infrastructure by 2030 and replacing most of the rest of it by roughly mid-century.

For a time, addressing climate change was a relatively bipartisan issue in the United States, but then denial of the climate threat captured the Republican Party and then the federal government. Today, climate denial is deeply entangled with the nation's larger political polarization, but it did not start there. Climate denial had been cultivated for years by the industries most heavily invested in selling and burning fossil fuels (merging later with other interests ideologically opposed to government regulation in general). Those industries worked hard to raise as much doubt as possible about the climate threat, even while the world's scientists grew more and more certain of it.

One such industry effort over two decades ago spurred my own interest in corporate denial. I was an assistant attorney general in Minnesota, helping implement air quality laws, when members of the coal industry intervened in an energy planning proceeding before our state utility regulators. I found myself cross-examining a handful of scientists brought to Minnesota to assure us we could safely ignore the climate warnings of the world's mainstream scientific authorities. That experience led me to write the 2003 book *Coal: A Human History,* and as I dug into coal's long history, I found similar examples of denial (like the nineteenth-century coal dealer who claimed that having coal particles lodged in your lungs was good for you because the carbon filtered the air as you breathed it in).

Later, as an advocate for nonprofit groups pushing for climate protection policies, I witnessed politicians and industry representatives engaged in what I can only describe as a jaw-dropping level of denial. Their claims became so divorced from scientific reality that I kept asking myself the (admittedly uncharitable) question, What is wrong with these people? How could they be so impervious to the mountains of evidence and so willing to expose the world to truly catastrophic risk? I could not simply write them off as evil or even as obviously less caring than the norm when it came to their other behavior—or at least not all of them. Nor could I write them off as unusually irrational; outside this one issue, their reasoning powers and risk perceptions seemed pretty normal.

Clearly, there was something else going on here. I started seeing this kind of denial as a powerful, dangerous, and surprisingly unexplored social phenomenon that could put both moral and cognitive blinders on basically rational, honest, ordinary people and that would surely make already irrational, dishonest, and uncaring people even worse. I wondered how far from reality this phenomenon had led people in the past. How much harm had it caused? How had it affected our laws and culture? How did society eventually overcome those denials—if it did? And is it possible to reduce the risk of such denial in the future?

To learn more, I started exploring and found a bounty of examples in the historical record, including many denials that were more outrageous than today's. Beyond that, I found a series of social dramas that were both disturbing and inspiring. They were disturbing in how they illustrated the human ability to deny evidence and cause harm under the right circumstances. They were inspiring in how, in most cases, society eventually overcame those denials. In some cases, corporations that once denied the harms in question eventually admitted them, though usually not until the benefits of continued denial had passed.

To collect these denials and put them in context I began with the existing literature around each profiled controversy, which is in some cases enormous. While these books and articles usually do not focus on corporate denials, they still include many denials, and they pointed me toward others. In most cases I then followed the paper trail of denials appearing in newspapers and other publications of the day, trade journals, hearing transcripts, court filings, and the broadcast media.

Although my focus was mainly on each industry's public denials and how they influenced social norms, in many cases these public denials are supplemented by private ones, expressed in interviews conducted by historians and other researchers or in internal corporate documents later exposed by litigators, whistle-blowers, or journalists. I owe a debt of gratitude to the many people who have collected these denials and preserved them for posterity; the sources I rely on most are identified in each chapter and all are identified in the endnotes and the Major Works Cited in the Notes.

The first of the eight campaigns of denial I chose to focus on—denials made by British slave traders and plantation owners in response to an abolition movement—may seem surprising to find in a book like this. I start there, though, because no exploration of industrial denial would be complete without this most extreme example of what an organized and lucrative industry is capable of rationalizing. The other seven campaigns deny the harms, or responsibility for the harms, associated with radium, automobile accidents, leaded gasoline, chlorofluorocarbons, tobacco, the financial crisis, and—returning to where I began—climate change.

I chose these eight campaigns partly because there was such a wealth of documented public denials around each harm, sustained over decades. As with climate change, each campaign rejected evidence so powerful that it pointed to something at work other than reasonable minds differing over uncertain evidence. To be clear, most disputes over evidence of harm do not amount to what I am calling denial. Debate over how to interpret data is critical to the scientific and policy process, especially when that data is new and most uncertain, and such debate must be respected. This book focuses on the mental and linguistic maneuvers that occur when people have left the realm of reasonable doubt and debate and find themselves trying to explain, say, how having a flesh-destroying element fused into your bones is good for you, how nicotine is not addictive, or how climate disruption is not caused by humans.

As with climate change, each of the denial campaigns played out in public. That means that in addition to the corporate harms they directly perpetuated, these campaigns had an insidiously corrosive impact on the culture. They distorted the public's sense of reality, diminished overall levels of social trust, and reduced how much social responsibility people expect from corporations. In short, these denial campaigns were shaping much broader social norms than just those around the disputed corporate product or activity.

And finally, as with climate change, almost all these denial campaigns involved harms utterly vast in scale, threatening severe global environmental destruction or contributing to the death, suffering, illness, brain damage, or financial ruin of millions of people (radium, which threatened merely thousands, is the one exception). These examples illustrate how profoundly corporate-caused harm and the denial of that harm affect humanity's well-being and hint at the future threats we may face as we deploy new technologies posing unimagined dangers.

LOOKING PAST THE BAD APPLES

There is a broad and valuable literature about corporate malfeasance, and various authors have written about one form of corporate denial: science denial. Within that, some focused on climate science denial, like journalist Ross Gelbspan in his groundbreaking 1997 book, *The Heat Is On: The High Stakes Battle over Earth's Threatened Climate* (as it happens, among the climate denial efforts Gelbspan wrote about was the Minnesota hearing I mention above, which he observed). Some focused on the particularly cynical role of the public relations industry in spinning science, like Sheldon Rampton and John Stauber in their 2002 exposé *Trust Us, We're Experts! How Industry Manipulates Science and Gambles with Your Future.*

Scientists and science historians have written about the role of scientists who, on behalf of various industries, promoted unfounded doubts about the strength of the data underlying a health or environmental threat. Epidemiologist David Michaels has described many such examples in his 2008 book, *Doubt Is Their Product: How Industry's Assault on Science Threatens Your Health.*

A prominent and particularly revealing treatment of the manipulation of science is the 2010 book *Merchants of Doubt: How a Handful of Scientists Obscured the Truth on Issues from Tobacco Smoke to Global Warming,* by science historians Naomi Oreskes and Erik M. Conway. They describe the careers of particular scientists who disputed scientific evidence of harm on behalf of more than one industry, either directly or through a growing crop of industry-funded think tanks. While Oreskes and Conway did not mainly focus on the social factors promoting denial, they did explain that the careers of some of the key scientists profiled (including one that I cross-examined in our Minnesota climate hearing) were launched by Cold War weapons programs. In the authors' words, "Somehow, somewhere, defending America against the Soviet threat had transmogrified into defending the tobacco industry against the U.S. Environmental Protection Agency."

While I follow in the footsteps of such books, I look at the issues from a different perspective. I look beyond scientists to include industry representatives generally and the range of moral rationalizations offered to justify corporate actions, like the tobacco CEO who sees smoking as an alternative to wife-beating and reckless driving.

I also look at corporate harms whose proof lies outside the realm of science, like the slave trade and the precrisis practices of the financial industry, hoping to provide a more complete depiction of this phenomenon. And while I do not allege that all claims of corporate harm are true or all corporate defenses invalid, it helps to have this historic backdrop in mind when we look at how corporations handle new charges against them, whether a pharmaceutical company charged with fueling the opioid crisis, the NFL responding to findings of brain damage to its players, or technology companies facing charges of violating user privacy or enabling online fraud.

I also focus more on the social context within which these denials take place. Many people, especially corporations themselves, attribute corporate harm-causing and deception to "bad apples." Given how often corporate denial happens, though, and how many people indulge in it, we need to ask what it is about the "barrels"—corporations operating in competitive markets—that might encourage individual apples to go bad.

Of course others have considered how the corporate form affects moral behavior, though not necessarily focusing on denial. In his powerful 2004 book, *The Corporation: The Pathological Pursuit of Profit and Power,* law professor Joel Bakan compares corporate behavior to that of a psychopath. He makes the comparison not because the people who work for corporations are psychopaths, he is careful to explain, but because the corporation is "a legally designated 'person' designed to valorize self-interest and invalidate moral concern. Most people would find its 'personality' abhorrent, even psychopathic, in a human being, yet curiously we accept it in society's most powerful institution."

Some of the most fascinating work on moral choices faced by individuals working within corporations was done by sociologist Robert Jackall in the 1980s. A number of corporations gave Jackall access to interview their managers about their moral choices; he granted the managers anonymity, and they spoke with remarkable candor. His 1988 book *Moral Mazes: The World of Corporate Managers,* concludes that some corporate managers fighting outside critics actually "half-believe realities they know to be fictive." Other managers frankly admit to deception but rationalize it as something they have no power or responsibility to resist. One public relations executive said, "Our society is the way it is. It's run on money and power, it's that simple. Truth has nothing to do with it. So we just accept the world as it is and live with it." (Chilling quotes like this may be why corporations have granted so few researchers similar access to study their employees' moral choices in recent decades.)

Jackall's findings do not mean such cynicism is universal in the business world. While writing this book, I happened to attend a business school graduation ceremony. I heard a series of speakers inspire the newly minted MBAs with assurances that they would go forward and make the world a better place. I saw hat-and-gowned graduates pose with big smiles, surrounded by proud parents and spouses. I believe that for virtually all of them the desire to personally prosper went hand in hand with a desire to improve the world or, at the very least, a disinclination to hurt and deceive it. And I know many in the business world are motivated to make their institutions more socially responsible, and not just for the public relations value.

I have little doubt that most humans start with an innate concern for others. Babies get distressed when other babies cry, and from a young age they may try to offer comfort. Toddlers typically want to help other people. If a researcher drops something and pretends to be unable to reach it, the toddler will usually pick it up and hand it to the researcher, with no request and with no reward. The existence of some basic prosocial instincts makes evolutionary sense. They would surely have enhanced our ancestors' survival by enabling them to bond with others in their small tribes to collectively gather food, kill prey, protect children, fight enemies, and share knowledge. And we are by no means the only species to show concern for others. Researchers like primatologist Frans De Waal have documented displays of empathy in many other social species, suggesting how deeply and biologically rooted our own empathy likely is.

Caring about others or the social group as a whole will often conflict, of course, with our innate concern for ourselves. Which of these coexisting and competing instincts gets expressed in our behavior—the self-interested or the prosocial—depends in significant part on the culture, circumstances, and incentives of the world we have built. And that world, or at least the part of it we identify with most, plays a huge role in determining what we believe is factually true and morally right—or in other words, what evidence and responsibilities we are capable of denying.

To better understand the influence of social context on corporate denial, I dipped into the psychological research, following a larger trend that has revolutionized economics. Economics was long built on the assumption that people are rational, entirely self-interested, and firm in their self-control. The study of actual human behavior has (not too surprisingly) shown how wrong these assumptions are. Richard Thaler, a Nobel Prize–winning pioneer in this new field of behavioral economics, has explained that humans are "dumber, nicer, and weaker" than economics has assumed—less rational, less selfish, and having less will power. Other researchers are revealing what profoundly social creatures we are, with views shaped by the groups we identify with, especially in times of conflict. Moreover, our attitudes can be subconsciously influenced by situational factors. You could say we are not only dumber, nicer, and weaker, but more tribal, less aware, and more malleable than we like to think.

Social psychology's findings often have strong media appeal and get particular attention in the business world; in fact, a great deal of the published research comes from psychologists employed by business schools. Some psychologists, business school professors, and business writers have begun trying to apply emerging psychological findings to create more ethical businesses (discussed more in the conclusion), though most of the business world's interest in social psychology seems to stem more from a desire to improve profits.

I tread carefully when wandering into the psychological research, because experimental psychology and especially social psychology are facing something of a crisis. Critics have pointed out that many studies use small sample sizes and show small effects that other researchers have been unable to replicate, perhaps reflecting a "publication bias," where studies with positive findings get published while studies with negative findings never get submitted.

Some of the psychological findings that have received widespread attention from the popular media and the business world do appear to rest on very thin evidence, especially when compared to the evidence of health and environmental impacts discussed in this book, which is typically based on vast bodies of research collected over decades by many different researchers, repeatedly scrutinized by independent review panels, and tested in litigation. So we should view some of the psychological findings with extra skepticism and patience, waiting to see if they are replicated and recognizing that we *Homo sapiens* are still in the early stages of using our rational skills to understand our many irrational tendencies. But we should still keep an eye on the emerging psychological research because of the profound importance of understanding whether and how our cognition and morality can be skewed by external factors.

Among the factors that bear scrutiny are those that appear to undermine objectivity and honesty, amplify self-serving biases, reduce empathy, diminish perceived risk, or weaken a sense of responsibility. Financial self-interest is obviously one bias-creating and denial-promoting factor, but it is by no means the only one. In addition to being tightly focused on profit, corporations are by their nature competitive, hierarchical, and often powerful. They let individuals act with relative anonymity and limited liability. By operating through global markets and often at the cutting edge of new technology, corporations can cause inadvertent, distant, and widely dispersed harms to unknown parties and do so through highly divided labor, management, and ownership. And corporations are steeped in a justifying market ideology that limits responsibility for social impacts.

Other forms of human organization—like political groups and movements, militaries, bureaucracies, and religions—share some of these features. Corporations are unique in having them all.

WHAT IS TRUE: DENYING EVIDENCE OF CAUSALITY

The corporate denials ahead can be put into two broad categories: causality and responsibility. Causality denials relate to whether the corporation actually causes a given harm. Responsibility denials relate to whether the corporation can or should do anything to reduce that harm, *even if* it causes it.

Causality denials may begin with denying that the problem even exists (like ozone depletion and climate change, two problems not yet detected when scientists first predicted them). Where the harm is acknowledged, corporations may try to minimize it, comparing it to risks society willingly accepts (unsafe cars compared to hardwood floors, smoking compared to the bacterial content of a kiss). And they will often point to alternative causes (the dissolving bones of radium workers caused by their predisposition to poor health, lung cancer in smokers caused by genetics, and climate change caused by the sun).

Are those offering such denials simply lying, or do they actually believe what they say? I will seldom try to parse outright lies from self-deceptions in this book. We may feel less judgmental of those who are deceiving themselves as well as others, but denials rooted in self-deception are no less dangerous. Moreover, I believe the two phenomena are usually entwined. Even the most blatant lies are often candy-coated with self-deception, as the speaker rationalizes both causing the harm and lying about it. Meanwhile, many delusions are surely accompanied by some inkling of the truth. Robert Trivers, an influential evolutionary biologist, argues that "deceit and self-deception are two sides of the same coin." He theorizes that self-deception evolved because it allows humans to more successfully deceive others by suppressing the signs of deceit that might otherwise give us away. Others argue that we evolved the ability to deny reality to help us cope with the consciousness of our own mortality, freeing us from dread and letting us more cheerfully carry on propagating the species; this more sympathetic explanation, however, would not stop us from also using our self-deception skills to better deceive others.

Causality denials inevitably shift from whether a product or practice *actually* causes harm to whether it has been *proven* to cause that harm. These denials assume that the burden rests with their accusers to prove harm, rather than with them to prove safety. Whether the burden of proof morally should or legally does fall on those alleging harm, as a practical matter it does indeed fall on them.

Many causality denials do not explicitly address issues of fact at all; they invoke personal character instead. In effect, the deniers argue that the allegation could not be true because they are good people who would never cause such a harm. These denials make sense on a psychological level if, as research suggests, people usually start with a moral feeling about a certain act and then rationalize their beliefs to support that feeling. Corporate executives might feel no guilt partly because most corporate harms are side effects of other actions, and side effects appear less likely to trigger our moral alarms. Or they might feel no guilt because the very power they hold could have narrowed their mental focus to their own goals, reducing their awareness of risk and social impact.

It would make sense, then, for corporate representatives accused of causing harm to check their gut, find a lack of guilt, and automatically seek reasons why the allegation must not be true. In their search to explain these false allegations, corporate defenders will naturally suspect their accusers' motives. In each denial campaign described in this book, corporations impute ulterior motives to their critics, suggesting it is a reflex rarely resisted.

Again and again, what should be factual disputes about causality become tribal conflicts, which should hardly be surprising. Outside the corporate world, researchers have shown how cultural loyalties shape people's views on socially disputed issues like climate change. Dan Kahan, a professor of law and psychology working with Yale's interdisciplinary Cultural Cognition Project, argues that people's views on such issues are motivated by their interest in conveying their loyalty to "affinity groups central to their personal well-being." A corporation is obviously an affinity group central to the well-being of those who work there, and one that can reinforce tribal loyalties with a paycheck.

Corporations are, after all, a form of tribe in competition with other tribes, and their critics will quickly be seen as members of a hostile tribe. Neuroscientists and psychologists have confirmed that our brains are highly tribal, immediately and automatically dividing the world into us versus them at the slightest provocation and highly inclined to agree with "us." Scientific claims are particularly vulnerable to tribal distortions, given the need for specialized training to judge their merits. Accepting scientific conclusions requires people to trust a foreign tribe of experts, and intertribal trust is an early casualty of conflict.

A corporate defender's public attacks on the motives of the corporation's critics may begin naturally enough. As the chapters ahead show, though, sowing a larger social distrust—of scientists, experts, media, and government—can evolve from an unconscious human reflex to a conscious corporate strategy. It can even spawn its own lucrative denial industry (encompassing public relations experts, industry lobbyists, and industry-funded think tanks) that sows distrust about the regulatory science behind issue after issue until such distrust becomes a core ideological belief of a significant segment of society.

This progression of distrust—from reflex to strategy to industry to ideology—fuels a larger corrosion of social trust that, as we see today, can paralyze a society's ability to solve problems, including its ability to effectively respond to even the most dire of scientific warnings.

WHAT IS RIGHT: DENYING MORAL RESPONSIBILITY FOR A HARM

Corporate denials related to responsibility argue that even if the corporation does cause a harm, the corporation should not be blamed or stopped.

Some argue that the harm is necessary to achieve a higher social goal (progress, national power, lifestyle, freedom). Some claim that the cure—stopping the harmful behavior—is worse than the disease and will lead to unintended consequences (seat belts will encourage people to drive carelessly; smoking will be replaced by drug addiction).

Some responsibility denials just try to redirect attention to other problems society should focus on (the plight of poor Britons rather than African slaves, air pollution rather than smoking). Some argue the futility of trying to stop the harm (because other nations will keep causing it, or because there is no affordable alternative). Some simply heap blame on the consumers of their products (smokers, drivers, subprime mortgage borrowers) or on society more generally (for not building safer roads). These denials may not address social responsibility explicitly, but they have the effect of shifting the uncomfortable spotlight of moral accountability away from the corporation.

The renowned psychologist Albert Bandura has identified various psychological maneuvers people use to turn off their moral self-sanctions, freeing them to hurt others, including through corporate actions. Among the maneuvers are the displacement and diffusion of responsibility. People feel less responsible for the consequences of their actions when they are just one part of a larger group effort and when they are following orders. Other researchers have found that people feel much less empathy for harms that fall on a distant and unidentified group of victims. Divided labor (and ownership divided from management) are key features of big corporations, and global markets facilitate distant harms to unknown victims.

Responsibility denials are also surely made easier by a certain masking effect inherent in incorporation. Indeed, anonymity is such a core feature of the corporate form that in much of the world it is built into the entity's name. In parts of Europe and elsewhere, instead of appending "Inc." or "Corp." to their names, corporations attach the letters *S.A.*, for a phrase that translates into English as "Anonymous Society" (for example, in French, *Société anonyme*).

The corporation by definition is legally recognized as an entity that exists separately from the warm-blooded beings who own or run it. The word *corporation* comes from the Latin word *corpus*, for "body" (as in *corporeal* or *corpse*). The corporation is in essence a pretend person with its own economic rights (and in the United States, with a growing list of constitutional rights previously thought to be possessed only by actual people). Its ability to operate in its own name—buying and selling, hiring and firing, suing and getting sued—surely makes it easier for those acting on the corporation's behalf or profiting from its actions to avoid feeling responsible for any harm caused by those actions. And of course, these pretend people are aggressively branded, increasing the moral illusion that they exist separately from those who control them.

The ability to psychologically detach from corporate-caused harm is enhanced by another core feature of corporate law: limited liability. It allows corporations to attract capital from shareholders without putting those shareholders at risk of losing their other assets if things go badly and creditors cannot be paid. This is not unfair to creditors because they understand that when doing business with a corporation, its shareholders' assets are off limits and provide no security. However, limited liability also protects shareholders if the corporation hurts someone—a customer, a neighbor, the environment—and is faced with having to pay for it. The "corporate veil," as it is called, can be pierced in rare circumstances, but it provides shareholders with enormous legal protection.

The corporate form, with its independent legal existence, ownership separated from daily management, and limited liability, has proven spectacularly successful by many measures: attracting capital, driving economic growth, shrinking poverty, advancing technologies, and industrializing the world. To be clear, while the widespread social benefits delivered via corporations are not the focus of this book, they are undeniable and ongoing. Corporations at their best create jobs, support communities, drive innovation, achieve efficiencies, inspire hard work, channel human effort in productive ways, provide a vehicle for collective action outside government, and can help check the abuse of government power.

It is important, though, not to let these benefits blind us to the harms corporations can also inflict nor to accept the notion that such harms are unavoidable. Society can confront and reduce such harms and may be more likely to do so if it recognizes how many features inherent in the corporate setting erode people's innate feelings of responsibility for damage done in the corporation's name.

Cultural expectations can counter some of the responsibility-draining impact of the corporate form. The corporate social responsibility movement has long sought to do just that, as consumers, investors, and others press corporations to factor social consequences into their decision-making. However, that movement runs counter to another cultural force: a free-market ideology that assures corporations that their actions will, through the invisible hand of the marketplace, automatically yield social benefits. Not only does this ideology give corporations permission to ignore the social harms they might cause, but in its most extreme form it says they must.

In a highly influential 1970 article, free-market economist Milton Friedman argued that corporations exist solely to maximize shareholder profit and that executives claiming any broader social conscience are not only "preaching pure and unadulterated socialism" but are "puppets of the intellectual forces that have been undermining the basis of a free society these past decades." In effect, this view insists that corporations must do whatever it takes to maximize shareholder profits, as long as it is legal. The chapters ahead show how dangerous it is to view corporate responsibility this way, at least while corporations have so much power to determine what remains legal. If corporations cannot voluntarily reduce their social harms, and if they can simultaneously block governments from mandating that they reduce those harms, then no social force can protect the common good against the dangers that commercial activity poses to our collective well-being, our planet, and our civilization.

Ideological and other denials related to a corporation's responsibility to advance the common good, or at least not undermine it, play a major role in the annals of corporate denial. They also help illuminate current debates, especially in the United States, over corporate power, the legitimacy of government regulation, and the level of responsibility people owe to each other as they pursue their own self-interest.

·   ·   ·   ·   ·

Chapter 1 recounts what is probably history's first and certainly its worst campaign of corporate denial—the orchestrated denials advanced by British slave traders and plantation owners when confronted in the late eighteenth century by an abolition movement. I do not mean to suggest, by including this chapter, a moral equivalency between selling and owning human beings and the other commercial enterprises profiled. However, this book is largely about how social norms and business contexts influence what people believe to be true and right, and nothing shows that more vividly than the astonishing defenses offered by an industry built upon enslavement.

The next seven chapters span the twentieth and twenty-first centuries. They describe the defenses raised by corporations faced with compelling evidence: that the fiercely radioactive element radium, used recklessly in the workplace and marketed casually for human consumption, was killing people, often by causing their facial bones to rot and crumble; that the rising carnage of auto accidents could be greatly reduced by changes in auto design; that leaded gasoline was causing measurable brain damage to generations of children; that chlorofluorocarbons were destroying a feature of the atmosphere vital to life on earth; that tobacco was both extremely addictive and killing millions; that subprime mortgages and the complex new investment products based on them would cause a global financial crisis; and that fossil fuels are driving the planet toward irreversible climate catastrophe.

I hope readers will ask themselves throughout this book what can be done to reduce the threat of corporate denial. The last chapter addresses this question, though only in part, given its vast scope. It touches on current efforts to promote social responsibility within the business and investment world and on efforts to create new corporate structures less single-mindedly devoted to profit. I applaud these efforts because I believe denial can be reduced by changes in culture, including a corporation's internal culture. Such experimentation may even, in the long term, lead to the widespread replacement of today's corporate structure with a different social construct—which we may or may not still call a corporation—less inherently prone to denial.

On the other hand, while some people will surely succeed in voluntary efforts to make their corporations more objective and responsible, others—and those most likely to indulge in denial in the first place—will fail or never try. They will create new societal dangers as they exploit new discoveries and perhaps inflict even greater harms than we have faced before as humanity's ability to alter the world crosses new frontiers.

If we want to truly reduce the risks posed by corporate denial in the foreseeable future, I believe we need to do so through checks and balances on a society-wide scale, countering that denial as we have in the past with independent science, journalism, activism, litigation, elections, laws, and agencies to enforce those laws. Daunting as this seems, the balance of power between corporations and other social forces has dramatically shifted before at moments in our history when corporate activity became widely viewed as intolerably destructive. There are signs this may be about to happen again.

It will be tempting for those working to shift the balance of power to view their efforts as a moral crusade, and it may even be necessary. Major social reforms seldom happen without the group morale that comes from a moral passion. Such passion seems particularly necessary to fight climate change, where the dangers of continued denial are so enormous. But reforms to check corporate power are equally justified by a dispassionate recognition that the social constructs we have put at the heart of our global economy reliably corrode objectivity and responsibility, putting cognitive and moral blinders on the *Homo sapiens* that run and own them. Confronting this industrial-strength denial with our other social constructs is essential to reducing the power of corporations to blind the rest of us.

1 A "More Pleasing Representation"

THE ALTERNATE REALITY CRAFTED BY
THE SLAVE LOBBY

*"Nine out of Ten rejoice at falling into our Hands. They
seem to be aware that they are bought for Labour, and by
their Gestures wish to convince the Purchasers that they
are fit for it."*

—Richard Miles, former official of the British Company of
Merchants Trading to Africa, describing African slaves to
parliamentary committee, 1789

In 1562, the English slave trade was launched with a voyage to Africa that had the financial backing of several prominent English officials. When Queen Elizabeth I later spoke with the leader of the expedition, she reportedly expressed her hope that no slaves had been carried off without their consent, because that "would be detestable and call down the vengeance of Heaven upon the undertakers." She must have been satisfied with his answer, because she sent one of her own ships along on his next slaving expedition.

In time, Britain would outcompete its European rivals and dominate the Atlantic slave trade. In the late 1700s, though, an abolition movement arose, stressing the brutal suffering inflicted on the slaves. The slave lobby—both slave traders and slaveholders in the British West Indies—launched a sophisticated campaign arguing that slavery was entirely consistent with the nation's self-image as humane and enlightened. In fact, they argued, they were helping the slaves, who enjoyed their captivity, who could not handle freedom anyway, and who were much better off than if they had been left in Africa.

Of course, an abolition debate would also rage in the United States, but there the rationalization of slavery would spread well beyond its commercial roots to become a deeply entrenched example of societal denial. Britain's defense of slavery can more fairly be seen as an early though extreme case of corporate and industrial denial, as an established industry tried to portray its behavior to a British public too far away to observe it.

Britain's slavery debate displayed tribalism in its most naked form, with people not merely drawing lines between their in-group and out-groups but literally debating who was human, who was not, and what being human meant. It also illustrates the overwhelming influence of the accepted behavior and attitudes *within* one's own tribe—the social norm—in shaping how evidence is interpreted. And it shows an industry scrambling to stay within a shifting social norm, partly by creating an interlocking web of denials so complete as to amount to an alternate reality.

RISE OF A RESPECTED INDUSTRY:
"DAZZLED" AND DEHUMANIZING

The Atlantic slave trade shared many features of modern commercial industries. It was carried out by competitive, profit-driven group enterprises, backed by complex capital arrangements, and integrated into vast global networks of commerce. The very earliest English slaving voyages, in the 1560s, were backed by an early form of corporations, with multiple stockholders who enjoyed limited liability. In the 1600s, when slave trading was dominated by national monopolies, England's Royal African Company became one of the world's largest corporations.

As a proslavery writer would note, slaving was not some "clandestine or piratical business, but . . . an open, public trade; encouraged and promoted by acts of parliament. For so, if being contrary to religion, it must be deemed a national sin." According to British historian Hugh Thomas, among those who owned shares in slaving corporations were members of the royal family, noblemen, members of Parliament, and such leading lights as Jonathan Swift, Daniel Defoe, Sir Isaac Newton, and Alexander Pope. Even John

Locke, whose writings on liberty would famously help inspire the American and French revolutions, was invested in the slave trade.

By the late 1700s, ten big firms and hundreds of small ones sponsored slave voyages just in the thriving slave port of Liverpool. A contemporary source claimed that the potential profits so "dazzled" the population that many of Liverpool's slave ships were "fitted out by attornies, drapers, ropers, grocers, tallow chandlers, barbers, taylors, etc.," each with a share in the enterprise. Profiting from slavery was considered respectable across Britain's lower, middle, and upper classes.

Slavery was deemed critical to fully exploiting the vast resources of the New World. Fabulously valuable tropical crops like cotton, tobacco, and sugar demanded back-breaking work in the tropical heat. The slave lobby argued that African slaves were necessary because white people could not handle the fatigue caused by cultivation in a tropical climate.

One New World industry created more demand for slaves than all the others combined: sugar. Modern scholars estimate that of eleven million Africans who survived the trip across the Atlantic, six million were brought to sugar plantations, including plantations on the various islands in the West Indies that Britain claimed as colonies. The British were eagerly embracing this sweet and exotic commodity. While some medical experts raised concerns about the nation's widespread sugar consumption, in 1715 one physician published a lengthy tract praising both the nutritional and medical benefits of sugar; in fact, he recommended not only freely consuming it and feeding it to babies but also cleaning your teeth with sugar, having it blown into your eyes to correct eye disease, and snorting it up your nose (as an alternative to using harmful tobacco snuff—another popular New World slave-grown product).

The work on sugar plantations was so harsh that roughly one-third of Africans died within three years of arriving in the West Indies. One plantation owner admitted that the planters on Antigua had carefully calculated the costs of giving slaves moderate work and ample food so they could live to old age versus the cost of effectively working them to death and then buying new slaves. They found the latter approach was cheaper, and that became their policy.

The slave lobby treated its human captives as just another commodity, or as livestock. One defender of the slave trade suggested not using the inflammatory word *slavery* at all and using the word *property* instead. Slave ships did not even record the Africans' names in their logs, just their assigned numbers. If the captives died along the way, their burial-at-sea would be recorded in the captain's log with entries like "buryed a girl slave (No. 172) of a flux." In a brutally literal example of corporate "branding" (harkening back to the word's original meaning), many of the Africans would have the initials RAC—for Royal African Company—seared onto their chests with branding irons.

Psychologists trying to understand such extremes of brutality have long pointed to the importance of both euphemism and dehumanization. The psychologist Albert Bandura has stressed that when people see others in terms of their common humanity, it is hard to brutalize them without feeling a distressing self-censure for violating their own moral standards. But people can reduce this distress and disengage from their moral standards by mentally stripping victims of their human qualities, including through language comparing their victims to animals. There is also experimental evidence suggesting that having power encourages the dehumanization of the powerless.

The slave traders and owners engaged in a sometimes literal form of dehumanization, focusing on race. One prominent slaveholder wrote that Africans were not actually human but a distinct species located between humans and apes. That view was extreme for the time, but it was not uncommon to compare Africans to animals. An anonymous writer defending the slave trade assured readers that Africa was populated by "unenlightened Hordes, immersed in the most gross and impenetrable glooms of barbarism, dark in mind as in complexion . . . ignorant, unteachable, lazy, [and] ferocious as their own . . . tigers."

While occasional moral challenges were raised over the centuries of expanding slavery, they were ineffectual. They were ignored or met by pointing to Bible passages accepting slavery or claiming economic necessity. Britain's right and need to make an economic success of its Caribbean sugar colonies was unquestioned. It would take tremendous courage to seriously challenge the slave industry's legitimacy, and something more than courage to actually stop it.

REHUMANIZING THE SLAVES: "AM I NOT A MAN?" AND "A NARRATION OF MISERIES"

A movement that finally challenged British slave trading (and later, slave-holding within the empire) gained tremendous momentum in the 1780s. In the words of Adam Hochschild, who vividly describes it in his book *Bury the Chains: Prophets and Rebels in the Fight to Free an Empire's Slaves*, this campaign "was something never seen before: it was the first time a large number of people became outraged, and stayed outraged for many years, over someone *else's* rights." And the campaign used many of the strategies that activists have used ever since: organizing a network of citizen committees; spreading information through books, flyers, posters, logos, newsletters, and speaking tours; strategic litigation; calls for investigative hearings; a petition drive; and even a consumer boycott.

The British abolitionists challenged head-on the dehumanization on which the industry depended. Josiah Wedgwood, the famous potter and industrialist, designed for the movement a widely reproduced image of a chained and kneeling African beneath the words "Am I Not a Man and a Brother?"

The abolitionists also focused on whether this industry was inhumanly cruel—something that could still be open to debate only because the slaving and slaveholding took place so far from public view. They knew that to change the social norm they needed to stir people's compassion and moral outrage. To do that they needed, in the words of one abolitionist, a "narration of miseries . . . which extend to millions of our fellow creatures." They needed to change slavery from a distant, hard-to-envision concept to a vivid physical reality, and so they collected specific stories and material evidence of the suffering the industry caused.

Some of the stories of inhumanity came directly from former African slaves, especially Olaudah Equiano, who wrote a widely read autobiography and toured the nation describing his own ordeal as a slave. Some came from Britons who had lived in the sugar islands and seen the inhumanity firsthand, like the minister James Ramsay, who wrote an important book describing life on the plantations. Some were collected by activists, like the minister Thomas Clarkson, who devoted years to the dangerous task of traveling around Britain interviewing slave-ship crew members and ship surgeons, reviewing ships' logs, and collecting samples of the whips, manacles, thumbscrews, and other instruments of torture used to keep the Africans terrorized. And with the help of their parliamentary champion, William Wilberforce, the abolitionists arranged for government hearings to investigate the slave trade and found dozens of witnesses who could testify from firsthand experience about the conditions in Africa, on slave ships, and on plantations.

The abolitionists' evidence of the slave trade's brutality shocked and mobilized the British public within just a few years. All around the nation, citizen committees in support of abolition were formed. Eventually, hundreds of petitions bearing nearly 400,000 names would be sent to Parliament, and more than 300,000 would join a boycott of slave-grown sugar.

This movement focused on the ongoing slave trade rather than slaveholding more generally. Still, the West Indian plantation owners also felt threatened, and they often acted in concert with the traders to oppose the abolitionists. In 1789, a committee of plantation owners even imposed a levy on its members' imported products to fund the antiabolition campaign. As Hochschild points out, "Just as the abolitionists were the prototype of modern citizen activism, so the West India lobby was the prototype of an industry under attack."

Unlike modern denial campaigns, though, this one took place largely through the publication of a flurry of books and pamphlets, and the industry's defenders did not hide behind their corporate affiliations. While some of the books were published anonymously, most of the authors—including slave traders, merchants, and plantation owners—signed their names. These books, combined with the testimony that industry members gave to government inquiries, amount to a vast, detailed, and appalling trove of deception and rationalization, foreshadowing almost all the types of denials that would follow and showing just how deep the rabbit hole can go.

AN ALTERNATE REALITY: "DANCING" ACROSS THE ATLANTIC AND THE "PECULIARLY COMFORTABLE" LIFE OF A SLAVE

In government hearings, the abolitionists' witnesses described with excruciating detail the horrors of the Atlantic slave trade. They testified to the anguish the Africans showed upon being brought onto the ships, the frequent rape of the women by crew members, the many captives who killed themselves by jumping overboard or refusing to eat, and the horrific conditions below deck. Historian Marcus Rediker, author of *The Slave Ship: A Human History,* reports that the abolitionists produced a widely seen diagram of a slave ship to show how its chained captives were wedged side by side into the tiny space allowed them. They described the many deaths from rampant disease and the vicious punishments, including routine whipping and torture, and showed the torture instruments used.

The industry could not fight such emotionally searing evidence merely by denying isolated facts. The slave lobby would need to oppose these gruesome reports with a vivid, detailed, and completely contrary narrative—a socially acceptable alternate reality. One plantation owner proclaimed, "As a contrast to the horrid and fictitious picture, which has been drawn of the state of the negroes in the West-Indies, I shall here exhibit a true and more pleasing representation, taken from the life."

The slave lobby surely had the psychological advantage when it came to persuading the public. People generally want to believe they live in a just world, and the abolitionists were raising accusations of horrendous injustice. Social psychologist John T. Jost and others have formulated what they call the theory of system justification, which holds that people are unconsciously motivated to view the existing social and political system as fair and justifiable. This bias toward justifying the status quo is heightened by criticism of the system, and it appears not just among those benefiting from the existing system but among those who hold lower status within it.

The evidence presented by the abolitionists was obviously a potent threat to the self-image of those profiting from slavery, but it seems likely that many others in Britain wanted to disbelieve evidence that their society had condoned such brutality (or that the delicious sugar sweetening their tea and coffee was derived from it). The slave lobby made that disbelief easier by offering a much happier fictional portrayal of conditions, complete with festive slave ships and comfortable plantations.

The British were told that the Africans wanted to be enslaved and even engaged in self-marketing. The quote at the beginning of this chapter from a prominent industry witness who had governed company-owned slaving forts on the African coast is an example. Another slave trader similarly described the slaves' general eagerness to be purchased. Some feared they would be eaten when first brought on board, he explained, "but, when from kind treatment and the attention paid to their health, and accommodation and comfortable living on board, such apprehensions are removed, they are quite at ease, and cheerful and happy."

A third member of the slave lobby offered assurances that the slaves' "lodging on board is made as comfortable for a long sea voyage, as it is possible for the ingenuity of man to effect . . . . Thus every possible care is taken to bring them in good health and spirits to the market." Yet another reported that "a Slave on Board a [slave ship] in respect of Food and Attention, is as well, perhaps better situated, than many Kings and Princes in their own Country."

A former slave ship captain told an official inquiry that that the slaves are comfortably lodged in rooms cleaned for them every day. He went on: "If the Weather is sultry, and there appears the least Perspiration upon their Skins, when they come upon Deck, there are Two Men attending with Cloths to rub them perfectly dry, and another to give them a little Cordial." After they eat "they are then supplied with Pipes and Tobacco . . . they are amused with Instruments of Music peculiar to their own Country . . . and when tired of Music and Dancing, they then go to Games of Chance. The Women are supplied with Beads, which they make into Ornaments; and the utmost Attention is paid to the keeping up their Spirits, and to indulge them in all their little Humours."

The repeated mention of slaves dancing on the ships was particularly perverse. The abolitionists' witnesses explained that when weather allowed, the Africans were brought up on deck, the men still shackled in pairs. To exercise them, one crew member testified, the crew would use a whip to force them to move to the beat of a drum, though they could only jump and rattle their chains. In an extreme example of industrial euphemism, the crews actually did call this whip-driven movement "dancing." One crew member's job was to "dance the Women," while another would "dance the Men."

Meanwhile, sugar plantations were portrayed by the slave lobby as an indulgent, cradle-to-grave welfare state, designed at each turn to ensure the slaves are "comfortable"—a favorite word among the industry's defenders.

Pregnant women were "cherished," were given ample time off before and after the birth, and were free to quit working to care for sick or teething infants, wrote the slave trader Gilbert Francklyn. Another slave trader, Robert Norris, explained that the slaves were provided with homes that are "comfortable and commodious, with a garden to each" where they can cultivate fruits and vegetables and raise a little flock of chickens, which they can consume for "their evening's repast; this, with a comfortable night's rest, enables them to return with vigor to the next morning's work."

Norris went on to stress the generous health care benefits the slaves receive, noting that as soon as one feels sick, "he is instantly exempted from all labor, and lodged in a house particularly constructed for the purpose, where he is visited daily by a practitioner of medicine; supplied with fresh viands, vegetables, and even wine." He is attended constantly by a nurse and not allowed to work until fully recovered. Meanwhile, the masters make sure that his grounds are worked by others, so that "he comes out of his hospital a richer man than when he went in." Francklyn similarly assured readers that the lucky hospitalized slave enjoyed wine, rice, and a variety of fruits that even wealthy Europeans could scarcely attain.

Elderly slaves were particularly well cared-for, wrote Norris, so that "old age, in this state, often wears away, and snaps its slender thread, as gently, and perhaps as imperceptibly, as in any country whatever." As for the relationship between master and slave, Francklyn reported that the confidence and freedom with which slaves asked their masters for favors had "more the appearance of those of a relation, to his parent and protector, than of a slave prostrating himself before his tyrant."

Witnesses less invested in the industry provided ample evidence that the planters' portrayal of the comforts of plantation life was just as cruelly ludicrous as it sounds to the modern ear. While some slaves did get an allotment of land, many who did were denied food from the slaveholders and were expected to grow their own food when not working in the sugarcane fields. One witness appearing before a parliamentary committee described hunger so prevalent among the slaves that dead mules and other carcasses had to be burned for fear that if buried, the hungry slaves would dig them up and get sick from eating the rotting meat.

Work in the sugarcane fields was harsh and compelled by the constant presence of the whip-bearing overseer. Work in the boiling houses where the sugar was made was so dangerous many slaves lost arms or hands in the mills. Witnesses testified that slaves too sick to work were sometimes whipped for the offense, and they also recounted cases of pregnant women whipped till they miscarried. Some of the industry's own defenses also undermined its rosy counternarrative: one plantation owner complained that the slaves "are so intolerably . . . inconsiderate, that they, at present, do no more work, in general, than they are compelled to do by the terrors of punishment."

As for those slaves too old or infirm to work, they could hardly count on the gentle treatment the industry described. Witnesses for abolition testified that it was not uncommon for slaveholders to drive such slaves off the plantation, leaving them to wander, beg, steal, and starve. So many cast-out slaves were "daily infesting the public streets" of Barbados that the island had to pass a law criminalizing the practice of casting them out, though many such slave-welfare laws in the sugar islands went wholly unenforced. Showing once again their flair for euphemism, slaveholders called driving sick and elderly slaves away "giving them free."

What are we to make of such a ridiculous counternarrative? Surely, no one with any direct knowledge of slave ships and sugar plantations could possibly have believed it; they were simply lying. But many back home in Britain—the public, members of Parliament, sugar consumers, and slave-enterprise shareholders—may well have let themselves accept this alternate reality, which was much more in keeping with the nation's self-image as enlightened and humane. Even when outright lies are at the center of an industry's narrative, there may still be a layer of motivated self-deception that surrounds and spreads those lies, provided by those who wish to believe them.

MEMBERSHIP AND GROUP CHARACTER: "ARE WE NOT YOUR BRETHREN?"

Much of the slavery debate had nothing to do with abstract notions of morality. Srividhya Swaminathan, a modern scholar of the era's rhetoric, describes how the slave lobby often focused instead on asserting its own membership in British society and claiming its consistency with British character. The allegations of brutality could not be true, they essentially argued, because we are one of you, and our standards of behavior are no worse than yours. In short, they were trying to secure their position within the national in-group and within its prevailing social norms.

This line of arguments makes sense when we recognize that our moral instincts are deeply rooted in our evolution as social beings. In the words of Joshua Greene, a professor of psychology at Harvard and a researcher into moral cognition, "Morality is a set of psychological adaptations that allow otherwise selfish individuals to reap the benefits of cooperation." But Greene stresses that these instincts evolved within a very tribal context, where groups of humans competed with other groups. Indeed, we are "wired for tribalism," intuitively dividing the world into us and them, favoring us over them, and cooperating with us but not them.

However, the all-important line between us and them—with such important implications for our moral judgments—is fluid. People can expand, narrow, and shift their definition of the in-group and the out-group. And, of course, the moral standards of the in-group can change (indeed, in the modern era it feels like they are constantly changing, causing clear discomfort among those most attached to the prior standards and fueling today's polarization). The slave lobby was threatened with losing its status as part of the in-group and of losing its moral legitimacy by having its behavior redefined as outside the social norm, and it responded accordingly.

The slave traders and owners repeatedly stressed that they, not the slaves, had the higher claim on the nation's sympathies. Slave trader Robert Norris wrote that "though the Liberty of Negroes seems now to be the favourite idea, the Liberty of Britons to pursue their lawful Occupations should not be forgotten." Trader Gilbert Francklyn, turning the abolitionist motto on its head, argued that the slandered plantation owners can say to their critical countrymen, "Are we not men? Are we not your brethren?" Almost all the criticized industries I have studied portray themselves as victims of unfair attack; the near universality of this portrayal, as well as its limited strategic value, suggests that it is a reflection of genuine group self-pity.

The West Indies slaveholders felt particularly at risk of being seen as outsiders because their world was far from Britain. They rushed to assure their compatriots that, despite their accusers' false accusations, the plantation owners "are not tyrants; . . . on the contrary, they are remarkable for urbanity of manners, liberality of sentiment, and generosity of disposition." Gilbert Francklyn assured that one could not even in England find a higher proportion of "men of better education, of more enlarged ideas, of more charitable, humane, dispositions" than the plantation owners of the West Indies.

However, one of the enlarged ideas that the British considered a defining feature of their identity was freedom. Historian Christopher Brown, in his book *Moral Capital: Foundations of British Abolitionism*, observes that during the last quarter of the eighteenth century "Britons' abiding need to think of themselves as a people uniquely dedicated to liberty would make it difficult for them to regard overseas slavery with complacency."

There was a striking conflict, then, between two aspects of the social norm: the dedication to liberty versus the support of the slave trade. The abolitionists tried to exploit that conflict, appealing to the principle of liberty (as well as basic human empathy and general principles of humane behavior) to redefine the slave trade as socially unacceptable. They drew a bright moral line around slavery, which they considered "one of the greatest evils at this day existing upon the earth."

The slave lobby tried the opposite: to reconcile the conflict by showing that in actual practice the nation's dedication to liberty and humane treatment of others was overstated, thereby erasing the bright moral line abolitionists were drawing. They did this by comparing slavery to the many socially accepted injustices suffered daily by the British poor. Where the abolitionists were saying with respect to slavery, "We Britons are better than this," the slave lobby was in effect saying, "Actually, no we're not."

One plantation owner claimed the slaves were far happier than "the poor peasant, or the indigent mechanic! who, bending beneath the weight of years, or of infirmities, is yet forced to toil for a small pittance," and who, along with his faithful wife and helpless children, is "sinking at once under the heaped up misery, the accumulated wretchedness, of sickness, hunger, and cold!" Gilbert Francklyn likewise claimed the slaves' lot was "to be envied, by the generality of the peasants in every part of Europe."

Moreover, West India's slaves enjoyed "infinitely better" working conditions than British coal and lead miners, argued one plantation owner. And

Francklyn argued that slaves were treated less cruelly than English factory workers exposed to lead, mercury, or other workplace hazards that in a few months or years "renders the life of the poor victim an unremitting scene of torture and misery, which death alone can relieve him from."

This line of comparison would be brought to bizarre heights decades later by one of the most prominent U.S. defenders of slavery, George Fitzhugh. He wrote rants worthy of a passionate Marxist over the way "the vulgar landlords, capitalists and employers" of the Northern states exploited the poor. But instead of the solutions offered by Communists (or less radical reforms, like better pay), he offered the model of Southern slavery, the "beau ideal of Communism," where the slave gets all he wants from a benevolent master, making the slave "as happy as a human being can be."

When Britain's proabolition witnesses testified that whippings, mutilations, and other punishments more gruesome than I can bring myself to describe were common on the plantations and sometimes fatal, defenders of slavery responded by claiming that the slaves faced punishments less harsh than those faced by the poor in Britain. One argued that "such thefts as would bring criminals to the gallows here, are frequently punished there with only a few stripes." Lest people think these slave whippings were done in a cruel or careless manner, one slave trader assured readers that "all these flagellations are inflicted with so much care, as rarely to disable the offender from work." Another defender of slavery reportedly dismissed the horror over slaves being burned alive by stating that those so condemned "are previously strangled."

Comparisons of this sort—where an industry favorably compares the harms it causes to greater harms that are accepted in a society—are a staple of corporate denial. (Advantageous comparison is also another psychological factor Albert Bandura identifies as enabling the moral disengagement that makes violent atrocities possible.) People judge their own morality and behavior largely in comparison to that of others, which is why social norms are so powerful in the first place.

For example, psychologist Dan Ariely and his colleagues have shown that people are much more likely to cheat on a test when they see somebody else doing so—a tendency he calls catching the "dishonesty germ." History strongly suggests we could apply the contagion metaphor to other kinds of beliefs and behavior, and that we can catch and spread an oppression germ, a cruelty germ, or a complacency germ. Fortunately, history suggests that freedom, empathy, and honesty germs can be contagious too.

In addition to helping the slave lobby position itself within the social norm, these advantageous comparisons could redirect sympathy away from the slaves to others. One pamphlet, attributed to "A Plain Man," was printed by the slave lobby and likely written by it too (apparently an early example of an industry making its case through messengers that the public deemed more credible). The author claimed to have signed a petition to abolish slavery but later changed his mind when he learned about the slaves' "little snug houses" and lives so much easier than those of English workers. One plantation owner urged those passionate about spreading the blessings of liberty to "begin at home—set open the prison doors to the poor debtor, who hath committed no crime, if misfortune be not a crime!"

THE NOBLE MISSION OF SLAVERS: "THE HOUSE OF BONDAGE MAY BE CALLED THE LAND OF FREEDOM"

In addition to favorably comparing slavery to poverty in Britain, the industry favorably compared slavery to conditions in Africa. By reframing the debate in this way, the slavers took their alternate reality to the next level, using language that reached truly Orwellian heights to exalt themselves as humanitarians.

The slave lobby argued that life in Africa was so horrendous that slavers were rescuing their captives from a worse fate. What exactly they were rescuing them from varied, though almost all claimed that the enslaved would have been killed as prisoners of war if they had not been sold to Europeans. Some also claimed that they were saving them from a harsher form of slavery in Africa, from death by human sacrifice or cannibalism, from idolatry (typically involving snakes), or simply from the arbitrary power of a tyrannical leader, which was conveniently characterized as worse than plantation slavery. Sometimes they argued that by removing from Africa "the refuse of her population," the captives were "snatched from the horrors of famine." All agreed that whatever the slaves' fate would have been in their home countries, life on the sugar plantations was a big step up.

One plantation owner explained that making Africans slaves in British colonies "is really a redemption of them from the most cruel slavery to a milder and more comfortable state of life;" it also lets them "live under just and wholesome laws, by which their lives and properties are secured from murder, rapine, or theft." The slave trader Robert Norris argued that "the house of bondage, strictly speaking, may be called a land of freedom to them: . . . where, although prevented from exercising cruelty on others, they are always protected themselves." Slave traders and owners thus portrayed themselves not as the agents of brutality and barbarism, but as agents of humanity and civilization.

And if slavery saves Africans, then of course abolition would doom them. Abolitionists, the industry argued, would "be the immediate instruments of the massacres, murders, and sacrifices" that would follow if Europeans did not transport these Africans to plantations. More specifically, "many thousands of people would be sacrificed or put to death, who are now saved and placed in very comfortable situations, and they and their offspring are made happy." The Duke of Clarence—who was a close friend of the West India lobby and would later become King William IV— insisted with a (presumably) straight face before the House of Lords in 1799 that the slave trade must be continued "for the sake of humanity" and that the West Indian slaveholders treated their slaves with the "milk of human kindness." (Ironically, it would be under his reign in 1833 that Parliament would finally abolish slavery in the British Empire, with the king's assent.)

Those using the salvation argument never explained why this humanitarian act had to be accomplished with manacles, whips, and thumbscrews, or why, once rescued, the Africans and their descendants should be perpetually kept in bondage. Even so, the argument gained surprising traction, even among those initially skeptical. Upon hearing the argument of the plantation owners that the Africans were made happier by being carried away to the West Indies, the famous biographer James Boswell reportedly said, "Be it so. But we have no right to make people happy against their will." Yet a few years later he parroted the industry's arguments, concluding that abolition would "be extreme cruelty to the African savages, a portion of which it saves from massacre or intolerable bondage in their own country." Abolishing the trade, he concluded, would be "to shut the gates of mercy on mankind."

The industry argued that the road from serfdom to liberty in Western Europe had taken centuries, and African slaves would similarly need centuries before they could handle freedom. In the meantime, slavery "suits their characters" and should not be disturbed by "sudden and violent laws" of abolition. And the industry assured the British public and Parliament that the Africans did not miss freedom, because having never experienced it, they lacked the "love of rational freedom" that exists in civilized parts of the world "where liberty is prized above all other enjoyments." Indeed, the push to abolish the trade amounted to an "attempt to cram liberty down the throats of people who are incapable of digesting it."

The slave lobby's defenders denied charges that its members sometimes kidnapped free people to transport into slavery. They stressed that usually the captives were brought to them already enslaved by their African trading partners. How and why did the slaves lose their freedom? In their daily practice, it is clear that the British traders did not know or ask. Whatever happened, it occurred upstream, on the other side of the market transaction, so that by the time they bought them, the slaves had already been transformed from people to property. The industry acted as if there was a veil over whatever took place before its purchases were made. This sort of "market veil" might be compared to the well-known metaphor of the corporate veil, but instead of making shareholders blameless for the actions of a corporation, this veil makes buyers blameless for the actions of the seller. The market veil is particularly effective when the buyers studiously avoid trying to see behind it.

Britain's abolitionist movement might be viewed, then, as an early attempt to pull back that market veil and let the blame flow through, making the British slave buyers (and even British sugar consumers) share culpability with the African slave suppliers. The movement forced the slave traders to expand their narrative and describe what might have happened on the other side of the veil. They typically used one of three explanations for how the slaves lost their freedom: they were prisoners of war (waged by brutal tyrants); they were part of a domestic class of slaves (owned by brutal masters); or they were criminals (justly convicted under the wise laws of Africa). Some of the captives had indeed been convicted of "crimes" like witchcraft, causing their entire family to be enslaved, with the profits going to the judge who convicted them. The first two explanations helped set up the rescue narrative and the third added a touch of victim-blaming.

The industry repeatedly denied that its insatiable demand for slaves in any way encouraged the wars or other violence necessary to supply them, or that it had any sort of corrupting influence on Africa. The abolitionists, however, brought forth ample evidence to a government inquiry that the Africans went to war precisely to acquire prisoners to sell to the slave ships, though often the attacks on villages and collection of captives were done not on behalf of any African king but simply by private marauders. It was well known in Africa that captives could be sold on the coast with no questions asked regarding how they had been acquired.

Interestingly, the widespread characterization of African leaders as tyrants who would kill thousands of prisoners if they could not sell them to slave ships did not prevent the slave industry's defenders from stressing the importance of respecting these tyrants' laws and customs, which included the selling of people: "No foreign nation ought to deprive the Africans of their natural privileges without their consent . . . to dispose of their slaves, prisoners of war and felons according to their own established laws and customs." In short, not only was bondage a form of freedom and kindness while abolition was a form of violence, but the enslavement of Africans showed respect for the rights of Africans.

IT'S NOT ABOUT US: ABOLITION WILL "RUIN THE KINGDOM," LEAVE FAMILIES "NAKED AND HUNGRY"

The slave traders and plantation owners strongly objected to the harm that the abolition movement was doing to their reputations as gentlemen, but when it came to making economic arguments, they clearly understood they would not get far arguing solely on behalf of protecting their profits, which in many cases had turned into conspicuous fortunes. They would be better off stressing the economic harm to others—either to the nation as a whole or to a more sympathetic class of victims.

There is no doubt that the slave trade and the plantations it supported were economically important to Britain. Abolishing the trade and eventually slaveholding within the British Empire is estimated to have ultimately cost the nation 1.8 percent of its annual income over more than fifty years. So unlike most of the denials listed above, industry claims about economic damage from abolition of the slave trade were not obviously untrue. Still, the predictions of sweeping national catastrophe—including economic, geopolitical and military catastrophes—due to abolition of the slave trade are early examples of an industry exaggerating the social costs of regulation and conflating its own fortunes with that of the nation.

One plantation owner argued that abolition of the slave trade would mean seeing "Britain itself become a poor, wretched, defenceless country, and very soon a province to France; and thus by setting free Africans, Britons become the more wretched slaves to arbitrary power." Another proslavery pamphleteer argued that ending the slave trade "would overturn our resources as a trading nation, and entirely ruin our naval powers" and ultimately "ruin the kingdom by a universal Bankruptcy." A Liverpool slave trader predicted that without his trade, Britain's "national importance would quickly decline, and be known to the next generation, only by the page of history."

Some defenders of the industry, referring to the violent slave insurrections that sometimes occurred and were understandably feared on the sugar islands, even suggested that abolition could leave the whites enslaved. "What calamities then must follow," wrote one, "should we admit these creatures at present on a footing with their Masters. Anarchy, Conflagration, Homicide, must be the hideous catastrophe, with the total extermination, or perhaps, (such are the strange vicissitudes of humanity) the subjugation and slavery of their white masters, and the revival of old African inhumanities."

There was also a not-so-subtle threat that if Parliament insisted on upending the power structure on the slave plantations, the nation might find its own class structure upended as well. "What would the people of England think of men, who, under a similar pretext of zeal for the rights of humanity, should erect themselves into a society, and endeavor, by preaching, writing, and publishing, to stir up the soldier, the sailor, the artisan, and the peasant, to assert their rights, to an equal portion of liberty with those who now lord it over them?" With the American and then the French Revolutions as backdrops to the abolition debate, the threat of a broader insurrection in the name of liberty was one that the powerful in Britain took seriously. We could call this the "help us or you're next" defense, a variant of the slippery-slope argument often used to claim that every action will invariably be carried to extremes.

And just like modern industries facing regulation, the slave lobby stressed the impact of abolition on the poor. One member pointed to the pensioners, widows, children, and other creditors of the plantation owners, who, along with those who manufactured the goods that were traded for the slaves, would be "left to starve," along with the shipbuilders and their wives and infants, who would be left "naked and hungry." And he pointed to the sailors, who, if the trade were abolished, would lose work that kept them from idleness and evil and therefore saved many from being hanged.

Meanwhile, opponents of the abolitionist-organized sugar boycott warned that eating less sugar would damage the nation's health. A defender of the sugar trade (who claimed not to be in the sugar business but remained anonymous) explained that sugar is "a mild, nutritious, vegetable substance; possessing a power of correcting the ill effects arising from a too free use of animal food."

IT TAKES A MOVEMENT: "I NEVER HAD A SCRUPLE UPON THIS HEAD"

The slave industry's denials and defenses surely played a role in stalling abolition. British abolitionists launched their public campaign in earnest in 1787 or so, and within a few short years the tide of public sentiment turned their way. But they still faced a fierce industrial denial campaign, and parliamentary opponents blocked bills for abolition year after year. Then, the French Revolution and the subsequent war between Britain and France diverted the nation's attention. Britain's slave ships would not be officially put out of business until 1807. Parliament would not vote to free the slaves in the British colonies until 1833, following a revived abolition campaign, another round of industry denials, and a major slave revolt in Jamaica that made widespread war seem the only alternative to emancipation.

The human cost of the delay was staggering. Between just 1800 and 1807, ships from Liverpool delivered more than a quarter million Africans into slavery. It is hard to say how much of the delay in abolition can be attributed to the industry's campaign to deny the realities of slaving, as opposed to its sheer economic and political power, but clearly the slave lobby felt its denials were important enough to invest heavily in propagating them.

The abolitionists understood that getting people to see the reality of slaving was key to their success and that the industry was interfering with that effort. In a famous speech to the House of Commons, William Wilberforce, the parliamentary champion of abolition, cited the industry delegates' description of singing and dancing on the slave ships as proof of "how interest can draw a film over the eyes, so thick, that total blindness could do no more, and how it is our duty therefore to trust not to the reasonings of interested men, or to their way of colouring a transaction."

In attributing the industry's testimony to blindness instead of conscious lying, Wilberforce was advancing a remarkably generous (and politically expedient) interpretation. Yet Wilberforce may have believed that those involved in the slave industry were indeed at least partially blind to its brutality, given his friendship with one man who seemed to personify that moral blindness more than any other: John Newton.

In his youth, John Newton was a slave ship captain, of average brutality and above-average religiosity. He spent an hour or two praying each day, felt that seafaring gave him a particularly "awakened mind," and appreciated how being a slave ship captain provided him so many hours of "divine communion." He credited a particular spiritual awakening to long theological discussions he had with another slave ship captain, from whom he learned about the concept of divine grace. Newton wrote about deeply regretting his own sins, but he was usually referring to his habit of swearing rather than to any pain inflicted on the people shackled below deck. After he fell ill and had to leave the trade, he became a minister, though he kept his savings invested in slave ships.

Newton would later rise to become a nationally renowned evangelical cleric. In the thousands of sermons and half dozen books he wrote in the next thirty years of his ministry, he failed to condemn slavery, even when cataloging the many sins of the nation (a list that ranged from blasphemy to the size of the national debt).

Finally, in 1788, after many of his friends and acquaintances (including William Wilberforce, who considered Newton a religious advisor) came out publicly against slavery, Newton added his highly influential voice to the cause. While condemning the trade in the strongest moral terms, he admitted that he had quit only because of his health. He wrote that it had simply not occurred to him at the time that slavery was morally wrong: "I never had a scruple upon this head at the time; nor was such a thought once suggested to me by any friend." He went on to suggest that the nation as a whole might have likewise been kept from seeing the evil of slavery by "inattention and interest."

After he had left the slave trade but many years before he spoke against it, John Newton wrote the lyrics to what is still one of the most beloved hymns in the English language and one particularly embraced by slaves and the civil rights movement: "Amazing Grace." The hymn must be the most famous song ever to touch on overcoming metaphoric blindness. Its lyrics celebrate how the singer "was blind, but now I see," thanks to divine grace. While these words are sometimes interpreted as describing how Newton's religious awakening turned him against his trade, in fact he continued trading in slaves for years after his awakening and did not preach against slavery for many years after writing the hymn.

Slavery had been part of his tribe's social norm, and Newton had blindly accepted it. His blindness persisted until that social norm was directly challenged on moral grounds by a movement dedicated to opening eyes—a movement that included people he respected. And if the beliefs and practices of those around us can cause a socially induced and socially endorsed moral blindness complete enough to make human bondage seem morally acceptable, imagine what other forms of motivated blindness it can foster.

2 "A Wonderful Stimulant"

RADIUM, RISK, AND RESPONSIBILITY

*"Radium for several years has been given internally and
by injection in large doses with absolutely no disturbing
symptoms. It is accepted as harmoniously by the blood
stream as is sunlight by plant life."*

—C. Everett Field, MD, Standard Chemical Company, 1915

In 1898, Marie and Pierre Curie were working in a Parisian laboratory so dilapidated that another scientist would compare it to "a cross between a stable and a potato shed." Marie, still a doctoral student, had recently found traces of an intensely radioactive new substance, but the Curies would have to process tons of ore to isolate it. It was hard physical labor— Marie sometimes spent entire days stirring a boiling cauldron with a heavy iron rod. That December they announced the discovery of a new element they called radium.

It was a fascinating, history-making discovery. Radium was a million times more radioactive than uranium. It actually glowed in the dark, and Marie described her joy at going into the shed at night and seeing "from all sides the feebly luminous silhouettes." And radium killed living cells; close contact with it left burns that appeared days later. Scientists immediately looked for cells that needed killing, like cancerous tumors, and developed an early version of the radiation therapy that continues today.

Soon, though, a new industry sprang up that promoted radium as a cure-all capable of doing everything from reversing insanity to restoring manhood to growing new teeth. The industry convinced desperate people to drink radium or have it injected into their veins, and it eventually sold products to squirt, splash, or poke into every human orifice. Meanwhile, factories arose in which workers applied radium-bearing, glow-in-the-dark paint to clock and watch dials. Those workers, mostly young women, were trained to sharpen the tips of their paint brushes with their lips and tongue. They were assured that the radium they inevitably consumed was good for them.

This chapter is about how that new industry raced to create a market for this glowing, flesh-burning element, heedless of the risks to consumers and workers. It is also about how, after those risks became gruesomely obvious, industry members found many ways to deny all responsibility for creating them.

FOOLS RUSH IN: FROM A MYSTERY TO AN INDUSTRY

In the first decade of the 1900s, radium was the world's rarest, most expensive, and most scientifically mysterious substance. Its phenomenal release of energy seemed to defy the laws of physics, and its decay challenged the long-held belief that elements were immutable. Thomas Edison, whose assistant had been mortally injured experimenting with x-rays, urged extreme caution and patience when it came to radium. He stressed that scientists needed to learn much more about the powerful element before trying to use it for the good of humanity. But he would not be experimenting with radium himself: he told a newspaper in 1903, "I am afraid of radium and polonium too, and I don't want to monkey with them."

In 1911, a former mortician in Pittsburgh named Joseph Flannery decided he did want to monkey with radium. That year, with the help of his brother James, he launched the Standard Chemical Company, the first corporation in the nation to commercially refine the element. Flannery was nothing if not ambitious. Between his years as an undertaker and those as a radium magnate, he made a fortune building a company that sold vanadium, a rare metal that fortifies steel. Flannery also sold vanadium-containing patent medicines to treat tuberculosis and for "general stimulation of cell activity." The American Medical Association (AMA) found that Flannery had no evidence for these health claims and that he employed a man who falsely claimed to be a medical doctor. Flannery nonetheless later told a Congressional committee that his vanadium remedy was considered "the greatest tonic in the world that is known to-day."

Flannery also told the committee that his interest in radium was a humanitarian one: "I was actuated by a motive to find out a cure for cancer." His sister had cancer, and around 1911 he learned that radium was being used in Europe as an experimental treatment. Radium was still refined only in Europe, though often using ores from Colorado and Utah, and Flannery was familiar with these ores because they were also a source of vanadium. So he set up the industrial facilities needed to mine and extract radium, and by 1913 Standard Chemical was selling it.

Radium is so radioactive that even infinitesimal amounts had market value, and for years a single gram of it was priced at $120,000. (Flannery once told a newspaper a tale about an employee who sneezed onto a receptacle containing radium, blowing away $25,000 worth of product.) It took a significant industrial enterprise, hundreds of tons of ore, and hundreds of workers to squeeze out just a pinch of radium. Between 1913 and 1921, Standard Chemical extracted less than three ounces of the element, yet that was enough to make it the largest radium producer in the world.

In Europe, a mix of governmental, academic, philanthropic, and commercial entities were involved in developing radium, though World War I would cripple European production. The Curies did not even patent their radium extraction methods, believing that profiting from their discovery was not in the scientific spirit. While there were commercial radium companies involved, European governments controlled the limited radium ores, academic scientists oversaw the industrial radium production, and philanthropic groups formed institutes to ensure radium supplies for scientific and medical uses.

The US government was initially involved in radium production as well. Experiments by the Bureau of Mines in 1913 developed a breakthrough in how to refine U.S. ores. There was a short-lived public-private partnership that for a few years successfully extracted radium at a third of the price Standard Chemical was charging. A bill introduced in 1914 would have put certain US radium ores under federal control, with the aim of ensuring affordable radium for US medical uses, preventing a radium monopoly, and stopping radium from falling "into the hands of quacks" selling "toenail cures" and other remedies.

Flannery opposed the legislation with a classic slippery-slope argument, claiming that since practically every mineral in the ground is somewhat radioactive, "if the Government wants to get all the radium in the country, where will it stop?" Ultimately, Congress yielded to the demands of the industry and left radium production to Standard Chemical and a few other private competitors.

Thus, this uniquely rare and confounding element would become just another commercial product—indeed, a consumer product—to be promoted like other products. Where the government worried about too little radium to meet medical needs, Standard Chemical worried about too little medical demand to meet its corporate needs. The medical market for radium would never take off if it was limited to tissue-destroying uses like cancer treatment, especially when such treatments used the same radium over and over. (Treatment typically involved positioning a vial or needle containing radium near a patient's tumor for a few hours.)

So Standard Chemical put its marketing skills to work. Flannery's earlier effort to sell vanadium-based remedies had failed for lack of any supporting medical evidence, but he was determined that would not happen with radium. Standard Chemical would make sure by collecting its own evidence of radium's health benefits.

INDUSTRIAL-STRENGTH QUACKERY: "AN INTENSELY STIMULATING EFFECT"

Flannery would later claim before a congressional committee that his company was doing more clinical work than anyone in the world to expand radium use beyond cancer. Standard Chemical pioneered "internal" therapy—one-time consumption of radium through drinking, injection, or other means—at the nation's "first free radium clinic," opened in Pittsburgh in 1913. There, patients suffering from a wide range of common chronic ailments drank radioactive water, spent hours inhaling the radioactive gas that emanates from radium (what we today call radon), and were apparently the first to experience radium injected directly into their veins, in increasingly larger amounts (for free!). Just one of the clinic's doctors estimated that over four years he had injected radium into 1,500 to 2,000 patients.

Standard Chemical's doctors would promote the use of internal radium and radon to treat arthritis, gout, diabetes, high blood pressure, low-grade joint and muscle pain, and all forms of anemia and to improve general metabolism, correct "faulty elimination," and stimulate the "body ferments." The company published its findings in its own scientific/medical journal, called *Radium*, which it sent to thousands of American doctors each month. Those doctors would not have necessarily known this journal was published by the makers of radium, and Flannery denied that the journal represented advertising. He said it was sent to doctors only to "enlighten" them to the fact that radium "will cure 25 times more people of different diseases more important than cancer." He told a Senate committee that radium injections cured epilepsy, and that radium would probably be very important in treating insanity and tuberculosis.

The company's physicians also treated cancer patients, though not necessarily in compliance with the Hippocratic oath. The clinic selected only the most gravely ill patients, and a critic suggested that it did so more for purposes of experimenting on them than extending their lives. In 1914, clinic chief William Cameron admitted to a Congressional committee that around two-fifths of his patients died as a result of his care. When pressed on these deaths, Cameron explained that cancer patients who might have lived for three or four more months would, thanks to his radium treatments, die just two or three weeks after he treated them. Cameron justified these deaths with astonishing candor: "I feel this way, that I have just shoved those patients over a little more quickly."

Cameron later claimed the private sector could produce radium ten times faster than the government could, to which one Congressman replied, "If it is going to kill the people, I think I should be opposed to putting it out as quickly as you want it."

Standard Chemical also hired Dr. C. Everett Field to reach out more directly to physicians. Field worried that the eight weeks of training the company gave him did not qualify him to teach radium therapy: "To Joe Flannery I said, 'My Gosh, if any of those professors ask me some questions, I'm sunk!" Flannery responded, "Dr., you have been trained more than anyone in America. . . . Answer them anyway you choose—nobody knows enough to refute you." Field would go on to have a lucrative private medical practice in New York City, where he later claimed to have administered radium intravenously some six thousand times. Field is also the source of the quote that begins this chapter, comparing injected radium to sunlight.

Field's sunlight metaphor was in line with the semimystical aura that had built around radium and radioactivity since early in the century. Much of that aura came from the resorts at natural hot springs in Europe and the United States. It had been discovered in 1903 that some of these waters were radioactive, and the resorts claimed that was the cause of their healing properties. The waters contacted radium deep underground, which infused them not with radium but with radon, the radioactive gas radium emits. Guests could drink or soak in the radon-infused water and inhale the gas in an "emanatorium," a special room that the spas built to concentrate radon. The radon reportedly had an "intensely stimulating effect."

One scientist reported that research had "succeeded in enhancing the secondary symptoms of sexual passion in water-newts by radium emanation," though without explaining what the secondary, or even primary, symptoms of newt passion are. The association of radioactivity with energy and stimulation would make radium a natural choice for quacks to market as an aphrodisiac in the years ahead.

Radon has a half-life of only a few days, so although the spas were exposing their customers to radioactivity, at least they were not making their customers permanently radioactive. By contrast, Standard Chemical was injecting people with an isotope of radium with a half-life of over 1,600 years, and although some of that radium left the body, some did not. By 1913, French and British research showed that some of the radium that entered the body became fixed in the skeleton.

Many doctors would have been alarmed at the news that this mysterious element accumulated in the bones, continuing indefinitely to expose patients to its powerful particles and rays with unknown long-term effects. Radium rays were known to be similar to x-rays, and x-rays had already been blamed for over fifty cancers among people working with them. However, Frederick Proescher—a Standard Chemical doctor who pioneered intravenous injection of radium—put an entirely different spin on the discovery in a January 1914 article in the company's journal, *Radium*.

As noted by Claudia Clark, a historian who wrote an important history of radium use in this era, Proescher managed to portray having radioactive bones as a *good* thing. He wrote that the radium deposited there would "render the organism not only passively but actively radioactive for a considerable period. . . . In other words, the body becomes a vital emanatorium due to the deposit of radium salts."

Also in 1914, the AMA began including radium solutions for drinking and injection in its annual list of new and nonofficial remedies. Flannery had succeeded in gaining for his radium potions a credibility that had been denied his vanadium potions. The stage was set for a new era of radium quackery.

Standard Chemical also encouraged the application of its radioactive waste to food crops. The company had lots of radioactive material left over from radium production, and it brought in a botanist to test it on plants. The results were published in 1914 in a full-page feature story in the *New York Times* (headlined "Radium a Wonderful Stimulant of Farmers' Crops").

The study, partly conducted in Joe Flannery's own garden, described how adding radioactive waste to the soil dramatically improved the yields of squash, carrots, radishes, turnips, beets, and many other vegetables. Moreover, "nearly all vegetables [were] wonderfully improved in their table qualities." The study's author, a renowned botanist named Henry Rusby, confidently concluded that most crops would benefit from radioactive fertilizer and that the beneficial effects would probably last for many years. A few weeks later, scientists at the University of Illinois Agricultural Experiment Station strongly disputed Rusby's optimistic findings; they had concluded from their own research that there was no foundation for expecting radioactive waste to increase crop yield. Fortunately, scattering radioactive waste across the nation's croplands never gained much traction.

OPPORTUNITY-SPOTTING, RISK-BLIND: WHEN A
VISIONARY SEES ONLY THE "PROMISES OF HIS OWN
VISION"

Joseph Flannery died in 1920 at the age of fifty-two, just nine years after launching the U.S. radium industry. (His body was brought to Flannery

Brothers undertakers, the very business he had left years earlier.) While some sources report the cause of his death as the Spanish flu, his death certificate does not bear that out. Rather, it blames a heart problem and lists anemia—a common consequence of radiation exposure—as a contributing cause of death. It is fair to wonder if Flannery's hands-on approach to radium refining, or merely eating the vegetables from his own radioactive garden, contributed to his early demise. Of course, his company promoted radium as a treatment for, rather than a cause of, anemia; I have seen no evidence that Flannery consumed his own radium potions, but if he believed his own marketing, he might well have.

Multiple editorials written upon Flannery's death praised his boldness, determination, and most of all, his remarkable ability to spot opportunities. One said that Flannery "saw what was denied others. He saw success and progress for himself and his native city where others saw nothing. He strode boldly into a new field until then unexplored and holding nothing except the promises of his own vision." His life proved, in the words of another newspaper, that "the gates of opportunity are ever open to the man with eyes to see and the courage to enter."

This was not just hyperbole: Flannery's life did indeed demonstrate unusual vision and drive. According to an obituary in *Radium*, upon leaving the family's undertaking business, Flannery bought a bolt company and then traveled to the world's leading steel centers to learn how to improve the bolts using stronger steel. He learned that the metal vanadium could help, so he tracked down and bought a small vanadium mine in Peru. He later sold the idea of using a vanadium-steel alloy in the Model T to Henry Ford (achieved, according to legend, by throwing a specially built car made with vanadium steel over a cliff to demonstrate its strength). As for radium, the US ore he used required a new method to refine it, and Flannery withdrew from the vanadium business to devote himself fully to developing it.

In short, Flannery had the qualities commonly celebrated in an industrial pioneer—he was innovative, bold, focused on pursuing rewards that others could not see, and uninhibited by risk. Most people have an optimism bias, seeing our goals as more achievable than they are and discounting the associated risks, and in entrepreneurs this bias is particularly prominent. It leads to overconfidence, but the markets tend to reward overconfidence, even when it causes bad decisions. As Daniel Kahneman, a psychologist and Nobel Prize–winning behavioral economist, explains in *Thinking, Fast and Slow*, "optimism is highly valued, socially and in the market; people and firms reward the providers of dangerously misleading information more than they reward truth tellers." In short, in our economic system, underestimating risk leads to power, as least for a while.

And more power may lead to further underestimating risk, according to a psychological model that governs much of the field's research into power's impact on the mind. It is built around two brain systems governing behavior: the Behavioral Approach System and the Behavioral Inhibition System. The approach and inhibition systems have been compared to the mind's "going" and "stopping" systems, and neuroscientists have tracked distinct brain processes and regions involved in each system.

The approach/inhibition theory of power, set forth by psychologists Dacher Keltner, Cameron Anderson, and Deborah Gruenfeld, proposes that power activates the approach system, which is focused on rewards and is associated with action, confidence, low levels of deliberation, and lack of inhibition. By contrast, powerlessness activates the inhibition system, which is focused on threats and linked to uncertainty, deliberation, vigilance, concern over consequences, and awareness of others' interests.

Under this theory, since powerful people are focused on reward and not threat, they would be less aware of risk. One study suggests this diminished risk perception applies not just to the risks faced by the power holders but to societal risk generally. Researchers primed subjects to feel powerful by having them recall an incident where they had power over others; the power-primed subjects then made much lower estimates of annual deaths from several causes, including lung cancer, tornadoes, and airplane accidents, compared to estimates by subjects not primed to feel powerful (and much lower than actual fatality statistics). This was a small study, and the use of priming is now controversial because many other studies using priming have made findings that other researchers failed to replicate. But if findings like those from this study do hold up, they have troubling implications: power, which enables people to impose new risks on society, also makes them less likely to see those risks.

Flannery clearly fits the archetype of a high-power, reward-driven, action-oriented figure high on the approach scale, not inhibited by a careful consideration of the risks he was imposing on others. We can imagine his inner voice saying, "Let's create a lucrative and glorious new industry selling health-giving radium to as many people as possible," drowning out any internal (or external) voice saying, "Wait, let's first find out if it's actually good for people to have this mysterious, flesh-destroying element lodged in their bones." A particularly strong approach motivation surely characterizes most founders of new industries, and it may well come with an impaired perception of risk that promotes denial.

THE RADIUM GIRLS: FROM GLOWING CHEEKS TO ROTTING JAWS

In 1906, an Austrian physician and physicist named Sabin von Sochocky immigrated to the United States. He was fascinated by radium; before he left Europe, he had met the Curies, and he may have also learned that Swiss clockmakers were applying a glow-in-the-dark paint containing radium to the dials. (Many substances glow for a limited time after exposure to light; what made radium special was that it kept glowing due to its radioactive energy.) In 1913, von Sochocky formulated his own radioluminescent radium paint, and it was so popular with U.S. clockmakers that in 1914 he launched a company called the Radium Luminous Materials Corporation (later, renamed U.S. Radium).

Demand for his paint skyrocketed when the United States entered World War I, and by 1918 nearly every American soldier wore a radium wristwatch. After the war millions of civilians bought them too. Soon, radium paint—which glowed green* and which von Sochocky's company called Undark—was used on a long list of products from doorbells and the buttons on bedroom slippers to fishing lures and crucifixes. It was even painted onto the eyeballs of toy animals and dolls, a particularly nightmarish idea seemingly guaranteed to terrify children who woke up in the dark.

---

*Radium in high enough concentrations glows blue, but radium paint contained zinc sulfide, which glows green when exposed to the energy released by just an infinitesimal amount of radium.

Von Sochocky's company eventually did everything from mining and refining radium to making the paint and hiring hundreds of workers to carefully apply it to watch dials and other products in its Orange, New Jersey, facility. A subsidiary of Flannery's Standard Chemical soon opened its own dial-painting center in Illinois, and a third major center of dial painting was set up in Waterbury, Connecticut. The dial painters were almost all women and girls, many hired when only fifteen years old or even younger. The unluckiest of them would become known in the head-lines as the "Radium Girls," the "Doomed Women," and the "Living Dead," as they became victims of one of the nation's most sensational workers' health disasters.

The dial painters mixed powdered paint with water or adhesive and then painted it onto watch faces with camel-hair brushes. They used their lips and tongue to keep a nice, sharp point on the brush, as taught. They inevitably swallowed some of the paint, and they came home with the powdered paint dusting their hair, skin, and clothes. That dust contained just a few parts per million of radium, but that was enough to make them glow in the dark, even after trying to scrub it off. One former dial painter, referring to a friend she worked with who got particularly dusty, recalled asking "the neighborhood kids in to watch Alice glow in a dark closet. They'd get a good laugh out of that." And some dial painters played with the paint; one "lively" girl reportedly painted her teeth with it whenever she had a date "so that they'd shine in the dark," though presumably the green tint of the paint limited the cosmetic appeal of this practice.

The dial painters had been told that the paint was not just harmless but good for them. And a government investigator was assured by a company supervisor that instead of being harmed by the paint, many dial painters were physically helped by it. A supervisor in the Illinois studio reportedly ate a bit of the paint off a spatula to demonstrate its harmlessness to the workers. Dial painters would later testify that they were told the paint would make them "good looking" and put a "glow in our cheeks."

The hype around the health benefits of internal radium therapy, largely fueled by Standard Chemical, supported the notion that consuming radium paint was beneficial. Von Sochocky—whose original interest in radium was a medical one—even sold the radioactive waste from his plant to parents to put in their children's sandboxes. He assured parents that it was "most hygienic" and "more beneficial than the mud of the world-renowned curative baths."

The dial painters might indeed have exhibited a certain healthy glow when first exposed to radium. The body's initial response to radiation is to defend itself by producing a large number of red blood cells, giving the victim a fleeting feeling of health. This transient stimulation of the blood has been credited with giving rise to the legend of the healing powers of radium, though the stimulation of the profit motive among radium companies, spas, and certain doctors surely helped too.

Before long, radiation exhausts the blood-forming processes, causing red blood cell production to drop, potentially leading to severe anemia. Like calcium, radium is taken up by the bones; once there, radium continually blasts the surrounding tissues with radiation. Despite the positive spin that Standard Chemical had tried to put on it in 1914, having radioactive bones is not good for you. In addition to damaging the blood-forming processes in the bone marrow, the relentless radiation kills bone tissue ("necrosis"), which then becomes infected, decays, and crumbles.

In many cases the dial painters' first symptoms began in their mouths. Instead of a healthy glow in their cheeks, they faced the disfigurement of lost teeth and rotting jawbones (sometimes presenting with a "gelatinous liquefaction" and opening holes into the sinuses or through the cheek). Many suffered crippling bone problems in their knees, hips, and spines as well.

The first death that would eventually be linked to radium dial painting was that of Mollie Maggia, who painted dials in von Sochocky's facility. She had an aching tooth pulled in 1921, but it never healed. More teeth became loose and were extracted from her badly infected and ulcerous mouth, and then even more teeth fell out on their own. She became anemic, suffered severe joint pains, and was too sick to work by early 1922. Later that year her lower jawbone was so disintegrated that her dentist lifted out the entire thing with his fingers. She died that fall. She had been misdiagnosed with syphilis, but later her bones would be exhumed and found to be highly radioactive, and the autopsy found no syphilis.

As more dial painters developed mysterious jaw problems, attention was drawn to the New Jersey plant. Local dentists suspected "phossy jaw"—a well-known occupational disease that plagued workers who handled phosphorus and that similarly caused horrible infections of the jawbone and anemia—but they learned there was no phosphorus in the paint. State and local officials got involved when the list of sick or dead dial painters grew to five; they found no legal violations and took little action, though one expert was immediately convinced the culprit was radium.

The dial painters' case is a story not just of women as victims but of women as activists, as historian Claudia Clark detailed in her 1997 book *Radium Girls: Women and Industrial Health Reform, 1910-1935*. The dial painters were helped by a growing industrial health movement largely propelled by women. In early 1924, a female local health official alerted the state branch of the Consumers' League—a women's reform organization concerned with industrial health—and it began a campaign to help the dial painters. (U.S. Radium would later blame the mental strain and worry suffered by one of its ailing workers not on radium poisoning but on "agitation" by the Consumers' League.) The Consumers' League worked behind the scenes with Alice Hamilton, an MD and Progressive-era social reformer often considered the founder of industrial toxicology in the United States. At the time, Hamilton was already a national expert on workplace poisoning and Harvard's first female faculty member. Hamilton had begun researching workers' health earlier in the 1900s, when, she later observed, it was considered a "subject tainted with Socialism or with feminine sentimentality for the poor."

There would be, in the years ahead, investigations, lawsuits, hearings, reports, and a great deal of press covering the suffering of the doomed young women. A few dial painters or the families they left behind got some slight financial compensation for their agonizing deaths after years of delay, though most did not. Throughout it all, the industry denied responsibility.

BLAMING THE VICTIMS: THEY WERE "ALREADY IN COMPARATIVELY POOR HEALTH"

By the time the dial painters' symptoms emerged, von Sochocky had been forced out of his company. The new president, Arthur Roeder, responded in 1924 to the claims of workplace poisoning by inviting Cecil Drinker, founder of Harvard's industrial health program, to visit the plant. The Drinker team was appalled to discover glowing dust covering workers' hair, skin, and clothes, and it found abnormalities in all the blood samples it took. The Drinker team reported to Roeder that it believed radium was the cause of the trouble and strongly urged additional precautions.

Roeder rejected these alarming findings, calling the evidence circumstantial and citing the lack of illnesses at other radium plants. The company concluded that "there is nothing harmful anywhere in the works" and even told state regulators that the report had cleared the plant of blame. When the Drinker team learned their work had been misrepresented, they published their report, even though the company threatened to sue.

Meanwhile, Roeder shopped for an expert to refute the Drinker report. Ross Mullner, author of *Deadly Glow: The Radium Dial Worker Tragedy*, reports that Roeder found Frederick Flinn, a former director of several mining companies who had recently obtained a PhD in physiology and was teaching at Columbia. Flinn sought out the sick dial painters and examined them, promising an unbiased opinion. He assured them they were not really sick (just suffering from nerves, he explained to the Consumers' League) or that their troubles were not caused by radium. Some were stunned to later learn that Dr. Flinn—who examined them, took blood, and opined on their health—was not in fact an MD. Flinn published an article concluding that "an industrial hazard does not exist" at the plant, disputing the Drinker study without disclosing that he was working for U.S. Radium.

By the summer of 1925, seven U.S. Radium employees had died. The first lawsuit was filed, multiple inquiries were launched, and the newspapers were paying attention. The company denied blame, citing the lack of problems in the past or at other radium plants. It argued that radium is harmful only in far higher exposures; at the diluted levels at the plant, if radium had any effect at all it "should have a beneficial and not baneful effect." However, slow poisoning causing symptoms only after years of exposure was common, as scientists knew already from experience with lead, mercury, and phosphorus, and it had been known for years that radium built up in the bones. Moreover, severe illnesses had in fact appeared in other plants; they had just been kept quiet.

If the company's arguments were shaky, at least they were not as absurd as what came next. The company went on to explain that since the work was such light labor, they had hired "a number who were unfit for more strenuous labor. Consequently when some of those already in comparatively poor health declined normally it was said that their handling of the paint was responsible."

Declined normally? The dial painters almost all shared the unique and horrific experience of having their bones, especially jawbones, rot and crumble in place. Moreover, that year it would be discovered and reported that the women themselves were radioactive, even if they had left the plant years earlier. They were exhaling radon and their bones emitted radiation. In 1927, even Flinn, the company's consultant, publicly admitted that radium was partly or wholly responsible for the workers' conditions.

Nonetheless, U.S. Radium still claimed it was being unfairly penalized for the generosity it showed in hiring illness-prone workers (with, apparently, a preexisting tendency toward radioactive breath and dissolving facial bones). In a blend of victim blaming, in-group aggrandizement and siege mentality that was especially jaw-dropping, Roeder's successor wrote in 1928 that "cripples and persons similarly incapacitated were engaged. What was then considered an act of kindness on our part has since been turned against us, as . . . regardless of what [previous employees] may have been suffering from or are suffering from at the present time, in the minds of the general public [it] can be attributed to 'Radium Poisoning.'"

By 1929, twenty-three dial workers (not all of them dial painters) were already known to have died from bone necrosis and anemia; more deaths would occur in the years ahead, including among the Illinois dial painters, who sued in the 1930s, though total deaths were not carefully tracked. Other dial workers were disabled by bone lesions, but we do not know how many. Around 1930, the rare cancers started emerging: eighty-six dial painters would be diagnosed with bone cancer or cancers of the nasal sinuses or mastoid cavities, which were clearly attributable to radium. Ironically, given the era, it is entirely possible that external radium application may have been used to fight the tumors.

It is worth noting that most of the dial painters did not die of radium poisoning or develop cancer of the bone, sinus, or mastoid. Even among the 1,600 or so workers hired before 1927 and who practiced lip-pointing, only a little over 5 percent developed these cancers, and even fewer died of necrosis or anemia. The fact that only a fraction of workers became so dramatically ill is not well explained, but may be due to different levels of susceptibility to radiation among the population. Whatever the reason, this fact probably made it psychologically harder for the companies to accept responsibility and easier to blame the victims for getting sick.

BLAME SHELTERS: AUTHORITY, DIVIDED LABOR, IGNORANCE, SIDE EFFECTS, AND LIMITED LIABILITY

The denials discussed above go to the heart of causation, disputing that the illnesses were caused by radium paint at all. Other denials accepted that radium made the workers sick but found other ways to evade moral responsibility and legal liability. We've all seen people trying to avoid the hot spotlight of blame when things go wrong, seeking shelter in the shadow of a good excuse. There are a number of what we could call "blame shelters"—common psychological rationales that effectively limit one's sense of responsibility (and liability) for causing harm the way a tax shelter lowers one's tax bill.

Perhaps the most well-known is the "just following orders" blame shelter, employed by war-crime defendants at Nuremberg. Famous and controversial psychological experiments conducted by Stanley Milgram in the early 1960s explored the scope of this blame shelter when he put study subjects into the role of "teachers," and asked them to administer a series of increasingly painful electric shocks to "learners." Subjects were told this was part of an experiment about teaching methods. In fact, the "learners" were in on the experiment, and they were not really being shocked, though they screamed convincingly. Over 60 percent of subjects were willing to inflict the maximum and apparently life-threatening shock on the screaming learners, illustrating the dark side of obedience to authority and a moral hazard inherent in any hierarchical group, whether it is an army, a corporation, or something else.

A second blame shelter is built around the "not my job" rationale, and Milgram explored this one too. He found that if he divided the labor—so that the subject did not directly inflict the simulated shock but merely enabled another to do so by administering the tests that the learner would get shocked for failing—more than 90 percent of subjects were willing to facilitate infliction of the maximum level of pain. Their reluctance to hurt another was diminished, apparently by not having to push the button themselves and by being a more distant part of a team of two involved in delivering the shock. One can imagine that the sense of responsibility would be diminished even more if there were more people among whom the labor was divided. (These first two blame shelters may also be seen as illustrations of the displacement and diffusion of responsibility that Albert Bandura links to the ability to morally disengage.)

Von Sochocky may have been employing one or both of these blame shelters when he failed to warn the dial painters of the danger they faced from his radioactive paint. At one of the trials, two dial painters testified that when they asked von Sochocky why he hadn't warned them, he'd said it was not his responsibility but that of the plant manager and later company president, Arthur Roeder (though von Sochocky denied saying this). If he did say it, it would suggest that this shelter is attractive not just to low-level employees but even to the man who invented the product and founded the company causing the harm.

Ignorance is a third commonly used blame shelter. Von Sochocky employed it when he testified that the danger of radium paint "was unknown to us." U.S. Radium president Roeder would even testify that he did not remember ever seeing the dial painters put the brushes to their lips, even though that was the standard practice. Years later, this ignorance shelter would prevent recovery by another dial painter's family when a federal court concluded that, while there were reasons to suspect the danger, the company did not *know* dial painting was dangerous until 1924. The value of ignorance as a blame shelter depends in part on keeping the burden of proof on the workers to show the company had knowledge of danger rather than on the company to show it had evidence of safety. As long as the burden stays with the workers, continued ignorance is encouraged and rewarded.

Did von Sochocky really believe radium exposure was safe? In years past he had been reckless in handling radium and cavalier about the consequences. He once had had part of a finger cut off due to radium necrosis, but he insisted that such dangers were hardly worth mentioning. In 1925, after the company chemist died of aplastic anemia, von Sochocky admitted that he felt sick but emphatically denied he had been poisoned by radium (though around that time he learned he too was exhaling radon). A few months after testifying in 1928, he died of aplastic anemia, at age forty-five. (*Time* magazine later reported that at the time of his death, von Sochocky's teeth and fingers were all gone, though other news accounts did not note this gruesome detail.) So it seems von Sochocky's ignorance, or his psychological denial, of radium's danger was at least deep enough to put him as well as his workers in mortal peril.

A fourth blame shelter relates to the "side effect" nature of corporate harm. A U.S. Radium official stressed that "no industry is in existence for the purpose of endangering human life and certainly not the radium industry, the main objective of which is to relieve human suffering." Indeed, in virtually any industry the harm to others is an unintended side effect of the pursuit of profit and other goals.

Whether or not an effect is intended may play a role in one's ability to emotionally recognize that effect. Joshua Greene at Harvard has for years studied moral sentiments by asking people what they would do if faced with certain unlikely moral dilemmas, often involving runaway trolleys. In his book *Moral Tribes: Emotion, Reason, and the Gap between Us and Them,* Greene suggests that our brains have a cognitive subsystem that monitors our plans and sounds an alarm when we contemplate harming others. Greene theorizes, though, that our innate alarm system "is *blind to harmful side effects*" of our plans. If our moral resistance to harming others does not get triggered when that harm is only a side effect of our main plan, it explains a great deal. All the harms discussed in this book could qualify as unintended side effects, even the anguish of slavery if we assume most of the slave traders and owners were not sadists and would have preferred it if the enslaved Africans were in fact contented.

I don't mean to suggest by listing these excuses that they are never valid. Organizations could not function if their members could not usually limit their focus and feelings of responsibility to their own job. And ignorance is a good excuse if the consequences of an act could not reasonably have been predicted even after an appropriate level of inquiry (and what level is appropriate can be fiendishly hard to define). As for the side-effect nature of most corporate harms, intent really is a morally and legally crucial question, even defining the border between an accident and a crime. And yet the psychological attractiveness of these excuses means they are applied in much less valid situations as well.

The availability of these blame shelters creates a moral hazard in any group that involves hierarchy and division of labor and that operates in the realm of unknown and unintended impacts, including corporations pushing the boundaries of existing practice and technology. Yet there is another blame shelter specifically designed for corporations and key to their ability to attract capital: limited liability. The protection it gives shareholders from being held personally responsible for harms the corporation causes makes the corporate form itself a legally established blame shelter. (The noted cynic Ambrose Bierce in the early twentieth century defined the corporation as "an ingenious device for obtaining individual profit without individual responsibility.")

U.S. Radium settled with five of the dying dial painters in 1928, still denying blame for their impending deaths but giving them a modest settlement "solely because of the humanitarian considerations." After that, the action largely shifted to Ottawa, Illinois, where since 1923 hundreds of dial painters had been employed by Radium Dial Company—a subsidiary of Joseph Flannery's Standard Chemical.

The Illinois cases hit the headlines in 1937, more than a decade after the New Jersey cases, but the parade of dying young women was no less tragic. There were years of legal machinations and delays, during which time the people running Radium Dial, facing a growing number of claims, shifted its assets elsewhere. The corporation was left a close-to-empty shell, limiting what poisoned workers could recover. What followed is complex and disputed, but a member of the family of Standard Chemical's founder Joseph Flannery ended up running a new dial-painting studio a few blocks away under a different corporate entity called Luminous Processes, which seemed to have preserved some of the original company's assets and had some of the same corporate officers but carried none of the previous company's liabilities toward its workers.

This is not how limited liability is supposed to work. It illustrates, though, how responsibility can be manipulated and evaded when it is deemed to attach only to an artificial entity rather than to the people who own and run it.

FUELING A HEALTH FAD: FLOODS OF SUNSHINE TO
REVIVIFY EVERY CELL

Despite the lurid coverage of the dial painters' radium poisoning, many people still linked this exotic element to health, and radium quackery flourished well into the 1930s. Internal use of radium (or of the radon gas it produced) was sold to treat conditions from the minor to the deadly, the common to the rare, including colds, headache, sunburn, nervousness, poison ivy, hay fever, asthma, insomnia, obesity, constipation, hemorrhoids, impotence, syphilis, schizophrenia, diabetes, malnutrition, tuberculosis, pneumonia, and both high and low blood pressure. Radium was even marketed to treat diseases it actually causes, like bone cancer, leukemia, and anemia.

No body part was considered too tender for exposure to radium. Radium products were sold as eyewash, toothpaste, earplugs, and something called "nose cups." One could smear radium on the skin using ointments and creams or just soak in radium bath salts, and a French company sold an elegant line of radium-bearing face creams, powders, and lipstick. Ads promised "weak discouraged men" that they could "bubble over with joyous vitality" and "perform the duties of a REAL MAN" by using Vita Radium rectal suppositories; not only would these cocoa-butter-based radium delivery devices restore sexual powers, but the package assured they were also "splendid for piles and rectal sores." Radium suppositories were also sold for vaginal insertion and even urethral insertion. If you simply wanted to swallow your radium, there were pills; the makers of Radio-X Tablets compared swallowing radioactive tablets to introducing "light, the enemy of all disease," into the human body. German companies also sold radium-fortified chocolate and bread.

There were two options for those who wanted to drink their radiation. One was to make radioactive water at home in a special crock made with radium, which infused the water with radon. Hundreds of thousands of just one brand of such crocks, the Revigator, were sold in the 1920s. Water without radioactivity, it was explained, was "devoid of its life element." One ad, unafraid of overstatement, simply called the water it produced "the greatest remedy and cure ever discovered for each and every disease."

The other way was to buy small bottles of water that contained actual, bone-seeking radium, not just the more fleeting radon gas. Flannery's

Standard Chemical had a subsidiary that sold such water for drinking, along with a radium solution for intravenous use. It advertised its solutions for arthritis, high blood pressure, and, incredibly, simple and pernicious anemias.

Standard Chemical's claims for its radium water were positively modest compared to those made by William J. A. Bailey, a true virtuoso of radium quackery. At the time, science was just starting to understand the role of the endocrine glands, and some claimed that restoring glands could reverse aging. The 1920s even saw a "monkey gland" fad, where some doctors grafted bits of monkey testicles onto the testes of men seeking to restore their youth and potency. Bailey merged the gland fad with the radium fad, arguing that radium could stimulate all the glands, not just the sexual ones, and could not only reverse aging but restore all aspects of health, including mental health.

In 1924, the *New York Times* quoted at length from a speech by Dr. William J. A. Bailey to the American Chemical Society, in which Bailey explained that curing the violently insane was just a matter of "a few minutes ionization a day" of the thyroid gland. Bailey took out ads featuring his own picture with a headline that screamed, "Science to Cure All the Living Dead: What a Famous Savant Has to Say about the New Plan to Close Up the Insane Asylums, Wipe Out Illiteracy and Make Over the Morons by His Method of Gland Control." In 1925 Bailey was believed enough of an expert on radium that the *Times* quoted him several times, including his denials that radium was killing the dial painters.

In fact, Bailey's scientific credentials were entirely faked. He had dropped out of college, been jailed for selling nonexistent mail-order cars, and was once fined for selling a male impotence medicine containing strychnine. When he became enthusiastic about radium, he granted himself the title of Doctor and eventually opened the Bailey Radium Laboratory in East Orange, New Jersey, near where U.S. Radium was operating. Some sources state he had worked at U.S Radium, but more detailed accounts of his life do not mention that, and he may have just set up operations in East Orange because U.S. Radium was a convenient radium source.

One of Bailey's early products was the Radiendocrinator, a gold-plated, credit-card-sized device containing radium and aimed at the high-end consumer; it originally cost $1,000 though the price later fell to $150. A woman could wear it on a belt around her hips to invigorate her ovaries, but it was mainly marketed to men, who were instructed to strap it beneath their scrotum at night where it could radiate their testicles as they slept. In addition to restoring sexual function, consumers were told it could help with flatulence and pimples and improve character and memory. (Radiendocrinators and other radioactive quack cures are displayed online in a fascinating collection maintained by the Oak Ridge Associated Universities.) It seems likely that Bailey and others selling quack cures targeted people who had sexual or other medical problems that embarrassed them, who might have preferred a remedy discreetly obtained by mail to a conversation with their doctor, and who would be less likely to publicly complain when the cure failed.

Bailey's most successful product was Radithor, radium-containing water sold in tiny bottles. It was like Standard Chemical's radium water, but Bailey marketed it with far more gusto. He claimed it treated over 150 ailments and was a powerful aphrodisiac, and he managed to sell over 400,000 bottles at a hefty markup between 1925 and 1930. A book Bailey ghost-wrote and sent to doctors explained that Radithor released billions of alpha rays that "liberate their energy throughout the entire system like floods of sunshine, reaching every cell, every gland, and every nook and corner of the body to revivify and quicken to action every fibre of the organism."

Bailey's most famous customer was Eben Byers, a prominent millionaire, athlete, socialite, and president of a Pittsburgh iron foundry built by his father. Byers hurt his arm when he fell out of a train berth in 1927, and when it continued to bother him, his doctor recommended Radithor. Byers drank several bottles of Radithor a day, his wealth allowing him to poison himself much more thoroughly than most could afford to do. He was so happy with the results that he sent cases of it to his friends and even gave some to his racehorses. According to Roger Macklis, a radiation oncologist who has studied the history of Radithor, the product seemed to have been "more a recreational drug than a medicine, a tangible symbol of the surging enthusiasms of the 1920s." Looking at it through the neurobiological model of approach and inhibition systems discussed above, we might say that Bailey, Byers, and the era itself were all especially reward-focused and threat-blind.

Not long after the Roaring Twenties came crashing to a halt, Byers started having headaches and jaw pain and began losing teeth. By 1931, he could barely speak. A government investigator would report that after two jaw operations, Byers's "whole upper jaw, excepting two front teeth, and most of his lower jaw had been removed. All the remaining bone tissue of his body was slowly disintegrating, and holes were actually forming in his skull." (Ironically, Bailey's ghostwritten book quoted the claim that radium would help the toothless, as "mouths will be equipped with their third set of teeth.")

Byers's death in 1932 was front-page news, and it was attributed to radium poisoning. Bailey disputed the diagnosis, arguing that he had drunk more radium water "than any man alive and I never have suffered ill effects." Besides, he noted, his product had been prescribed by a physician, so he could not be held responsible—a version of the "not my job" blame shelter. In fact, Bailey had done all he could to construct that blame shelter himself: he had marketed heavily to doctors, mailing pamphlets describing his theories to every physician in the country, much like Standard Chemical had been sending its journal *Radium* to every physician. Bailey also gave doctors a $5 kickback for every $30 case of Radithor they ordered, a practice condemned by the AMA as "fee-splitting quackery."

At the time, the Food and Drug Administration (FDA) did not have the authority to stop the sale of radium nostrums. They did test various consumer radium products in 1926 and found that 95 percent of them contained either no radium at all or what the FDA considered too little radium to have a "therapeutic" effect. Radithor was among the 5 percent that did contain significant radium, making Bailey both more honest and more likely to kill people than many competitors. The FDA warned that radioactivity could be dangerous, but ultimately, it was the Federal Trade Commission, spurred by Byers's illness, that went after Bailey for false advertising and ended his Radithor sales by 1930.

The people at Standard Chemical or U.S. Radium would probably have viewed Bailey as a con man and a quack, and indeed he and many other marketers of radium products went much farther than these corporations in their unhinged health claims. And yet Standard Chemical, a self-declared pioneer in promoting the internal radium "therapy," sold equally dangerous radium drinks, along with radium solution for injection, and

U.S. Radium promoted radium as an internal medicine as well. These larger corporate enterprises helped establish the social norm of radium consumption, providing a legitimacy—not to mention the actual radium— that the even more blatantly divorced-from-reality quacks of the world would fully exploit.

SUNSET OF AN INDUSTRY: DEATH, CLEANUP, AND BURIAL

The market for radioactive remedies and consumer products largely dried up in the 1930s. This was probably due to the combined effect of the Depression, national coverage of the Byers case, and more attention paid by the medical profession and regulatory agencies. State and local health departments cracked down on radioactive products, while the FDA issued new warnings and sought more regulatory powers. The market did not entirely die, though: as late as the 1950s a contraceptive jelly at least claimed to contain radium.

We don't know how many people were sickened or killed by radium drinks, injections, and other products. Researchers found it harder to trace the fate of these consumers and patients than to trace the dial paint- ers, though it was learned that one doctor who commonly treated patients with radium had among his patients six people who developed bone or mastoid cancer. We also know that one of Byers's friends drank Radithor and died from radium necrosis a few months before Byers, though her death gained less media attention. And the doctor who prescribed Radithor for Byers—and who denied it caused Byers's death, blaming it instead on gout—drank Radithor as well, and according to one source he later died from a radium-induced sarcoma. (Madame Curie herself would die of radiation-induced anemia in 1934.)

After the Radithor scandal, William J. A. Bailey went on to sell other radioactive products and then on to a variety of other careers. He died in 1949 at age sixty-four of bladder cancer, which is not generally linked to radiation exposure. His bones, studied two decades later, were highly radi- oactive. Apparently, he did indeed drink his own product and maybe even swallowed his own bogus claims; he just proved more physically resistant to the dangers of radiation than many of his customers.

As for the dial workers, the deaths and cancers that could be clearly attributed to radium—including at least twenty-three from bone necrosis and anemia and eighty-six cancers of the bone, sinus and mastoid—no longer appeared in workers hired after lip-pointing was stopped around 1926 or 1927. (The first generation of dial painters are sometimes hailed as martyrs whose ordeal helped scientists set safety standards for the future nuclear weapon and power industries, protecting thousands of future workers.) Radium paint was still applied to dials using other methods in the decades that followed, especially during World War II. Workers, assured that the workplace was safe now that lip-pointing had stopped, still accumulated radium in their bodies through dust and other routes of exposure, often exceeding the newly set radium body-burden limits.

Dial painting with radium continued in Illinois until the mid-1970s, where the last generation of workers reportedly experienced an overall cancer rate double the expected rate. When some of the workers sued their employer, Luminous Materials, it closed the plant. (It actually donated radioactive dial painting desks to a local school, though the company was forced to take them back.) Corporate assets were shuffled about—as they had been in the 1930s—and there was not enough left to pay worker claims or clean up the contamination.

More lawsuits were brought in the 1970s and 1980s—by homeowners in New Jersey, where nearly 750 homes were built on radioactive fill from U.S. Radium; by landowners who bought former radium facilities; and by governments left to deal with contaminated sites around the country. Ultimately, though, hundreds of millions of dollars in cleanup costs would be borne by taxpayers, the federal Superfund, or private landowners rather than by the radium industry.

Radium is now barely used and no longer mined. Safer radioactive materials made in particle accelerators and nuclear reactors made radium almost entirely obsolete for both cancer treatment and paint. Radium is still sometimes used to treat certain tumors—tissue destruction being radium's first and last medical use—but our long-lived stocks are more than ample to meet that limited demand, making it unlikely radium will ever be mined again. In fact, by the 1980s, radium—once the costliest substance in the world—was considered merely a waste product of uranium mining, to be fixed in a form suitable for reburial. Radium researcher and geologist Edward Landa noted that in less than a century this element went from buried treasure to buried waste.

The story of radium might be seen as a cautionary tale of what happens when the brain's reward-focused "going" system (the Behavioral Approach System) is not kept in check by its threat-aware "stopping" system (the Behavioral Inhibition System). The potential rewards of exploiting radium drove entrepreneurs and the corporations they built to race ahead to create new markets for it, ignoring the predictable risks that would harm so many and finding many ways to deny responsibility for those harms.

An industry that would symbolize such a forward-drive mindset for much longer was the auto industry. Unlike with radium, the risks that came with driving automobiles were immediately obvious in the climbing highway death toll. But as the next chapter shows, just like the radium industry, the auto industry would long deny that it could be blamed for those deaths or expected to do much about them.

3 "The Nut behind the Wheel"

CARMAKERS AVOIDING BLAME FOR HIGHWAY DEATHS

*"Until we have substantially more information I find it
difficult to believe that the seat belt can afford the driver
any great amount of protection over and above that which
is available to him . . . if he has his hands on the wheel and
grips the rim sufficiently tight . . . and also takes
advantage of the shock absorbing action which can be
achieved by correct positioning of the feet and legs."*

—Howard K. Gandelot, GM chief auto safety engineer, 1954

In the mid-1950s, when General Motors' chief auto safety engineer, Howard Gandelot, expressed the above opinion—doubting the value of seat belts over just bracing oneself in a crash—he was working for the richest and most powerful industrial corporation on the planet. The US auto industry was booming in the postwar era, and GM dominated it, making more than half the cars sold. GM's president, Harlow Curtice, would be named *Time* magazine's 1956 Man of the Year as he and his company were hailed for helping bring America to "an all-time crest of prosperity, heralded around the world."

Meanwhile, in 1955 alone, traffic accidents killed 38,000 Americans and injured perhaps 2 million more, including an estimated 100,000 who were totally disabled, and the toll was rising. Since 1900, far more Americans had died in car accidents than in all the wars in the nation's history. Congress was just starting to pay attention to what one member called the "wholesale slaughter on our highways," a tragic loss that "staggers the imagination."

GM was uniquely equipped to find out if seat belts or other design changes could in fact help reduce these staggering losses. It had the biggest nonmilitary research and development staff in the nation, surely capable of finding out how its customers were harmed when they crashed in its products and of inventing ways to reduce that harm. Moreover, one of the core founding principles of GM was to collect facts and objectively analyze them. GM was the first in the industry to build proving grounds—mammoth facilities to scientifically test its cars—because "it is always sound philosophy to recognize that the most effective attack is the determination of facts without prejudice and using an open mind," according to the legendary Alfred P. Sloan Jr., whose decades of leadership shaped GM and strongly influenced the nation's philosophy of business management. Gandelot espoused the same personal philosophy, once reportedly telling an inquirer, "I delight in living my life each day, realizing that the information I give out is extremely factual."

And yet—despite public assurances that cars were as safe as it could make them—for decades the auto industry failed to find and make simple design changes that could have saved the lives of thousands and greatly reduced human suffering. Why didn't the industry devote more of its ample resources, sophisticated fact-gathering practices, and celebrated engineering prowess to making car accidents less lethal?

This chapter discusses how the industry avoided feeling (and being held) responsible to make cars more crashworthy, while simultaneously dismissing or minimizing the findings of others who identified safer auto designs. Key to the industry's approach was keeping the public's focus on the cause of the *accident,* not the cause of the *injury,* and stressing that the cause of the accident was usually bad drivers. This episode of denial also shows an industry reacting and contributing to a landmark shift in the historic debate over the role of government in holding private corporations responsible for acting in the public interest.

BLAMING DRIVERS: "ACCIDENTS ARE PRIMARILY CAUSED BY ATTITUDE"

Roadway deaths and injuries had been seen mainly as driver failures from the very beginning, and not just by carmakers. In 1902, when cars were a novelty but already subject to lavish media attention, one journalist wrote, "The accident which happens to the automobile is seldom due to the machine itself, but almost wholly to the loss of control or presence of mind of the operator."

In 1935, when the death toll was already in the tens of thousands yearly, *Reader's Digest* published a gruesome piece about the risks of motoring called "—And Sudden Death." It would become one of the most widely reprinted articles in the magazine's history. Its stated goal was to help readers understand the "pain and horror of savage mutilation" from car crashes, and it lingered on descriptions of decapitation, broken bones, flayed skin, and searing pain. It described dangerous aspects of car design, like driver-impaling steering columns and the "lethal array of gleaming metal knobs and edges" inside the car, and the article sparked what the auto industry later called an explosion of public concern. But it did not spark a sustained movement for safer cars, nor was that its intent. It was commissioned by the magazine's editor, who had recently witnessed the aftermath of an accident, to "bring some of the reckless drivers and speed maniacs to their senses."

Blaming drivers for highway carnage was easy, because some accidents were obviously caused by reckless drivers. Then, as now, such drivers made a memorable impression, speeding, weaving, cutting other cars off, and leaving a trail of angry people behind them. When the issue of traffic safety came up, those conspicuously dangerous drivers would naturally leap to mind.

The readiness of society to attribute car accidents to bad drivers might have been partly propelled by the same psychological forces behind other types of victim blaming. Basically, if we can attribute terrible events to the foolish behavior of the people who suffer them, we feel less worried that such events will happen to us and we can better maintain the belief that the world is just. The auto industry would have had the extra incentive to blame drivers in order to keep the blame off its products and itself, just as the radium industry wanted to blame its workers for having a preexisting sickliness that caused their symptoms.

Excessive driver-blaming may also reflect another much-studied cognitive bias. Psychologists have for decades examined attribution—how people think about what causes certain behavior and outcomes—and found that people are inclined to overestimate the importance of another person's disposition or choices and to underestimate the causal role of external situational factors. This tendency—dubbed the "fundamental attribution error" by psychologist Lee Ross—has appeared in scores of studies over the decades. (There is even neuroscientific evidence suggesting that it is easier for the brain to attribute events to persons than to situations, because that requires less elaborate information processing.) While much of the research deals with social behavior, the tendency also applies to accident attribution: if a person slips on a wet floor, observers are inclined to blame clumsiness or carelessness rather than the condition of the floor. In the field of safety management, the tendency to blame individuals for accidents rather than seeking systemic or engineering solutions was more prominent in decades past, but psychologist and engineer Richard Holden argues that it persists and continues to inhibit safety advances.

Conceivably, society and industry could have *attributed* accident causation to drivers without *blaming* them—that is, without adding any gloss of moral judgment by assuming the accident-causing behavior was somehow willful or inappropriate. After all, never before had humans been in the position of hurtling through space at such speed, propelled by such force at such proximity to each other, in devices requiring unnatural physical motions and unfailingly sharp reflexes, in an environment designed for much slower transportation. (A 1956 report found that "more continuous attention from moment to moment is required of the motor vehicle driver than of the operator of any other type of transportation, including the airplane.") Accidents could be seen as the inevitable result of this dangerous new interaction of human, machine and environment, particularly when virtually the entire adult population is driving, not just those with the most training and skill.

And yet accidents were more typically attributed to something willful: the driver's failure of attitude. In 1939, the head of the industry's safety advocacy foundation wrote that "a safe driver is one who is expert *and wants to avoid accidents*. It is that desire, a feeling concerning the urgency, smartness and sporting character of safety, that education must inculcate."

In 1956, Ford issued a statement explaining that "accidents are primarily caused by attitude. One cure for accidents is to make them social errors." Ford's statement explained that the car had created a new social order on the streets and that new social customs would evolve in response: "The time is coming when traffic accidents will be looked upon much as lying, rudeness, or dishonesty is now and people will refrain because of social pressure."* GM's chief engineer urged that same year that high school driver education programs were needed to teach drivers a sense of responsibility for their fellow man. In short, the US auto industry—perhaps the nation's largest collection of engineers—responded to the rising highway death toll not with mechanical engineering solutions but with suggestions for something closer to social engineering.

And something like social engineering had been taking place. Thousands of new driver training classes appeared in high schools. States required driving tests and licenses, imposed speed limits, and invested in traffic enforcement. A massive private, nonprofit safety movement led by the National Safety Council (NSC) launched major safety campaigns largely devoted to continually reminding people of the risk of accidents and urging them to drive safely. The auto industry supported all these efforts and helped fund the NSC, which often echoed the industry's philosophy on auto safety. The NSC's president said in 1956 that the key to stopping the rising death toll was for the public "to stop doing the things that are causing these accidents. Courtesy, commonsense, and care will do the trick."

Apart from making a huge investment in new highways, the federal government's role in traffic safety was mainly to support traffic laws and driver education at the state and local levels, through the President's Highway Safety Committee. This committee, formed by President Eisenhower, was never likely to confront the automobile industry over auto design. Its first chair was Harlow Curtice, president of GM. Thanks to his work on this committee, Curtice said, he had "reached the firm conclusion that driver education offers the most fertile field by far" for improving auto safety. The president's committee freely used the presidential seal, even though its executive director and two assistants were chosen and paid by the auto industry, something that was not made clear even to the committee's other members.

---

*This statement is surprising coming from Ford, which was trying—genuinely if temporarily—to promote and sell safer car designs in its 1956 models, as discussed later in this chapter.

Of course, social norms do have tremendous power, and trying to create safer norms around driving through education, laws, and public relations campaigns was entirely reasonable. What was unreasonable was the failure to simultaneously look for and deploy engineering solutions to make cars less lethal during the millions of crashes that continued to happen every year, despite all these other efforts.

By continually shifting the focus back to accident causation and driver culpability, the industry could draw a sort of veil over the violent unpleasantness of the accident itself. This would let them enjoy the psychological benefits of not thinking about—or taking responsibility for—what actually happens to the humans inside their products once the driver loses control and physics takes over.

THE FAILURE OF ENGINEERING GENIUS: TRAINING KIDS TO JUST BRACE THEMSELVES

In 1936 an auto industry representative assured the public that "our cars are the safest we know how to build. We will continue to build into them every sound safety factor developed by engineering genius." And, in fairness, cars were getting safer in many ways. The kind of dramatic mechanical defects that obviously caused accidents (and lawsuits)—like wheels that snapped off or steering that suddenly failed—became much less common as automotive engineering advanced. But when it came to engineering for crash protection, there was a decided lack of engineering genius at work.

Howard Gandelot, the chief GM auto safety engineer quoted at the beginning of this chapter, was not unique within the company or the industry when it came to a dismissive attitude toward proposed safety designs. Still, a lack of faith in safety engineering is particularly troubling in a safety engineer, and perhaps the world's most powerful one. In other auto companies, safety engineers advocated for safer designs, pushing against other divisions more interested in styling, sales, and costs, but there is little evidence that Gandelot championed safety within GM during this era.

Gandelot was described in a 1955 magazine article as "at once charming, brusque, adept with words, and generally self-assured." He was a former test driver, and according to others in the auto safety field interviewed by historian Joel Eastman, Gandelot's experiences convinced him that accidents were acts of God and it was little use to design with crashes in mind. He urged people to recognize that when it came to safety, "there's a ceiling on what the automotive engineer is going to be able to do."

Gandelot's lack of confidence in crash design may have had something to do with some primitive crash-testing that GM did at its proving grounds shortly after World War II. Remotely controlled cars were rolled down a steep hill and smashed into a concrete barrier. They hit at only about 30 miles per hour (mph), but apparently suffered great damage, according to what was written many years later by another GM safety engineer, Kenneth Stonex. Stonex wrote that the "catastrophic nature of these tests resulted in the belief that the threshold of serious and probably fatal injury is far below normal highway speeds. These tests led to the conclusion that it is impossible to provide secure protection during impacts of this nature by any amount of design modification, or by any restraining devices that the average driver would be willing to use."

This passive acceptance of technological limits was way out of step with the can-do technological spirit of the postwar years. Global fascism had just been defeated thanks in no small part to US technology, from its atomic bombs to the vast output of its auto industry, which had stopped making civilian cars during the war in order to churn out a tremendous flow of tanks, trucks, jeeps, and plane engines. The postwar age brought new technological anxieties but also a sense of empowerment through technology.

Unlike its self-serving fatalism about safer car design, GM was extremely ambitious when it came to the nation building safer highways. In 1956 the United States launched its greatest public works project to date, the interstate highway system, and GM contributed useful ideas for safe highway standards. But GM engineer Stonex wanted even more; he proposed that the government also rebuild almost all the rest of its millions of miles of public roads, and his vision of a society redesigned around the automobile went beyond just safety. Given all the unused roof space in cities, Stonex saw no practical reason why planners could not build new roads "over the buildings in commercial districts and heavily congested residential districts so that the road pavement serves as the roof deck. In central business districts, we might even have to think of horizontal tunnels through the buildings to carry automotive traffic, just as we have vertical tunnels to carry elevator traffic."

Yet GM found plenty of practical reasons why it could not design simple safety features into its cars, though this is not to suggest its engineers had no ideas about crash safety. Howard Gandelot had many; he just seemed to favor self-help suggestions over engineering solutions. As the quote at the beginning of the chapter says, he suspected that drivers who held the wheel tightly and correctly positioned their legs were as safe as those with seat belts, and he applied this same just-brace-yourself advice to children. A 1955 article described a customer's letter to GM about how he had suddenly stopped his car to avoid a kitten, and his young son flew into the dashboard and broke a tooth. The customer suggested that if the company would just pad the dashboard—something doctors had been urging for years—it would help "save faces and maybe lives."

Gandelot wrote back with an alternative suggestion for keeping the little ones safe. He noted that as soon as they get large enough to see out when standing up, that is what they want to do, and he did not blame them. With his own youngsters, he said, "I made it a practice to train them so that at the command 'Hands!' they would immediately place their hands on the instrument panel if standing in the front compartment, or on the back of the front seat if in the rear, to protect themselves against sudden stops." He explained that he frequently gave these commands even when there was no occasion to do so "just so we all keep in practice." (Gandelot also wrote later that padded dashboards would "make it impossible for front-seat passengers to cross their legs.")

Gandelot did not overtly claim that seat belts were useless or dangerous. He told journalist Harold Mehling in a 1955 interview that "General Motors hasn't said they're no good. We're just waiting to find out if they are any good. Nobody knows." Gandelot had his suspicions, though; asked about Ford's and Chrysler's experiment of offering seat belts as an optional feature, he said, "We don't think they're going to work out," and dismissed people in favor of them as "seat-belt evangelists." There was, in fact, compelling evidence by this time that seat belts saved lives. Research at Cornell University and elsewhere had shown, among other things, that when occupants were ejected from a crashing car, they were much more likely to be injured or killed, that seat belts prevented ejection, and that injury by a seat belt was so rare as to be nonexistent.

The need to keep people from being flung from crashing cars was also why auto companies had been urged to make latches that would keep doors from flying open during an accident, as Cornell's research showed they often did. However, Gandelot doubted that Cornell was correctly interpreting its accident data. Failing once again to appreciate the sudden violent forces that hurl people around during a crash, he said, "You take all this talk about door openings. No one knows exactly what happens in an accident. A lot of people probably figure that the best thing is to get out of the car as fast as they can. They reach over and open the door and fall out. Then the Cornell people tell us it's a door opening and they were thrown out." He added, "A lot of people fall on hardwood floors and hurt themselves, don't they? Should we take the hardwood floors out of houses?"

GM often fueled doubts about the safety of seat belts. In 1955, GM's vice president of engineering, Charles A. Chayne, said that safety belts "just define where you will fold under pressure, and the sudden pressure of the belt in many types of accidents can cause serious damage," and he told another audience he thought seat belts "offered little promise." That same year, Gandelot had written a draft report for the safety committee of the Automobile Manufacturers Association concluding that "until it is factually known whether seat belts, during major collisions, provide increased protection for the wearer or cause increased bodily injury, it would be unethical for the engineers on the vehicle safety committee to recommend their use; further, it would not be legally justifiable for auto manufacturers to equip their cars with seat belts or offer them as optional equipment." This draft report was never released, though, due to a brief but dramatic split among major carmakers on the safety issue, which is discussed later in this chapter.

LEAVING IT TO OTHERS: STUDYING THE "SECOND COLLISION"

Gandelot's claim that "no one knows exactly what happens in an accident" was unwittingly an indictment of his own company and industry for averting its gaze from this critical question for so long. It was also only partly true. Not only were some things entirely predictable given basic physics, but people outside the industry had by then learned much by actually studying how the human body responds to sudden impacts.

In a frontal collision, for example, the vehicle hits something and suddenly decelerates. After this first impact, the car's occupants keep moving forward at the speed the car had been going until they hit something that stops them; this would become known as the "second collision." The steering column posed an obvious threat; critics described it as a spear pointed at the driver's chest. The poorly attached steering wheel could snap off in the crashing driver's hands or when hit by the driver's body and leave the chest exposed to puncture by the hub. (Some auto stylists actually designed the hub to rise a few inches above the wheel, or even topped it with a pointed end.) If the crash crumpled the front of the car, the forward end of the steering column could be hit, thrusting the column back toward the driver just as he or she was flung forward, increasing the likelihood of impalement.

All occupants of the car were at risk of being catapulted onto hard, often sharp-edged instrument panels, which would come to be called "meat cleavers" by some within the industry for their effect on crashing passengers. Occupants could crack their skulls or puncture their facial bones on protruding metal knobs or other design elements. Back-seat passengers would collide with the back of the front seat, which might also be hard and sharp. Sometimes the seats ripped free of the floor, or simply folded forward if the car was a two-door. Then the weight of both the seat and the back-seat passenger would add to the force smashing the front-seat occupants into the unyielding steering column or sharp-edged dashboard.

If the car was rolling over, all occupants were at risk of being crushed by a collapsing roof. It was common in many types of accidents for doors to pop open, flinging passengers out of the car. And of course sometimes people exited the car through the windshield. In the years before safety glass, this was a particularly grisly outcome, as slivers of broken glass could pierce through eye sockets, and sharp edges could slice across necks or limbs.

While some dangers were obvious, there was still much to be learned about the exact forces and designs that injured people and about how designs could be changed to reduce injury. For the most part, though, the industry had little interest in learning about them. Fortunately, a few people outside the industry stepped into that knowledge vacuum, willing to take a close and sustained look at what happens to the human body in those few brutal seconds.

One such person was Dr. Claire Straith, a Detroit plastic surgeon who treated accident victims. In the 1930s, he started campaigning for collapsible steering columns and smooth, padded dashboards. He met with auto company executives and designers and showed pictures of crash victims whose facial gashes mirrored dashboard features. In 1937, Chrysler actually responded with a car with a safer dashboard. In the highly competitive postwar atmosphere, safer designs were largely forgotten, though Straith and other doctors, the American Medical Association, and various medical committees would keep pressing the industry for decades to make the interiors of cars less lethal.

In the 1940s, Colonel John Stapp of the Air Force started researching how people could better survive plane crashes, and then he expanded his team's focus to auto crashes. The research included extensive crash testing using dummies, human volunteers, and anesthetized animals. (The animals of choice were hogs and chimpanzees, because as Stapp explained to a congressional committee in 1957, "Some people are more like hogs; others more like chimpanzees.") Stapp himself volunteered for some of the crash tests, which used a specially designed rocket sled. He also made the important finding that lap belts could put thousands of pounds of pressure on the pelvis without causing injury; he installed them in his own car and said he "could not afford to be caught dead without one." His crash tests found that people could walk away from a 60-mph crash into a solid object if they were adequately restrained and if the vehicle would absorb enough of the energy to crumple two or three feet. This was just the opposite of what GM had found in its apparently abbreviated postwar crash testing.

Some of the most revealing research in the field of crash injury was launched by an inventor and researcher named Hugh DeHaven, who got into the field, well, by accident. He had been the sole survivor of a plane crash during World War I and then briefly studied how and why some people survive crashes. A couple decades later, after a career doing other things, DeHaven happened to witness a car skid off a road and land on its side. The driver had been thrown into a sharp steel knob that pierced his right frontal sinus and tore across his face, leaving him with a disfiguring and disabling injury. DeHaven would later call it a "frightening demonstration that engineers in 1936 had no more contact with causes of injuries than they had in 1917. I again realized that engineers didn't know—and that nobody knew—how many times people were hurt or killed by things that could be easily changed."

In 1938, DeHaven began to devote himself to studying what impacts the human body could survive, including why some people survive falls from great heights. Like Stapp, he found that people could withstand tremendous impacts if the forces were distributed and if what they hit would bend or deform. With federal funding, he set up a small aeronautic-crash-injury research project at Cornell Medical College. He and his staff of three gathered data from hundreds of small plane crashes; by 1944 he published a paper concluding that seat belts caused no injury, and he argued that many of the lessons from plane crashes applied to cars too.

In 1951, Corporal Elmer Paul, an Indiana state police official who had investigated many auto accidents, oversaw a large study of the state's fatal car crashes. Indiana police and doctors gathered data on over six hundred fatalities that year, and the study found that people were often killed by "the placement and design of equipment and furnishings in vehicle interiors." By 1952 Cornell expanded on this extremely useful number-crunching, gathering detailed car accident data from other states. Cornell's database of thousands of car accidents enabled it to publish important reports with the weight of data drawn from actual experience.

The data from the Indiana survey and then the Cornell studies held some surprises, including the finding (mentioned above) that people are statistically much better off if they are not thrown from a crashing car. And by matching accidents where people had no seat belts to very similar accidents where people wore belts (there were a few because some people had installed them at their own initiative), the Cornell researchers could show how dramatically belts reduced injuries. They found, for example, that accident victims wearing seat belts were 87 percent less likely to experience dangerous or fatal injuries than were unrestrained people in similar accidents who were thrown from the car. They also found that cars were getting less crashworthy; accident victims were more likely to die in cars built in the 1950s than those who had a similar accident in cars built in the 1940s.

SPLIT IN THE INDUSTRY: "WE DON'T BELIEVE YOU SHOULD BE CONSCIOUS OF ACCIDENTS"

Data like this encouraged medical activism promoting auto safety. In 1955, a number of state and national medical groups formally urged the industry to design safer cars. Carmakers' different responses to those recommendations illustrated a growing split within the industry. A representative of the American College of Surgeons told a congressional committee in 1956 that Ford and Chrysler responded well to its resolution calling for design changes. However, he added, "We had some resistance with the safety engineer of General Motors for some reason, and they took a curious reaction. He berated us for getting out of our field into the field of automobile design."

Ford and Chrysler had also shown more genuine interest in Cornell's findings than GM had. In 1951, Gandelot had been assigned to contact Cornell to see if "any degree of control could be exercised [on] behalf of General Motors to mitigate their statements." By contrast, Ford's head safety engineer, Alex Haynes, responded to Cornell's and Indiana's preliminary data by starting to research better steering columns and door latches. Ford also conducted or sponsored its own crash testing and lab studies, and the research wasn't always pretty. To test new energy-absorbing materials to use in dashboards, for example, Ford partnered with Wayne State Medical School to drop human heads and then entire cadavers from six stories onto different materials.

Haynes—who had worked in the aviation industry, where seat belts had saved many lives—could see the value of seat belts in cars. In the spring of 1955, Ford, Chrysler, and AMC announced they would offer seat belts as an option in 1956 models, leaving GM isolated among the major carmakers on the issue. Then, despite having urged the industry a few months earlier to announce that seat belts were potentially dangerous and it would be unethical to offer them until more was known, GM began to offer seat belts as a dealer-installed option. However, even a few years later a safety engineer would comment that installing front seat belts in four-door GM cars was "exceedingly difficult."

But Haynes and his boss, Ford vice president Robert S. McNamara, wanted to go further, adding a few more safety features to their cars and then actually marketing the concept of safety. Years later they told historian Joel Eastman, author of *Styling vs. Safety,* that by that time, they felt the industry had a responsibility to deal with the auto accident problem, and if they did not do so, the government might intervene (congressional hearings had already been proposed). And they thought their safety campaign would increase sales. While the auto industry was booming, Ford's 1955 model-year sales were lagging in comparison to GM's Chevrolet, and with only minor styling changes in 1956 models, Ford faced a potentially disastrous year of sales. McNamara felt that an aggressive safety push could prevent that, and he and Haynes overcame resistance from an older generation of executives.

So Ford made some changes to its 1956 model cars. Safer steering wheels and better door latches were standard. Customers could pay extra for an energy-absorbing dashboard, a safer rearview mirror, and seat belts, which could now be factory-installed. In an even greater break from industry practice, Ford launched a massive advertising campaign highlighting crash safety, earning an enthusiastic response from many in the media and from safety advocates like Claire Straith, Hugh DeHaven, and John Stapp. One Ford employee would say of Ford's safety effort, "It isn't often that you can be on the side of God and profits."

It was understood within the industry that the greatest opposition to safety design came from GM. An executive identified only as a "vice president of one of the auto giants" (perhaps McNamara) told a journalist in 1955, "Whenever I'm asked why a certain company is being so stiff-necked about this safety business, I say: 'Maybe they've gotten so big they're smug and arrogant. On the other hand, maybe they're up to something we don't know about. I can't be sure. The important thing is that we don't care what they do. We're going ahead with safety and we're going to sell the pants off them.'"

Ford's safety campaign left GM "dumbfounded—and then furious," according to a *Fortune* magazine article written years later by journalist Dan Cordtz, "and many an outraged telephone call went out" from GM to

Ford, trying to get them to stop it. Why would Ford listen to its competitors at GM? There was a saying at Ford at the time that Chevy could drop its price $25 to bankrupt Chrysler and $50 to bankrupt Ford, suggesting how threatened people at Ford felt about GM's tremendous market power. Moreover, a number of top executives at Ford had formerly worked at GM and may have shared GM executives' attitude or at least been more willing to take their outraged calls.

But why would GM bother to pressure Ford? If customers really did not care about safety, as GM had long argued and would claim for years, Ford's gamble on safety would fail in the market, to GM's advantage. Why not just let the experiment play out?

Apparently, GM officials opposed Ford's campaign because they felt that talking about crashes would frighten buyers away from all cars. In 1955, at McNamara's initiative, Ford and then Chrysler had agreed to contribute funding for expanded auto-safety research at Cornell, but GM refused to join them. The Cornell program's director, John Moore, remembered it as "a harsh refusal" to recognize that outsiders had any legitimate interest in car design. A person involved in that dispute told Cordtz that GM had a strong feeling "that if you said or did anything that made it look like driving was anything but fun—the most fun of anything in the world—you were hurting the business."

Surely GM was wrong about this. America was investing billions in interstates and suburbs, strip malls and drive-ins, reshaping its communities and its national identity around the automobile. It would take more than a few ads reminding people of the unfun possibility of crashing to quench the nation's passion for cars. After all, that passion hadn't been quenched by years of highway death toll predictions printed in the papers before each holiday weekend; those predictions were made by the National Safety Council, which was partially funded by the auto industry. And it hadn't been quenched by the harsh reality of people crashing by the millions and dying by the thousands each year. How could drawing attention to such an obvious reality and adding a few features designed to reduce that death toll hurt sales more than the death toll itself?

Valid or not, the belief that reminding people of crash risks would hurt the industry kept emerging. The influential GM auto stylist Harley Earl said in 1958, "We are trying to make the slogan 'Driving for Fun' a reality. . . . We don't believe you should be conscious of accidents. If you were on a boat, you would not want life preservers all over the table; it suggests too much." An unnamed industry official told the *New York Times* in 1965 that "people don't like to be reminded that you can have a wreck in an automobile. It is not in our interest—it is not logical—to say, 'If you get in a wreck, you're probably not going to be killed in this car.'"

After a few months of devoting about a third of its advertising budget to safety, Ford changed course, switching its ad focus back to performance, styling, and speed. There were rumors McNamara would be fired. He not only held on though, but he later became president of Ford, then John Kennedy's secretary of defense, and then a prime architect of the Vietnam War.

Explanations for why Ford shelved its safety campaign varied. Industry outsiders, including *Fortune* magazine, pointed to the behind-the-scenes pressure from GM. Industry insiders pointed to sales: Ford's 1956 model-year sales started strong but then began to lag behind Chevy's, and for most in the industry, Ford's experiment hardened their belief that "safety doesn't sell." However, the evidence that safety didn't sell was ambiguous at best. Ford had been expecting a disastrous sales year, and the safety campaign's supporters would later claim the campaign helped Ford hang onto its market share. The safety features themselves actually proved much more popular than Ford expected. The padded dash, which cost extra, was ordered by 43 percent of customers, catching on faster than any option in the company's history, and one in seven buyers ordered the extra-cost seat belts. This demand for seat belts was so much higher than expected that the company at first could not keep up.

Whatever the reason, Ford's shift away from marketing safety meant that an opportunity for the auto industry to make greater strides in this area and to increase customer demand for safety was lost. Future historians would see this reversal as delaying the advance of auto safety for years.

CONFLICT BLINDNESS: "WHAT'S GOOD FOR THE COUNTRY IS GOOD FOR GM, AND VICE VERSA"

GM's greater resistance to safety design had deep roots, as illustrated by the story of safety glass—a partial exception to carmakers' general disinterest in crashworthiness. In 1927, Henry Ford was about to release his new Model A, but he knew it posed new dangers because it went so fast—up to 60 mph, compared to the Model T's top speed of only 45 mph. Then a Model A test car collided with another car at 50 mph; a prominent Ford designer smashed through the windshield and was badly cut. Afterward, Ford reportedly said, "We can't put that car out on the public! We'll kill them," and decided to use more costly, shatter-resistant safety glass in the Model A's windshields. Other carmakers, like the head of DeSoto, would soon credit such glass with preventing "thousands of accidents from causing grievous bodily injuries" every year.

The president of DuPont pressed GM in 1929 correspondence to add safety glass to Chevrolets, its lowest-priced cars; DuPont owned much of GM's stock, and it would have made the glass. GM head Alfred P. Sloan Jr. refused. "Accidents or no accidents, my concern in this problem is a matter of profit and loss." Safety glass, he feared, would threaten "the comparatively large return the industry enjoys and General Motors in particular." Sloan apparently had some qualms about so clearly putting profits over safety, but he overcame them, noting, "I believe that when any of us are dealing with safety matters, we should perhaps not be commercial yet it is hard to avoid that phase of the question." In 1932, when the two executives again debated safety glass, Sloan again refused, writing, "I am trying to protect the interest of the stockholders of General Motors and the Corporation's operating position—it is not my responsibility to sell safety glass. . . . You can say, perhaps, that I am selfish, but business is selfish. We are not a charitable institution—we are trying to make a profit for our stockholders."

If GM had openly acknowledged at the time that it had shrugged off responsibility for making cars (at least the cheaper cars) less lethal when they crash, then society might have understood sooner that others would have to fill that vacuum. In the case of safety glass, within a few more years many states did step in, requiring it by law in windshields, but this state action was made possible only by this unusual split within the industry.

Sloan would become perhaps the most influential corporate manager of the twentieth century, his management philosophy widely studied and copied, so it is worth delving a bit into his thinking. In 1941, he defended the need for big companies, refuting those concerned about concentrated economic power. He argued that such concentration simply means that "industrial management must expand its horizon of responsibility. . . . It must consider the impact of its operations on the economy as a whole in relation to the social and economic welfare of the entire community. For years I have preached this philosophy. Those charged with great industrial responsibility must become industrial statesmen."

On the other hand, Sloan was a great believer in free market ideology, which assures market actors that they can concentrate on pursuing their own self-interest, secure in the knowledge that, thanks to the invisible hand of the marketplace, the public interest will automatically be advanced. No expanded horizons of responsibility are needed. Sloan's free market beliefs appear to have predominated over any expanded-responsibility beliefs, not just when considering the fate of Chevy customers who might someday smash through their windshields but when deciding how helpful GM should be in militarizing Nazi Germany. GM had a highly profitable subsidiary in Germany. When a shareholder complained that the subsidiary was aiding Hitler's militarization, Sloan responded in 1939 that Nazi Germany's politics "should not be considered the business of the management of General Motors." Of course, the phrase "minding one's own business" suggests a kind of deliberate blindness to broader considerations or a conscious narrowing of one's horizon of responsibility.

Given GM's hundreds of thousands of stockholders and employees, Sloan may well have viewed anything that boosted GM's profits as automatically helping society as a whole. A blindness to any conflict between the company's interests and the public's would be expressed most famously by GM president Charles E. Wilson, who was nominated to be secretary of defense in 1953 (while Sloan still chaired GM's board). Wilson still held stock in GM, and when asked in congressional hearings whether he could make a decision that hurt GM if it was good for the country, he said, "I cannot conceive of one because for years I thought what was good for our country was good for General Motors, and vice versa. The difference did not exist. Our company is too big. It goes with the welfare of the country. Our contribution to the Nation is quite considerable."

The power that Sloan and Wilson held as leaders of the world's biggest industrial enterprise may have made it even less likely they would see how the interests of the nation might differ from GM's. The research into power's effect on cognition indicates that, rather than expanding power holders' horizon of responsibility, power tends to narrow their focus to their individual goals. Psychologist Dacher Keltner, in his book *The Power Paradox: How We Gain and Lose Influence,* stresses that power tends to reduce our empathy and compassion and makes us more "self-focused rather than focused on the greater good"—at least when that power is unchecked.

Fortunately, there is also some evidence that these selfish tendencies might be checked and even reversed by our preexisting values. One study found that a heightened sense of power makes people who hold a communal orientation—with a strong sense of responsibility for the needs of others—*more* prosocial. By contrast, it found that more exchange-oriented individuals—who expect a return on their investment when they do things that benefit others—respond to power by acting in a more self-interested way. Like much of the psychological research into power, this study used the now-controversial method of priming, but even if it had not, this topic—how power interacts with social values to influence behavior—is so important that more research into it would be warranted.

Ironically, Alfred P. ("we are not a charitable institution") Sloan Jr. is now perhaps best known by the public for the Alfred P. Sloan Foundation, the charitable institution he founded in 1934 to promote science and technology, among other things. Peter Drucker, the well-known management consultant and author, was given access to study GM's management closely in the 1940s and knew Sloan well. He would write that Sloan had "tremendous personal warmth and was unbelievably generous." Drucker also wrote, surprisingly, that Sloan devoted "long, loving hours" to the cause of auto safety. Yet despite his evident interest in social welfare and alleged interest in auto safety, with his corporate hat on, Sloan defined his responsibility so narrowly that it did not include trying to reduce thousands of deaths every year by making GM's products less lethal when they crashed. These inconsistencies illustrate how a person's values can change when that person is wearing the mantle of a corporate leader, with all the norms and incentives that come with it.

NEW WAYS TO BLAME DRIVERS: THE SEAT BELT
"JUST ENCOURAGES THE NUTS"

Pressure on the industry kept building after 1956, but slowly. Doctors kept highlighting the lethality of car interiors, and lawyers began arguing that cars were defective since they failed to include reasonable safety designs (a standard that applied to other manufactured products). More data was collected on auto-crash injuries, including at Cornell, though the industry funding that it accepted after 1955 threatened its independence. (Within a few years, after a researcher there wrote an article discussing how to make cars safer, he got "very bitter calls from Detroit" and noted that the Cornell program got "very nervous, especially around grant-renewal time.")

And Congress got involved. In 1956, Kenneth Roberts, a little-known representative from Alabama, began holding nearly annual hearings on auto safety. Roberts initially hoped Detroit would improve safety voluntarily, but he later told Jeffrey O'Connell and Arthur Myers, authors of *Safety Last: An Indictment of the Auto Industry,* that the industry was "never going to do anything unless you made them do it. They just didn't want to be bothered. They would come around with the business of putting the blame on the driver." By 1958, he told an audience, "I, frankly, am tired of hearing that our drivers are delinquents, alcoholics, and incompetents." Industry resistance kept Roberts from passing safety standards for all cars, but in 1964 he managed to push through a law requiring cars bought by the federal government to meet certain safety standards.

Meanwhile, states became more active in considering and passing auto safety measures, especially New York. By 1963, twenty states had passed laws over industry opposition requiring standard front-seat lap belts. Faced with this wave of legislation, the industry announced it would make such belts standard nationwide, acknowledging that "it is good customer relations to heed the inevitable." But few were satisfied, and the push for a federal safety law kept rising. In 1964, auto clubs in several states started campaigning for a law mandating minimum safety features.

By the summer of 1965, traffic safety polled as one of the six or seven problems Americans worried about most, possibly the all-time peak of concern. Congress took up auto safety again, this time in hearings spearheaded by Senator Abraham Ribicoff of Connecticut. Ribicoff said,

"Detroit will holler blue murder" over the prospect of federal regulation but added that "whether safety sells cars isn't the issue; we're talking about life and death."

Yet despite clear warnings that Congress was serious, industry executives at the hearings were unprepared to answer safety questions. The *Wall Street Journal* would report that "the hostile Congressional reaction evidently came as a shocking surprise to the auto magnates," noting that "two auto titans [from GM and Chrysler] stubbornly refused to admit even the possibility that car design may play a significant role in the traffic toll." One senator said of the industry leaders, "I really wouldn't have believed they could be so bad."

There was reason for the senators' increased concern and anger. By 1965, highway deaths had risen to 48,000 per year, and for three years in a row the rate of deaths per miles travelled had risen as well. The death rate was always a somewhat unreliable value because it required estimating how many miles Americans drove each year. Still, success in bringing it down over the decades even as annual deaths kept rising was a sign that something was improving: cars, drivers, laws, roads, or even just the ability of modern medicine to keep crash victims alive. Now, though, even the rate of death was rising, so this was no time for the industry to appear cavalier about safety.

An advisor to the Ribicoff hearings that summer was Ralph Nader, a young lawyer who had devoted himself to the cause of auto safety. Nader would later explain that his interest in auto safety had begun in the mid-1950s when he saw a little girl who was decapitated by a glove compartment door that had opened in a 15-mph crash. (In the early 1980s, I spent a year working at one of the many groups Nader went on to found; I did not work directly with him, and I did not focus on auto safety issues.)

In late 1965, Nader's book *Unsafe at Any Speed* was released. It was a blistering attack on the auto industry's failure to employ safer designs, at the cost of thousands of lives. It got considerable attention upon publication, and the auto industry's defensive reaction to it would ensure it got vastly more in the months that followed.

Frustrated lawmakers were ready to focus on the car, not just the driver or road, and on what caused injuries, not just accidents. Annoyed carmakers, by strategy or just reflex, kept changing the subject back to drivers, roads, and accident causation. In 1965, GM's vice president for engineering, Harry F. Barr, said, "The driver is most important, we feel. If the drivers do everything they should, there wouldn't be accidents, would there?" The next year, Henry Ford II, the founder's grandson and chairman of Ford's board, would make the same point: "The driver is the most important factor, because, if you drive safely, accidents won't happen." David R. Jones, a *New York Times* journalist who interviewed many in the auto industry in early 1965, reported that "the rising chorus of criticism infuriates auto men, who contend that poor highway design and bad driving are the main reasons for accidents." One executive stressed that "the number of accidents caused by failure of the product are pretty damned small."

None of the industry's critics were suggesting that society should abandon training, licensing, and regulating drivers, but the industry, using a classic straw-man rhetorical technique, sometimes portrayed the debate that way. The president of General Motors, John. F. Gordon, once said, "The suggestion that we abandon hope of teaching drivers to avoid traffic accidents and concentrate on designing cars that will make collisions harmless is a perplexing combination of defeatism and wishful thinking."

One troubling industry argument blamed drivers in a new way, suggesting that if drivers had a safer car, their resulting overconfidence would make them drive more recklessly. It was a neat reframing of safety advances as inherently dangerous (reminiscent of the way abolition was once reframed as cruel to the slaves). In 1963, for example, GM director of styling William Mitchell would argue that "the seat-belt craze isn't doing anything for the brains of the guy driving the car. . . . This just encourages the nuts. Put belts and shoulder harnesses on them and they think they can do anything." Of course, this argument ran counter to the industry's other fear: that awareness of safety devices would take the fun out of driving.

Concern about inadvertently triggering dangerous driving did not inhibit carmakers when it came to building tremendously fast and powerful cars. In fact, the industry portrayed higher horsepower as a safety feature. GM's head of engineering claimed in 1956 that the chief reason for putting a powerful engine in cars is that it "makes them safer to drive." Of course, lacking the power to accelerate quickly when merging or passing is dangerous, especially in a world where other cars are moving fast, but cars that could often go well over 100 mph were hardly necessary for safety. And surely the temptation to unleash all that thrilling power and speed caused more reckless driving than did overconfidence caused by seat belts.

This temptation was especially likely given that the industry had for decades expertly appealed to our thrill-seeking instincts with ads that made cars symbols of freedom, excitement, empowerment, and even aggression. In 1957, facing criticism for pushing dangerous speeds, the major carmakers formally resolved among themselves to stop marketing cars based on speed and racing performance (and they had already informally agreed not to mark speedometers higher than 120 mph). In 1965, GM chair Frederic Donner assured senators his company was still complying with the spirit of that resolution. And yet, as Nader noted in *Unsafe and Any Speed*, this self-imposed restraint did not stop GM from running an ad for one of its cars asking: "Ever prodded a throttle with 445-pound-feet of torque coiled tightly at the end of it? Do that with one of these and you can start billing yourself as The Human Cannonball."

Given the industry's saturation advertising, with many ads fueling a sense of personal invulnerability, it is hardly surprising that many people truly were uninterested in safety design (though as Ford showed in 1956, many other people were interested). The industry also exaggerated the demands of safety advocates and then portrayed the vehicles that would result as slow, ugly, and unsellable. "Look, we could build the safest car in the world. We could build a tank that would creep over the highways and you could bang 'em into each other and nobody would ever get a scratch. But nobody would buy it either. We'd last about two months putting out stuff like that," said Henry Ford II.

After largely ignoring safety in its ads for decades, the industry then blamed customer disinterest for its lack of standard safety features. A GM executive said one of the "startling problems so far as crash injury is concerned is the utter refusal on the part of the American motorists to be strapped into a seat," pointing to "a real disinterest on the part of the public in their own safety." GM's Donner assured Ribicoff's committee in 1965 that "in the engineering, development, and testing of our automobiles no consideration is more important to us than safety." But he also explained that until they deem a safety feature essential, it remains an extra-cost option to protect the "basic freedom of the customer to pay the cost of tailoring a car to his own specifications." Otherwise, GM "would face a customer revolt, and we want to stay in business." Nader would point out that, by contrast, many costly styling features were standard, whether customers wanted them or not.

Of course, federal standards that applied to all carmakers would protect each company from a customer revolt over safety features, but opposition to such standards was virtually universal within the industry. GM's president James Roche warned in 1966 that "anything that might be done to hamper the industry in carrying out its tasks—any form of regulation, controls or imposition of unrealistic conditions—would have a serious impact on the industry. That impact would be speedily felt throughout the economy." He added, "We can't afford to indulge in what might seem like lofty ideals at the cost of immobility, a lower standard of living and the risk of falling behind in the world-wide competition." Several of the industries profiled in this book, from the eighteenth-century slave traders to the twenty-first-century fossil fuel industry, have similarly tried to tap into larger tribal and nationalist sentiments by arguing that changing their behavior would advantage other countries.

The auto industry also warned that federal standards could actually impede safety advances by restricting the research and experimentation that leads to safer cars. This would have been more persuasive if the industry had a history of actually leading on safety rather than resisting advances identified by others.

TRIBAL RESPONSE TO NADER AND OTHER CRITICS: "SOME PIPSQUEAK COMES ALONG"

Tribalism would, unsurprisingly, shape the auto safety dispute. The auto industry was known for its clubbiness. GM, in particular, famously promoted from within and even educated many of its employees and executives at its own school, General Motors Institute (GMI). Critics in this era charged that this system helped create "an extreme form of corporate inbreeding." Moreover, there is evidence that power itself makes people less open to persuasion, so GM's status as what *Fortune* magazine called "the mightiest industrial enterprise in man's history" may also have blunted the ability of its leaders to understand the criticism. Even Henry Ford II, chair of a considerably smaller automaker, viewed his high profits as evidence he must be right. In his book *Car Safety Wars: One Hundred Years of Technology, Politics, and Death,* Michael Lemov reports that Ford said to a Senate counsel at a 1968 meeting about the company's lack of safety innovation, "I am making 18 percent in profit a year. I can't be making any mistakes." Ford might have considered it a joke, but it was a revealing one.

The carmakers felt themselves unfairly attacked, especially in 1965 and 1966. GM's Roche said in a speech that the industry was being irresponsibly singled out as the "scapegoat." Henry Ford II complained that the industry was "being attacked on all sides," and that the "harassment" was unfair. An unnamed industry executive told the *New York Times* that "we in the industry are disturbed at being the goat. . . . We're the goats because we're the easiest to get at."

Some in the tire business, which was also feeling the heat of legislative attention at this time, came to the carmakers' defense. One article in a trade journal with the bouncy name *Rubber World,* argued that politicians had given the existing safety groups a "facile and potentially popular rationale for their failure to reduce accidents: the *vehicle* is at fault. At a period when the theory that society itself is to blame for individual failure, this is a view that is not only acceptable—but fashionable. Detroit is a symbol of success throughout the world—and like all such symbols, arouses ambiguous emotions." In short, the movement for safer cars was written off as a trendy rejection of personal responsibility and jealousy of the car industry's success.

Auto industry leaders did not think much of their critics and particularly resented outsiders interfering with what they considered their field of expertise. Critics were dismissed as "amateur engineers" and "self-styled experts" by the head of GM, and as "amateur experts" by a Ford public relations executive.

Ralph Nader provoked particular ire: Henry Ford II told an author that Nader was "full of crap," complaining, "We spend a hell of a lot of time trying to make [cars] better and safer, and then some pipsqueak who doesn't know a thing about the industry comes along and tries to tell us how to do what we've dedicated our lives and billions of dollars to doing."

Critics were also dismissed for being emotional and biased, rather than fact-driven. GM's Roche told the press that solutions need to be "based on facts, experience, and research. The problem is serious and important. It should not be distorted by emotionalism, misinformation, or biased opinion." He added that a "scapegoat, while it may serve as an emotional substitute, is not a solution." Of course carmakers had their own emotions, which could flare up in response to their critics' data: when Dr. Paul Gikas, a pathologist who had methodically studied fatal car accidents for years, showed a government committee pictures of car interiors and explained how certain features injured people, a Ford vice president angrily dismissed his presentation as an "inflammatory, vindictive, totally biased attack." Safety critics were, in fact, drawing on a great deal of accident data, virtually all of which had been generated from research outside the industry. GM had gathered some data on crash safety, but safety engineer Gandelot said in the 1950s that it was classified as "engineering data and not for public distribution."

In February 1966, Senator Ribicoff held more auto safety hearings. This time Nader was a witness, and he directly challenged the industry's tendency to blame drivers for accidents. First, he questioned the basic factual premise of driver-blaming by quoting Secretary of Commerce John T. Connor. Connor had said in a 1965 speech that the interstate highway system succeeded in reducing accidents because highway engineers "relied on facts and rejected the emotional and widely held but fallacious belief that almost all accidents are somehow caused by driver error or failure, through carelessness or irresponsibility." A recent federal analysis had found that the great bulk of accidents happened to generally good drivers. Connor stated that "in our pursuit of safety the emphasis on remedial engineering rather than reprimand represents an important breakthrough."

Nader then questioned the morality of driver-blaming. He said, "The best that can be said about such thinking is that it is primitive. A civilized society should want to protect even the nut behind the wheel from paying the ultimate penalty for a moment's carelessness, not to mention protecting the innocent people who get in his way." He was articulating a growing societal perspective about corporate social responsibility, just as an older perspective was fading. As it happened, exactly a week later, Alfred P. Sloan Jr. died at the age of 90. He had remained active on GM's board until the end and was hailed upon his death as the "archetypal corporation man of his age."

INVESTIGATING NADER AND ENSURING REGULATION: GM'S "MOST UNWORTHY" STUNT

Nader's testimony was greatly overshadowed by what was then going on behind the scenes. In the weeks before and after this testimony, Nader perceived he was being followed. He was also getting harassing anonymous phone calls, sometimes several a day. Twice he was abruptly approached in stores by young women: the first one invited him to her apartment for a "foreign affairs discussion," and the second one asked for his help moving heavy articles at her home. He declined both invitations and suspected someone was trying to lure him into a compromising situation.

Nader also learned from friends and colleagues that they had been contacted by a detective claiming that Nader was being considered for a job and they were doing a prehiring investigation. The investigator had asked questions about Nader's political views, whether his Lebanese ancestry made him anti-Semitic, whether he drank, and whether he was a homosexual, among other things. Nader contacted the media, blaming the auto industry for the investigation, and his charges hit the headlines. The *New York Times* reported that "spokesmen for the major manufacturers in Detroit dismissed Mr. Nader's charge as ridiculous." Some industry sources were particularly indignant to be accused of such a clumsy investigation, and one added, "You can bet that if one of us was doing it, it would be a lot smoother. . . . If we were checking up on Nader he'd never know about it."

It is a crime to harass or intimidate a witness before a congressional committee, so Ribicoff asked the Justice Department to investigate. Soon after, GM released a late-night statement admitting that it had indeed initiated an investigation of Nader but denying involvement in the harassment reported in the papers. GM stressed that it was a "routine investigation" that

was "limited only to Nader's qualifications, background, expertise and association with" attorneys then suing GM over the Corvair, a car whose design
failings Nader had featured in his book.

Next came the very public spectacle of GM's CEO Roche and its general
counsel Aloysius F. Power appearing before the Ribicoff committee in
March 1966. GM claimed the investigation had nothing to do with Nader's
role as a congressional witness, but Ribicoff pointed out that the detec-
tives began constant surveillance of Nader soon after it was announced he
would appear before the subcommittee. Ribicoff stressed that most of the
questions the investigators asked, such as ones about his sex life and political views, had nothing to do with litigation against GM and called them
just an attempt to "downgrade and smear a man." Fifty or sixty people
were questioned by the investigator GM had hired through an intermedi-
ary, including Nader's neighbors, boyhood friends, and the high school
principal in his small hometown. Senator Robert Kennedy expressed the
committee's concern about whether the investigation was really about
"harassment, intimidation, and possibly blackmail."

Roche apologized to Nader before television cameras, noted for the
record that no derogatory information about him had been found, and
had to admit that the investigation as it was carried out was "most unwor-
thy." GM's general counsel (whose name, Mr. Power, is remarkably apt in
light of the above-mentioned insights about how power affects thinking
and behavior), was less conciliatory. He argued that under the circumstances it would have been irresponsible of him not to order the investigation of Nader. Power tried to distance GM from the seamier side of the
six-week investigation—even though it was being done on GM's behalf
and people on his staff were getting ongoing reports of the interviews—
claiming he had initially *intended* it to be narrower (but then, as Power
put it, "it went the other way . . . with the surveillance and the rest"). It was
a bit like GM putting unsafe cars on the road and then not feeling any
responsibility for the consequences when later some of them predictably
spun out of control since, of course, GM did not *intend* for them to crash.

Roche urged the senators not to view this unfortunate episode as a sign
that GM did not care about traffic safety, assuring them that the company
gave safety "a priority second to none." But it was too late to stop the
momentum for a traffic safety law. President Lyndon Johnson had called

"the shocking and senseless carnage" on the highways the nation's gravest problem next to the war in Vietnam and had already submitted a proposed bill. Members of Congress would soon make the bill much stronger. One senator would recall, "Everybody was so outraged that a great corporation was out to clobber a guy because he wrote critically about them. At that point, everybody said the hell with them." A top executive with one of GM's competitors said, "I get mad every time I think about that stunt. . . . They made the entire industry look bad, and we're all going to suffer for it."

A NEW ERA: LIVES SAVED AND A MOVEMENT LAUNCHED

By August, the landmark National Traffic and Motor Vehicle Safety Act of 1966 was passed. The industry had tried hard to get a weaker bill, but it mostly failed and ultimately gave in and supported the bill, which was passed unanimously in both houses. Nader described the bill as "a good start," and a Ford vice president said, "I think we can live with" it.

The act created a new federal agency to set and enforce minimum safety standards for new vehicles. The first standards—relating to such things as brakes, tires, door latches, seat belts and anchorages, rearview mirrors, and steering wheels—had to be met starting in 1968. Industry tried to weaken and delay many of the standards, often successfully, and sometimes claimed that if proposed standards were not changed, factories would have to be closed. There would be epic battles over safety design in the years ahead, including a decades-long fight over airbags, and many fights over defects and recalls.

Today's cars are clearly much more crashworthy than those in decades past. The highway death toll peaked in 1972 at over 54,000. It fell, nonlinearly, to under 33,000 deaths by 2014, even though the miles driven more than doubled over those years (however, deaths have since risen again, to over 37,000). The rate of deaths per 100 million vehicle miles driven—still an imperfect measure—fell from 5.5 in 1966 to 1.16 in 2017.

Some of that reduction is due to factors like safer roads, less drunk driving, better medicine, and demographic changes. After factoring out those causes, though, the National Highway Traffic Safety Administration (which sets the safety standards) estimated that auto safety technologies saved over 27,000 lives in 2012 alone. Over 10,000 of the lives saved were directly attributable to seat belts. In total, safety technology and standards are estimated to have saved over 600,000 lives between their adoption and 2012. One can only imagine how many lives could have been saved if the auto industry had taken responsibility from the beginning for designing safer cars.

GM's actions not only helped ensure passage of the 1966 legislation but contributed greatly to the consumer movement to come. Ralph Nader sued GM for invasion of privacy and in 1970 settled for $425,000. He used some of the money to launch a network of nonprofits, including the Center for Auto Safety, which would keep pushing for safer cars, and many other watchdog and consumer groups. He also founded Public Citizen and its Health Research Group, where I worked for a year after college in the early 1980s, focusing on the dangers of workplace chemicals. While I did not work directly for Nader, I was among many in my generation influenced by his message that citizens and the government should hold corporations responsible for the social impact of their actions.

This same belief in corporate social accountability helped propel the rise of the modern environmental movement. One of that movement's earliest accomplishments involved getting the lead out of gasoline. This only occurred, though, after the auto industry and its fuel-selling partners had denied for decades that exposing the entire population to a known toxin posed any threat at all.

4 "How Wrong One Can Be"

BIAS, TRIBALISM, AND LEADED GASOLINE

*"The whole proceeding against an industry that has made
invaluable contributions to the American economy for
more than fifty years is the worst example of fanaticism
since the New England witch hunts in the Seventeenth
Century."*

—Lawrence Blanchard, vice president of Ethyl Corporation, on
rules phasing lead out of gasoline, 1976

In 1921, Thomas Midgley was a young engineer at General Motors. GM
was already an exciting place to be; cars were transforming the world and
GM was transforming the car. Its engineers believed, though, that more
powerful cars needed improved gasoline to stop the annoying "knocking"
that plagued engines of the time. So Midgley—described as a convivial,
whimsical, and highly inventive man—spent years tossing different chemicals
into gasoline hoping to solve the problem. Many additives stopped
the knocking, but each had its drawbacks. Some were too costly or corrosive.
One promising option was dropped because it made the exhaust
smell like "a devilish mixture of garlic and onions."

On December 9, Midgley and his colleagues tried yet another additive,
and to their delight just a tiny bit made the test engine purr like a kitten.
As important, it was cheap and patentable. (Yes, the additive would harm
engine parts, but that difficulty could be largely overcome.) In one recounting
of the day, all the men danced a "non-scientific jig around the laboratory."
Midgley's boss, Charles Kettering, himself a celebrated inventor,
remembered the day as the most dramatic of his career. The magic

ingredient was a substance called tetraethyl lead (TEL), and it was soon clear that this breakthrough—the invention of "leaded" gasoline—was worth a staggering amount of money.

There was only one problem. Lead was known since antiquity to be a slow, cumulative, insidious poison. A Greek physician observed over two thousand years ago that "lead makes the mind give way." In the 1920s, lead was perhaps the world's single most well-recognized, indeed conspicuous, occupational and environmental toxin.

GM was not deterred. With its corporate partners and subsidiaries, it went ahead and added lead to the nation's fuel supply. In time leaded gasoline was used worldwide, and as our gas became leaded, so did our blood, bones, and brains. Use of Midgley's discovery would ultimately spew millions of tons of a fine poisonous dust across the planet over several decades, concentrated in the most populated areas. Generations of children were exposed to enough of this neurotoxin to dull their minds, shorten their attention span, weaken their impulse control, and diminish their chances in life. In adults, lead would push blood pressure higher, adding to the heavy death toll from strokes and heart attacks. We are still calculating the full human cost of this utterly predictable (and repeatedly predicted) global poisoning.

This chapter shows how a grave public health risk was warned of, denied, reframed as serving a greater good, imposed on the world, and then forgotten about for decades while the relevant field of science was dominated by those with the greatest incentive to remain blind to the danger. When others finally identified the ongoing global contamination, it triggered tribal attacks on those scientists and complaints of a witch hunt.

AN INAUSPICIOUS START: "INSANITY GAS" AND A DELUSIONAL CORPORATE RESPONSE

When word got out of GM's plan to put lead into gasoline, the company received a flurry of warnings from experts at Yale, MIT, Harvard, and elsewhere. The first medical opinions "were full of such frightening phrases as 'grave fears,' 'distinct risk,' 'widespread lead poisoning,' and the like," reported one of Midgley's colleagues. Some of these warnings related to the use of tetraethyl lead itself, a volatile liquid that can be absorbed through contact with the skin or by breathing its fumes, making it an occupational hazard for those asked to work with it. A German chemist warned Midgley early on that the death of one of his colleagues was the direct result of exposure to this "malicious and creeping" poison.

Many of the warnings, though, were about the long-term danger to the general public from breathing the lead dust that would be released through cars' exhaust systems and accumulate along the roadways. The surgeon general, alerted to GM's plan, wrote with a polite and reasonable question: "Since lead poisoning in human beings is of the cumulative type resulting frequently from the daily intake of minute quantities, it seems pertinent to inquire whether there might not be a decided health hazard associated with the extensive use of lead tetra ethyl in engines."

Midgley informed the surgeon general that although the problem "had been given very serious consideration . . . no actual experimental data has been taken," according to correspondence cited by David Rosner and Gerald Markowitz, experts in the history of public health whose work has been crucial to keeping the early lead controversy from fading away. Despite this lack of data, Midgley remained confident that "the average street will probably be so free from lead that it would be impossible to detect it or its absorption." Midgley's response suggests the deeply unscientific attitude that what you can't see can't hurt you, which is particularly dangerous when the science of detection is not well advanced and the people looking for harm are those who least want to find it.

A few weeks later, Midgley left on a six-week trip to Florida to recover from his own case of lead poisoning from his work with TEL. He described having "lead-lined lungs" and a body temperature so reduced that he was at risk of being "classified as a cold-blooded reptile." He wasn't too worried, though, because he was sure the cure would require only a few weeks golfing in a warm place.

Midgley was wrong about his quick recovery: when he returned to work, his body temperature was still suppressed. But this cheery bravado in the face of his own lead poisoning may help explain his equally cavalier approach to the risk to workers and the threat of chronic lead poisoning to which the public would now be exposed. He seemed more worried about the *perception* of a health risk than about actual risk. Indeed, while recovering from his own lead poisoning, he assured a fellow engineer that poisoning from handling leaded gasoline was almost impossible and the exhaust would not have enough lead to worry about, "but no one knows what legislation might come into existence fostered by competition and fanatical health cranks."

In February 1923, leaded gas went on sale in Ohio. GM and Standard Oil of New Jersey soon formed a new corporation called the Ethyl Gasoline Corporation, with Kettering as president and Midgley as vice president. It would market TEL-spiked gasoline as "Ethyl," a friendly-sounding brand name that avoided the loaded word *lead*. Word spread quickly among "automobilists" of the satisfying boost of power Ethyl gave their engines, and soon it was being sold at more than ten thousand filling stations.

And then the deaths began. In the summer of 1924, two workers under Midgley's close direction at a GM plant in Dayton, Ohio, died from TEL poisoning, and dozens were hospitalized. According to the Ethyl Corporation's official history, published in 1983, Midgley was "tremendously upset." He had hired these employees, socialized with them, and "was depressed to the point of considering giving up the whole tetraethyl lead program." However, Charles Kettering's "calmer approach" won the day, and production continued.

Within a couple months of the deaths in Dayton, Kettering was pushing to greatly expand production of TEL at a DuPont plant in Deepwater, New Jersey. DuPont owned a large share of GM and manufactured most of the TEL the Ethyl Corporation would sell. Poisonings at the DuPont plant ultimately killed several workers and affected perhaps hundreds. These poisonings, as with those in Ohio, were effectively hushed up at the time.

But in October 1924, men at a third facility—a Standard Oil refinery in Bayway, New Jersey—started falling ill. Because the plant was located just across the river from New York City, several of the city's papers got wind of the story and covered it with alarming headlines like "Odd Gas Kills One, Makes Four Insane," "Another Man Dies From Insanity Gas," and "Gas Madness Stalks Plant; 2 Die, 3 Crazed." As the Ethyl Corporation's official history would later state, "if ever a company started its corporate life under bleak circumstances, it was Ethyl Gasoline Corporation."

The newspapers described in vivid detail how in the course of a few days a number of workers had suddenly become delusional, suffered hallucinations, shouted about being persecuted by attackers, and ultimately become "violently insane." Some of the stricken became suicidal and one jumped out a window. Some were carted off screaming in straitjackets. It was reported that even before these incidents the plant workers had been calling TEL "loony gas," but the *New York Times* called it by a less light-hearted name, "insanity gas."

In one week, five workers died and another thirty-six were hospitalized. Their doctor soon reported they were "doing nicely," though they were continuing to "have fits of insanity," suggesting a rather loose definition of "nicely." In fact, at least one of the survivors would reportedly spend the next forty years locked in a mental hospital. This chemical psychosis would be described as similar to "delirium tremens" or even, because of the violent mania it provoked, rabies. TEL's effect on the mind was so dramatic that the Army Chemical Warfare Service had a few months earlier been testing the chemical to see, in the words of one reporter, if "this reason destroyer had any promising possibilities for war."

Given the earlier poisonings, it is hard to understand why the executives of Standard Oil were so hopelessly unprepared to handle the public attention that followed the Bayway crisis, but they were. Perhaps they assumed they could sweep the news under the rug as successfully as Ethyl and DuPont had done at their facilities. Indeed, Charles Kettering was reported to be very upset that his partners at Standard Oil had failed to keep this news quiet.

One of the first responses to the disaster made on behalf of Standard Oil came from a physician who had been consulting for the company. Not realizing that the horse had already left the barn, he told a newspaper reporter that "nothing ought to be said about this matter in the public interest."

Small-town papers have a long history of agreeing to ignore spectacularly violent workplace accidents upon the request of locally dominant employers. In 1767, the *Newcastle Journal* had been asked by coal mine operators to stop covering the frequent deadly explosions at their mines; the paper announced that because paying attention to such accidents "could have very little good tendency, we drop the further mentioning" of them. Alas, it was Standard Oil's bad luck to have its plant located close to Manhattan, a city with newspapers that could not be quieted as easily as smaller papers in company towns.

A subsequent response issued the first day of the crisis came from the chief chemist at the plant, Dr. Matthew D. Mann. When asked by journalists to comment, he left the room for several minutes and returned with a written statement saying that "these men probably went insane because they worked too hard." While major corporations were not as good at presenting plausible denials in the 1920s as they are today, their denials were hardly ever this preposterous. However, Dr. Mann was himself later named among the victims of TEL poisoning, and William Kovarik, a communication historian who has researched the 1920s controversy in depth, concluded that Mann "had probably made the statement while in a delirious state of mind." If so, this would be a rare example of a corporate denial caused by the very product whose dangers were being denied.

What was not rare was for employers to blame workers for getting poisoned. When the story did not go away, that is what Ethyl and Standard Oil tried next (though at least they admitted that the symptoms were caused by workplace exposure, unlike US Radium which a few months later would blame its workers' poisoning symptoms on their inherent weaknesses). Midgley raced to New York for a press conference at the Standard Oil headquarters on Broadway, where he said that despite warnings, the Bayway workers "had failed to appreciate the dangers of constant absorption of the fluid by their hands and arms." Other company officials at the press conference insisted that they had constantly admonished workers to wear rubber gloves and gas masks, and said the workers had plenty of reason to know they were engaged in "a man's undertaking." A few months later the company would employ a stricter worker-protection protocol, which Midgley described like this: "The minute a man shows signs of exhilaration he is laid off. If he spills the stuff on himself he is fired. Because he doesn't want to lose his job, he doesn't spill it."

At that New York press conference, though, Midgley demonstrated his own failure to appreciate the dangers of TEL. For the benefit of reporters, he opened a bottle of it and rubbed some on his hands (a performance he repeated at other press conferences too, assuring reporters there was no risk). Perhaps the Bayway workers had been sent similarly mixed messages about the dangers of TEL. Indeed, it would later be revealed that safety precautions at the Bayway facility were "grossly inadequate," according to DuPont engineers who had visited the plant just weeks before the poisonings. (Recall that DuPont's own TEL plant was so dangerous it had already poisoned many of its workers).

VIEWING RISK THROUGH A TRIBAL LENS: SHAPING THE SCIENCE

There were red warning flags that might have stopped things: the well-known toxicity of lead, the early alarms raised by national experts, Midgley's own poisoning, the deaths of so many plant workers, and the lack of scientific studies showing the safety of TEL and low-level lead exposure. Despite all these, Midgley, Kettering, and others went forward with their plans, exposing additional workers to TEL and the public generally to a fine and cumulative spray of lead dust.

Their willingness to keep going may have been partly due to the strong "approach" systems often seen in powerful and ambitious people, as discussed in chapter 2, on radium. Midgley and his colleagues would have been keenly focused on their potential reward (more powerful cars and more impressive profits) and relatively blind to the larger social risk (violent insanity in the workplace and slow poisoning around the globe). However, their denials also show that the industry was looking at the dispute through a very tribal lens.

Psychologists have long studied the strong human tendency to draw a line between our in-group and out-groups, including our desire to agree with the views of our in-group and resist out-group efforts to persuade us otherwise. More recently, researchers like psychology professor Mina Cikara, head of the Harvard Intergroup Neuroscience Lab, have used neuroimaging to observe how such group dynamics automatically and subconsciously change the way our brains work. They have identified neural processes linked to the reduced empathy people feel for out-group members and the joy we sometimes find in out-groups' misfortunes, and they have detected brain activity that can help explain why humans are typically more aggressive and less aware of our own moral standards when we compete as groups rather than as individuals.

One of the surprises coming from the research is how very little it takes to provoke a psychological division between *us* and *them*. Our brains are so eager to draw this line that they will apparently latch onto almost any flimsy excuse to do so. Researchers know this because they create "minimal groups" in the laboratory, assigning people to one group instead of another at random or based on arbitrary factors. Even the most trivial psychological investment—with no preexisting group bonds and little or nothing at stake—can create in-group bias and alter the way people perceive out-group members and their actions.

Of course, the stakes for Midgley, Kettering, and the other decision-makers promoting leaded gas were anything but trivial. Their financial and reputational investment was tremendous, and they would have surely felt themselves very much an in-group. Midgley's initial concern about worker deaths in Dayton suggests he might have briefly considered these workers part of his in-group, but the speed with which he shifted gears— supporting accelerated TEL production using still-dangerous methods at other plants—suggests he quickly adopted the more traditional business mind-set of the time, which viewed workers as members of a different tribe with interests quite distinct from management's.

Among the earliest clues that the backers of leaded gas were thinking in tribal terms comes from their secrecy around the health dangers of their product. Kettering understood back in 1923, the year before the worker poisonings, that his team would eventually need actual data to address the concerns the surgeon general and others had raised. If they had wanted the most expert analysis possible of the risks of TEL and leaded gas, they could have hired one of the national experts who had already weighed in on the dangers (including the prominent experts GM had initially contacted at Harvard and Yale). Instead, a few months after sales of Ethyl began, GM funded a study by the federal Bureau of Mines. The bureau was known for its close relationships with industry, so it was subject to some control, and yet it could still give public credibility to the research.

Kettering persuaded the Bureau of Mines to keep news of the research secret, insisting that it withhold the usual press and progress reports because he feared "the newspapers are apt to give scare headlines and false impressions." The bureau also agreed to use the word *Ethyl* in its research rather than the scientific term *tetraethyl lead*, because if news of the research leaked, it was thought it would be less prejudicial if the word *lead* were omitted. Ultimately, the bureau agreed to submit its findings to the Ethyl Corporation for approval before they were made public.

Who performed the research was crucially important, because understanding the long-term risk to the public would take some very careful science. Lower-level lead poisoning of the type that the public was being exposed to was far less eye-catching (and thus far more deniable) than the sudden-onset madness that put TEL on the front pages. It could appear in various subtle forms easily overlooked or blamed on other causes, which the experts knew even then. Spotting it would take a sustained, properly designed experiment run by keen-eyed researchers who were both well trained and objective.

The study that the Bureau of Mines conducted for GM and Ethyl failed to meet this standard, but from its sponsors' perspective, it was a great success. For some months, the bureau exposed rabbits, monkeys, dogs, and other animals to measured amounts of the exhaust of engines burning leaded gasoline. Just days after the Bayway crisis, presumably at Ethyl's request, the bureau stated that based on its preliminary results, it considered the public health threat from car exhaust "seemingly remote." Newspapers ran reassuring headlines—"No Peril to Public Seen in Ethyl Gas"—even as independent experts were highly critical of the study's design, which, among other things, failed to allow the lead dust to accumulate in the way it would in the real world.

In short, from the very beginning, the risk of putting lead in gasoline was viewed from within a tribal mind-set. Kettering and his associates distrusted the newspapers, the "fanatical health cranks" in the medical community, and the workers they were continuing to expose to TEL (and of course many people within these groups, in turn, deeply distrusted the industry). Given this lack of trust, those backing leaded gas played their cards close to their chest, including initially suppressing the news of the deaths at the Dayton and Deepwater facilities—news that might have prevented the poisonings at Bayway if the health authorities and workers had known it. This us-versus-them mind-set would become even more apparent as the public debate over leaded gasoline advanced.

EXALTING THE IN-GROUP: AN INDUSTRY WITH THE
"INTERESTS OF THE PUBLIC AT HEART" SELLING A
"GIFT OF GOD"

When criticism of leaded gas began, the industry naturally wanted to defend itself and its motives. As is often the case, that defense involved both denying any potential self-interested bias and exalting itself by claiming a much loftier social mission than mere profit-seeking. In effect, it was denying that it viewed the issue through any sort of tribal lens.

With so much invested financially and otherwise in TEL, it would have taken tremendous effort for the product's promoters to achieve anything close to objectivity in assessing its health risk. That effort would have required, at a minimum, an awareness that they had a private interest in leaded gas that could conflict with the public's interest and bias them, and yet the industry repeatedly claimed it had no such bias because its interest in the public good was so strong. This claim foreshadowed the claim of GM's Charles Wilson in 1953, when he famously said that what's good for the country is good for GM and vice versa.

In 1925, the surgeon general held a high-profile one-day conference to discuss the risks of TEL, inviting representatives from industry, government, academia, and labor. Drawing attention to the risk of leaded gasoline was about all the federal government had the statutory authority to do at the time. The surgeon general and the federal Public Health Service he ran could hold hearings, make recommendations, and issue warnings, but actual regulation of industry actions was still almost entirely the purview of state and local governments.

One of the attendees at the conference was Yale physiology professor Yandell Henderson, a nationally recognized expert on the effects of gases on the body. Henderson had become a widely quoted thorn in industry's side since the Bayway poisonings. He had prophetically warned in an April 1925 speech of the likelihood that "conditions will grow worse so gradually and the development of lead poisoning will come on so insidiously (for this is the nature of the disease) that leaded gasoline will be in nearly universal use and large numbers of cars will have been sold that can run only on that fuel before the public and the Government awaken to the situation."

At the conference, Henderson pointed out that they had in the room "two diametrically opposed conceptions," with "industry, chemists and engineers" taking one perspective, and "sanitary experts" taking the other. When he suggested that the industry representatives were not giving health the priority they should, Dr. Robert Kehoe rose to object.

Kehoe was a young medical doctor that Kettering had hired the year before to look into the poisonings at the GM plant in Ohio. He assured the group that the decisions about TEL "have been not in the hands of the industries; they have been in the hands of medical men, who have had the interests of the public at heart." He claimed that the company's "attitude is one of complete regard for facts," and if an "actual danger" to the public could be shown, "the distribution of gasoline with lead in it will be discontinued from that moment. Of that there is no question." Kehoe was not just assuring others that there was no reason to worry about company bias but revealing his unquestioned presumption that the burden of proof fell on those alleging danger to show it, rather than on the company to show safety. (Public health scholar Jerome O. Nriagu would later call this show-me-the-data approach to environmental risk the Kehoe Paradigm.)

Midgley would also assert his company's lack of bias. More than that, he called a suggestion that industry-funded research was not sufficiently objective an attack on his company's morals. In an article about TEL, he would make the counterintuitive and unexplained claim that "no one is more anxious to discover if any health hazard exists in the use of tetraethyl lead than the people who are interested in extending its use."

Kehoe and Midgley were likely inclined to believe their claims about objectivity; such a lack of bias awareness is by no means rare, especially among those who feel under attack. There is something deep within most of us that will resist the notion that we are being influenced by factors outside our consciousness, especially by something like rank self-interest. Studies have shown that the average person believes he or she is less biased than the average person. Yet whether we see Kehoe and Midgley as the rational profit maximizers described by classical economics (devising a cynical corporate strategy) or as the flesh-and-blood humans described by evolutionary psychology (trying to apply a brain evolved for tribal conflict to complex questions of systemic risk), or as some mixture of the two, circumstances were pushing them toward bias and denial of that bias.

The industry went on to argue that while the health experts only had to worry about public health, the industry bore the heavy responsibility of advancing our industrial civilization. Charles Kettering was not just the nation's foremost automotive engineer; he was on his way to being celebrated as the "prophet of progress," a widely sought speaker famous for his folksy mix of technological optimism and can-do spirit. One of his widely quoted sayings was "the price of progress is trouble, and I don't think the price is too high." At the 1925 Surgeon General's Conference, Kettering made the case that TEL was indispensable for getting more work out of gasoline, letting the nation extend its dwindling supply of petroleum. (Even Kettering's critics acknowledge his genuine concern over a feared oil shortage.)

Frank Howard, of Standard Oil, but speaking on behalf of its corporate partners too, went further. He stated that "our continued development of motor fuels is essential in our civilization," and by letting a gallon of gas go further, TEL was a "gift of God." A scientist who consulted for Ethyl expressed a similar view in a letter to a federal official; while acknowledging the health risks of leaded gasoline, he was "afraid human progress cannot go on under such restrictions and that where things can be handled safely by proper supervision and regulation they must be allowed to proceed if we are to survive among the nations."

Reframing a harmful action as serving a greater good is another psychological mechanism Albert Bandura identified that enables people to more easily violate their own moral codes. The industry's defenders may well have convinced themselves they were serving the larger good when they made their statements, but there is evidence that the larger good was not the dominant motive.

For example, the first nation with which this gift of God would be shared was Hitler's Germany. In 1936, a TEL plant would be built in Germany and jointly owned by an Ethyl affiliate and IG Farben, a powerful German chemical trust that was crucial to the rising Nazi war machine. The deal would be negotiated by the same Frank Howard, and as a congressional investigation would later reveal, the TEL technology was shared despite warnings that Germany was secretly rearming and TEL would help it. Indeed, an IG Farben official wrote during the war that "without lead-tetraethyl the present method of warfare would be unthinkable," and the Nazis' ability to produce TEL was entirely because "the Americans had presented us with the production plants, complete with experimental knowledge."

Moreover, the indispensability of lead as an antiknock compound had been challenged even in the 1920s. Gasoline could have been blended with ethanol (grain alcohol), as Midgley and others at GM knew because they had successfully experimented with it. But ethanol could be made by "any idiot with a still," in the words of journalist and automotive historian Jamie Lincoln Kitman. Ethanol could not be patented and did not offer a revenue stream the way TEL did. In his award-winning article in 2000 about the history of leaded gas for *The Nation*, Kitman would write that the benefits of leaded gasoline "were wildly and knowingly overstated in the beginning, and continue to be."

Ultimately, the parties at the 1925 conference voted to hand the issue over to the surgeon general, who would appoint a committee of experts to look at all the evidence and make some recommendations. A few months later the committee members said there were no good grounds to ban leaded gasoline for the time being. They warned, though, that their conclusion was based on limited short-term data, and longer exposures might indeed cause detectable lead poisoning. The committee stressed that the long-term investigation "must not be allowed to lapse" and strongly urged that Congress appropriate money to continue the investigation.

The federal authorities never sought, and Congress never appropriated, money to continue the investigation. The use of leaded gasoline expanded until nearly all gasoline sold in the United States contained lead, and it eventually spread into global markets. The acute poisoning of workers was reduced by more careful manufacturing practices, keeping that issue out of the news.

The nation seemed to forget about the hazards of long-term public exposure to lead. When it was finally suggested many years later that Americans, especially children, were being harmed by widespread low-level lead exposure, that brought out another dimension of tribalism: the instinctive desire to denigrate our adversaries.

ATTACKING THE OUT-GROUP CRITIC: A NAÏVE,
IGNORANT, BRASH, PASSIONATE, DOGMATIC,
ABSURD ZEALOT

Robert Kehoe—the young physician who in 1925 assured critics that the
industry would stop selling TEL if the facts showed an actual hazard—
would utterly dominate the search for such a hazard for the next forty
years and never spot one. In the meantime, his career would become a
symbol of the intimate ties between business and academia, as he simultaneously worked for the University of Cincinnati as head of its industry-
funded Kettering Laboratory and as medical director of the Ethyl
Corporation. Industry not only built his lab and financed most of his
research, but it paid his salary (except for the one dollar per year he
received from the University of Cincinnati).

While Kehoe's prominence extended to the field of occupational medicine generally, about lead he was the long-unquestioned authority. To an
astonishing degree, virtually all research into lead's effect on the human
body between the 1920s and 1960s was conducted at the Kettering
Laboratory under Kehoe's direction. After he sent colleagues a compilation
of his lectures on the subject in 1960, one colleague wrote back, "You are
God in the field," and another wrote, "The last word has been said on lead."

Kehoe's data largely came from studying workers, and he helped develop
protocols for greatly reducing worker exposures to TEL, surely saving lives
by reducing acute occupational poisonings. He also conducted experiments where he had young men eat lead salts and breathe the exhaust of
engines burning leaded gasoline, and then measured how much lead was
excreted in their waste and how much was left in their blood. He championed two particularly important conclusions drawn from this work. First,
he concluded that relatively high levels of lead were naturally present in
both the environment and people's bodies. Second, he argued that as long
as blood lead levels stayed below the threshold associated with clinical
symptoms of classical lead poisoning, lead posed no harm. The threshold
Kehoe identified was 80 micrograms of lead per deciliter of blood ($\mu g/dL$),
because he had never seen symptoms of lead poisoning below that level.
For decades, these basic principles limited the scope of the discussion
about lead poisoning, to the extent there was any discussion.

Eventually, though, Kehoe's reassuring views were directly challenged by someone entirely outside his field who had arrived at the issue indirectly: Clair Patterson. Patterson had no medical training, was not a biologist, toxicologist, or industrial hygienist, and at least initially he was not driven by concern over health or the environment. He was a geochemist trying to determine the age of the planet; since uranium decays into lead over time, precisely measuring lead levels in minerals offered a way to calculate Earth's age.

In the late 1940s and early 1950s, Patterson devised the technological means to measure various lead isotopes in increments far tinier than had been measurable before. In so doing, though, he realized that lead was everywhere in our environment—so prevalent even in the laboratories that he had to build a special, ultraclean laboratory to make his measurements. Ultimately, Patterson was able to calculate that our planet was formed 4.5 billion years ago—a groundbreaking calculation he published in 1953, which has held up over the decades.

Patterson turned his attention to the seas to further develop his lead-dating technique. By measuring the lead in different depths of the ocean and in seafloor sediments, he could determine how lead levels have changed over time. This work was partially funded by the American Petroleum Institute, which had been convinced by a mentor of Patterson's that the geologic history revealed by lead measurements could someday help to locate more oil. Patterson's measurements revealed that lead had risen dramatically during the industrial age, and especially in the previous few decades, and he concluded that the source of this extra lead was probably leaded gasoline. He knew his findings would anger the oil industry, but he published them anyway.

Journalist and author Lydia Denworth, in her engrossing book *Toxic Truth: A Scientist, a Doctor, and the Battle over Lead*, quotes Patterson claiming that the industry's first response was to try to buy him off by offering continued funding only if he would change the focus of his research. He declined, and as he explained years later, "Wham! They stopped my research. They not only stopped funding me, they tried to get the Atomic Energy Commission to stop giving me anything. . . . They went around and tried to block all my funding." Someone within the petroleum industry also tried, unsuccessfully, to get Patterson fired from his job at Caltech.

Patterson's willingness to risk the wrath of the oil industry and jeopardize his funding was just another illustration of a fiercely independent nature. In many ways he was Robert Kehoe's opposite—an eccentric and somewhat detached outsider who cared little about worldly status or how he was viewed by those in power, including by those funding his research. He was much more interested in pure science than in its application, and he largely depended on others to obtain the federal and other grants he needed. (Patterson would years later decline a professorship at Caltech for a time because he didn't support the concept of tenure.)

Patterson was invited to publish his findings in the medical journal *Archives of Environmental Health,* and in 1965 he submitted an article in which he presented his calculation that average Americans probably had one hundred times more lead in their bodies than prehistoric humans, based on what he knew about lead levels in the prehistoric environment (later, he and his colleagues would adjust this estimate to six hundred times more lead).

It was an extraordinarily provocative claim—arguing that we humans had contaminated the world and ourselves with potentially dangerous levels of lead. One of the scientists who reviewed the paper for the journal prior to its publication rightly noted that it "impugns the life work of Bob Kehoe." Even so, Kehoe, who also reviewed the paper, did not try to stop its publication. He wrote, "I should let the man, with his obvious faults, speak in such a way as to display these faults." Kehoe knew it was too late for the issue Patterson had raised to be "swept under the rug," so his views "must be faced and demolished."

Kehoe warned an executive at Ethyl that Patterson's forthcoming article could lead to a ban on leaded gas. He also urged "that there be little or no obvious effort on the part of those who have an important stake in the lead-using industries to discredit Dr. Patterson, for such effort will be a boomerang." Kehoe himself, though, did not hold back in trying to discredit Patterson. In reviewing Patterson's work for the journal prior to publication, Kehoe called his inferences "remarkably naïve. . . . It is an example of how wrong one can be" when he steps into a field "of which he is so woefully ignorant and so lacking in any concept of the depth of his ignorance, that he is not even cautious in drawing sweeping conclusions.

This bespeaks the brash young man, or perhaps the not so young, passionate supporter of a cause."

After the article came out, Kehoe wrote a response chastising Patterson for venturing "without caution, humility, or appropriate critique" into a new field. He accused Patterson of "the boldness, passion, and disregard for troublesome facts that more befit zeal in the advocacy of a cause than the attitude of the serious investigator" and called his conclusions "astonishingly dogmatic (and absurd)."

Kehoe's response echoed an earlier defender of leaded gas, who in 1925 had accused those warning of its dangers of offering "incompetent and hysterical testimony" and being "misguided zealots." Industries frequently accuse their critics of hysteria and emotionalism, portraying the business world as ruled by nothing but reason and pragmatism, beset by irrational and emotional critics.

Kehoe's attack on Patterson might have run counter to his own advice to industry, but it would be no surprise to the psychologists who study how people react to a threat from an out-group. If you are engaged in a tribal conflict, even if you don't consciously recognize it as such, you don't just defend your own tribe; you instinctively want to criticize the outsiders threatening you. Psychologists dryly call this "out-group derogation."

There is research suggesting that even a minor and symbolic threat to a group we identify with can lower our self-esteem. In one small but interesting study, psychologists Nyla R. Branscombe and Daniel Wann manipulated the collective self-esteem of their research subjects using, surprisingly enough, a six-minute clip from the movie *Rocky IV*. They showed subjects a dramatic fight scene in which Rocky boxes the villainous Russian fighter Ivan Drago. (The year was 1989, before the Soviet Union broke up.) The researchers edited the clip so that half saw Rocky win and the other half thought they saw Ivan win.

The collective self-esteem of those subjects who identified more highly as Americans dropped if they'd seen Ivan win. Then the researchers gave the subjects the opportunity to disparage Russians by asking a series of questions about US policies toward the Soviet Union, Russian exchange students, and aspects of Russian character. Those whose self-esteem had dropped were most eager to tear down Russians, and doing so helped their collective self-esteem bounce back. Insulting those who pose a threat to one's group identity—even just a symbolic threat—appears to be a mood-altering activity.

Of course, when a critic raises charges that actually threaten our financial interests, not to mention our reputations, we have a strategic incentive to discredit that critic in order to undermine the validity of the charges. But research like this points to an emotional inclination to do so quite apart from any conscious corporate strategy.

RISING SKEPTICISM OF INDUSTRY DENIALS: "I SEEM TO BE A BIT UNDER THE GUN"

After publishing his 1965 article, Clair Patterson wanted more evidence of changes in lead deposition over time, and he went to extraordinary lengths to get it. He visited a US military base in Greenland to meticulously collect ice formed from snow that fell centuries ago, so that he could learn how much lead had made it into the Arctic atmosphere in the past. Then he took a team to Antarctica for another arduous sample-collecting expedition. Now Patterson had even more persuasive evidence that atmospheric lead had risen dramatically during the industrial era, especially in the previous few decades.

Meanwhile, Patterson's article about global lead contamination had attracted attention, including from the *New York Times*, which ran two articles about his claims that leaded gasoline was causing an alarming increase in lead pollution and human exposure. Amazingly, there was no mention that public health experts forty years earlier had warned of precisely this problem in the pages of the same newspaper.

In December 1965, the Public Health Service, the same federal agency that had hosted the first conference on leaded gas in 1925, held another conference that ended up largely focused on Patterson's findings. Robert Kehoe, now seventy-two, was likely the only person to attend both meetings, and he delivered roughly the same "no evidence of danger" message he had delivered in 1925. Patterson, still in Antarctica, missed the meeting, but a handful of his scientific colleagues represented his views, and one reported that it was an angry and emotional affair.

As in 1925, the question of the objectivity of industry-funded research was raised, but this time it focused on Kehoe personally and it was a different era. Kehoe could not bat it away, as he had done four decades earlier, by assuring people he had only the public interest at heart and a complete regard for the facts. In a press conference after the meeting, Kehoe was subjected to enough questioning about industry funding of his salary and research that Harriet Hardy, head of MIT's occupational medical clinic and a committed ally of Patterson's, "almost felt sorry" for Kehoe. This giant in his field was unaccustomed to such questioning ("I seem to be a bit under the gun," he said) and was reportedly quite upset.

Of course, Kehoe had just attacked Patterson's objectivity in the strongest terms. This back and forth occurs in almost every dispute over corporate harm. The industry's defenders are assumed to have a financially driven bias (as I assume in this book). This bias is not always openly mentioned, especially in official conferences, but industry members understand they are generally viewed as biased. Industry in turn accuses its critics of being biased due to some ulterior motive beyond just preventing the harm they have identified. Corporate defenders sometimes accuse their critics of having a hidden financial motive (of being, in effect, an "industry" just like them), and commonly they see their critics as motivated by some political cause. Rarely does either side acknowledge the possibility of their own bias, even while accusing the other side of it.

As noted, people naturally resist the idea that they may be biased, but readily assume that others are. Psychologists call this "naïve realism," since it combines a realistic recognition of the biases of others with a naïve denial of one's own potential biases. Indeed, our assumption that we are objective gives us reason to look for and even overestimate the bias of others, since it is the most obvious explanation for their failure to agree with our own clearly correct views.

Patterson did not come to the question of lead contamination with any sort of "cause" in mind, but when his research revealed what he considered an alarming problem, he had to make a choice that scientists generally hate to make: raise the political alarm and face the charge that you have lost your objectivity, or have your findings and the problem you have identified ignored.

Patterson may have been happier sealed in his ultraclean laboratory or off collecting polar ice samples, but he was worried enough about industrial lead exposure to jump into the political fray. This might have been an easier choice for Patterson than for most scientists, though, given his demonstrated disregard for conventional opinion and the names he was occasionally called. He was already seen as something of a "kook," even among his friends, and had been known to walk about his Southern California campus wearing a gas mask on smoggy days.

So Patterson sent his findings to health officials and politicians, including to Senator Edmund Muskie, chair of a US Senate subcommittee on air and water pollution. In June 1966, Muskie held hearings on air pollution, including lead. Robert Kehoe appeared, repeating his views that relatively high lead exposure was inevitable ("there is no way in which man has ever been able to escape the absorption of lead while living on this planet") but that its accumulation in the body was harmless below the 80 μg/dL threshold of clinical poisoning. When Muskie asked if medical opinion agreed with him on the latter point, Kehoe responded, "It so happens I have had more experience in this field than anybody else alive."

Patterson also appeared at the hearing, and he did not pull any punches in his testimony. He challenged Kehoe's idea that what he called today's "typical" lead levels were natural, as well as the idea that lead exposure was harmless below the threshold of recognized poisoning. In fact, he argued, the evidence strongly suggested that the average American was "being subjected to severe chronic lead insult." He did not blame just industry; he accused public health agencies like the Public Health Service (PHS) of violating their duties to the public by collaborating with the lead industry and accepting the industry's health research as objective science.

While Patterson had some friends within the Public Health Service, he had opponents too, and Muskie put into the record a letter from one of them. It was written by a PHS toxicologist objecting to the publication of Patterson's "rabble-rousing" article and asking if he was "trying to be a second Rachel Carson."

In 1962 Carson had published her groundbreaking exposé about pesticides, *Silent Spring*—a book that unleashed a wave of public concern about pollution and that helped spark the modern environmental movement. Like Patterson, Carson had been accused of unscientific zealotry on behalf of a cause. The head of the nation's top producer of DDT claimed she was writing not "as a scientist but rather as a fanatic defender of the cult of the balance of nature." A lawyer for another pesticide maker invoked Cold War tensions, suggesting Carson was somehow associated with "sinister parties" who wanted to reduce America's and Western Europe's food supply to "east-curtain parity."

Neither Carson nor Patterson were actually involved with cults or Communists, and neither showed any interest in rabble-rousing for its own sake. However, they were both part of a larger societal shift in thinking that was changing how business in America was viewed. Indeed, the resurrected debate over leaded gasoline was happening against the backdrop of the higher-profile debate over auto safety. Nader's *Unsafe at Any Speed* came out just days before the 1965 Public Health Service conference on lead, and the June 1966 Muskie hearings where Kehoe and Patterson testified took place just weeks after the Ribicoff hearings where the head of GM had to apologize for having Nader followed. It was an era of rising skepticism about corporate motives and impacts, shrinking acceptance of corporate denials, and growing demands for government regulation of industrial threats.

AN INDUSTRY UNDER SIEGE: "THE WORST EXAMPLE OF FANATICISM SINCE THE WITCH HUNTS"

Patterson's data ensured that the emerging environmental movement— along with medical researchers, civil rights groups, and antipoverty activists—paid long-overdue attention to lead, to the dismay of the industry. The year 1970 was a particularly rough one for the Ethyl Corporation. Just a few days into the new decade, the president of GM announced that to cut smog-creating emissions, GM was turning to catalytic converters. Since catalytic converters were ruined by lead, new cars would have to burn unleaded gasoline. Both GM and Standard Oil of New Jersey, who had been there at the birth of Ethyl, had sold their shares in the early 1960s; one Ethyl executive compared GM's announcement to being disowned by your father.

The Ethyl Corporation reacted to the announcement with a flurry of denial. It argued the plan would backfire: unleaded gasoline would actually increase smog and had more cancer-producing agents. It argued impossibility, with one official opining that "lead is going to be in gasoline until they stop using gas in internal combustion engines" (an ironic expression of technological pessimism from a company launched by Charles Kettering, the prophet of progress). The company claimed there was "no proof whatsoever" that lead in gasoline hurt public health, echoing wording the tobacco industry had long used about smoking.

Ethyl's chair suggested the shift away from lead was driven by irrational forces, saying the nation needed to "proceed only on the basis of established facts and not to be stampeded into condemning proven products or embracing untested theories." One Ethyl official deployed the comparative-risk defense to point to other industries, asking, "Who kills the most people in the United States yearly? The auto makers—not the leaded gasoline. Let's get in proper perspective who is doing the damage." He added, for good measure, "If people were really interested in clean air, why not make them stop smoking cigarettes in the Los Angeles area? That is where much of the particulate matter . . . comes from." The tobacco industry would similarly try to redirect attention to air pollution.

The year 1970 also saw the first Earth Day—a stunning outpouring of public support for environmental protection that caught many in government and industry by surprise. Public concern over pollution was so strong that later that year President Nixon launched a new regulatory body called the Environmental Protection Agency (EPA). By year's end, the newly minted EPA was given vastly more authority when Congress passed a strong new Clean Air Act. This sweeping landmark law addressed almost all forms of air pollution, but it paid particular attention to cars. The auto industry opposed the law, but the spirit of the times was for the law; it not only passed but did so with virtually unanimous support in both houses of Congress.

Finally, the federal government had the authority, resources, and personnel to regulate lead emissions, along with a social movement pushing it for action. It was the beginning of the end for leaded gasoline in the United States, though it would take another quarter century before it was actually banned.

The EPA required gas stations to make unleaded gas available to fuel cars with catalytic converters, but it was not eager to confront the contentious issue of lead in gasoline head-on, so a newly formed environmental group, the Natural Resources Defense Council (NRDC), sued and won a court order requiring EPA to act. When EPA did adopt rules in 1973 requiring a three-quarters drop in the lead content of leaded gasoline over five years, it was promptly sued by Ethyl, DuPont, and others. (This pattern—regulatory inaction, environmentalist suit, regulatory action, industry suit—would become depressingly common in the realm of environmental regulation and is one reason it takes so many years to convert scientific evidence of harm into a reduction of that harm.)

Studies were starting to link relatively common blood lead levels to subtle brain damage in children, but the evidence was still fairly thin and it was hard to connect all the dots between that damage and lead in gasoline. However, the DC Circuit Court, in a landmark opinion by a 5–4 vote of the entire court, rejected the industry's argument that the EPA needed a single definitive study showing that leaded gasoline causes harm, noting that "science does not work that way." The EPA was allowed and even required to look at the suggestive results of numerous studies and act to prevent potential future harm.

Lawrence Blanchard Jr., an executive of the Ethyl Corporation, was livid; his quote at the beginning of this chapter compares the proceeding to the New England witch hunts of the seventeenth century. He added, "Those deaths of innocent people who couldn't prove that they weren't witches were also upheld by the courts swept up in the emotions of the day. That chapter in American history soon came to be an embarrassment to all intelligent people, and so will this proceeding."

In fact, the evidence of the damage done to children by low-level lead exposure kept mounting, with no apparent effect on the industry members' view of their product. They simply dismissed the evidence of harm, while proffering at least one study suggesting lead was actually an essential micronutrient. A 1983 panel of experts found that study unpersuasive, and the EPA concluded that given the pervasive extent of global lead contamination, the idea of "lead deficiency" was "virtually inconceivable" anyway. The industry was not without allies, though. The *Wall Street Journal* also claimed that lead was good for kids, but on different grounds. It editorialized in 1982 that adding "a bit more lead" to gasoline would, by creating a stronger economy with more jobs, "likely do more for ghetto children" than emotion-driven environmental protections.

Even during the antiregulatory Reagan administration, restrictions against lead grew stronger (following a congressional backlash to an initial effort to weaken lead regulations). A lengthy cost-benefit analysis prepared by EPA showed that further slashing lead content in gasoline would yield vast health and economic benefits, far outweighing the costs. Reagan's Office of Management and Budget judged the analysis a very fine example of how such regulations should be approached. Blanchard of the Ethyl Corporation disagreed; he was "simply shocked" by the "juvenile and simplistic" analysis, calling his foes at the EPA "novelists" and "bastards." He assured shareholders the company was "not about to surrender to our intellectually fraudulent opponents."

Public health historians Gerald Markowitz and David Rosner write that by the mid-1980s the lead industry "would abandon its effort to win the scientific argument over lead's effects on its merits and revert to attempting character assassination and manufacturing uncertainty about the emerging scientific consensus." Its chief target for years would be the pediatrician and researcher Herbert Needleman, a pioneer in the discovery of how low-level lead exposure affects children. Like Clair Patterson, Needleman was tenacious in drawing attention to the threat. Industry consultants formally challenged not just Needleman's findings but his integrity, even accusing him of professional misconduct. Ultimately, both he and his data were exonerated, but Needleman told biographer Lydia Denworth that defending himself "took three years out of my professional life."

There was also considerable finger-pointing during this era. The Ethyl Corporation blamed the lead levels in children's blood on kids eating lead paint, while the paint industry—with its own long history of exposing children to lead and denying the harm—was blaming leaded gasoline (among other things). In the end, there was plenty of blame to go around.

Ethyl officials felt themselves at war, and the company's continued denial of the science surely fueled its growing sense of unfair victimization. The CEO of Ethyl complained that his "good product" had been turned into a "sacrificial lamb." Another Ethyl official claimed that the atmosphere was preventing "objective scientists from coming forward" because they would be "crucified" by the press, EPA, and environmentalists. A spokesman for a lead industry trade group said in 1981 that "for the past decade or so the lead industry has seen itself as an industry under siege." When the Reagan EPA tightened lead regulations even further, he said the industry felt "wronged" and blamed skillful manipulation of the media by "five or six scientists, together with the rabid environmentalists." It was a slightly ironic charge given how much the TEL poisonings in the 1920s resembled actual rabies, though by this time that history was long forgotten.

Almost all the industries profiled in this book complain about being victimized by unfair processes and irrational critics. This seems to be a highly effective way for them, or probably members of any tribe facing criticism, to minimize any feelings of remorse about the harms their tribe has caused. Focusing instead on the wrongs they perceive to have been done to them (and those in the bunker with them) lets an energizing anger obliterate any emerging guilt that might otherwise threaten to demoralize them.

LEAD BURDEN: THE GIFT THAT KEEPS ON GIVING

While the lead in gasoline dropped precipitously in the late 1970s thanks to EPA regulations, leaded gasoline was not actually banned for on-road vehicles in the United States until 1995—over seventy years after it was introduced. The industry had argued that there was no proven link between lead in our gasoline and lead in our blood, but as lead in gasoline fell between 1976 and 1980, so did average blood lead levels, almost in lockstep.

The lead sprayed from engines over all those decades—millions of tons of it—has not disappeared. Some dispersed globally, which is why Patterson was able to read the rise of leaded gas in the ice of Greenland and Antarctica. But a bit remains deposited in the soils of our cities and towns, and when the wind blows on dusty days, we and our children can breathe it once again.

The health community's celebration over falling blood lead levels was muted by a deepening understanding of just how harmful even a little lead really is. A long and heartbreaking parade of studies over the years would find children being harmed at lower and lower levels of lead exposure. Needleman and others showed that lead was associated with lower IQs, lower verbal ability, shortened attention spans, and more disruptive behavior in grade school children. Studies have linked lead exposure to impulsivity, hyperactivity, depression, and anxiety, and even to higher rates of criminal offenses.

The blood lead level threshold that Robert Kehoe argued was safe—80 micrograms per deciliter (µg/dL)—has proven to be way, way off. Health authorities and regulators have lowered the level of concern multiple times over the years, with industry resistance. Today, subtle but permanent neurologic damage and behavioral disorders have been associated with childhood blood lead levels of less than 5 µg/dL.

In 1976–1980, the *average* blood lead level for American preschoolers was 15.1 µg/dL; by 2008 it had fallen tenfold, to 1.5 µg/dL. It is estimated that most US adults born before 1980 had blood lead levels over 10 µg/dL when they were children, with many far higher. Screenings of children decades ago in Chicago, New York, and other cities found that between 20 and 45 percent of them had blood lead levels in the range of 40–50 µg/dL. It appears that most of the lead exposure even for low-income, inner-city kids, who also had considerable lead paint exposure, came from gasoline. By way of comparison, it appears that even in those parts of Flint, Michigan, that faced the greatest lead contamination during that city's recent water crisis, 10.6 percent of the children had blood lead levels that exceeded 5 µg/dL.

The lead burden borne by the public at large was so widespread that it raises some heavy questions. For example, what sort of people might we have been if we had all developed to our full potential and been a little smarter, more attentive, less anxious, and less impulsive than we have been? If you slide the bell curve of a population's intelligence to the left a few IQ points—meaning, among other things, that more people are severely impaired and fewer are geniuses—how does that alter a society? The next time you see an inexplicable sign of mass stupidity (insert your own political jokes here), you may find yourself wondering if it might in some way reflect a collective mental impairment caused by the lead that so many of today's adults absorbed at a very tender age.

Separate analyses by Rick Nevin and Jessica Wolpaw Reyes ask whether, given the strong correlation between lead exposure and delinquency, lead may have contributed to the midcentury surge in violent crime experienced in the United States and many other nations. Their studies show that reductions in violent crime correspond remarkably well with the removal of lead from gasoline, which took place at different times in different states and nations, factoring in a two-decade or so lag for the exposed children to reach the prime criminality age. However, other researchers using a different series of crime statistics have not found a correlation to lead exposure in the United States, so we can expect this debate to continue.

Less attention has been paid to the impact of lead on adults, but lead exposure—even in decades past—is a major risk factor for premature death from cardiovascular disease. A major international research effort estimated that in 2017 over a million deaths worldwide could be linked to lead exposure (from all sources, not just gasoline), and yet this number may be way too low according to an astounding new study. Thousands of US adults had their blood lead levels tested between 1988 and 1994 as part of a larger medical survey. A 2018 analysis found those with higher lead levels in the earlier period had a significantly higher risk of death in subsequent years, especially from heart disease. Based on this finding, researchers estimated that just in the United States, about 400,000 deaths are attributable to lead exposure every year—ten times more than previously thought. If this estimate is correct, it would put lead exposure in the same ballpark as tobacco, which is linked to about 480,000 early deaths in the United States yearly.

What happened to the corporations behind leaded gasoline? GM, DuPont, and Standard Oil of New Jersey (now Exxon) would, of course, remain giants of the auto, chemical, and oil industries. And the Ethyl Corporation actually managed to survive America's ban on what had once been its sole product. First, Ethyl diversified, mainly into other chemicals; its executives once considered buying a tobacco company but thought better of it. Second, it relied more on selling leaded gasoline in other countries where, as Ethyl's president said in 1970, "We don't face the hysteria that we do here."

It turns out that children in other countries, particularly developing ones, were exposed to brain-damaging leaded gasoline for years after American kids no longer were. International campaigns by health activists, the United Nations, and others would eventually help drive leaded gas almost entirely out of the global market. The only nation still using leaded gas is Algeria, though five other nations—Iraq, Yemen, Afghanistan,

North Korea, and Myanmar—phased it out only in the last few years. Although there are obviously a host of factors driving the violence in war-torn Iraq, Afghanistan, and Yemen, being among the last to stop spreading a brain poison potentially linked to violence surely has not helped.

As for the individual players in this drama, Clair Patterson remained active for years in the push to get the lead out of not just gasoline but food (it was used to solder cans) and other sources. He was showered with prizes and honors for his work on lead and in 1987 was elected to the National Academy of Sciences, the nation's preeminent scientific association (though one he did not hold in particularly high regard). In 1995, at the age of 73, this man who had done so much to clear the air died of a severe asthma attack. He left unfinished a book about a new question that consumed him for years before his death—namely, what is it about human consciousness and the thought processes of *Homo sapiens* that could allow us to poison the earth so profoundly?

Charles Kettering, ever the technological optimist, probably did not struggle with that question. He achieved fame and fortune at GM and retired as something of a living legend. Much of his money he would devote to philanthropy, with a particular focus on science and health. His name is perhaps best known for its association with the Sloan-Kettering Institute, which he cofounded with Alfred P. Sloan Jr. and which has been a world leader in cancer research. (Lead and lead compounds, incidentally, have been officially classified as "reasonably anticipated to be human carcinogens," though the evidence is not nearly as strong as the evidence for lead's other harms.) Kettering died in 1958, years before Patterson changed the way the world thought about lead. Robert Kehoe, on the other hand, lived long enough to learn how dangerously wrong he had been, though he may not have accepted it. He died in 1992, at the age of 99.

Like Kettering, Thomas Midgley would die before he could learn the tragic consequences of his discovery. He had become one of America's most celebrated and award-winning chemists, which is particularly impressive given that his training was as a mechanical engineer. In 1940, at the age of 51, Midgley developed polio. He devised a rope and pulley system to lift himself from bed, and one morning in 1944 his wife found him strangled to death in the ropes. The newspapers were told it was a freak accident, but cemetery records called it suicide. A few months earlier, in a speech to the American Chemical Society, Midgley had argued that the best discoveries are made by the young, and older scientists should get out of their way.

One of the other world-changing discoveries Midgley made during his inventive younger years was chlorofluorocarbons—a family of chemicals that would be widely used in refrigeration, air conditioning, and spray cans. In 1974, scientists warned that these chemicals posed a grave threat to the stratospheric ozone layer, which we and other surface life forms depend on to shield us from dangerous radiation. It would launch yet another dramatic chapter in the annals of corporate denial.

5 "Our Free Enterprise System Is at Stake"

CFCS, IDEOLOGY, AND MANIPULATED
UNCERTAINTY

"My theory is that the whole thing is orchestrated by the
Ministry of Disinformation of the KGB in Moscow, to
damage our economy and our faith in democratic
government."

—George Diamond, president of Diamond Aerosol, 1977

In the 1920s, people started replacing their old iceboxes with mechanical refrigerators, sometimes called icebox machines. Then a problem emerged: the new devices used toxic gases for cooling, and the gases occasionally leaked out and killed people. Chicago health authorities in the summer of 1929 announced that the mysterious recent deaths of eighteen city residents could be blamed on leaks of methyl chloride, one of the three commonly used refrigerants.

Newspapers wrote of growing "icebox anxiety" caused by the reported deaths, and within weeks federal authorities rushed out a statement to prevent undue excitement over the issue. The US Public Health Service reassured consumers that deadly refrigerant leaks were quite rare given how many refrigerators were already in use. However, it did note that unlike other common refrigerants, which have strong and irritating odors, methyl chloride had a "slight and rather pleasant odor, which probably would not awaken a sleeping person." The overall message—that home refrigerators can indeed kill people in their sleep but do so only rarely—was not exactly the ringing endorsement that the makers of this new consumer product probably wanted.

By then, though, the refrigeration industry was already looking for a solution. The company Frigidaire was owned by General Motors, and in 1928 GM's Charles Kettering had asked Thomas Midgley to find a refrigerant that was both nonpoisonous and nonflammable. It did not take Midgley long to synthesize a new family of chemicals we now call chlorofluorocarbons, or CFCs, which nicely met the criteria. To demonstrate CFCs' safety at an American Chemical Society meeting in 1930, the ever-dramatic Midgley inhaled some CFCs and then blew out a candle. He would note that while not poisonous, CFCs were a little intoxicating, but not in a fun way; unlike alcohol, they did not "rouse a desire to sing or recite poetry."

The new compound was dubbed Freon, and GM and DuPont formed a corporation to make it. Frigidaire marketed it as a miracle refrigerant, "one of the most outstanding scientific achievements of our times," and within a few years virtually all refrigerator manufacturers were using Freon. CFCs would allow widespread use of both refrigeration and air conditioning—two technologies that would transform modern life.

Later, CFCs would be central to the emergence of the new aerosol spray industry. CFCs were nonreactive; they would not interact with the product being sprayed, making them the perfect propellant in spray cans. During World War II, CFCs were used to disperse a widely hailed new pesticide called DDT to kill malaria-carrying mosquitoes, and this spraying is credited with saving many lives during the Pacific campaign.* In the postwar years, though, rather than saving lives, CFC propellants were largely just saving hairdos and preventing embarrassment by propelling hairsprays and deodorants. Propellants that would not burst into flames when sprayed at one's body were especially handy in this era of increased smoking.

So leaded gasoline and CFCs were both invented by the same guy working for the same company in the same decade. Thomas Midgley and his team, and the new industries they helped create, managed to leave a lasting chemical mark not only on our land, oceans, and bodies but on the vast reaches of the stratosphere as well.

---

*Rachel Carson would later point out that mosquitoes quickly built resistance to DDT and it built up in the environment, causing harms including declines in bird populations.

Yet for the purposes of this book, there are differences worth noting between Midgley's two inventions. Leaded gasoline spread a known, cumulative poison through society, not to mention exposing workers to a notoriously toxic gas. By contrast, CFCs replaced deadly chemicals in consumer products with something much less likely to kill the products' users. And where the long-term threat posed by leaded gasoline had been tragically obvious even in the 1920s, the long-term threat posed by CFCs would have been virtually unfathomable.

When the alarm was raised about CFCs decades later, industries were threatened by science they did not understand. The tribal attacks with which many responded were heavily tinged with the anticommunist ideology of the Cold War and with resentment over the rising environmental expectations of the era. More sophisticated industry players would focus on the scientific debate, exploiting every uncertainty and keeping the burden of proof on those alleging a world-threatening danger.

Eventually, the drama around CFCs would yield a rare example of corporate denial actually overcome by—among other things—scientific evidence. Unfortunately, this victory for science would be quickly followed by an ideological, antiscience backlash that haunts us today.

DISCOVERING OZONE AND ITS VULNERABILITY: DEATH RAYS AND HAIRSPRAYS

Life on the surface of the earth could never have evolved without the shelter provided by the stratospheric ozone layer. It would have been killed by ultraviolet light coming from the sun (in particular, the shortwave part of the spectrum called UV-B). Fortunately, the primitive oceans started releasing oxygen—a waste product of underwater life forms. When this oxygen rose up and was blasted by ultraviolet light, the two-atom configuration that oxygen is typically found in was broken up and reconfigured into a three-atom molecule known as ozone.

The ozone molecules accumulated miles above the surface, and like a natural sunscreen, they began to absorb enough of the UV-B rays to allow life to finally emerge onto land. But stratospheric ozone is not static; its continual formation by radiation is kept in balance by a continual destruction by other natural forces, maintaining a relatively steady state though one that varies significantly by latitude and season. (Ozone is also the prime component of smog; although we want ozone in the stratosphere to absorb radiation, ozone down at the surface is an air pollutant that causes lung damage and other harms.)

Scientists were just learning the importance of the ozone layer when Midgley synthesized the first CFCs, and it would be explained to the public in sensational terms. *Popular Science* magazine thrilled its readers in 1934 with the announcement that "an armor plate of invisible gas surrounds the earth and protects us against death rays from the sun!" The *New York Times* explained that, but for ozone, these death rays would "blind and blister and eventually destroy all earthly life." Dr. Charles Abbot, the secretary of the Smithsonian, said that "it is astonishing and even terrifying . . . to contemplate the narrow margin of safety on which our lives thus depend. Were this trifling quantity of atmospheric ozone removed, we should all perish."

But as Seth Cagin and Philip Dray note in their fascinating 1993 book about the CFC controversy, *Between Earth and Sky: How CFCs Changed Our World and Endangered the Ozone Layer,* despite the apocalyptic tones, no one then suspected that our all-important ozone layer was vulnerable: "Knowing how fine a thread safeguarded mankind did not inspire fear, but only increased one's awe and appreciation of nature's intricacies." It would be some decades before anyone imagined that the miraculous chemicals then making refrigeration safer might also weaken Earth's shield against solar death rays.

In the early 1970s, the British scientist Dr. James Lovelock invented a device that vastly improved our ability to measure gases in the atmosphere and determined that nearly all the CFCs ever released since Midgley first made them were still floating around in the sky. Lovelock was unconcerned by this discovery, almost as a matter of personal principle. He would later say, "I'm not a doomwatch sort of person," and he bent over backward to avoid triggering a "doomwatch scare" over CFCs. When he published his atmospheric measurements in 1973, he wrote that "the presence of these compounds constitutes no conceivable hazard."

Dr. Sherwood (Sherry) Rowland, a chemistry professor at the University of California, Irvine, learned of Lovelock's CFC measurements from a DuPont scientist he happened to speak with at a conference. Rowland had what he called the "casual thought" that those CFCs might keep rising, in which case they would eventually come apart due to their exposure to ultraviolet radiation. He registered no alarm at the thought, just interest, and the next year he sought funding from the federal Atomic Energy Commission (which had funded his earlier work) to research the question. His postdoctoral research associate, Dr. Mario Molina, was curious about the fate of CFCs too.

Molina looked for natural mechanisms that might keep CFCs from reaching the stratosphere but found none. He and Rowland concluded that CFCs would eventually, after decades of drifting through the lower atmosphere, reach the stratosphere and be blasted with ultraviolet radiation, breaking up the CFC molecules and releasing chlorine atoms. And based on their understanding of chemical reactions, they calculated that once set free, each chlorine atom would trigger a chain reaction that would destroy many thousands of ozone molecules. In short, thanks to their much-celebrated nonreactive nature, CFCs could rise undisturbed into the sky and thereby deliver to the stratosphere chlorine atoms that were, by unfortunate contrast, fiercely reactive.

Molina really started to worry when he looked at the CFC industry's annual production figures. He calculated that even if CFC emissions stayed at 1972 rates, they could lead to an alarming depletion of the Earth's ozone over the next few decades. He and Rowland assumed there must be some mistake but could find no error in their calculations. Rowland reported to his wife, "The work is going well. But it looks like the end of the world."

Rowland and Molina published their findings and presented them to a conference of the American Chemical Society in 1974, and the *New York Times,* network news, and others covered the story. While there was definitely concern and attention, in some ways the surprise was how little alarm was caused by the potentially catastrophic implications of depleting the critically important ozone layer. Surely part of the lack of alarm was the fact that, unlike most questions of environmental impact, this was not a story about the cause of a known problem; it was a prediction of a problem that had never been detected. But there were other factors that probably inclined people—including the industry and the public—toward disbelief.

Those who study how our minds perceive risk have identified mental shortcuts and cognitive biases that tend to make us underestimate some risks while overestimating others. One factor that influences our perception of a given risk is its "imaginability." We tend to underestimate dangers that are hard to conceive of; depletion of the ozone layer—something that had never happened in human experience—would surely fall into that category.

And the threat was likely made even more unbelievable given the alleged role of the familiar cans of hairspray and deodorant sitting in Americans' bathrooms. How could chemicals used to transport a product just a few inches from can to body end up travelling the globe and accumulating miles above our heads? How could products that delivered at best the one-day benefit of stiffer hair and dryer armpits cause harm for decades? How could chemicals prized precisely because they are so non-reactive end up wreaking such chain-reaction havoc? And how could such mundane and trivial products threaten a vital, mysterious, life-sustaining feature of the planet? Something in the mind reels at the wild disproportionality between such fleeting benefits and such profound costs.

This may well have made it easier to dismiss the warnings as absurd, especially for those inclined to trust their gut over science. In 2016, long after CFC's were banned, one skeptic with notably stiff hair told an audience, "I said, 'Wait a minute, so if I take hairspray and I spray it in my apartment which is all sealed, you're telling me that affects the ozone layer?' Yes? I say no way folks. No way." Later that year that speaker would be elected president of the United States.

ATTACKING CRITICS OF THE PUSH-BUTTON AGE: VIGILANTES, HYSTERICS, TRAITORS, AND THE KGB

Ideally, when confronted with scientific claims of a hazard posed by its product, a corporation would engage on the scientific merits. In this case, though, the science was so rarified that the makers and users of CFCs had no special expertise in it. DuPont and other manufacturers had made some efforts to determine CFCs' environmental impact but failed to track the chemicals to their ultimate fate in the stratosphere. Indeed, when Rowland went to discuss his findings with DuPont scientists in the fall of 1974, he saw they lacked expertise in stratospheric science. "We understood that we had a terrific responsibility, because we did not see sufficient scientific competence in our opposition," Rowland said. "If there were flaws in the theory, we would have to find them ourselves."

And if a large and sophisticated company filled with chemists, like DuPont, could not understand the science of ozone depletion, the aerosol industry was certainly in way over its head. That industry included small and medium-sized businesses that filled aerosol cans with various products, often on a contract basis. It also included larger companies that made the cans, made the spray nozzles, or made and marketed the products that would ultimately go into the cans, and none of these companies had any particular expertise in stratospheric chemistry. The aerosol industry was flying in the dark, unable to really engage in the merits of this all-important scientific debate, and yet it knew that its recently rocketing industry faced a serious threat.

The aerosol industry had been growing at a breakneck pace since WWII, and it saw itself as helping create the modern era of push-button convenience. Between 1960 and 1972, production of spray cans globally had risen by over 20 percent per year. In 1973, Americans bought nearly three billion aerosol cans, or about fifteen for every person in the country. About half of spray cans sold globally were sold in the United States, and about half of US aerosols used CFCs as their propellant, especially hair-spray and deodorant.

The saturation of the American household with aerosols had drawn criticism even before the ozone issue arose. The Center for Science in the Public Interest (CSPI), a new consumer group, sought federal regulation of spray cans in 1973, pointing to occasional explosions and poisonings and noting that the fine mist that aerosols create could penetrate deeply into the lungs with unknown health effects. And the intoxication that Midgley joked about in 1930 was now being actively sought by some; CSPI claimed in 1974 that "hundreds of aerosol sniffers have died."

And so the aerosol industry was on the defensive for other reasons by 1974. It dismissed its critics' health claims as "distorted and alarmist" and was already planning to spend a couple million dollars singing the praises of spray cans. One trade journal at the forefront of the dispute was *Aerosol Age*, a publication that was "unexcelled in the humorless stridency with which it denounced all who had anything bad to say about spray cans," according to Lydia Dotto and Harold Schiff, who wrote a lively 1978 account of the spray can wars. An *Aerosol Age* editorial argued that if we were so worried about household risks, we would be better off dulling the edges of all our kitchen knives, not unlike an earlier auto industry defense comparing crash injury risks to living with hardwood floors. As it happened, the aerosol trade press also encouraged people to worry instead about the "hundreds of thousands of people being killed and injured on the highways."

Soon after the ozone issue hit the headlines in September 1974, the Natural Resources Defense Council (NRDC)—the same environmental group that had recently sued the EPA to reduce lead in gasoline—urged federal regulators to ban CFCs from aerosol cans. The NRDC's petition claimed that within twenty-five years there could be an additional 1.5 million cases of skin cancer in the world annually, causing as many as 60,000 deaths. Skin cancer was not necessarily the worst consequence of ozone depletion. Dialing up the amount of biologically active radiation beaming down on Earth's surface had the potential to cause a vast array of changes, from suppressing our immune systems to reducing our crop yields to depleting the plankton that forms the first link of the oceans' food chain. Moreover, both adding CFCs and removing ozone changes the climate— another confounding problem scientists were just starting to understand. Rather than trying to grapple with all these imagination-straining existential threats, though, the ozone debate would come to focus on the more easily quantified impact of extra human skin cancers.

In December 1974, the first of many congressional hearings were held on the threat to the ozone layer. Meanwhile, an interagency federal task force and the National Academy of Sciences launched reviews of the science. The focus fell on aerosols rather than refrigeration and air conditioning. Half the CFCs used in the United States went into spray cans, and while refrigerators and air conditioners used CFCs in a closed loop for years until they leaked, spray cans released their CFCs with each and every use. And of course, most spray cans were less vital to society's well-being and far easier to imagine replacing.

It is hardly surprising that many in the aerosol industry, already feeling besieged by alarmists, would respond to the new science in tribal terms, seeing the issue not as inadvertent harm caused via complex stratospheric chemistry but as a conflict between us versus them, good guys versus bad guys.* Industry members stressed that they were the good guys; they had been "parent-like" in their concern for safety and were not the "unfeeling monster-types" they were portrayed as. They denied any bias, claiming the goal of their PR campaign was to "create an atmosphere of objectivity," in contrast to the hysteria of their critics.

Industry members alleged ulterior motives behind the charges against them. Two scientists at the University of Michigan, Ralph Cicerone and Richard Stolarski, were also deeply involved in ozone research. An *Aerosol Age* article called a news release about their work "particularly sensational-ized" and "probably designed more to get newspaper space than to solve a potential problem." It dismissed the results of computer models more gen-erally by arguing that "when some computer jockeys take their giant machines and feed into them material designed to prove a preconceived idea, they likely will come up with what they want, not what is valid." As for regulators, they were "young, anxious to build their own image and they rel-ish power."

The aerosol trade press provided a steady diet of articles nourishing readers' sense of victimization. They faced a "stacked deck," their industry had become a "whipping boy," and the media had an apparent "vendetta against pressure packaging." Industry members complained of "vigilantes" and feared a "lynching party." The editors of *Aerosol Age*, after sitting in on various hearings, claimed to have been "made ill by the pious concern for the atmosphere by the inquisitors comfortable in their climate-controlled environments."

Some members of the aerosol industry linked the dispute to a much big-ger battle between much bigger tribes. "Everything and everybody in the U.S.A. seems to be under attack," wrote the president of one aerosol company in a 1975 newspaper ad. Claims brought against their industry by nonprofit groups were dismissed as just "another group of crusaders . . . being forced by its conscience to demand that Washington save the American people from another evil created by money-grubbing businessmen." The aerosol industry reflected a business culture that had not yet come to terms with federal

---

*One notable exception was Samuel Johnson, the environmentally inclined head of Johnson Wax, whose company removed CFCs from its aerosol products while others in the aerosol industry were working to keep them, shattering what had been a united industry front of opposition.

authority over its actions, much less with the nonprofit groups drawing negative attention from the once-friendly media that had received so much advertising revenue from the aerosol industry over the years.

Linking their battle to a loftier struggle likely delivered an energizing jolt of moral righteousness beyond what could be had from simply defending a particular means of propelling deodorant. (The importance of a sense of moral purpose to group conflict is often forgotten, but it can be seen in both the words *morale* and *demoralize*.) Moreover, hitching onto existing cultural disputes can expand the size of the team coming to the corporation's defense, bringing important allies into the fight.

Darkly hinting or outright claiming that your critics are in league with the nation's enemies is one obvious way to elevate the dispute to a larger plane. George Diamond, president of the Diamond Aerosol Corporation and one of the most conspiratorial of aerosol industry executives, was particularly inclined toward this approach. He wrote in 1975 that politicians are "hysterical . . . and behaving in a suspicious manner," that various pressure groups are "somehow interlinked and are at best brainwashed and at worst traitors," and that the scientists are "at best incompetent fools or at worst are traitors and subscribers to political philosophies hazardous to the public health and well-being." Similar accusations had been made a few years earlier against scientists pointing out a potential threat to ozone from supersonic transport: a chief engineer for Boeing said that scientific opponents of the planes his company sought to build were perpetrating "the 'Big Lie' on the American public" and were "scientifically dishonest if not treasonous."

In 1977, Diamond would even more directly connect the dots between critics of his and other industries and the Soviet Union. In the quote at the beginning of this chapter, he is complaining to a local TV crew that "the whole thing" is the work of the KGB, whose goal is "to damage our economy and our faith in democratic government."

DEFENDING CFCs THROUGH IDEOLOGY: "OUR FREE ENTERPRISE SYSTEM IS AT STAKE"

While George Diamond's explicit invocation of a KGB-driven conspiracy might be fairly dismissed as the extreme views of one industry bit-player, those at the top of the multibillion-dollar aerosol industry similarly portrayed aerosol's critics as being not just against ozone depletion but against capitalism itself.

The single most prominent member of the aerosol industry was Robert Abplanalp. In the late 1940s, Abplanalp had invented a better aerosol valve that would revolutionize the aerosol industry. He then founded Precision Valve Corporation to make and sell his invention, eventually employing thousands and making millions by selling billions of tiny valves. In the 1960s, Abplanalp became a close friend of Richard Nixon, and this made Abplanalp something of a household name. Nixon would vacation on Abplanalp's private island while president, and when Nixon resigned in disgrace in August of 1974, Abplanalp flew to California to comfort him.

It was the next month, September 1974, when the ozone issue hit the headlines, and a few weeks later Abplanalp gave a speech to his industry colleagues upon receiving the award for Packaging Man of the Year. His speech celebrated the character of the aerosol industry ("a great industry, but not a self-serving one") and disparaged the motives and honesty of those raising concerns about aerosols ("headline-grabbing critics" practicing "deliberately inaccurate science"). His company would later run an advertisement calling ozone scientists "academic terrorists."

Moreover, Abplanalp saw defending aerosols as part of a larger defense of capitalism. Part of the greatness of the aerosol industry, he said, was that it opened doors to "anyone who wants to try his hand at the free enterprise system; let us all be reminded that the system with all of its faults is still the shining light that has attracted people from all over the world to a better way of life," in contrast to "the dismal Bolshevik collectives." In the United States now, though, he claimed that "extremists in the areas of ecology and consumer protection are today waging a more effective war on American industry than the most capable hosts of enemy saboteurs ever dreamt of doing during World War II."

A few months later, Ralph Engel, the head of the Chemical Specialty Manufacturers Association, would argue at an aerosol industry seminar entitled "Aerosols under Attack" that regulatory agencies like the Consumer Product Safety Commission were "a real threat to the free enterprise system." He urged "those who believe in free enterprise and capitalism" to fight back because "our free enterprise system is at stake."

Another prominent industry member, the head of the Can Manufacturers Institute, similarly argued that industry associations like his should be more aggressive not just in defense of themselves but in defense of something much bigger: "All of us are poor disciples for business and the free enterprise system." He urged his colleagues, "Let's get mad." Invoking the long-used national-standing argument, he added, "We will remain the best nation in the world only if we stay in front."

For aerosol's defenders to invoke ideology in this way is entirely consistent with research into the psychological function of ideology. Social psychologist John Jost has for years researched what he calls "our species' uncanny enthusiasm for abstract belief systems." Following a review of decades of research from around the world, Jost and his colleagues Christopher Federico and Jaime Napier theorize that ideology helps satisfy three core psychological needs: security, solidarity, and certainty.

Security comes from ideology's ability to promote people's belief that they are part of a meaningful universe that transcends the self. Indeed, studies have shown that if subjects are made insecure by reminding them of their own mortality, they hold tighter to their belief system, showing greater patriotism, more hostility to critics of their nation, a stronger endorsement of the unique validity of their religion, and more stereotyping. Members of the aerosol industry, facing economic, reputational, and self-esteem threats, could be expected to hold more tightly to a free market ideology that gave their dispute a meaning transcending their own profits or the specifics of spray-can propellant chemistry.

Solidarity is strengthened by ideology because it enhances tribal bonds. People feel more positively toward those with whom they share beliefs and attitudes; indeed, research suggests that finding out that we disagree with a valued in-group about something (or that we agree with a stigmatized out-group) can reduce our self-esteem, encouraging us to change our views. It seems we need to bond with others over a shared worldview, particularly in times of conflict. Sharing a common ideology around business and markets would help strengthen the morale of members of the beleaguered aerosol industry, especially if they believed their critics were truly motivated by a desire to undermine capitalism.

Certainty, the third psychological benefit, comes from the larger narrative that an ideology provides and into which we can fit new information to help us understand the world. Uncertainty is uncomfortable, tiring, and inhibiting; certainty is comfortable and invigorating. And psychological studies that try to measure people's need for certainty find that those with the greatest intolerance for uncertainty tend to be the most ideological. Of course, there was profound uncertainty surrounding the question of CFCs' effect on the ozone layer and regulation's effect on the industry, likely increasing the appetite for an uncertainty-reducing ideology. If you can categorize your critics as coming from a hostile ideology, it provides an understandable explanation for why they are accusing your company of doing harm, and it offers an escape from the uncomfortable uncertainty that comes from wondering if they may be right.

EXPLOITING THE UNCERTAINTY: UNWARRANTED CONFIDENCE THE PROBLEM WILL GO AWAY

Of course, another response to scientific claims is to find a scientist who can defend you, ideally with certainty, verve, scorn, and a sophisticated accent. When such a scientist appeared, the aerosol industry embraced him like a life preserver.

Shortly after CFCs' threat to the ozone layer hit the headlines, a British scientist named Richard Scorer wrote to *New Scientist* magazine to denounce the theory as "preposterous" and "simple-minded," arguing that for the "scaremongers" to predict disaster was "quite silly." Before long, the Council on Atmospheric Sciences—an industry trade group that was formed to defend CFCs but, despite its name, was at first lacking in actual scientists—sent Dr. Scorer on a six-week tour of the United States to explain why the ozone theory was "utter nonsense." Scorer's powerful certainty was not persuasive to other scientists, even within the industry, but that was beside the point. The tour's target was the media, and Scorer generated enough headlines that the aerosol industry hailed his visit as one of their most successful attacks on the scientific validity of Rowland and Molina's work.

Scientific uncertainty is something that nonscientists have a hard time with. Nonscientists often seem to believe that scientific assertions fall into one of two baskets—"facts," which are definitively proven and universally recognized, and "theories," which are entirely speculative. And in this black-and-white view of scientific understanding, if an assertion is not yet a proven fact, it does not need to be given any weight at all. Moreover, if there are any scientists at all who dispute a fact (even if, like Scorer, they are disputing facts outside their field of research), it must be an unproven theory, so it can be safely ignored until the scientists all agree.

In reality, scientific understanding usually emerges in frustratingly tiny steps, taking us through many shades of gray. This is especially true when we are trying to understand and predict extremely complex systems. A huge portion of what we know about the natural world and our impact on it, including a great deal of policy-relevant science, falls in the vast space between the definitively proven and the entirely speculative. Fortunately, people do have the cognitive ability to weigh levels of certainty; indeed, we make personal decisions based on what we consider unlikely, likely, or highly likely all the time. But this kind of nuanced thinking is tiring, and when the subject is something we care about—because of money, self-image, tribal loyalties, or ideology, for example—it's much easier to succumb to the lure of easy, self-serving certainties.

Industries do not need to find a dishonest scientist to support their views; in most areas of emerging science, there will be disagreements. They simply need to find a scientist on the spectrum of opinions whose views they prefer and amplify his voice. That will create the impression that there is far more disagreement within the scientific community than there actually is. Scorer may well have been in earnest, but he was very much an outlier in his views. By the time of his media tour in the summer of 1975, consensus was building among experts in atmospheric chemistry that the threat to the ozone layer was anything but nonsense, and a federal task force, after months of review, found there was indeed "legitimate cause for concern." Yet the aerosol trade press uncritically trumpeted Scorer's findings, fueling the contempt that industry members already felt for the science and the scientists behind the ozone warnings.

The scientific grounds on which Scorer dismissed the ozone depletion theory were particularly attractive. He argued that there were natural sources of ozone-depleting chlorine that reached the stratosphere, like volcanoes, so there must be some natural mechanisms that keep ozone levels in balance. Scorer argued that the atmosphere is far more robust than many believe and that human activities could have little impact on it. Sherwood Rowland would describe and dismiss the theory by saying that "some people have the belief that the Lord designed an atmosphere that can take this kind of abuse. I live too close to Los Angeles to agree with that." Yet one can imagine the draw of such a reassuring perspective—not just to the CFC-invested industries but to any polluting industry, or indeed to any person made anxious by the growing number of environmental warnings (and growing regulatory response) that marked the era.

DuPont officials endorsed the concept of a robust, self-balancing atmosphere early in the debate. Most of the company's public defense on the ozone issue came from Dr. Raymond McCarthy, technical director of the company's Freon Products Laboratory. McCarthy said to *Newsday* in December 1974, "I'm personally convinced that the atmosphere of the planet has cycle and feedback mechanisms that are conducive to life on this planet. I think it's conceivable, and this is theory, that nature has long since developed a cycle in which chlorine does not have deteriorating effects." It is notable that McCarthy did not claim to have evidence in support of this theory, yet he was "personally convinced." Robert Abplanalp, who likely knew nothing about atmospheric chemistry, would similarly declare his personal confidence that the Rowland-Molina theory was "nonsense."

Notably, DuPont's embrace of this theory was expressed without the contempt for Rowland and Molina expressed by Dr. Scorer and other industry members. Indeed, DuPont showed conspicuous restraint (notable within the broader history of corporate denial) in not attacking the character or competence of Rowland and Molina, who it conceded were good scientists. Dr. Peter Jesson, a research director at DuPont, told a British science magazine that he had accepted the main elements of the Rowland-Molina hypothesis by fall of 1975—namely, that CFCs rise to the stratosphere, where chlorine atoms will attack ozone; he just disputed estimates of how much damage would be done. When Jesson was asked why industry had not started checking out the possibility of ozone depletion earlier, he said no one in the industry had thought of it. "Putting all the factors together was a stroke of genius by Molina and Rowland. I give them great credit for that." The aerosol trade press, having recently quoted with approval Scorer's judgment that the Rowland-Molina theory was utter nonsense, did not confuse its readers by repeating this DuPont official's statement that their theory was "a stroke of genius."

When corporate defenders attack the character of their critics, they are in effect inviting their audience to stop trying to make complex science-based judgments about risk and to instead make the kind of simplistic personal character judgments that come more easily to us. We might call this the these-claims-can't-be-true-because-our-critics-are-bad-people argument. And while DuPont generally resisted the temptation to indulge in this line of argument, on at least one occasion it indulged in a softer, less offensive attempt at character-based social influence: a these-claims-can't-be-true-because-we-are-good-people argument. In 1975 Senate hearings, a senior DuPont executive informed the senators who were worried about the ozone layer that he had four small grandchildren. "I would not want this advertised, but they call me, the two older ones, Papa Sweetie Pie. Now, if I felt that there were any problem or danger, believe me, to the children down the way, I would want to pull the plug right now and be precipitous."

Such an argument makes complete sense if you believe that systemic harms are only caused by bad people acting intentionally. It makes much less sense, though, if such harms can be caused by regular people (even those beloved by their grandkids) acting unintentionally and perhaps under the influence of biased risk perception.

THE BURDEN AND STANDARD OF PROOF: WHO HAS TO PROVE WHAT?

In the summer of 1975, DuPont ran full-page ads in many newspapers promising that "should reputable evidence show that some [CFCs] cause a health hazard through depletion of the ozone layer, we are prepared to stop production of the offending compounds." In the same advertisement, though, the company complained about the unfairness of what it called a "cloud of presumed guilt" over aerosol products and a disturbing "ban now—find out later" approach in headlines and legislative proposals.

In this ad, DuPont raises critical questions: in a dispute over a social or environmental harm, who bears the burden of proof? What must the parties with the burden prove? And with what level of certainty must they prove it? By way of example, in a first-degree murder case, the state must show the defendant is guilty (the burden of proof), that the defendant purposely killed someone with premeditation (the elements of the case), and that guilt is established beyond a reasonable doubt (the standard of proof). However, the rules about burden and standard of proof are relatively nimble tools that can be altered to fit the circumstance; for example, most civil cases use a lighter standard of proof, requiring plaintiffs prove the elements of their claim only by a preponderance of the evidence.

These rules of the road guiding legal disputes determine who gets the benefit of the doubt, so the more doubt there is, the more these rules matter. Should an industry putting a chemical into the world have the burden of proving it safe (as those marketing new drugs must now do under US law)? Or should those seeking to limit those chemicals be required to prove them dangerous (the more common approach, described as the Kehoe Paradigm by a scholar of the leaded gas dispute)? DuPont's ad did not acknowledge that society can and sometimes does put the burden of proving safety on the industry allegedly causing the harm. Rather, it just assumes the burden of proof should fall on the industry's critics, and it should stay there while questions remain.

Many industry members claim that the well-known presumption of innocence we give to individuals facing criminal charges also applies to industrial activities facing regulation. An ad by Abplanalp's Precision Valve company explained, "We believe in what US law holds clearly and we cherish dearly: you are innocent until proven guilty." A DuPont official, in a 1976 letter to the president of the National Academy of Sciences, which was then studying CFCs' threat to the ozone, argued that basing legislation on "unproven theory" would put the nation on "the road to the rule of witchcraft where, by definition, the accusation proves the charge." (This was, as it happened, just a few weeks before the president of Ethyl would similarly invoke witch trials to describe the regulatory process then phasing lead out of gasoline.)

In fact, many scientists had been trying since the ozone theory was published to find holes in it, including Rowland and Molina themselves. While they had no definitive proof that CFCs depleted ozone, the theory was based on several scientific building blocks that were now widely accepted, and nobody had identified a scientific mechanism that would protect the ozone layer from the predicted effects of CFCs. "Industry says it is just a hypothesis," said Rowland. "But their position is just hypothetical, too. They have a hypothesis that it is safe to release fluorocarbons, but no data to back up their position. We have a hypothesis that it is unsafe, but we do have some scientific data, and are coming up with more." Industry's position, as Rowland would describe it to a Senate hearing, depended on some "missing factor" that had been left out of the calculation and assumed that this missing factor would not make the situation worse but would render CFCs innocuous.

By this time, the federal government had already asked the National Academy of Sciences[*] to study the validity of the ozone depletion theory, and two reports were issued in September 1976 (one by a panel focusing on atmospheric science and one by a committee focusing on impacts and policy). CFCs had by now been measured in the stratosphere as predicted, and the panel concluded that it was "inevitable" that these CFCs would release chlorine that would destroy ozone; the hard part was predicting by how much. The NAS panel acknowledged great uncertainty on this point but said that if CFC use stayed at 1973 levels, it estimated that global ozone would ultimately be depleted by about 7 percent (within a range of 2 to 20 percent) over a period of decades. The committee concluded that regulation of CFCs "is almost certain to be necessary" at some time, but that regulation could and should be delayed for a year or two during which time the size of the risk would become clearer.

Just three days after the NAS report, Russell Peterson, chair of President Ford's Council on Environmental Quality, gave a speech calling for immediate regulation of CFCs. Peterson had spent twenty-six years as a chemist for DuPont, and he acknowledged the ongoing doubts about the quantitative effect of CFCs on ozone. When considering public policy, though, he argued that "we cannot afford to give chemicals the same

---

[*] The National Academy of Sciences, which plays a role in many of the disputes described in this book, is not just another scientific association. It was formed under a federal law signed in 1863 by Abraham Lincoln to create a formal way for the nation's top scientists to give the government independent advice on scientific issues. Members are elected by their peers for their original research and are widely considered leaders in their fields; nearly five hundred National Academy members have won Nobel Prizes.

constitutional rights that we enjoy under the law." He added, "Chemicals are not innocent until proven guilty." A few weeks later, the head of the FDA said, "It's a simple case of negligible benefit measured against possible catastrophic risk. . . . Our course of action seems clear beyond doubt." Within a few months, regulations were adopted banning CFCs for virtually all spray-can uses; industry had two years to replace them.

DuPont called the swift regulatory action "astonishing" since the NAS report had supported some regulatory delay. And yet, within a few months, many in industry were meeting the imminent ban with a collective shrug. DuPont explained that aerosol propellants were only about 0.5 percent of their total sales. *Aerosol Age* reported that despite all the problems faced by the industry, "there is a surprising upbeat feeling." One company president reported, "We feel that the aerosol situation will work itself out and we have completed new formulas, without [CFCs], which will enable us to continue marketing all present products." Robert Abplanalp remained convinced that the ozone threat was a "hoax," but even so, he had already invented a new spray valve that he was excited about and that did not require the use of CFCs.

THE POLITICAL WINDS SHIFT AGAIN: ANTIREGULATORY SENTIMENT AND THE "WAIT-AND-SEE" APPROACH

Once CFCs disappeared from spray cans in the United States, the ozone issue fell off the radar screen. The problem was by no means over. Most other nations still used CFCs in their aerosols, and there were no regulations in the United States or anywhere else on CFC use in refrigeration or air conditioning or on other increasingly significant uses of CFCs, like the manufacture of foam products and the cleaning of electronic parts. However, the 1977 amendments to the Clean Air Act required the EPA to regulate activity if in the EPA administrator's judgment, it "may reasonably be anticipated" to affect the ozone and endanger public health or welfare. In October 1980, EPA floated a regulatory approach to limit other CFC uses, but it was too late. The next month, Jimmy Carter lost the presidential election to Ronald Reagan. The antipollution sentiment of the 1970s was being replaced in Washington by the antiregulatory sentiment of the 1980s.

Even before the election, industry had mobilized to oppose additional regulation. It had formed the Alliance for a Responsible CFC Policy, a coalition of CFC manufacturers, such as DuPont, and CFC users, such as refrigerator and air conditioner makers and companies that made foam products. The EPA's regulatory plan was met by over two thousand written comments, of which all but four opposed the plan. By contrast, at one point in the 1970s Congress reportedly got more letters from concerned citizens about the effect of spray cans on the ozone than about any issue other than the Vietnam War.

Congress switched its focus from the impact of CFCs on ozone to the impact of CFC regulations on industry, even in the Democratic-controlled House. In 1981, in hearings held by a subcommittee of the House Committee on Small Business, business representatives argued that CFC regulations would economically devastate them. Their opposition was not merely on cost grounds, though; it tapped into deeper ideological currents. The former owner of a company that used CFCs to make polystyrene egg cartons testified that she was there "because I believe in the free enterprise system," and she found it "incredibly irresponsible" for the EPA to propose regulation based "solely on the theory" that CFCs may harm the ozone layer.

James Watt, Reagan's highly controversial interior secretary, would say with respect to environmental regulations more generally that "the battleground is not what our critics would like you to believe it is, protecting the environment. It is over ideology, over forms of government that lead to a centralized, socialized society," and he would charge that the real objective of environmentalists was centralized planning and control, as in Nazi Germany and Communist Russia.

It is true that scientific uncertainty persisted and even increased in this era. NAS reports raised the estimated ozone loss in 1979 and then dropped it in 1982. If by law or custom, the industry had the burden of proving that CFCs were *not* endangering the planet, the lingering uncertainty would not have weakened the argument for regulation. But it was a new political era, regulators faced more-sophisticated industry opposition, and there was no obvious way to replace the remaining CFCs. The Clean Air Act may have required regulation if harm could "reasonably be anticipated," but the de facto standard of proof that fell on those who wanted stricter limits on CFCs (a group that no longer included EPA leadership) was going to require much more certainty.

Industry tried to move the goalposts farther back for would-be regulators by pushing for a law that would prevent regulation until there were either actual measurements of ozone depletion directly attributable to CFCs or an international regulatory treaty. The Alliance assured members of Congress that the "statistical technique of time-trend analysis, applied to actual measurements of ozone concentration, will provide an 'early warning system' capable of detecting even small changes in the stratospheric ozone concentration." In short, the industry was arguing that the world could take a wait-and-see approach without much risk.

In fact, requiring regulators to tie CFCs to actually detected losses represented "an extreme stance on the standard of proof required to justify regulation," according Edward Parson, a Harvard professor of public policy who wrote the 2003 book *Protecting the Ozone Layer: Science and Strategy*, a deeply researched analysis of the controversy. Ozone levels vary naturally by season, by latitude, and in response to sunspot cycles. Detecting a global decline distinct from natural fluctuations would be no easy task.

Moreover, ozone depletion is not the sort of problem that lends itself to a wait-and-see approach because CFCs take decades to reach the stratosphere. That means that even after depletion is finally detected, depletion will persist long after emissions are cut. One congressional committee staffer witnessing these efforts later complained that "here were people who were willing to say they ought not be required to modify their behavior one scintilla until they had massively disturbed one of the fundamental parameters under which life had evolved on earth." The bill in question failed to pass, yet the standard of proof it embodied—the need to measure actual depletion—would in practice be the one that was applied to the question in the years ahead.

As the science of ozone depletion continued to progress, the industry trumpeted every development that seemed to reduce the risk while ignoring or attacking every development that seemed to increase the risk. This was another situation where corporate strategy and psychological biases would align and no doubt reinforce each other. Human objectivity and judgment are vulnerable to the well-known confirmation bias, which inclines us to seek, accept, and remember information that supports what we want to believe while inclining us to ignore, dispute, and forget information that undercuts our beliefs. Those with the most invested in CFCs turned that innate bias into a PR strategy.

In the early 1980s, industry felt that the risk of future regulation was so low that it moved ahead with new, long-term CFC investments. By 1982, the Pennwalt chemical company announced it was investing millions to expand an existing CFC plant. In 1986, DuPont revealed it was expanding its CFC production in Japan and starting production in China.

A GLOBAL SHOCK: THE OZONE HOLE AND HOLES IN INDUSTRY'S ARGUMENT

In the beginning of 1985, CFC makers and users may well have felt that CFCs' economic prospects were bright, but those prospects would darken with remarkable speed. Within three years much of the world would agree to drastically limit CFCs under the Montreal Protocol. That landmark environmental treaty would be ratified by the US Senate without a single dissenting vote and be signed by President Reagan, who would overcome his antiregulatory preferences and hail the treaty as a "monumental achievement." By 1990, an alarmed world would go further, agreeing to ban CFCs more or less entirely. Even more surprising, by then CFC manufacturers would mostly be on board with the ban. How did things change so utterly in just a few years?

It was in part due to a shocking discovery: an area of severe ozone depletion over Antarctica that came to be called "the ozone hole." Members of the British Antarctic Survey had been quietly collecting ground-based ozone readings from Antarctica since 1957. In May 1985, the British team published findings alerting the world that it had found ozone plummeting to a dramatic 40 percent below normal in the atmosphere above its station in the springtime.

Atmospheric scientists were stunned, and many assumed there was some mistake. Sudden losses of this magnitude were far outside what the models anticipated, and surely NASA's satellites would have detected such a dramatic loss. But NASA soon confirmed that the hole was not just real but enormous, about twice the size of the continental United States. Its satellites had missed the hole because ozone readings were so far outside what had ever been measured that the NASA computers had been programmed to treat them as instrument error rather than as alarm-inducing evidence of extreme ozone depletion.

The ozone hole put the issue back on the radar of the media, the public, and policy makers and created a big hole in industry's argument that we could afford to just "wait and see." Still, industry was not ready to accept regulation of CFCs. Dr. S. Robert Orfeo, a scientist with Allied Signal chemical company who also represented the influential Chemical Manufacturers Association, would call linking the ozone hole to CFCs "sheer speculation." He argued we should take a couple years to study it, assuring a Senate subcommittee that "continued releases of CFCs will not pose a significant threat to the environment" during this delay.

On what grounds could the chemical industry possibly base its certainty that continued pollution caused no significant threat, when it had no plausible explanation for the sudden and severe ozone depletion that had already occurred? Even at this moment of what should have been profound scientific humility, the industry's confidence in the harmlessness of ongoing pollution was apparently shatterproof. This kind of blatantly unwarranted confidence is the opposite of the skepticism that should characterize science, and it is one of the more common and dangerous forms of corporate denial.

A second hole in industry's argument related to the future growth of CFC production. Industry forcefully opposed any assumption by the EPA that global CFC production would grow significantly, arguing that various factors, including the risk of regulation, would prevent CFC production from growing much at all. For years, the scientific assessments and policy makers quietly incorporated the unsupported assumption that CFC emissions would stay at current levels. After the global recession of the early 1980s, though, production of the most widely used CFCs did rise, and by 1984 had exceeded the earlier peak in 1974. The EPA—including a handful of staffers who had never stopped worrying about the ozone layer— began to insist that CFC emissions be more realistically represented in computer models.

A third hole that appeared in industry's arguments at this time related to whether CFC alternatives could be found. In the 1970s, the threat of regulation did prompt research into alternatives. However, the industry's Alliance for a Responsible CFC Policy warned the EPA and Congress in 1981 that there were "no commercially available, acceptable alternatives for most uses of CFCs." What it did not announce was that in 1981 the industry largely stopped investing in the development of the alternatives it had found. There certainly was no proof in the early 1980s that continuing to pump millions of tons of CFCs into the atmosphere was safe, and there was plenty of reason to worry that it was not. Yet the CFC industry clearly did not believe its continued operations required that proof of safety or that it had any obligation to continue searching for substitutes once the risk of regulation had eased.

In March 1986, the EPA held an important workshop on CFCs with industry and other stakeholders. (This workshop was part of a two-year period of consultation and assessment that EPA agreed to conduct to settle a suit brought by the NRDC under the Clean Air Act.) At the workshop a DuPont representative announced three important facts: first, that the company had stopped its research into CFC alternatives five years earlier; second, that there were several options that were feasible alternatives to CFCs; and third, that these alternatives could likely be commercialized in roughly five years. Later that year, another DuPont executive would explain with remarkable candor that the "development of alternatives is going to happen at a rate that corresponds to the amount of pressure that is applied. Right now there is no economic or regulatory incentive to look for other routes."

In short, DuPont was not investing in substitutes for CFCs because of the lack of the very regulations it and its industrial colleagues had worked so effectively to prevent. Perhaps DuPont realized around this time that it had been *too* successful in blocking regulations. CFCs had not been a particularly profitable product for DuPont for years. A DuPont official would later say about its CFC business, "Since the early 1970s, I can only describe our performance in an economic sense as abysmal. It's been a cash trap for the company." In opposing CFC regulation, DuPont had also eliminated its incentive to develop and market safer and potentially more profitable substitutes.

RISING PRESSURE: THE UNRAVELING OF
INDUSTRY OPPOSITION

At this same workshop Lee Thomas, Reagan's third EPA administrator,* explicitly rejected industry's wait-and-see argument. A recent international assessment of the science, led by NASA and the World Meteorological Organization (WMO), warned of substantial ozone loss if CFC emissions grew even modestly. EPA's own analysis of the data was alarming; it would later predict millions of extra skin cancer deaths from ozone loss among those born before 2075, just in the United States. The agency calculated that global CFCs needed to be cut by 85 percent just to keep stratospheric chlorine concentrations from rising further. Under its settlement with NRDC, EPA soon had to make a decision, and industry saw it would likely pursue deep cuts.

Some industry representatives already felt personally uncomfortable with their strict antiregulatory position. Richard Barnett, head of the industry's Alliance, was starting to feel like a "shill for the chemical companies," according to interviews conducted by Harvard public policy professor Edward Parson. Barnett was also under intense pressure from his own family to change course after his views had been quoted in an influential *New Yorker* article by Paul Brodeur. In the summer of 1986 both the Alliance and DuPont were reconsidering their blanket opposition to any further limits on CFCs.

In September 1986, the Alliance announced it would support global limits on the growth of CFC emissions, citing the NASA-WMO assessment as an important reason for the change. Soon, DuPont announced its support for not just a limit on the rate of growth of CFC use but a global cap on emissions. The NRDC hailed the shift as a breakthrough, though industry was far from supporting the deep cuts the EPA said were needed. In explaining their changed positions, the Alliance and DuPont both used

---

* Reagan's first EPA administrator, Anne Gorsuch Burford, was dismissive of concerns over ozone depletion. Her controversial tenure ended when she resigned in 1983 following a dispute with Congress over her handling of the Superfund program. In February 1986, she published a memoir that asked, "Remember a few years back when the big news was fluorocarbons that supposedly threatened the ozone layer?"

wording that effectively shifted the burden of proof. In the Alliance's words, "The science is not sufficiently developed to tell us that there is no risk in the future." One could say the same thing regarding current emission levels, but that was a step too far.

Meanwhile, the dots were connecting between CFCs and the ozone hole. A 1986 expedition to Antarctica organized by NASA concluded that the ozone hole was probably caused by a chemical process rather than by natural causes. (One member of the expedition later noted about these findings, "In retrospect, we were probably too timid. We didn't want to say it was CFCs. We were all scared at being labeled sensationalists.") NASA scientists were also starting to detect disturbing ozone loss over the populated parts of the globe.

To the surprise of many, in early 1987, the US delegation took a strong stance in international treaty negotiations, seeking to phase out 95 percent of CFC use. This position, advanced by the EPA and the State Department, was strongly opposed by the Alliance. EPA's Thomas later speculated that "industry got exercised because I had taken this thing farther than they wanted to go." Soon there was a backlash from other branches of the Reagan administration.

In May 1987, news was leaked that Interior Secretary Donald Hodel had argued at a cabinet-level meeting that a "personal protection" plan— apparently the widespread use of hats, sunglasses, and sunscreen—was a reasonable alternative to pursuing global CFC cuts. In response to the EPA's estimates of increased cancer deaths, Hodel told the *Washington Post* that "people who don't stand out in the sun—it doesn't affect them." Hodel was widely ridiculed in the media and the news seems to have provoked a backlash to the backlash: the Senate passed a resolution by eighty votes to two urging the administration to seek deep CFC cuts. Even the industry seemed to retreat from its opposition.

The Montreal Protocol, under which the major nations agreed to cut CFC consumption in half by 1999, was agreed to on September 16, 1987. A vice president of CFC maker Kaiser Chemicals said the treaty "borders on being catastrophic for our CFC business." Many in industry opposed the protocol at first, but opposition soon waned. The Alliance thought that the schedule might be "too tight" but said that the agreement was a "significant step." A DuPont representative said the company would urge the protocol's ratification.

The protocol was not officially a response to the ozone hole because its cause was still disputed. While negotiators met in Montreal, though, scientists were back in Antarctica on a mission to gather more data. Pilots flew specially modified planes higher into the brutally cold Antarctic stratosphere than anyone had flown before, collecting air samples. One pilot, Ron Williams, called the mission "more dangerous than anything any of us ever flew over Vietnam. If you punch out over Antarctica, you are going to die . . . [but] this is probably going to be my last chance to make my mark in history." And history was made: their samples showed quite strikingly that as stratospheric chlorine went up, ozone went down. In the words of science writer John Gribbin, this evidence was not just a smoking gun; it was "more in the nature of a signed and witnessed confession."

DuPont had promised in the 1970s to stop making CFCs if reputable evidence showed a threat to ozone, but it still disputed whether enough evidence existed. In March 1988, though, things changed. The Ozone Trends Panel—over one hundred scientists organized by NASA to laboriously reanalyze the science—confirmed that ozone was decreasing not only over uninhabited Antarctica but over our heads, and faster than models had projected. In the winters over northern Europe and much of Canada and Russia, ozone had fallen over 6 percent since 1969. Over the mainland United States, ozone had fallen from 1.7 to 3.0 percent on a year-round basis since 1969, and up to 4.7 percent in the winters.

This was the magic moment when DuPont, still the world's largest producer of CFCs, decided to stop making its product. DuPont's own scientist, Mack McFarland, was a member of the Ozone Trends Panel, but he had been sworn to secrecy until the panel's findings were made public. Once the panel's findings were released, there was a flurry of meetings at DuPont, and within a few days, the company's top officials had agreed that DuPont should stop making CFCs entirely by 1999. One DuPont executive said that "not one time that week did anyone discuss what effect this decision could have on the financial end of the business." Their decision earned widespread praise. (McFarland would later be listed by a former EPA official as among a "handful of honorable and honest corporate scientists who steered their management away from deceptive defense" of CFCs.) Pennwalt, another major CFC producer, announced support for a global phaseout the same day, and later other companies followed suit.

The evolution of the industry—from opposing all limits to supporting limits on growth in 1986 to supporting the Montreal Protocol's 50 percent cuts and then supporting a total phaseout of their product in 1988—stands as a rare example of an industry that had long publicly denied a threat changing its mind in response to scientific evidence and then agreeing to stop making the threatening product.

The CFC story shows that when confronted with enough scientific evidence, even companies that have long denied a threat can change their position. At least they can when the consequences of continued pollution are potentially catastrophic; when actual harm to a vitally important planetary feature is underway and attributable to the product; when scary global surprises draw public, media, and political attention; when regulation seems imminent anyway; when the product in question is only a sliver of the company's revenues; when the company has an unusually high respect for science; and when there are profits (potentially greater ones) to be had selling replacement products instead of the existing one.

This case study does not tell us what would have happened if other members of our pluralistic society had not seen the threat and pushed to address it. What if independent scientists had not spotted the accumulating CFCs and figured out the implications? If scientists like Rowland and Molina had not been willing to risk their reputations by advocating for solutions? If the British Antarctic Survey had not discovered the ozone hole? If NASA had not organized the critical global scientific expeditions and assessments? If EPA had not pursued regulations and a treaty? If Congress had not held hearings, amended the Clean Air Act, and made a bipartisan push for emission cuts? If NRDC had not sued, if the media had not paid attention, or if the UN had not organized international negotiations?

That is, what would have happened if it had been entirely up to the industry to detect, admit, and correct the problem its product caused? Fortunately, the world did not have to find out.

BANNING CFCs: A DISASTER AVOIDED BUT
A BACKLASH LAUNCHED

By 1990, falling ozone levels led to a stronger Montreal Protocol; CFCs were banned in the developed nations by 2000, while giving poor nations an extra ten years. In 1992, the United States accelerated the ban to 1996. It had unanimous support in the US Senate and from the industry's Alliance, which considered the sped-up ban "warranted by the scientific evidence." Later that year, the faster phaseout was endorsed by the eighty-seven nations involved in a yet-again strengthened protocol.

It proved far cheaper and easier to move away from CFCs than early industry opponents or even the EPA had predicted, as industries got creative. Electronics firms, which had become big consumers of CFCs, found ways to clean electronic parts using alternatives like water or a chemical made from orange rinds. Air conditioning and refrigeration manufacturers found ways to redesign their equipment to use CFC alternatives and simultaneously improve efficiency. The main chemical alternatives to CFCs used in refrigeration and air conditioning, while considerably safer, still posed some threat to ozone or the climate, so the Montreal Protocol has been amended over the years to phase down these substitutes too, often with support from industry. DuPont has captured much of the market for CFC replacements, though apparently less than it expected to in 1989.

Global *emissions* of ozone-depleting chemicals (largely but not only CFCs) peaked in 1987 and then fell steeply. However, given the long lifetime of CFCs, global *concentrations* in the atmosphere will take decades to return to 1980 levels. Global ozone averages—about 5 percent depleted at their worst in the early 1990s—are bouncing back (they were only 3 percent depleted in the early 2010s). Ozone is on track to return to 1980 levels around midcentury. The ozone hole in Antarctica that so alarmed scientists in 1985 got worse in the 1990s. It was always understood it would take decades for the ozone hole to "heal," but scientists believe they have found the first evidence of that healing, with close to full recovery expected sometime between 2060 and 2080.

How bad would things have gotten with continued pollution? Various models try to predict the "world avoided," and all show alarming ozone loss over the entire planet if CFC use had kept rising. A much-cited NASA model projects that by 2065 two-thirds of the Earth's ozone layer would have been gone if CFCs and similar compounds had kept rising at 3 percent annually. Already by 2020, 17 percent of global ozone would have been destroyed, and in the 2050s there would have been a sudden and severe collapse of ozone in the tropics. The EPA estimates that the Montreal Protocol will prevent more than 280 million cases of skin cancer in the United States alone among people born before 2100. However, it is quite possible that skin cancer would have been the least of our worries in this avoided world, given estimates that the increased radiation might have cut global agricultural production in half. The dramatic rise in mutation-causing "death rays" would have affected surface life across the planet.

Sherwood Rowland was treated as something of an outcast within the field of chemistry in the first decade after raising the alarm about CFCs, but after depletion was documented in 1988, he suddenly found himself swamped with speaking requests. In 1993 he was elected president of the large and prestigious American Association for the Advancement of Science, and in 1995, he and Mario Molina shared a Nobel Prize in Chemistry with Dutch scientist Paul Crutzen. Rowland died in 2012; his work with Molina was credited with helping create a whole new field of scientific research. Molina has continued his work and was awarded a Presidential Medal of Freedom in 2013.

Credit for saving the ozone layer also goes to the collective efforts of hundreds of scientists working on the largely thankless task of preparing assessment reports for policy makers. These reports were apparently critical in reducing industry denial and building support for the Montreal Protocol. In effect, the ozone layer was saved because of an important social norm related to how society handles scientific uncertainties: we pull together large groups of nearly all the most qualified scientists to review all the relevant data and present collective advice to policy makers. This collective review process is slow, demanding, and surely sometimes dull, but it got us past the uncertainty and conflict that had been preventing action on CFCs.

The Montreal Protocol has been widely hailed as a phenomenal success. In addition to protecting the ozone layer, it has helped slow global warming because CFCs are also potent greenhouse gases. Even when first negotiated, it was seen as a model of how the world could address global warming. This may be one reason why—just when the link tying CFCs to ozone depletion was being confirmed and the industry was giving up on trying to dispute it—there emerged a fierce new backlash of ideologically driven denials. It came from right-wing sources that loved free markets, hated Communism (and the environmental regulations they saw as a path to it), and claimed sinister conspiracies behind mainstream science.

The most bizarre manifestation of this wave of denial was reflected in a 1992 book by Rogelio A. Maduro and Ralf Schauerhammer, published by a group connected to Lyndon LaRouche, a figure from the distant edges of U.S. political thought. The book claimed that the global scientific community was wrong about CFCs, relying on already debunked scientific arguments. It then carefully explained that the ozone "hoax" involved a coalition that included major chemical companies like DuPont,* environmental groups like NRDC, the Trilateral Commission, America's top patrician families, Henry Kissinger, Ralph Nader, Margaret Thatcher, the British royal family, a rising "green gestapo," green pagans, and an "elite neo-Satanic organization." It argued that environmental leaders promoted the hoax because they actually wanted to restrict refrigeration, hoping it would kill millions of people and thus reduce overpopulation.

A less absurd and more dangerous strand of ideological denial came from people like Fred Singer, an atmospheric scientist featured in the 2010 book *Merchants of Doubt* by Naomi Oreskes and Erik M. Conway. The authors explain how the same handful of scientists, including Singer, would over the years manage to sow doubt over the science of CFCs, tobacco, climate change, and other issues. These scientists and the right-

---

* A sad but rather spectacular chapter in the CFC story involved an heir to the DuPont fortune named Lewis du Pont Smith, who became a follower of Lyndon LaRouche and who (according to the Maduro and Schauerhammer book, at least) distributed a pamphlet at DuPont's 1990 shareholder meeting urging the company to resist CFC regulation because of the millions it would kill through starvation. It also called for the release of LaRouche, then in prison. After Lewis made large donations to LaRouche's political movement, his parents succeeded in getting him declared mentally incompetent to prevent more of the DuPont fortune from being used this way. Lewis's father later faced federal criminal charges for allegedly planning to have Lewis kidnapped and deprogrammed, but the father was acquitted.

wing groups they worked for and with were, in Oreskes and Conway's words, constructing a larger "counternarrative." Rather than letting the world celebrate the CFC/ozone story as a successful model of how to solve a global environmental crisis, it was cast as a story of deception, hysteria, and overreach by forces that had what Singer would call a "hidden political agenda" against "business, the free market, and the capitalistic system."

This new wave of denial around CFCs would find various outlets in the conservative media, including the *Washington Times* (founded by the anticommunist leader of the Unification Church, Sun Myung Moon), the *Wall Street Journal,* the *National Review,* and Rush Limbaugh's books and radio program. With surprising speed it would reach the congressional leadership. Whereas in 1992 Congress had strongly supported accelerating the CFC ban, by 1995, the House—run by a newly elected Republican majority with an actively hostile view of environmental regulations—held hearings on "scientific integrity" to expose the "myths" around ozone.

Fred Singer told the representatives they were being "bamboozled" by the federal scientists presenting the latest international ozone assessment. Singer claimed they twisted the science "to achieve certain political objectives." But by then the carefully hammered-out assessments of the international scientific community mattered less and less in Congress. Majority Leader Tom DeLay would state at this hearing that he had not looked at the latest official scientific assessment, but rather got his assessment "from reading people like Fred Singer."

This new ideological backlash against the ozone science did not change industry support for the CFC phaseout. At the 1995 House hearing, Kevin Fay of the Alliance for Responsible CFC Policy found himself in the strange position of defending the evidence that his industry's product depleted ozone and even defending the phaseout.

While the rising backlash did not slow down ozone protection efforts, it represents an important part of the legacy of the CFC saga. The important social norm of respect for collective scientific assessments would prove surprisingly vulnerable to attack by a handful of people sowing distrust. The science-denying counternarrative—with its blatant appeals to ideology and political tribalism—would go beyond regular corporate denial and sometimes outflank it. And yet, as later chapters further explore, the counternarrative has deep roots in corporate denial—particularly the tobacco industry denial that helped create and fund the counternarrative, and the climate denial, where it has had its greatest political impact.

6 "Psychological Crutches"

TOBACCO'S MASS PRODUCTION OF DENIAL

*"I think that if the company as a whole believed cigarettes
were really harmful, we would not be in the business. We're
a very moralistic company."*

—Dr. Helmut Wakeham, head of research and development,
Philip Morris, 1976

In 1999, the US Justice Department brought a massive lawsuit against
nine cigarette companies, charging them with civil violations of the racketeering law usually used to fight organized crime. In 2006, after seven
years of litigation and a lengthy trial, the court made a landmark ruling:
the companies had knowingly engaged in a scheme "to defraud smokers
and potential smokers, for purposes of financial gain." Overwhelming evidence showed that for over fifty years the tobacco companies had lied
about the health effects of smoking to support an industry that, in the
court's words, "survives, and profits, from selling a highly addictive product which causes diseases that lead to a staggering number of deaths per
year, [and] an immeasurable amount of human suffering."

This powerful legal and moral judgment was greeted with a yawn. Wall
Street saw it as a win for the tobacco companies because it would not hurt
their profits. How could that be? A higher court ruling had stopped the
judge from ordering the billions in damages and other remedies the
Justice Department had sought; she could only restrain future violations.
As for the industry's reputation, it could hardly go lower. Polling that year
showed that only 2 percent of Americans would normally believe a state-

ment by a tobacco company, making tobacco the least trusted among the nineteen industries asked about.

And yet, the people leading those companies often spoke of how clean their consciences were. For decades, they claimed that they didn't believe the evidence that smoking killed people because it was "not proven." After they finally admitted that they sold a deadly and addictive product, there were many other rationalizations they had cultivated over the years and could still embrace.

This chapter is about how these masters of rationalization manufactured psychological crutches both to help smokers deny the danger they faced and to help themselves deny any responsibility for that danger. They showed that even an industry with little public credibility could delay social action by raising doubts about science and eroding trust in government, especially if it mobilized other industries threatened with regulation. And they showed how industry members could reduce guilt by nursing a resentful bunker mentality and shifting all responsibility for their product's astounding death toll onto their addicted customers.

CREATING A NEW SOCIAL NORM: "TORCHES OF FREEDOM"

Native Americans had been smoking tobacco for thousands of years before Columbus showed up, but purposely sucking smoke into the body was unheard of elsewhere. Still, some Europeans gave tobacco a try, and smoking and snuff spread through the Old World. Over the centuries, tobacco provoked both passionate defenses (as a cure-all, as civilizing, inspiring, and divine) and condemnations (as disease-causing, barbaric, enslaving, and satanic). Many kings and church officials initially condemned tobacco, but they would come to make peace with it as a source of ample tax revenue. Some of the American colonies were formed with tobacco-growing at their heart, and like the West Indies sugar colonies, they would come to depend on that other emerging social norm, New World slavery.

While the history of tobacco is long, the history of cigarettes is not. They were not a widespread social phenomenon until the twentieth century, and they brought tobacco consumption to a whole new level.

Cigarettes were mass-produced, mass-marketed, and mass-consumed like no other tobacco product. They cost less and were more quickly lit and smoked than pipes or cigars. And cigarettes were more acceptable in public than cigars, which were smellier, or than chewing tobacco, which involved lots of unsanitary spitting. In a way, the cigarette was the fast-food of tobacco—cheap, widely available, easy to grab, quick to consume on the go, even in public, lending itself to frequent use, and particularly appealing to children.

There were forces opposing the rise of cigarettes as a social norm in the late nineteenth and early twentieth centuries, especially among those pushing for the prohibition of alcohol. By 1909 seven states had banned cigarettes and dozens had debated such a ban. There were definitely health concerns at the time, but it was clearly the moral objections that gave the crusade its juice, with cigarettes seen as strongly linked to overall moral degeneracy. Henry Ford vowed not to hire cigarette smokers, arguing that those "addicted to this habit . . . were loose in their morals, very apt to be untruthful."

The tobacco industry pushed back against this opposition, of course. As Richard Kluger explains in his groundbreaking and Pulitzer Prize–winning history of cigarettes, *Ashes to Ashes: America's Hundred-Year Cigarette War, the Public Health, and the Unabashed Triumph of Philip Morris*, the industry "fielded a small army of lawyers, lobbyists and other persuaders who appealed to the hearts, minds, and pocketbooks of legislators being asked everywhere to crack down on cigarettes." The industry also had great influence with key congressional committees, some of whose members owned large blocks of tobacco stock. And then came World War I. General Pershing told the public that his army needed tobacco as much as bullets. Cigarettes were no longer seen as sources of degeneracy but as sources of solace to the brave lads in the trenches, and many veterans returned home addicted.

The industry spread cigarettes further into the mainstream by expanding its already aggressive advertising. The public was bombarded with ads that linked cigarettes to youth, health, freedom, success, sex, and—depending on the ad—to ruggedness or sophistication, individualism or sociability, masculinity or femininity. Many ads addressed background anxieties about health by making unfounded claims about one brand being more healthful or less irritating than others. The tobacco industry also encouraged the film industry to exploit the dramatic possibilities of smoking, and it did, further normalizing and glamorizing cigarettes. The industry was consciously aiming to tap into consumers' unconscious desires, drawing on the psychological insights of the era, such as they were.

In one famous example, Edward Bernays, often called the father of public relations, was hired by the tobacco industry to attract women to smoking in the late 1920s. Bernays, the nephew of Sigmund Freud, wrote candidly about influencing the masses using psychological manipulation and propaganda, noting that those "who understand the mental processes and social patterns of the masses . . . pull the wires which control the public mind." When Bernays learned from a psychoanalyst that women saw cigarettes as symbols of freedom, he secretly recruited female socialites to violate the taboo against women publicly smoking by marching in a New York City parade, their cigarettes held high and hailed as "torches of freedom." It was symbolic of much cigarette promotion—a corporation using the banner of individual freedom to encourage people to surrender some of their freedom by getting addicted to the company's product.

Cigarette use grew between the wars, and it skyrocketed again during World War II, when cigarettes were included in military rations. Some 80 percent of men who were teenagers or young adults during the war years became cigarette smokers, and smoking rose among women too. The social norm of cigarette smoking was now deeply entrenched—aided by the convenience and addictiveness of the product but also by the social influence of mass media, the political clout of the industry, and by that most socially bonding of endeavors, fighting wars together. And that new social norm would prove astonishingly resilient in the face of growing evidence that cigarettes were causing a public health catastrophe of astonishing proportions.

WINNING THE BURDEN OF PROOF GAME: "ULTRACONSERVATIVE ABOUT CAUSE AND EFFECT"

Cigarettes did not penetrate just modern society more deeply than cigars and pipes—their smoke penetrated people's bodies more deeply. Compared to cigars and pipes, cigarette smoke is milder and easier to inhale, and most cigarette smokers draw the smoke deeply into their lungs. In this way, the rise of cigarettes opened vast new frontiers of disease causation and addiction, as millions of people started drenching their highly absorptive lung tissue with tobacco smoke, usually many times a day.

Tobacco was linked to disease long before cigarettes were prevalent. Often, as the industry would remind people later, the early accusations had been ludicrous, like a home medical book that in 1901 warned that the children of heavy tobacco users are "liable to insanity." But some doctors had correctly linked tobacco to cancer since the 1700s, when it was noted that several people with cancer of the nostrils used tobacco snuff. In 1923, Sigmund Freud's doctors diagnosed him with oral cancer that they confidently blamed on his heavy cigar smoking. While his nephew Edward Bernays was using Freudian insights to expand the pool of tobacco smokers, Freud himself was suffering through thirty-three painful operations and was eventually forced to wear a denture-like prosthesis to keep his oral and nasal cavities separated. Freud tried several times to quit smoking, but his friend and biographer said he found it a "torture . . . beyond human power to bear." Freud died of cancer in 1939.*

Lung cancer had been an extremely rare disease, but it started appearing at alarming rates that echoed the steep twentieth-century rise of cigarettes, but a couple decades later. The few studies linking cigarettes to lung cancer that appeared between 1928 and 1950 drew little attention. In 1950, though, two major studies—one in the United States and one in Britain—looked at hundreds of lung cancer patients and found that virtually all of them were cigarette smokers. The statistical correlations were not subtle. According to Allan Brandt, author of the sweeping history *The Cigarette Century: The Rise, Fall, and Deadly Persistence of the Product That Defined America* and professor of the history of medicine at Harvard,

---

* Freud is frequently quoted as having said that "sometimes a cigar is just a cigar," as a way of suggesting that—despite most of his theories—not everything has a deeper psychological meaning. Some see the quote as a hypocritical loophole in his theories created for his beloved cigars. However, there is no contemporaneous evidence Freud actually said this. Freud wrote that smoking reflected an oral fixation caused by too-early weaning off the breast, despite the simpler explanation of chemical addiction, with which he was personally all too familiar.

the odds that the British study's results were by chance were less than one in a million.

At first, there was little coverage by the media, but then the nation's largest-circulation magazine, *Reader's Digest,* highlighted the issue in a widely read article. (Unlike most magazines, it did not at this time accept advertising, so it had more freedom to be critical about tobacco, auto safety, and other issues.) Then, in late 1953, researchers published a study showing that painting tar derived from cigarette smoke onto the shaved skin of mice caused cancerous tumors. The media paid more attention, tobacco stock prices dropped, and the industry was alarmed. Thanks to a trove of internal industry documents pried loose through litigation or leaked by whistleblowers, mainly in the 1990s, we have a real-time written record of how the industry responded. (The University of California San Francisco Library has created an extraordinary public resource by archiving and posting millions of these documents online in a collection called Truth Tobacco Industry Documents).

The top executives of the major US tobacco companies held an emergency meeting in late 1953 with the public relations firm Hill and Knowlton, brought in to help manage the crisis. One of the firm's employees thought, rather quaintly in retrospect, that the burden had now shifted to the industry to prove cigarettes safe, which they knew they could not at that time do. "But, naturally," he wrote, "that is something almost too terrible for most of the industry's men to realize, even yet." As it happened, the tobacco industry would succeed in keeping the burden of proof on its critics for decades more.

The campaign began with a full-page ad, "A Frank Statement to Cigarette Smokers," in hundreds of papers in January 1954. It said there was "no proof" cigarettes caused lung cancer and assured smokers that the companies "accept an interest in people's health as a basic responsibility, paramount to every other consideration in our business." The companies announced they would fund outside research into the health issue through a new Tobacco Industry Research Committee (TIRC), to be run by a scientist of "unimpeachable integrity" and advised by a "disinterested" board. There were skeptics, but newspapers around the country commended the industry for taking such a responsible stand.

The industry announced with great fanfare that prominent biologist Clarence C. Little would head the committee. Little told the press that he was "ultraconservative about cause and effect relationships"—as if that could only be a good thing—and assured them that he didn't have "any personal preconceived notions at all" about tobacco's health effects. He had just claimed, though, without evidence, that tobacco was "very good therapy for a great many nervous people. I don't have to tell you that. You all know it."

Little also had a preconceived attachment to a genetic explanation of cancer, suggesting that the type of people genetically inclined to get cancer may also be genetically inclined to smoke. (In fact, Little believed so deeply in heredity that in the 1930s he was a founder of the National Society for the Legalization of Euthanasia and the Race Betterment Congress, and he urged the compulsory sterilization of "the misfit.") Despite the galloping lung cancer epidemic, Little was in no hurry to find its cause, noting "it is a long, slow business, and that is another good thing—that there is no rush about this." Little was the perfect person to head TIRC and to keep rejecting proof of causation while perpetually calling for more research.

Within a few years an avalanche of evidence linking smoking to lung cancer and other diseases followed. A major study by the American Cancer Society, tracking nearly 188,000 healthy men between age fifty and sixty-nine, had by 1954 found that the smokers were dying from all causes at a rate about one and a half times higher than the nonsmokers. By 1956 these researchers reported that the heaviest smokers were dying of lung cancer at a rate ninety times higher than nonsmokers. By this time a prospective British study showed nearly identical results, and there were at least fourteen retrospective studies, all linking lung cancer and smoking.

Still, the industry claimed there was "no proof" that smoking caused cancer, or no proof that was "conclusive" or "definite," hinting at a standard of proof that was never clearly defined. Industry members objected that the evidence was "merely" statistical, as opposed to something observed in a laboratory. But as the head of the American Cancer Society would argue in 1956, it was not reasonable to insist that cigarettes be shown to cause lung cancer in living humans under laboratory conditions, and "no standards of proof in the entire world of research demand as much as that." The top scientist at British American Tobacco, Sidney Green, would years later accuse his own industry colleagues of having "publicly retreated behind impossible, perhaps ridiculous, demands for what in their public relations is called 'scientific proof.'"

In fact, it appears that by 1958 it was widely recognized among researchers within the tobacco industry that smoking causes cancer. Three members of the British tobacco industry came to the United States in 1958 to meet with dozens of researchers working in US tobacco companies, in academia, and elsewhere. They reported back that "with one exception [in academia], the individuals whom we met believed that smoking causes lung cancer if by 'causation' we mean any chain of events which leads finally to lung cancer and which involves smoking as an indispensable link."

On the other hand, there is evidence that industry members' fixation on proof was not solely for public consumption; behind the scenes they often stressed the same point. For example, one proposal within tobacco company Brown and Williamson for countering the attacks of the "totally unprincipled" anticigarette forces, apparently from 1969, asserted that "within the business we recognize that a controversy exists," adding, "Truth is our message because of its power to withstand a conflict and sustain a controversy. If in our pro-cigarette efforts we stick with *well documented fact*, we can dominate a controversy and operate with the confidence of justifiable self-interest."

Statements like this show industry employees, or at least some, working internally to justify their continued denial, propping up their morale by finding a way to claim morality. The general themes of most of the industry's public denials were echoed privately, suggesting the denials were meeting a psychological need as well as a strategic one.

MAINTAINING THE CRUCIAL DOUBT: WE MUST "GIVE SMOKERS A PSYCHOLOGICAL CRUTCH"

In 1963, a panel of scientists met privately in Washington, with guards to keep the curious away. "It was almost a Manhattan Project mentality," a participant recalled. The panel had been brought together by the surgeon general, Luther Terry, to review the thousands of studies then available on smoking and health.

None of the panel's members had taken a position on the subject, and they had been chosen almost like a jury, with both health advocates and the tobacco industry given veto power over their inclusion. The panel was carefully constituted to include five smokers and five nonsmokers, and its deliberations took place in a smoke-filled room. In January 1964, the surgeon general, himself a smoker, released the panel's consensus report to an auditorium full of journalists. It confidently linked smoking to lung cancer in men, to emphysema and bronchitis, and, with less confidence, to coronary artery disease. Future historians and judges would view this report as a landmark, resolving the basic question of whether smoking was harmful. (One of the heaviest smokers on the panel, as if to demonstrate its conclusions, would the next year be diagnosed with lung cancer, emphysema, bronchitis, and heart disease; only then would he quit cigarettes.)

The industry had seen it coming, and some members assumed they could no longer get away with the denials they had been using. Addison Yeaman, the chief counsel of Brown and Williamson, predicted that after the surgeon general's panel linked smoking to cancer and cardiovascular disease, "one would suppose we would not repeat Dr. Little's oft reiterated 'not proven.'" He thought that now the burden of proof would truly shift, forcing the industry to either disprove the causal link to cancer (noting that "the odds are greatly against success in that effort") or find and remove the carcinogens. But once again, this assumption was wrong. The industry's response to the evidence barely budged, and it mattered little.

This may be because—as expressed in a memo by George Weissman, an executive and future CEO of the tobacco giant Philip Morris—after the report's original "propaganda blast," the "public reaction was not as severe nor did it have the emotional depth I might have feared." Still, Weissman felt it was important for the industry to "in the near future provide some answers which will give smokers a psychological crutch and a self-rationale to continue smoking."

Providing that crutch to smokers would prove remarkably easy. Their basic confirmation biases were surely amplified by their addiction to nicotine. (Back in 1955, even doctors had proven less likely to agree that cigarettes caused cancer if they themselves smoked; one prominent researcher had complained that "their own addiction to this drug habit . . . blinds them.") All that many smokers needed going forward would be some shred of reason to doubt the science of causation or the wisdom of quitting. The same 1969 Brown and Williamson presentation quoted above, asserting that "truth is our message," also argued that "doubt is our product since it is the best means of competing with the 'body of fact' that exists in the mind of the . . . public. It is also the means of establishing a controversy."

In fact, the industry had long been offering a psychological crutch to smokers in the form of filters, promoted by ads implying greater safety ("Just What the Doctor Ordered!") even while the industry denied that its unfiltered product was unsafe. (Lorillard sold for a few years in the 1950s a new filter that was particularly good at removing tar and nicotine; unfortunately the novel ingredient in the filter was asbestos, described as a "completely harmless material" but adding yet another potent carcinogen to the mix.) Filtered cigarettes of all types were widely advertised and embraced by consumers during the 1950s, but filters and reduced-tar-and-nicotine cigarettes generally did not actually reduce smoker risk much. Smokers almost completely compensate for tar and nicotine reductions by smoking more or differently to get the nicotine their brains crave. The federal racketeering judgment of 2006 would find that the industry's sophisticated understanding of compensation meant the defendants had long known their supposedly "safer" cigarettes offered no clear health benefit.

Another way the industry created that crucial shred of doubt was to point to alternative potential causes of lung cancer. Both before and after the surgeon general's report, the industry would point to its long-standing "constitutional" theory: that something about the constitution of smokers—their genes, their hormones, their nervous personalities—predisposed them to both smoking and lung cancer. The industry also tried to blame the lung cancer epidemic on occupational hazards and especially air pollution—two of the "ready-made credible alternatives" that one industry strategist told his colleagues they should supply the public.

The industry also pointed to stress as a cause of cancer, which let it then claim (or arrange for others to claim) that cigarettes actually *reduced* the risk of cancer by alleviating stress. In 1968, the ironically named *True* magazine published an article by a writer named Stanley Frank that presented a tour de force of all the discredited pro-smoking theories. Frank suggested that just maybe the era's rising divorce rate, causing "frustrated sex drives and unhappiness stemming from a feeling of rejection," was behind the lung cancer epidemic. Frank also criticized the surgeon general for not considering that "a heavy smoker is more likely to get cancer if he is deprived of cigarettes which serve the important function of relieving his tensions."

The Tobacco Institute—formed by the industry in 1958 to "go on the offensive in bringing the truth about cigarette smoking to the public"—had over 600,000 copies of the article sent to doctors, the media, and political leaders. It did not reveal that, in fact, the tobacco industry had secretly paid for and placed the article, causing some controversy when the subterfuge was revealed a few weeks later through investigations by the *Wall Street Journal* and others. The blowback must have surprised the industry, since it had long succeeded in hiding its fingerprints and using more credible voices to convey its messages.

As we saw among the industrial defenders of CFCs, the defenders of tobacco frequently just expressed their unwavering personal belief in the safety of their product. Such unsupported expressions of confidence would be a useless tactic if we humans were always rational, conscious, and evidence-based in forming our views. The success of the tobacco industry, however, is partly due to its early understanding that we are also social animals powerfully swayed by social influence. Merely expressing an opinion with confidence can persuade others, at least when the speaker's and listeners' interests are aligned. While tobacco companies and smokers did not have aligned interests when it came to actual health impacts, their biases were surely aligned as they shared the desire to believe smoking was harmless.

And so tobacco executives confidently opined away for decades. The 1954 "Frank Statement to Smokers" stressed that "we believe the products we make are not injurious to health." The chairman of R. J. Reynolds Tobacco Company, in a cover story in *Time* in 1960, dismissed the cancer scare, saying, "I just don't believe it." The head of Philip Morris in 1963 told shareholders, "I think that eventually cigarettes will be exonerated." In 1986, the CEO of R. J. Reynolds told a magazine that if he saw evidence that "conclusively" proved tobacco was harmful to people, "and I believed it in my heart and my soul, then I would get out of the business." But he hadn't, so he claimed to have "an extremely clear conscience."

Most famously, when the heads of several tobacco companies were asked under oath before a congressional committee in 1994 if nicotine was addictive, most said they "believed" it was not. (The Justice Department later considered bringing perjury charges, but this belief-based wording appears to be what stopped them.) Geoffrey Bible, who became Philip Morris's CEO after the 1994 hearings, would later complain that each CEO answered with "his own personal opinion," so it was unfair that this became "the birth of the tirade against us for being liars."

In short, the doubt-promoting strategy was linked not to the idea of reasonable doubt but to personal doubt, letting industry executives shroud themselves in a kind of protective personal ignorance. When Geoffrey Bible was asked in 1998 his company's view on whether smoking causes disease, he testified, "I just don't know. It may, but I don't know" (though he did "not believe" it caused cancer). When asked if he was aware of any reputable scientific organization anywhere in the world that said smoking doesn't cause disease, Bible answered, "No, I am not."

The tobacco executives had taken the ignorance shelter discussed in chapter 2 to new extremes, no longer discussing what society or scientists knew or what their company should reasonably have known, but focusing on what they personally believed. You might say they were raising the already ridiculously high standard of proof one notch higher, demanding proof that convinced them personally, in their hearts and souls.

VIEW FROM THE BUNKER: FASCIST KILLJOYS IN THE ANTISMOKING INDUSTRY

Like other industries profiled in this book, the tobacco industry responded in a tribal way to outside criticism, enthusiastically denigrating its critics and seeing itself as unfairly victimized. Even internal documents over the decades show industry members referring among themselves to the "attacks" as baseless "propaganda," made by scientists just seeking publicity and funding. It was an industry "harassed" by "dedicated opportunists," forced to "suffer public condemnation along with litter bugs and forest fires." The industry was threatened by "lynching parties" and "witch hunts" and had been "unfairly pilloried." Its critics were engaged in a "reckless campaign of propaganda, mistruths, half-truths, innuendo, false piety, and downright deceit."

In public, members of the industry often insisted that they themselves were good people who did not feel guilty; on the contrary, they felt proud of their work and companies. Philip Morris's Geoffrey Bible said in 1999, "There is going to be a Day of Judgment. If there isn't a day up there, it's when you're lying on your deathbed. And you're going to say to yourself: 'Well, what did I achieve in my life?' It's not how much money you've made, or how big a house you've got, or how many cars. It's what you did for your fellow man. It's 'What did I do to make the world better?' That's what it's going to come down to." And he could apparently reconcile his industry with this moral standard.

Perhaps claims of a clean conscience were just a public ploy, hiding crippling guilt, but I have not seen such guilt expressed in the industry's internal documents (nor, indeed, actual concern over the health of its customers). I suspect these statements actually give a glimpse of how the human mind works. Psychologist Jonathan Haidt explains in his book *The Righteous Mind: Why Good People Are Divided by Politics and Religion* that people have moral intuitions and they conduct moral reasoning, but the reasoning is done largely just to rationalize the intuition; as he puts it, the intuitive dog wags the rational tail. So if something feels immoral, we find reasons to condemn it, and if it does not feel immoral, we find reasons to justify it. This theory suggests that if you are a tobacco executive and you don't feel any guilt, your mind will find reasons to interpret your behavior as morally acceptable.

In 1994, to fight growing antitobacco sentiment, Philip Morris allowed journalist Roger Rosenblatt to interview some of its executives about how they personally justified selling cigarettes. Rosenblatt concluded, in his *New York Times Magazine* profile, that the executives "remove themselves from most of the rest of the country and create their own moral universe of explanations and justifications." One executive spoke of the "incredible family feeling" at the company; another spoke about feeling "under siege." Steven C. Parrish, the company's general counsel, stressed his affection for the "really good people" that worked there, saying he saw more people "locking arms and getting together behind a business strategy than ... worrying about the externalities of charges about tobacco and health." Years later, though, Parrish would write with surprising candor that the tobacco industry's culture had long been one of "arrogance, bred by insularity and enabled by spectacular business success. . . . There was a bunker mentality, an 'us-against-them' attitude, a belief that anyone who disagreed with us was an enemy out to destroy us."

From within that bunker, many seemed to imagine the industry was replaying the battles of the early twentieth century, viewing their critics as prohibitionists and killjoys, both publicly and in private. In 1958, the president of the Tobacco Institute blamed "a few people who are fanatically prejudiced against tobacco. Not liking it themselves, they are opposed to its use by others." In 1963, a Philip Morris executive called industry critics "do-gooders who want to attack the pleasures of life, be it drinking, smoking or even Arthur Murray dancers." In 1979, William Dwyer of the Tobacco Institute called them "a joyless tribe . . . who want to manage everyone else's life, perhaps because they've been incapable of managing their own." (Dwyer would later tell author Richard Kluger that he "liked being in a battle—it was like a political contest—a head game.")

But Prohibition was apparently not a compelling enough historical analogy. Dwyer also linked the struggle against nonsmoking sections in airplanes to the struggle for civil rights, complaining about putting smokers in the rear of planes after we "broke down those barriers that used to divide people on pretty untoward bases." He defined his advocacy as a defense of "the free market system," tapping into anticommunist sentiments. And he compared the persecution of smokers to the persecutions of the Holocaust, warning about what might come next by repeatedly quoting the famous words of Pastor Martin Niemöller ("In Germany, the Nazis first came for the Communists and I didn't speak up because I wasn't a Communist. Then they came for the Jews and I didn't speak up because I wasn't a Jew. . . .").

As the tobacco industry became more embattled in the 1990s, references to fascism arose more often, including among the industry's leaders. Geoffrey Bible roused a gathering of his Philip Morris employees in 1996 by reminding them that "it took Winston Churchill and Roosevelt" more than five years to prevail over "these bad guys." Lawrence Tisch—the billionaire philanthropist and co-CEO of the company that owned Lorillard Tobacco Company—complained in 1998 to journalist Jeffrey Goldberg that "when the truth is undermined in America, then you've accomplished everything the fascists will want to try to do 20 years from today. . . . The

Big Lie is that these companies were ever marketing to kids. What worries me is that if you can get away with this against a legitimate industry, what could be the next big lie? This is McCarthyism."

Industry members' views about their critics often seem to reflect what psychologists would call projection. Tobacco's critics were often referred to as the antitobacco or antismoking "industry." One 1983 consultants' analysis done for Philip Morris hypothesized that the "anti-smoking industry," which apparently included scientists, educators, nonprofits, public health officials, activists, and many others, had "its own motives and rewards for appearing to prove that heart disease and cancer are caused by smoking," even though it is "equally plausible" the diseases were genetic or constitutional (a statement that by 1983 was beyond ridiculous). The antismoking industry, therefore, "can't claim any moral superiority, social superiority, scientific superiority, or any other kind of superiority."

It was an artful and surely appealing rationalization for tobacco executives stung by accusations of dishonesty, greed, and immorality, letting them privately fling each accusation back at their critics (except the one about causing all those deaths). And like all deeply cynical attitudes, it presented a certain moral danger. If, behind the "false piety" of their critics, everyone were in fact biased, dishonest, and greedy, then it would be easy to believe that was the true social norm. In that case, there would be no reason to try to overcome or minimize one's own bias, dishonesty, and greed. On the contrary, to do so would be to let the bad guys prevail over the good people with you in your bunker. If you believe that a system is entirely corrupt and rigged against you, then even obviously deceptive practices—like, say, hiding your influence behind front groups or purging your files of documents showing your company's knowledge of cigarettes' dangers—can seem justifiable.

Social psychology has not done nearly as much research as one would expect into how a siege mentality, or a collective resentment over perceived unfairness, affects moral behavior. (The current political situation, with so many groups feeling resentful and claiming the system is rigged, would seem to provide a rich opportunity to study the behavioral consequences of collective resentment.) Still, there is some evidence that, not surprisingly, individuals who feel themselves unfairly treated are more likely to behave dishonestly. One can imagine the distortion of the moral compass of a group of people who have been collectively nursing a resentment over unfair treatment for decades.

GOVERNMENT-BASHING: CONCENTRATING "ALL OF THE EPA'S ENEMIES AGAINST IT AT ONE TIME"

The industry's cynicism—combined with a grave new threat it faced in the 1980s—may be what gave the tobacco industry the chutzpah to take its arguments about the science to the next level. In 1986 the surgeon general released a bombshell report finding that carcinogens in secondhand smoke, or Environmental Tobacco Smoke (ETS), were causing lung cancer in nonsmokers. Some states and many localities were already limiting public and workplace smoking. The industry's defense that smokers knew the risk and chose to take it was useless against ETS, and the industry feared the issue would have a devastating effect on sales.

And so the industry that had become the poster child for scientific bias and deception decided to position itself as a champion of scientific integrity. Anticipating the surgeon general's report on ETS, the Tobacco Institute released a report in 1986 entitled "Tobacco Smoke and the Nonsmoker: Scientific Integrity at the Crossroads," and publicly called for an investigation of the surgeon general for "censorship and abuse of science." The report argued that the claims that tobacco smoke "compromises—even slightly—the health of nonsmokers will only intensify the current climate of emotionalism and impede the progress of scientific integrity." At the time, the industry's confidential polling showed that only about one in ten Americans thought the industry was telling the truth when it said it didn't believe mainstream health claims; virtually all the rest thought the industry knew or suspected the claims were true. Perhaps the industry thought its strategy posed no risk to its credibility, since it was already so damaged.

It was a particularly outrageous strategy given the industry's history of blatantly suppressing harmful science. For example, one day in 1970, R. J. Reynolds abruptly shut down the "mouse house" where it had been quietly exposing animals to cigarette smoke, fired the researchers, collected their notebooks, and presumably killed the animals. One researcher said he was told that the surgeon general was already "slitting our throats;

we don't need to do it ourselves." Industry members had taken many overt steps to keep its scientific findings secret, like doing certain experiments only abroad, getting or keeping incriminating research findings out of company files, running scientific research through lawyers so they could claim the findings were protected under attorney-client privilege, and trying to sanitize or suppress negative results by scientists it had funded.

By inventing or exaggerating the scientific sins of others, the industry could avoid looking at its own. In 1987, Philip Morris executives gathered for a three-day, high-level meeting to brainstorm ways to respond to the ETS threat. Participants complained that few scientists were "willing to remain impartial because of threat to their careers," that the "morality of scientists is appalling," and that data was "crooked." The long list of brainstormed solutions stands as a revealing group rant, showing not just a sense of grievance but lots of aggression and a willingness to deceive, including "sue the bastards!," "create a bigger monster (AIDS)," "make it hurt (political risk) to take us on," "get Nader-like group to examine anti funding," "organize 'spontaneous' protests on our issue," and "establish ties with libertarian and conservative groups."

While many of the listed options were not pursued, the industry did establish ties with libertarian and conservative groups by pushing a larger, anti-EPA agenda. In 1992, the EPA declared ETS responsible for thousands of deaths among nonsmokers yearly, with serious regulatory implications for workplaces. The Tobacco Institute charged the EPA with preferring "political correctness over sound science." By 1993, Philip Morris had the PR firm Burson-Marsteller develop an "ETS Media Strategy." It pointed optimistically to "growing perceptions about and animosity to EPA as an agency that is at least misguided and aggressive, at worst corrupt and controlled by environmental terrorists." It suggested pushing stories that focused on "general EPA bashing by credible, authoritative sources (i.e., scientists, mayors, etc.)" and "EPA ineptitude and, when possible, corruption." Noting the industry's own lack of credibility, it argued that the anti-EPA effort "must be part of a larger mosaic that concentrates all of the EPA's enemies against it at one time."

It is not clear how much of this particular proposal was implemented, but as Naomi Oreskes and Erik M. Conway point out in *Merchants of Doubt,* the tobacco industry played a substantial role in creating and funding antiregulatory "think tanks" and developing the strategies that other industries would use to challenge the science of ozone depletion, climate change, and other grave threats.

After the Republican takeover of Congress in the election of 1994, there would be no more hearings embarrassing the tobacco industry. The House subcommittee formerly led by Henry Waxman, before which industry leaders testified that they did not believe cigarettes were addictive, now held the hearings on "scientific integrity and the public trust," mentioned in chapter 5, where Fred Singer told members they had been "bamboozled" by federal scientists on ozone. When the head of the FDA asserted regulatory authority over cigarettes as nicotine-delivery devices, he was dismissed as a "thug" and a "bully" by new Speaker of the House Newt Gingrich. (The industry would years later persuade the Supreme Court to reject the FDA's assertion of authority by a 5–4 vote.)

The tobacco industry failed to improve its own scientific credibility with the public; it was probably too late, given the decades of deception made even more evident by recently released industry documents. But the industry may well have succeeded in dragging down the government's scientific credibility, contaminating a broader political audience with its own cynicism, and helping popularize the notion that regulators rely on "junk science." Moreover, it showed other industries that they didn't have to convince the public they were right about the science to delay regulation; they just needed to create doubt about whether the government was right. Part of the legacy of tobacco industry denial is the toxic residue of a broader science denial in the body politic, like a tarry buildup of cynicism preventing democracy from functioning as it needs to.

RELAX AND ENJOY IT: BETTER THAN CRACK,
NO WORSE THAN APPLESAUCE

Members of the tobacco industry also employed a sort of alternate-reality risk-benefit analysis that focused on smoking's "benefits" while minimizing the risks and that drew not on evidence but psychology.

Cigarettes had long been sold as a source of "satisfaction." After the cancer news of the early 1950s, Hill and Knowlton felt the industry had to free Americans "from the guilty fear that is going to arise deep in their biological depths" when they light up. Soon after the industry published its "Frank Statement to Cigarette Smokers" in 1954, there appeared a booklet, "Smoke without Fear," secretly written with the help of Hill and Knowlton and published by the editors of *True: The Man's Magazine* (the same magazine that would publish the 1968 Tobacco Institute–sponsored article mentioned above). It encouraged worried smokers to "relax and enjoy it," advising those who had found it hard to stop smoking to just "quit trying." "Smoking satisfies some inner needs you have. These needs may be unexplainable, unreasonable, preposterous. We may create them ourselves and might be better off without them. However that may be, you continue to smoke because smoking gives you more satisfaction than not smoking."

Soon the industry gave its satisfaction argument a more scientific spin, focusing on stress relief. In the 1960s, in particular, the benefits of smoking were seen in pharmaceutical terms. A top scientist for British American Tobacco (owners of US tobacco company Brown and Williamson) told his colleagues in 1962 that "nicotine is a very remarkable beneficent drug that both helps the body to resist external stress and also can as a result show a pronounced tranquillising effect." Modern life is stressful, and people "must have drugs available which they can take when they feel the need." Industry commonly expressed this view, giving little thought to the possibility that the only need that cigarettes satisfy is the very one they create through nicotine addiction. (Later research would find that smoking actually increases long-term stress.)

The 1964 surgeon general's report included a glancing reference to the "comparatively inconsequential" purported benefits of smoking, including the "intangible and elusive" mental health benefits. It said smoking meets the need for a "psychological crutch," and at least smoking posed less threat to society than narcotics and other illegal drugs. Philip Morris executives immediately urged that the industry build on this tepid support by emphasizing the mental health benefits of smoking. An internal R.J. Reynolds memo would in 1972 posit that "in a sense, the tobacco industry may be thought of as being a specialized, highly ritualized and stylized segment of the pharmaceutical industry," selling products that "contain and deliver nicotine, a potent drug with a variety of physiological effects." The industry would regret the revelation of documents like this in the 1990s when the FDA tried to regulate cigarettes as a nicotine-delivery device.

The tobacco companies continued to pay close attention to smoker psychology. A Philip Morris researcher summarized various studies that by 1972 had found that, compared to nonsmokers, smokers were more energetic and independent but also more antisocial, impulsive, anxious, and emotional, with "poorer mental health," less "strength of character," higher alcohol use, more divorces, job changes, and auto accidents, poorer academic performance, and lower socioeconomic status. (Of course, these unflattering descriptions of their customers hew more closely to the charges brought against cigarette smokers by Henry Ford and the moralists of an earlier era than they do to the winning images of smokers portrayed in cigarette ads.) Understanding the smoker's psychology would let the industry "help our consumer rationalize his decision to smoke in light of increasing external pressures," said an Imperial Tobacco executive to a 1984 industry gathering.

As for rationalizing their own decision to continue selling cigarettes, industry leaders routinely viewed smoking as preventing much worse behavior. One retired head of Philip Morris told author Richard Kluger that "I felt we were performing a real service—that ours was a product helping the public through the rigors of living," noting that tobacco was not nearly as bad as opium or crack. "We have fulfilled a need," he added, "and it's very naïve to assume that nonsmokers don't fulfill that need in other and more destructive ways," including antisocial acts of aggression. As noted at the beginning of this book's introduction, Philip Morris CEO Geoffrey Bible argued in 1998 that "nobody knows what you'd turn to if you didn't smoke. Maybe you'd beat your wife. Maybe you'd drive cars fast. Who knows what the hell you'd do?"

The flip side of industry's alternate-reality risk-benefit analysis was to minimize the risk. For one thing, who's to say certain physical impacts are unwelcome? In 1971, Joseph Cullman III, chairman of Philip Morris, dismissed evidence that women who smoked gave birth to lower-birth-weight babies by stating that "some women would prefer having smaller babies." Two years earlier, Mr. Cullman had inexplicably noted upon questioning by a congressional committee that "there are a lot of people that like to cough."

More commonly, though, the industry just compared the risks of smoking to other accepted risks, in the same vein as the auto industry comparing unsafe cars to hardwood floors or the aerosol industry comparing ozone depletion to sharp kitchen knives. The author of the industry-sponsored 1954 article "Smoke without Fear" argued that declining to smoke on risk grounds would be like refusing to drive a car, ride in a train, cross a street, carry matches, sit under a tree, own a dog, drink milk, or kiss someone because "the bacterial content of a kiss is horrifying." Helmut Wakeham, head of research and development at Philip Morris, said in a 1976 British television interview that "all kinds of things . . . are unhealthy. . . . Cigarettes are one, so what are we to do? Stop living?" He later added that "applesauce is harmful if you get too much of it."

The point, of course, was to encourage a fatalistic acceptance of risk as simply inevitable, unknowable, and unavoidable, even risks as large and by then obvious as smoking. Ross Millhiser, yet another former CEO of Philip Morris, told Richard Kluger in 1989 that he had confidence in the cigarette business because the "desire to die in good health will wane." Helmut Wakeham enhanced his applesauce comparison by helpfully explaining that "the best way to avoid dying is not to be born, you know."

Perhaps the ultimate example of the industry's skewed approach to risk and benefit was its attempt to recast the early death of its customers as a benefit to society. Even while still denying they caused smokers' deaths, tobacco companies argued before various courts that they should get some offsetting credit for shortening smokers' lives, thereby saving governments the financial burden of caring for them in old age. When this "death benefit" argument was raised before a Minnesota judge in 1998, he dismissed it as "abhorrent and horrendously contrary to public policy." (Three years later Philip Morris faced a political backlash for again pushing this argument; CEO Geoffrey Bible apologized, admitting it was "a complete and unacceptable disregard of basic human values.")

PERSONAL RESPONSIBILITY, ADDICTION, AND
CHILDREN: "THESE PEOPLE HAD BEEN TOLD"

The tobacco companies were often sued, and for decades they never settled and never lost. Since they denied cigarettes caused disease, plaintiffs had to pay experts to prove it and go through years of litigation, after which most dropped out, their funds exhausted. A lawyer for R. J. Reynolds once admitted that "the way we won these cases was not by spending all of RJR's money, but by making that other son of a bitch spend all of his."

Congress responded to the surgeon general's 1964 report with a 1965 law requiring that cigarette packs include the bland warning "Caution: Cigarette Smoking May Be Hazardous to Your Health." The industry publicly opposed it but secretly wanted the law because, as one industry lawyer later said, "It got us assumption of risk." That is, it would let the companies defend against future lawsuits by saying that smokers had been warned about the dangers of smoking and "assumed" the risk when they chose to smoke anyway, relieving the industry of any share of responsibility for the consequences. Industry won with this defense even while denying disease causation, essentially claiming that their denial did not matter because nobody believed them anyway. The Tobacco Institute's Bill Dwyer would say in 1979 that you would have to be a "cave dweller" not to have heard the health warnings. Dwyer suffered no guilt pangs because, he would later say, "I really believed that these people had been told." Another industry advocate would say, "People think there's something a little tawdry about deciding to smoke and then turning around and suing the tobacco companies."

The industry often expressed this blame-the-smoker defense in terms of individual responsibility, individual choice, and individual freedom. William Campbell, head of Philip Morris USA, would tell Roger Rosenblatt in 1994 that people "have to take a step back and say, 'Isn't individual freedom and individual choice an important characteristic of our society?'" A Philip Morris International lobbyist recently spoke of how proud he is of what he does, explaining that the tobacco industry is "the commercial manifestation of some of my most deeply held beliefs on personal choice, personal responsibility, and individual freedom." This simplistic, all-or-nothing perspective on responsibility suggests that blame for a dangerous product must fall either on the seller or the buyer and cannot be shared.

No More Addictive than Twinkies

Unfortunately for the industry, the personal-freedom-and-responsibility defense always had two major weaknesses, and the first was the addictiveness of nicotine. The tobacco industry's lawyers had warned it by 1980 that "we can't defend continued smoking as 'free choice' if the person was 'addicted.'" (They would also advise the industry to stop researching nicotine and addiction because the results were creating "dangerous implications for litigation.") In 1988, a new surgeon general's report found that nicotine was indeed addictive, similar to illegal drugs like heroin and cocaine. Some industry executives had been acknowledging nicotine's addictive nature among themselves for decades; a 1963 memo by the Brown and Williamson general counsel says, "Nicotine is addictive. We are, then, in the business of selling nicotine, an addictive drug." In public, though, industry leaders went to absurd lengths to deny it.

As noted, several company CEOs testified in 1994 before a House committee that they did not "believe" nicotine was addictive. James Johnston, the CEO of R. J. Reynolds, stated in his written testimony that if the elements of addiction are "carefully analyzed in an unbiased manner, it becomes clear that cigarette smoking is no more 'addictive' than coffee, tea or Twinkies." Three years later, Philip Morris CEO James Morgan, in testimony later featured on CBS's *60 Minutes*, said that cigarettes "are much more like caffeine or, in my case, gummi bears. . . . I love gummi bears. . . . And I eat gummi bears, and I don't like it when I don't eat my gummi bears. But I'm certainly not addicted to them."

Statements like this—trivializing an addiction that was leading to the agonizing death of hundreds of thousands of their fellow Americans yearly—surely helped fuel the sharp spike in public scorn toward the tobacco companies in the mid- to late 1990s. By this time polls showed that about seven out of ten smokers considered themselves addicted and wanted to quit. They knew nicotine held a far stronger grip on the mind than Twinkies and gummi bears.

During the 1990s, the public also learned just how sophisticated the industry's understanding of nicotine and addiction had long been. They heard whistleblowers, the media, politicians, and others accuse the industry of having purposely manipulated the nicotine content of their cigarettes or of adding chemicals to make the nicotine reach the brain faster. The industry would eventually be found, in the 2006 federal racketeering decision, to have carefully controlled the impact and delivery of nicotine to create and sustain addiction, though they continued to deny it.

A Pediatric Disease

The other major flaw in the "individual choice" defense was the tender age of almost all smokers when they first succumbed to the addiction. The head of the FDA, pediatrician David Kessler, labelled smoking a "pediatric disease" in 1995, citing studies showing that 90 percent of smokers began before age eighteen. The tobacco companies had long known their future success depended on the choices of teenagers. An R.J. Reynolds document from 1976 stressed that the "14 to 18 year old group is an increasing segment of the smoking population. RJR-T *must soon* establish a successful *new* brand in this market if our position in the industry is to be maintained over the long term." The federal court found the tobacco companies studied young people carefully so they could target youth with sophisticated marketing campaigns "to lure them into starting smoking and later becoming nicotine addicts."

Philip Morris researchers writing in 1969 concluded that "the 16 to 20-year old begins smoking for psychosocial reasons. The act of smoking is symbolic; it signifies adulthood, he smokes to enhance his image in the eyes of his peers." Then, "as the force from the psychosocial symbolism subsides, the pharmacological effect takes over to sustain the habit." A Brown and Williamson researcher, writing in 1973 about new brands for beginning smokers, recommended self-image enhancing themes because "the fragile, developing self-image of the young person needs all of the support and enhancement it can get." (He also recommended, oddly enough, a careful study of "high school American history books" for good brand name ideas.)

One of the many industry efforts to bare "that much-investigated but still mysterious adolescent psyche" involved interviewing sixteen- and seventeen-year-old smokers in the 1970s about why they smoked. The kids told about peer pressure to smoke, often as early as age twelve ("You've got to start to be in with the crowd"); about peer goading ("What, are you scared?"); about emulating someone older they admired ("I looked up to him . . . so I started smoking like him"); and about the lure of forbidden fruit ("You feel older. Sophisticated"). Most started around age twelve or thirteen. Fear of disease did not motivate them ("I think it would be really boring being a very old person so I might as well kill myself"). Most of these teenagers already wanted to quit, and while they still believed they would someday, the researchers noted (ominously for the kids but happily for the industry) that "it is likely that few will." A follow-up study in 1982 stressed that the kids know the dangers of smoking, but "they almost universally assume these risks will not apply to themselves because they will not become addicted."

Nine out of ten smokers in the United States say that if they could do it over again, they would not have started smoking. Their initial choice to smoke may have been an exercise of personal freedom, but it was probably made when they were children, and it is widely regretted. And for most, continuing to smoke is less an exercise in personal freedom than a reflection of the limits to freedom imposed by addiction.

One apparent way industry members avoided feeling guilty for marketing to youth a deadly addiction they would quickly regret was to morally disengage from what their companies had done in earlier eras. Geoffrey Bible stressed that when he became CEO of Philip Morris in 1994, he decided not to spend much time looking at the company's past. This is another benefit corporations have: they can and do reap the financial rewards of past misbehavior while their current employees are able— psychologically, if not always legally—to avoid responsibility for that misbehavior.

They may also benefit from the "side effect" blame shelter discussed in chapter 2, which draws on the hypothesis that our instinctive moral alarm system is blind to the harmful side effects of our intended action. The R.J. Reynolds executive behind the wildly successful campaign built around the cartoon character Joe Camel would say they were aiming for smokers eighteen and older, though she knew it might attract kids too. "Is it likely that some children would like that campaign? I would be the last person in the world to tell [sic] that that's impossible." But if they did not explicitly intend to attract younger teenagers, under this theory their moral alarms would not be triggered.

And they also used what we might call the "inevitability" blame shelter. Industry members denied they were encouraging young people, or really any nonsmoker, to smoke; they were just fighting for market share. Since most "of the '21 and under' group will inevitably become smokers," wrote an RJR researcher in 1973, there is "certainly nothing immoral or unethical about our Company attempting to attract those smokers to our products." This is essentially the if-we-don't-do-it-someone-else-will argument that works so well in competitive market scenarios. In this case it justifies addicting children to nicotine; centuries earlier it justified selling slaves. It is particularly dangerous when the industry simultaneously ensures that inevitability by fighting social efforts to, in these cases, reduce smoking rates or abolish slavery.

SEEKING SOCIAL LEGITIMACY: "A PLACE AT THE TABLE LIKE ANY CORPORATION"

In the mid-1990s, the tobacco industry's social legitimacy and financial future were threatened like never before by a new wave of litigation. Hundreds of billions in damages were being sought by dozens of state governments suing to recover Medicaid spending, and class action suits were mounting. Incriminating industry documents were coming to light, especially through a massive legal proceeding in my home state of Minnesota.* These documents, as well as those leaked by whistleblowers or released in earlier litigation, partly just confirmed what the public had long believed about the industry's deception, and yet seeing it in black and white—including new details about marketing to kids and manipulating nicotine levels—fueled a growing public scorn. One tobacco CEO would say the industry underestimated "the emotional content, how angry people have been over this issue."

Company stock prices were hurting, and some industry leaders feared society could yank their license to operate. Shortly after the 1994 Waxman hearings, every one of the CEOs who had denied the addictiveness of nicotine had been replaced. "A new breed of CEOs, eager to move past the high pitch of passions in the tobacco wars and to relegitimate and stabilize their industry, had taken over," reported Allan Brandt.

---

*This case was brought by Minnesota's attorney general, Hubert Humphrey III and by Blue Cross Blue Shield of Minnesota. I worked at the time at the attorney general's office as an environmental lawyer, but I had no role in the tobacco case. I did go to court to witness some of the testimony of Philip Morris CEO Geoffrey Bible to see if I could glean any particular insight into his moral reasoning by seeing him in person. It did not help.

And so in 1997, an industry famous for never settling finally sought settlement. The four largest major tobacco companies—Philip Morris, R.J. Reynolds, Brown and Williamson, and Lorillard—entered secret negotiations with the states. Steven Goldstone, CEO of the parent of R.J. Reynolds, led the way, explaining to journalist Jeffrey Goldberg that "we could not continue to be seen as a renegade industry." A settlement, Goldstone said, would acknowledge that the "tobacco companies have a legitimate right to exist in our country."

The companies reached an agreement with almost all the suing states that required the companies to pay $386.5 billion over twenty-five years and restricted their marketing. The deal needed congressional approval because the states also wanted the FDA to regulate cigarettes, and the companies wanted protection from class action lawsuits and punitive damages. Many public health advocates opposed the grant of legitimacy that the liability protections represented, and by the time the action shifted to Congress, public hostility toward the industry was so high that even former congressional friends were no longer supportive. Speaker Newt Gingrich kept the industry out of the bill-writing process, saying that the industry's "deliberate mendacity for a generation earned them exclusion."

With Congress seeking higher damages and refusing to limit liability, the industry pulled out of the deal: its bid for legitimacy had gone down in flames. Goldstone blamed health advocates for seeking "vengeance" and the "eradication" of his industry, which they had long demonized. The next year, the tobacco companies entered into a smaller settlement with forty-six states for $206 billion (they had already settled with four other states), stopped some forms of marketing most likely to reach kids, and shut down the Tobacco Institute. This deal reduced the immediate threat to the industry but did not confer the liability protections or social legitimacy it had sought.

Surely, one reason an industry cares about its social legitimacy is that being viewed as legitimate by others increases the industry's power. By contrast, being seen as illegitimate—as violating society's shifting moral norms—can threaten an industry's survival, as we saw with the British slave trade. But it also seems important for industry members to actually believe in their own moral legitimacy. There is some psychological research suggesting that power's invigorating impacts on the brain (discussed in chapter 2)—like the heightened inclination to pursue goals and take risks—are diminished if the power holders feels their power is illegitimate. Whether the motive is to preserve a sense of power, achieve tribal belonging, or something else, the very pervasiveness of moral rationalization points to a widespread human need to consider oneself morally good. Having one's livelihood judged immoral by society is distressing.

In 1999, *Business Week* published an article describing just such distress, titled "Philip Morris: Inside America's Most Reviled Company." The company's stock price had fallen by half within a year, and the company had "retreated into itself, creating a self-defensive culture to wall itself off from attack." Its employees were still highly compensated, but an in-house survey showed they wanted management to try again to repair the company's tattered reputation. CEO Geoffrey Bible told *Business Week* that the company was "filled with decent, hard-working people, no different than any other. We go to church. Our children go to school." He added, "We need to do more to restore self-pride amongst our employees . . . and to have our place at the table like any corporation."

Back in the 1950s, industry members said that if they believed smoking was truly harmful, they would not sell cigarettes, and this statement was repeated over and over again into the 1990s. It seems likely these executives had assumed the existence of a social norm that would deny legitimacy to corporations that sold a product they knew caused so much suffering and death. If such a norm ever existed, though, the industry helped demolish it by continuing to sell a product widely known to cause lethal illness.

Some time in the 1990s, tobacco executives started to realize they could openly admit that yes, of course they would keep selling cigarettes even if they knew they were deadly, as long as they were legal. Steven Goldstone, speaking for R. J. Reynolds, said in 1998 of the public health community, "I know these guys love to put this in moral terms, but if they can't convince Congress to ban this product, we don't have any choice but to sell it." This no-choice argument was somewhat surprising from an industry that had for so long defended itself by championing personal freedom of choice and responsibility.

In 2000, with the Justice Department suing the industry for fraud and racketeering, Philip Morris finally stated that it agreed with the overwhelming medical consensus that smoking is addictive and causes lung cancer and other fatal diseases. It would take some of the other companies a few more years to reach this point, but eventually the industry's denials around these essential points of disease causation and addiction crumbled away. (There would remain, though, much denial about the industry's history of deception, manipulation of nicotine levels, and marketing to kids.)

In the new millennium, there was a split within the industry. Philip Morris announced in 2000 that it was ready to accept some kind of FDA regulation. Steven Parrish, the company's general counsel, would explain that the industry was "acutely aware of our poor credibility" and supported regulation partly to "regain respectability." Parrish himself, after years as an aggressive warrior in the tobacco wars, said that when he finally sat down to negotiate with his opponents in 1997, he had found he liked them. He would later tell *New York Times* business columnist Joe Nocera that he found himself agreeing with much of what they said and began to feel ashamed of his past advocacy. "As long as I can remember," he said in 2006, "I thought smoking caused lung cancer, and I said that internally. And I said it was addictive and we should say that." As for his earlier public statements to the contrary, he said he had lapsed into "corporatespeak." He added, "I said a lot of things back then that make my blood curdle now."

In 2009, the Family Smoking Prevention and Tobacco Control Act—a law granting the FDA authority to regulate cigarettes—was finally passed, over the objections of other tobacco companies but not Philip Morris. Indeed, it passed with relatively strong bipartisan support at a time hardly known for bipartisanship. The law does not allow the FDA to ban cigarettes; despite industry claims, there has never been much support for prohibition. But it lets the agency regulate cigarette design and marketing. It also requires the FDA to make tobacco companies put color graphics depicting the health consequences of smoking on its packs and ads. The law essentially recognizes that written warnings can be overwhelmed by the positive images of smoking the industry has long mastered. With images illustrating the written warnings, the government could come closer to fighting fire with fire.

The images the FDA chose were indeed gruesome: tumor-clogged lungs, a cancerous mouth, and an autopsied cadaver, among others. The nation's second-largest tobacco company, R.J. Reynolds, as well as some smaller ones, sued, claiming the pictures were compelled speech that violated their First Amendment rights. In 2012 a federal court agreed, partly because it found the images were designed to evoke a "strong emotional response" rather than to convey "purely factual" information. The court left room for the FDA to try again with other graphic images. The FDA—perhaps because it was having trouble finding images of attractive tumors—delayed for years, got sued by health groups, and in 2018 was ordered by a different federal court to hurry up.

AN UNCERTAIN SOCIAL NORM: IS IT OKAY TO SELL A DEADLY ADDICTIVE PRODUCT IF YOU ADMIT IT?

What does this history tell us about how much dishonesty and how much harm society will tolerate from the people it authorizes to operate under the corporate form? Clearly, causing harm and being dishonest about it can put you on the wrong side of the social norm, though it might take decades for that to happen if your product is hugely popular and addictive. When that dishonesty is finally revealed—even if it was already widely assumed—it will fuel public hostility (as we saw with the documents released in the 1990s), though perhaps only once (as we saw with the lack of fresh outrage over the federal court's 2006 racketeering finding).

To what extent did the industry's dishonesty even matter? How much do scientific facts themselves matter to consumers, especially for a product so dependent on subconscious desires and addiction? The surgeon general's report of 1964, with all its publicity, caused only a small immediate dip in smoking rates. On the other hand, it did mark a turning point for American smoking; the multidecade rise of per capita cigarette consumption and of smoking rates turned into a multidecade fall. In 1965, when the Centers for Disease Control began tracking smoking rates, 42.4 percent of American adults smoked; by 2017, that rate had fallen to 14 percent.

During that period, of course, smoking rates were influenced not just by more information about the danger but by the *social denormalization* of smoking. That process was the result of an antismoking movement, limits on cigarette advertising, antismoking ads, and public smoking restrictions, among other things. Gradually, smokers were bombarded with social signals that their behavior was unwelcome and dangerous to themselves and others, which helped counter the tobacco marketing linking smoking with success, health, and happiness.

So, maybe scientific facts do not have much direct influence on whether someone starts smoking, especially since most smokers start when they are children. And maybe the facts directly persuade only a few people to quit smoking, especially since addiction gives them a powerful incentive to deny those facts. We know factual information can be overwhelmed by social cues in shaping the behavior of individuals (indeed, both recklessly starting smoking and guiltlessly selling cigarettes are hard to understand without viewing the behaviors in light of social signals). But factual information can either be reinforced by social cues or undermined by them. The industry's deceptions over the decades certainly hindered society's attempts to send antismoking cues that would reinforce the facts, delaying the denormalization process. So the industry's denials likely cost some lives because they directly swayed some individuals, but the denials likely cost many more lives because they slowed the critical social denormalization of smoking.

Now that the industry is more honest about the issues of disease causation and addiction, society can focus not so much on the industry's dishonesty as on the harm smoking causes. What is the social norm for an industry that sells a phenomenally dangerous product and admits it? The scientific director of British American Tobacco (which now owns what used to be the second, third, and fourth largest cigarette makers in the United States: Reynolds, Brown and Williamson, and Lorillard) admits that "for a lifetime smoker, about half can expect to die prematurely as a result of their cigarette smoking." Will society keep granting the advantages and protections of the corporate form—an artificial personhood complete with constitutional rights in the United States—to profit-driven enterprises whose success inevitably means widespread suffering and death?

Apparently so, at least for now. As a recent *Wall Street Journal* article put it, tobacco companies in the United States today are "rolling in money," even as ever fewer Americans smoke. The industry is thriving because the remaining smokers—presumably more hard-core than those who have quit—are willing to pay so much; the average price of a pack of cigarettes in the United States rose from $3.73 in 2001 to $6.42 in 2016. While a large share of the added cost goes to government, the tobacco companies are also making a killing, enjoying more revenues while selling far fewer cigarettes.

At the same time, smokers are more likely to be poor; while the national smoking rate may be down to 14 percent, it remains 27 percent for those living below the poverty line. Given the industry's claims about the mental health benefits of smoking, it is worth noting that those with serious mental illness are also much more likely to smoke, including 59 percent of those with schizophrenia (a fact that either strengthens or undermines industry's claims, depending on how you look at it).

THE DECLINE OF SMOKING: CHANGING POLITICS, CHANGING TECHNOLOGIES

The death toll associated with cigarettes is catastrophic. Tobacco is blamed for causing one hundred million deaths worldwide in the twentieth century, more than those killed in both world wars, and during the twenty-first century cigarettes could kill one billion people. The World Health Organization estimates that over seven million people die every year from smoking-related illnesses.

In the United States between 1964 and 2014, nearly twenty-one million people are estimated to have died from smoking-related causes, including over six million from cancer, over seven million from cardiovascular and metabolic diseases, nearly four million from pulmonary diseases, and over two million from secondhand smoke exposure. More than 480,000 people die each year in the United States from smoking-related causes, a figure that dwarfs the nation's combined deaths from all accidents (169,936), suicides (47,173), and murders (19,510).

But things are changing, and not just in richer nations. Although globally nearly a billion people smoke (and the number is growing as the population grows), the share of the population that smokes has fallen steadily since 1990. That year, 35 percent of men and 8 percent of women smoked; in 2015, 25 percent of men and 5 percent of women smoked. This decline is at least partly due to the global antismoking movement and antismoking policies. In 2005, the world's first global health treaty went into force: the Framework Convention on Tobacco Control. At least eighty-eight countries have adopted antismoking measures, often over tobacco company opposition; one study credits these measures with already reducing future smoking-related deaths by twenty-two million.

Another major change is technological—the rise of new nicotine-delivery technologies, like battery-operated e-cigarettes from which users inhale vaporized liquid nicotine. Invented by a Chinese pharmacist whose father died of lung cancer, vaping delivers the nicotine that smokers crave without all the tar that we know causes cancer, heart disease, and other illnesses from combustible cigarettes. E-cigs are considered far less likely to kill their users than regular cigarettes, but that does not mean e-cigs are safe. In September 2019 the Centers for Disease Control launched an investigation into the growing outbreak of a mysterious and severe lung disease among hundreds of "vapers," many of whom were hospitalized and a few of whom died. It is unclear at this point if this disease is caused by vaping nicotine products, marijuana products, or both, but the American Medical Association is urging Americans to stop using all e-cigs until the cause is known.

Research into the long-term effects of vaping is in its infancy, but nicotine is known to establish a particularly powerfully grip on the still-developing brains of teenagers. Alarmingly, vaping among high school kids is surging. The surgeon general calls it an "epidemic," warning that nicotine exposure in adolescence can harm brain development; impair learning, memory, and attention; and increase the risk of addiction to other drugs. A surprising share of the young people taking up vaping are not even aware that these products contain nicotine. Moreover, many e-cigs contain potentially dangerous flavoring additives. E-cig makers claim they do not intend to attract youth, but their products come in kid-appealing flavors like "tutti-frutti," "cupcake," and even "gummy bear."

The public health community has been divided over e-cigs. Some see them as a potential exit ramp helping smokers quit cigarettes, and others as an entrance ramp creating an addiction that will lead toward smoking or prevent smokers from quitting by giving them a way to maintain their addiction when they can't smoke. Suspicion is also being raised by the fact that the giant tobacco companies have moved into the e-cig market, buying up existing brands. The president of the R. J. Reynolds subsidiary selling e-cigs said the company was going down a new path and wants to "make sure we can put this industry on the right side of history." Altria, the parent company of Philip Morris USA, now owns a 35 percent stake in Juul, the dominant e-cig maker; Altria described the deal as part of its effort to "prepare for a future where adult smokers overwhelmingly choose noncombustible products over cigarettes."

Philip Morris International is also talking about a "smoke-free future." The company is betting not just on nicotine-delivering e-cigs but on a different electronic technology that still uses tobacco but heats rather than burns it, which the company claims is much less risky than cigarettes. Its website now says its goal is to "develop, market, and sell smoke-free alternatives, and switch our adult smokers to these alternatives, as quickly as possible around the world." How quickly? The company's CEO, in an interview with the *Wall Street Journal*, suggested that the transition will be "much longer" than forty years. Meanwhile, the company is still marketing cigarettes aggressively around the world and working to oppose the spread of antismoking policies, sometimes covertly.

For a time it seemed the US FDA might accelerate the shift from cigarettes to e-cigs through regulation. FDA commissioner Scott Gottlieb announced a revolutionary plan in 2017 to require cigarette makers to reduce the nicotine in cigarettes to levels that make them "non-addictive." If the plan is actually implemented, cigarettes would surely lose much of their appeal to remaining smokers, and those who couldn't just quit would presumably turn to e-cigs. Gottlieb, who initially delayed e-cig regulation, later proposed steps to reduce youth vaping, but even if those steps failed, removing so much of the nicotine from cigarettes would at least prevent the many new young nicotine addicts from graduating from e-cigs to combustible cigarettes since the latter would no longer be able to satisfy their cravings.

Gottlieb's proposal to force cigarettes to become nonaddictive was astonishing, especially coming from the Trump administration, and it provoked loud objections from the tobacco industry and the political right. In March 2019, Gottlieb abruptly resigned. While he denied any "intrigue" behind his departure, his leaving seems to have halted the agency's push to radically transform the cigarette. E-cig regulation, however, is advancing. After another alarming increase in vaping by youth, in September 2019, the FDA announced plans to ban all e-cig flavors other than tobacco. Juul seems to accept the ban, but the Vapor Technology Association accused President Trump of following the lead of "far left anti-business extremists."

As for the tobacco companies that have created and profited from a product killing seven million people around the world per year, they stand to profit enormously from the products that replace cigarettes. And history tells us that tobacco employees selling these (presumably) less dangerous nicotine products will not do so with any sense of penance for the millions of their customers killed by cigarettes. They will not worry much about the residual or novel risks their newer products may pose or about the addiction they certainly create. Now, in addition to using the traditional categories of denial, they can focus on how many lives they are saving by getting people addicted to something less lethal than cigarettes. Part of the legacy of the tobacco industry's denial of the extreme dangers of cigarettes is that the selling of other dangerous products will be that much easier to rationalize.

Just as the tobacco industry advanced the social norm of smoking cigarettes, it also advanced the social norm of corporate denial. First, it trained society to accept corporate dishonesty by denying the dangers of smoking long after they were obvious. Then, when forced to admit those dangers, the industry trained us to accept corporate irresponsibility as it happily continued to promote and profit from a product that it admitted kills millions. Finally, by rallying other industries to the longer-term project of discrediting science and regulation, the tobacco industry contributed to our current era of social paralysis and distrust. The social norm may have shifted when it comes to cigarettes, at least in many places, but the work to rebuild social trust in government is just getting started.

Another industry that fought regulation was the financial industry, and with great success. While tobacco companies struggled to prevent new laws in the 1990s, the financial industry convinced Congress and key regulators not only to reject new laws designed to prevent systemic risk to the economy but to repeal Depression-era laws. Banks argued that the industry's own profit motive put it in the best position to manage both its own risks and systemic ones. It was an argument that ignored the fact that corporations sometimes willingly profit from actions that hurt their customers and society, as the tobacco industry's predatory behavior had so vividly illustrated.

7 "Bottom Line. Nothing Else Matters"

THE FINANCIAL CRISIS AND A CULTURE OF EXPLOITATION

"We are all here to make as much fucking money as possible. Bottom line. Nothing else matters."

—email from Ameriquest manager to sales force selling subprime loans

In 2008, the world was thrust into the greatest economic crisis since the Great Depression. In economic terms, it caused trillions of dollars in losses. In human terms, it caused tremendous suffering, as millions of people lost their homes, jobs, and life savings. And without an extraordinary and costly effort by the government to prop up the collapsing banks and markets, the impact would have been vastly worse.

The turmoil was triggered by the bursting of housing and credit bubbles, which crippled a global financial system that had become dangerously dependent on high-risk subprime mortgages deceptively packaged into supposedly low-risk securities and derivatives. These financial products hid, amplified, and concentrated financial risk until it inevitably detonated, triggering the global crisis.

The crisis was fueled by broad changes in the incentives, norms, and government oversight of the financial services industry, creating a dangerous culture of runaway greed, recklessness, and exploitation. And both before and after the crisis, there was plenty of denial of the obvious.

This chapter is about how the financial industry (and regulators) denied the existence of a housing bubble, denied the risks of historically lax lending standards and rampant mortgage fraud, denied the dangers of investment products so complex nobody really understood them, and denied the need for regulations to curb the rising risk taking. It is also about the particularly corrupting influence of money on the mind and about how industry members have avoided feeling too badly about causing this global crisis.

SUBPRIME LENDING: "EVERY CLOSING REALLY WAS A
BAIT AND SWITCH"

Key to the financial crisis was the explosion of subprime mortgage lending. Subprimes were costly mortgages designed for people with poor credit who could not qualify for cheaper prime ones because they posed a higher risk of default. Millions of such inherently shaky mortgages would become the ground floor of the financial house of cards that collapsed in 2008.

Subprime lending was spearheaded by a new breed of lenders that would transform the culture of the mortgage industry. Traditionally, mortgages had been made by stodgy banks and savings and loans, who carefully lent out their depositors' money. That all changed with the rise of new nonbank subprime mortgage lending corporations in the 1990s. Many were recently founded by fiercely competitive people in a hurry to get rich. A spokesperson for the Mortgage Bankers Association would say in 1997 of the new entrants, "It's a high-risk, high-return market. . . . It stands to reason you'll have flashier types who worry less about bending the rules."

This would prove a gross understatement. One former loan officer for Ameriquest, the nation's largest subprime lender by 2005, admitted that "every closing that we had really was a bait and switch . . . 'cause you could never get them to the table if you were honest." The industry preyed upon the low-income and financially unsophisticated, but many of them had relatively good credit and could have qualified for cheaper mortgages.

Subprime lenders targeted people who already had a home but needed money. They were urged to refinance their existing low-cost mortgages with new ones and to cash out some of their home equity to help pay bills. The high costs of these refinancings were often hidden. One subprime lender, First American Mortgage Company (FAMCO), was particularly egregious. FAMCO routinely charged 20 points or more—that is, 20 percent of the loan amount—as a fee, adding it to the mortgage. That was an eye-popping fee even for subprime, and when state regulators started poking around, they found that borrowers had no idea the fee was there. "People had no clue," said Prentiss Cox, a Minnesota assistant attorney general who sued FAMCO for violating consumer laws. "They had no clue they had adjustable rate loans. They had no clue they had a teaser rate on the adjustable rate loans. They had no clue they had paid twenty percent."

Hiding a mortgage's true costs was done at Ameriquest too, explained investigative journalist and author, Michael W. Hudson, in his powerful 2010 exposé of the subprime industry, *The Monster: How a Gang of Predatory Lenders and Wall Street Bankers Fleeced America—and Spawned a Global Crisis.* Hudson described Ameriquest salespeople learning to put a document showing a fixed-rate loan at the top of a stack of papers while burying another document with the true adjustable rate near the bottom; once the lender signed the whole stack, they threw out the fixed rate documents. Borrowers would be surprised when, two years later, their payments jumped as their low teaser rate expired. They could refinance again, but would have to pay more hefty fees and a prepayment penalty.

Some loan officers became experts at simply forging customers' signatures or doctoring their tax forms to inflate their incomes. "Whatever you had to do to close a loan, that's what was done," said a former Ameriquest loan agent from a Kansas branch in 2005. "If you had to state somebody's income at $8,000 a month and they were a day-care provider, who's to say it wasn't?" One branch dubbed its break room the "Art Department," because that is where they kept the Wite-Out, tape, and other tools needed to alter documents.

After the first subprime loan, borrowers were often targeted again a year or two later. One former Ameriquest employee said, "The reality was you were screwing people again and again and again." For example, Hudson tells the story of Carolyn, a retired nursing assistant on Social Security who had never finished high school and suffered from heart disease. She owned a small house in Florida and was deluged almost daily with calls from subprime lenders. She finally responded to a pitch from Ameriquest in 2001. The agent promised to lower the interest rate and payments on her existing mortgage, but the papers he persuaded her to sign in fact raised her rates and payments.

In the next three years, as Carolyn struggled with the higher payments, she twice more fell for hard-sell pitches. In the third case, in 2004, two salespeople from Ameriquest showed up unsolicited at her door with a stack of documents. "They just said sign some papers and we'll help you," she recalled. They told her, she said, that they were just preliminary documents to get the process started, but in fact they were binding. Each refinancing put Carolyn deeper in debt, and her payments more than doubled, finally exceeding her Social Security check.

Ameriquest had thousands of salespeople aggressively pushing subprime loans, and some raked in huge commissions. In their illuminating 2010 book *All the Devils Are Here: The Hidden History of the Financial Crisis*, business journalists Bethany McLean and Joe Nocera write that at the height of the subprime bubble recent high school graduates might earn $30,000 to $40,000 per month at Ameriquest. A corporate educator who trained thousands of new hires per year for Ameriquest and others said most of his students were fresh out of school or had been "flipping burgers," but the best at selling subprime mortgages could "easily" earn millions. When salespeople started earning fat commissions, they were urged by managers to buy an SUV or a Mercedes, locking themselves into payments that demanded continued sales.

Ameriquest also cultivated a casino atmosphere by giving prizes to its top sellers, including trips to Vegas and Hawaii and expensive vehicles. Some were flown to corporate headquarters in Orange County, California, where they could play a roulette game called the Big Spin and win cars and other prizes. One loan officer, just out of college, won a Hummer in 2005; he was not that excited, though, saying, "Well, yeah, I've already got one." But for others, the incentives worked; one loan officer told of a colleague who admitted that she got a borrower to buy a high-cost mortgage by flirting with him so he wouldn't notice the hefty fees. The colleague felt bad about it, but she did it because she "wanted to go to Maui so bad."

In addition to the incentive of huge paydays and prizes, employees were under relentless pressure to sell or be fired. Ameriquest salespeople spent long hours on the phone making cold calls, hounded by their managers to sell or leave. One seller who worked in an Ameriquest branch in Michigan in 2003 and 2004 said, "I don't think there's a day that went by that I wasn't told I was going to be fired. . . . I was told I was going to be fired at least 200 times." Another former Ameriquest employee said his office was "a chop shop, and the whip was always being cracked for more." A FAMCO loan officer in Minnesota described how his manager would monitor his conversations with clients and scream at him if he deviated from the script or was hesitant to deceive customers.

Many subprime companies worked with independent mortgage brokers not on their staff. More than 200,000 new mortgage brokers flooded into the field during the housing boom. A past president of the National Association of Mortgage Brokers said about 50,000 of the newcomers were willing to do whatever it took to sell loans, and some were "absolutely" corrupt. Many had criminal records; the *Miami Herald* reported that in Florida alone some 10,500 new brokers had previous criminal convictions, including thousands with a record of fraud, racketeering, or extortion.

In some offices, the frenzied push to sell got a chemical boost. Some Ameriquest employees reportedly kept themselves energized with cocaine. Even without the cocaine, though, loan agents would have been getting a potentially addictive rush from the money they got. Money can stimulate the same primitive, dopamine-releasing reward systems stimulated by drugs. Indeed, brain scans of people who think they are about to make money look virtually the same as brain scans of an addict craving cocaine.

Even in settings not devoted to frenzied profit-seeking, financial incentives will encourage people to lie and cheat, though not as much as traditional economics would suggest. Dan Ariely is a professor of psychology and behavioral economics at Duke University and author of *The (Honest) Truth About Dishonesty: How We Lie to Everyone—Especially Ourselves.* He and his colleagues conducted tests where subjects (college students) were given the opportunity to cheat for money. They found that lots of people cheat a little, but not nearly as much as they could; rather, Ariely explains, their results suggest "we cheat up to the level that allows us to retain our self-image as reasonably honest individuals."

That internal struggle between getting money and feeling good about ourselves can be influenced by situational and social factors. For example, as noted in chapter 1, Ariely's tests found that their subjects cheated more when they saw others cheating. Studies by others suggest cheating goes up when subjects feel they are being underpaid compared to others.

MAKING EXPLOITATION THE NORM: "NOTHING ELSE MATTERS"

Hiring young and inexperienced people likely made it easier to get them to replace their own value system with that of the workplace. Company values were conveyed by rewards and punishments, and in other ways too. In 2000, a Hollywood movie called *Boiler Room* came out; it was about hyperaggressive, hypermacho young salespeople getting rich tricking customers into buying stock in fake companies. The movie became something like a training film or cultural touchstone for Ameriquest, with some new hires actually shown the movie on their first day at the office. Managers hoped, said one former employee, that workers would pick up "the energy, the impact, the driving, the hustling." And in case the message was too subtle, there were reminder emails from managers like the one beginning this chapter.

If you were trying to create a workplace that would get workers to set aside their morals and aggressively exploit others, you might well model it after some of these subprime salesrooms. You would monitor employees closely, continually threatening to fire them if they failed, building a perpetual sense of fear and time pressure. You would reward them lavishly if they succeeded, but you would deliver some of the reward in the form of prizes rather than predictable paychecks to intensify competition and maximize the dopamine jolt. You would encourage a costly lifestyle to make them financially dependent and promote the use of stimulants to keep them working and perhaps to create a costly chemical dependence. And you would show your young hires movies like the *Boiler Room* to suggest that exploiting others is not just an acceptable social norm but even an admirable one (and hope your employees don't dwell on the fact that the movie's characters end up in prison).

Who would try to create such a workplace? Most subprime lenders were founded by outsiders to the mortgage world with a sky's-the-limit attitude toward money and market dominance. Roland Arnall—founder of Ameriquest and often considered the godfather of subprime lending— had set his sights on outdoing Citibank even before he made his first home loan, asking a prospective manager, "How soon can we get to a billion a month?" Russ Jedinak, founder of another subprime lending company, "wanted to be the biggest, richest person in the world," according to a former associate. Brian Chisick, founder of FAMCO, told his new hires, "We are best in the business. FAMCO is going to change your life. Is there anybody here who thinks you can make too much profit?"

The subprime industry really took off between 2001 and 2006, both riding and helping inflate the housing bubble. With housing values rising so fast—especially in cities along the coasts and in the Southwest—there was more equity that homeowners could cash out. And of course, the bubble psychology that has afflicted markets periodically over the centuries took hold. Angelo Mozilo, the cofounder of the massive mortgage lender Countrywide, would later point to a "gold rush" mentality: "Housing prices were rising so rapidly—at a rate that I'd never seen in my 55 years in the business—that people, regular people, average people got caught up in the mania of buying a house, and flipping it, making money."

Now, instead of just trying to hang onto their modest homes and pay their bills, some subprime borrowers were trying to buy homes beyond their means or buy more than one home—an act of either "investment" or "speculation," depending on how you look at it. However, throughout the housing bubble, most subprime loans still went to refinancing existing homes, and most of those buying too-expensive homes or more than one home were prime borrowers. While lots of borrowers made foolish purchases (and millions of them later lost their homes and savings as a result), clearly, the mortgage lenders were more than willing partners in these risky transactions.

Michael Lewis, in his 2010 bestseller, *The Big Short: Inside the Doomsday Machine*, tells the story of certain investors who foresaw the coming financial crisis, in part because they saw how lending standards had plummeted. One investor discovered that the immigrant woman working as his nanny had, with her sister, bought six townhouses. After the first one rose in value, lenders suggested they refinance and use the profit to buy another, until they had six. As Lewis explains, subprime lenders targeted low-income immigrants because their short credit histories gave them high credit scores: they had never defaulted on a debt because they had never been given a loan. For reasons explained below, these high credit scores made them particularly valuable to the mortgage lenders, even though their low incomes made it unlikely they could pay the loans back.

Lending standards dropped in other ways, too. Subprime lenders started offering "stated income" loans, requiring little or no documentation; in the industry these were known as "liar's loans" and were, as one former regulator put it, "open invitations to fraud." Lenders offered "ninja loans"—industry slang for loans to borrowers with no income, no job, and no assets—and "interest-only" loans, meaning that for the first two or three years, borrowers did not have to pay any principal. In October 2005, consumer lawyer Sheila Canavan told the Federal Reserve governors that 61 percent of recent loans in California were interest-only loans. "That's insanity," she warned. "That means we're facing something down the road that we haven't faced before and we are going to be looking at a safety and soundness crisis."

While Ameriquest was large, its influence on the lending culture was even larger. Countrywide had become the nation's largest mortgage provider through prime mortgages; its CEO, Angelo Mozilo, believed the subprime industry was full of "crooks." But Mozilo hated losing market share to Ameriquest, McLean and Nocera reported, so Countrywide waded into subprime, dropping its lending standards to compete. Many traditional commercial banks and thrifts did the same. Some of the biggest banks and thrifts, like Citigroup and Washington Mutual (WaMu) plunged into the subprime market aggressively. WaMu dropped lending standards, pushed high-rate loans, sent top-selling employees to lavish pep-rally-type sales gatherings in Hawaii, sidelined risk officers who warned of a housing bubble, and ignored allegations of widespread mortgage fraud. In this hypercompetitive market, the predatory lenders were so profitable that they helped drag down the standards of the whole industry.

The Financial Crisis Inquiry Commission (FCIC)—an independent panel created by federal law to investigate the causes of the crisis—would note in its 2011 postmortem that the new mortgage operations created by the banks and thrifts were almost always sequestered in nonbank subsidiaries, "leaving them in a regulatory no-man's-land." By 2005, this poorly regulated system would flood the nation with hundreds of billions of dollars' worth of loans at high risk of default.

Of course, the industry I have been describing would make no sense if this was all there was to it. Lending lots of money to people who cannot pay it back is not a winning business strategy. No lender, whether a traditional bank or a flashy new nonbank, would do this if it expected to take the hit when these borrowers defaulted, which many would obviously do when their teaser rates rocketed up in a couple years or when the housing bubble stopped inflating, preventing another refinance.

What let this sketchy industry thrive long enough to create this vast river of high-risk debt was Wall Street's eagerness to take the risk off the lenders' hands and pass it on to others.

INFLATING AND IGNORING LONG-TERM RISK: "I'LL-BE-GONE, YOU'LL-BE-GONE"

When Eric Hibbert, a vice president of the Wall Street investment bank Lehman Brothers, went to visit the FAMCO headquarters in California in 1995, he was disturbed by what he saw. In a memo to his colleagues he wrote, "It is a sweat shop. High pressure sales for people who are in a weak state." He called it a place that requires you to "leave your ethics at the door."

Apparently, though, Lehman Brothers had no problem partnering with an unethical sweatshop. Author Mike Hudson reports that Hibbert's colleagues at Lehman wrote to FAMCO saying, "Lehman Brothers would enthusiastically welcome the opportunity to become a partner in your future growth," and set up a line of credit for it. In a few years, Lehman had become FAMCO's main financier, giving it the money it needed to make its risky loans and then taking those loans off its hands.

Lehman and many other Wall Street banks wanted these loans in order to "securitize" them. The mortgages, as later explained by the FCIC, "would be packaged, sliced, repackaged, insured, and sold as incomprehensibly complicated debt securities to an assortment of hungry investors." They were, in effect, creating a pipeline of toxic mortgages filled with players who, the FCIC concluded, "all believed they could off-load their risks on a moment's notice to the next person in line."

The appeal of subprime mortgages was that while inherently riskier than prime ones, they were also far more profitable on their face, with much higher interest rates and prepayment penalties. Wall Street could sell the securities based on such mortgages at a premium to investors.

What about the risk? Well, by packaging thousands of subprime loans together into securities, the theory went, they were reducing the risk while keeping the high returns. People traditionally defaulted on their mortgages following major personal setbacks like illness, divorce, or unemployment; but those setbacks would hit only a small percentage of the subprime borrowers at a time, so pooling their loans reduced the risk.

But what if something happened to all of them at once that pushed them toward default, like, say, housing prices crashing, making it impossible to refinance yet again? The possibility of the bubble bursting—inevitable as it seemed to many at the time—was ignored. The FCIC found that subprime lenders were "betting that home prices would never stop rising. This was the only scenario that would keep the mortgage machine humming." And the Wall Street bankers enabling those lenders made the same bet. Jamie Dimon, the CEO of JPMorgan Chase, would make this jaw-dropping admission to the FCIC: "In mortgage underwriting, somehow we just missed, you know, that home prices don't go up forever."

Wall Street was so thirsty for subprime mortgages to securitize that it urged lenders to keep dropping their lending standards. One executive of a subprime lender described to McLean and Nocera a meeting in 2003 with representatives from investment bank Bear Stearns. The bankers asked the lender if he could increase the flow of loans. The lender proposed, tongue in cheek, that he could give loans for no down payment and no income documentation to people with very low credit scores. As this lender described it, Bear Stearns enthusiastically accepted this suggestion, and the lender went on to sell the bank massive quantities of such loans. Another, more traditional mortgage lender was told to loosen his standards by a Wall Street bank wanting to buy more subprime mortgages. When the lender asked how he would know if the borrower would pay, he was told, "You don't need to worry about that."

Anecdotes like this illustrate Wall Street's shifting approach to risk in the years before the crisis. Laws enacted after the Depression created two types of Wall Street banks, distinguished largely by different levels of risk and regulation. The first was commercial banks, which took in deposits and made loans to businesses and others. Since these deposits were now federally insured, the banks were more heavily regulated to keep their risk-taking low.

The second type was the investment banks. They were not federally insured so needed less regulatory oversight. They took greater risks, but largely with the money of richer investors willing and able to accept greater risk in search of greater returns. Investment banks also traded in securities, both in their own name and on behalf of clients. The five most prominent investment banks in the precrisis era were Goldman Sachs, Merrill Lynch, Morgan Stanley, Lehman Brothers, and Bear Stearns.

For decades, risk-taking by investment banks was kept in check by the fact that they were private partnerships. If the investment banks lost money, the partners themselves took the hit. One banking veteran told author Joris Luyendijk that early in his career, when his bank was still a partnership, he had proposed a clever trade to one of the partners; that partner "looked at me and said: 'Don't forget, this is my money you're fucking with.'" After the crisis, Luyendijk interviewed over two hundred members of the financial industry, promising them anonymity to get them to speak freely about their experiences and quoting them in his revealing book *Among the Bankers: A Journey into the Heart of Finance*. (Although his subjects worked in London, the financial cultures of London and Wall Street are intertwined, and the leading firms in each city have branches in the other.)

Over the years, the private partnerships had transformed themselves into publicly traded corporations. Merrill Lynch went public in 1971, and most of the others went public in the 1980s; Goldman Sachs, the last holdout among the major firms, went public in 1999. Their new corporate structure flooded these firms with capital. It also ushered in a seismic shift in culture. In the words of business writer William D. Cohan, the "small, intimate petri dishes of greed and caution" that were the Wall Street partnerships were turned into a "Darwinian free-for-all, where bankers, traders, and executives were rewarded for taking big risks with other people's money." In fact, Luyendijk reveals, industry members adopted the expression "It's only OPM—Other People's Money."

Knowingly or not, they were quoting Adam Smith, who predicted this precise shift in risk-taking attitudes centuries ago. Smith worried that corporations would never be as prudent with money as partnerships, noting that the directors of joint stock companies, as he called corporations, "being the managers rather of other people's money than of their own, it cannot well be expected, that they should watch over it with the same anxious vigilance" as partners in a partnership.

Going public also shortened investment bankers' time horizon. Partners work together over the years to build something both profitable and lasting, but shareholders are not so patient. They pressure bank managers to show profits every quarter, and they care less and know less about long-term risk. (Of course, Wall Street had been putting just such pressure to show short-term earnings on the rest of the corporate world for years, so it could hardly complain.) The bank executives in turn pressured their employees to close a high volume of deals with big up-front payments. Soon Wall Street pay packages were tied to short-term income regardless of long-term risk.

This short-termism was reflected in another commonly heard code that emerged on Wall Street in the precrisis years. Bankers who expressed worry about what might happen with an investment in the future were told to relax: IBGYBG, or "I'll be gone, you'll be gone."

A VICIOUS HYPERCOMPETITION: "RIP OUT THEIR HEART AND EAT IT BEFORE THEY DIE"

While recent high school graduates were chasing bonuses in the thousands at the subprime lending companies, recent Ivy League graduates were chasing bonuses in the millions on Wall Street. The major banks recruit only from the most elite schools, and over the years Wall Street has vacuumed up a colossal share of their graduates. In 2005 and 2006, for example, 40 percent of Princeton graduates went into financial services. They were attracted partly by the lure of, as one recent hire put it, being surrounded by the "smartest and most ambitious people."

But, as in the subprime lending world, money was surely the biggest draw. Karen Ho—an anthropologist who worked briefly on Wall Street and then studied its culture and wrote *Liquidated: An Ethnography of Wall Street*—attended an employee orientation at an investment bank in 1996. A managing director shouted, "Show me the money!" and "You will be making more money than you ever dreamed possible," to a standing ovation from the fist-pumping, cheering new hires. Ho asked a hundred or so investment bankers why people worked on Wall Street; every one of them listed the money, though not necessarily as the only reason.

Certainly, nobody would have listed job security. When the investment banks became corporations, they started viewing their employees through a shorter-term lens, to be quickly hired and fired as firms chased the latest market trend. Ho describes how bankers were in constant danger of losing their jobs, often within a couple years of being hired, even during boom times. Journalist Joris Luyendijk, who also has a background in anthropology, described how London bankers are similarly subject to routine rounds of sudden firings (which they called, with a kind of bovine acceptance, "the cull"). One of the bankers said his boss used to tell him, "Every day you're getting closer to getting fired." The message is clear: your work for the bank is not a long-term relationship; it is a series of short-term financial transactions. If one day you are not making money fast enough, the transactions abruptly end and you are escorted from the building.

This utter lack of job security, which Wall Street shared with the subprime industry, has a predictable consequence: employees feel an urgency to milk the present, taking home as much money as possible as quickly as possible. It also corrodes any larger loyalty to the firm. One recently laid-off Lehman Brothers analyst told Ho that she had not fit in because "you need to be thinking I'm going to get as much as I can today because you don't know what is going to happen tomorrow. . . . You've just got to be that way. Think about yourself and only yourself."

Making lots of money fast is also a way to rationalize the personal sacrifice represented by the notoriously brutal work hours (often over one hundred hours a week). Ho was told by many she interviewed that Wall Street "deliberately recruits college graduates straight out of the gate (not those who have taken time off) in order to pick the most eager, fresh-faced, driven, young, unattached analysts, so they can be worked to the breaking point." As at the subprime lenders, it would be easier to get such people to accept the moral norms of the workplace, isolated as they become from family, friends, and competing meaningful pursuits.

Wall Street's annual bonus system increases the insecurity, competition, and urgency to make deals. After the first few years, the bonus becomes the lion's share of one's pay, but unlike a simple commission system, the actual amount is unknown until paid. Top executives extract their own hefty share of the bonus pool and then use their discretion to slice up the rest, considering the performance of the firm, each department, and each person. The process erodes any sense of team loyalty; at bonus time, according to one vice president, people are "trying to shove each other out of the way, saying 'I did the most. I spent the most hours. . . . I made the biggest contribution.'"

In time, those who stay see the money as no more than they deserve, given their long hours, stress, and sacrifice. And comparing themselves to other bankers lets them still feel underpaid. Sam Polk, a former Wall Street trader, explained in an article for the *New York Times* that "when the guy next to you makes $10 million, $1 million or $2 million doesn't look so sweet." Polk described the money as addictive, but also as a crucial marker of power, status, and a person's innate value. Another trader explained to Luyendijk that after a big bonus: "You think, *wow, so this is what I am worth.* That term in itself is telling: 'worth.'" A former Goldman Sachs banker described the bank's culture to the *London Times* in 2009 as "completely money-obsessed. I was like a donkey driven forward by the biggest, juiciest carrot I could imagine. Money is the way you define your success. There's always room—need—for more. If you are not getting a bigger house or a bigger boat, you're falling behind. It's an addiction."

Neuroscientists have indeed shown that, as with addictive drugs, the thrill of making money wears off with repetition; as the brain adapts, it takes more and more money to release the same amount of dopamine and deliver the same high. But research also suggests, like these quotes, that it is not just the money but the social signal of worth that comes with it; one study has shown that money acquired by chance does not trigger the same insatiability as money we view as a signal of our skill.

It is also important to understand the front-loaded nature of the bonus. An investment banker told Luyendijk that many of the securities he sold ran over several years, creating an anticipated stream of income. The banker's share of those expected profits are booked the year of the sale. "Obviously if you can book the future revenue of the next seven years in one go, that's a huge number." He added, "You don't need to maintain a relationship over many years. Sell a client one product and bang, you're there." That "bang"—the relative immediacy of the reward—is also neurologically relevant: a quick buck activates the primitive brain systems linked to impulsiveness and addiction; delayed income activates the calmer brain systems linked to deliberation.

This short-term perspective means people have much less reason to care about their customers' welfare. Adam Smith famously wrote that "it is not from the benevolence of the butcher, the brewer, or the baker that we expect our dinner, but from their regard to their own interest." But the theory of an invisible hand turning people's pursuit of self-interest into public benefits assumes those people have an eye to the future. We trust the butcher not to sicken us with contaminated meat partly because it could destroy his reputation and future sales; he has a financial incentive (beyond whatever benevolence he may also feel) to keep his customers happy *if* he plans to stick around. That's why it is so dangerous when the most powerful institutions in the financial world are filled with people who can't see past short-term profits. Their incentive to treat others well fades, while the incentive to exploit others grows blindingly bright.

Wall Street investment banks apparently used to pride themselves on their culture of client service. In the words of one former banker at Goldman Sachs—Wall Street's most powerful investment bank—the firm once embraced "teamwork, integrity, a spirit of humility, and always doing right by our clients." This employee, Greg Smith, left Goldman in 2012 because he felt there was virtually no trace of that culture left. And he didn't go quietly. In a blistering *New York Times* op-ed the day he quit, he wrote that it made him "ill how callously people talk about ripping their clients off," and how rather than trying to help clients—who Goldman's managing directors routinely referred to as "muppets"—they were interested only in making the most money possible out of them. (It is worth noting here that at least one psychological study has found that people who report a strong attachment to money are also much more likely to objectify other people. Of course, objectified or dehumanized people are easier to harm without moral qualms.) Smith later explained that when selling derivatives to clients, the company would bury the risk warnings "in the fine print of the ten-page disclaimer at the end of the contract," not unlike subprime lenders burying the true cost of a mortgage.

The language bankers used to describe their work to Luyendijk did not exactly suggest a nurturing culture of client service. Bankers told him that given the chance you should "rip your client's face off." A lucrative deal or trade was described as a "rape and pillage" or "slash and burn." People remarked that in the world of finance it was "have lunch or be lunch," and that the "sheep get slaughtered." Journalist and author William D. Cohan, in his book *House of Cards: A Tale of Hubris and Wretched Excess on Wall Street*, quotes a source who explained that, following a trade with a customer they expected to profit from, Bear Stearns traders might say, "I just ripped that fucker's head off."

This brutal attitude toward their clients may be a spillover from investment bankers' general hypercompetitiveness. A chilling video recorded at Lehman Brothers shows Dick Fuld, the firm's famously combative CEO, telling a room full of employees that, when it came to investors who were depressing his company's stock price, "I want to reach in, rip out their heart and eat it before they die." The look on his face indicated he was not entirely kidding.

Maybe we cannot count on the butcher's benevolence to feed us, but it is not too much to expect that the butcher will not want to rip our faces off. Surely, some fraction of this flesh-ripping talk is just posturing, but if bankers hear enough of it, the message gets through and a social norm develops. In its mildest version the norm is "Don't let empathy for others slow down your chase for money." A harsher version is "Rip off others because it is thrilling and proves your dominance."

It makes sense that investment banking would attract people who are aggressive, enjoy risk, and are especially motivated by money, and the profession itself enhances these traits. John Coates, a former Wall Street trader turned neuroscientist, studies the biology of market bubbles, and his focus goes beyond dopamine to testosterone. He notes that when male animals compete, their testosterone rises in anticipation of the contest, and afterward the winner's testosterone rises even more, causing a spiral that in time can make the animal more aggressive, oblivious to risk, and more likely to die. Similarly, successful trades raise traders' testosterone and increase their confidence and appetite for financial risk; a long winning streak can make traders as "delusional, overconfident and risk-seeking" as the aggressive and danger-oblivious animals. (In Coates's experience, women, with 10–20 percent of the testosterone levels of men, were relatively immune to such bubble-inflating mania.)

Social psychologists, too, have been studying how money affects the mind, especially people's attitudes toward others, with findings that are disturbing but controversial. They have set up experiments where people are primed to think of money, often in some subtle way like seeing images or words related to money while doing other tasks. Studies like these suggest that reminders of money make people more willing to accept social inequality, less prosocial, and less helpful and charitable, while also making them more self-sufficient and less likely to ask others for help. However, some of these findings have been challenged by other researchers who have tried but failed to replicate them, an example of the larger controversy within psychology. The heightened scrutiny is leading to stronger protocols that will presumably put such research on a firmer scientific footing, but meanwhile a question mark hangs over some findings, especially the more statistically marginal ones.

Of course, the financial world itself gives ample evidence that people will exploit each other for money. Defenders of the system—those who do not object to bankers trying to exploit trading partners and clients—turn to the justifying principle of caveat emptor, or let the buyer beware. Bankers say the principle is especially used when dealing with other "professionals," and they stress that their clients—largely pension funds, hedge funds, and other institutional investors—are sophisticated professionals (when they are not dismissing them as "muppets"). "With them it's anything goes, really," explained one banker. "The assumption is that professional counterparties should know what they are doing."

INNOVATING INCOMPREHENSIBLE PRODUCTS: "A THING WHICH HAS NO PURPOSE"

In fact, the professional counterparties did not know what they were doing, partly because the products Wall Street was selling them were so opaque. Investors depended on the three companies that have cornered the market on ratings—Standard and Poor's, Moody's, and Fitch—to analyze them and judge the risk.

Those high-risk subprime mortgages that homeowners took out from Ameriquest and other lenders were bought and "structured" by Wall Street into a dizzying array of financial products sold to investors. The new products were considered a form of technological innovation because they were devised using complex computer models. Thousands of mortgages would be combined into a mortgage bond that was divided into slices, or "tranches," creating a sort of tower of debt. The lowest tranches gave investors the highest yield but faced the highest risk. Like people living on the ground floor being the first submerged in a flood, they suffered the losses first if borrowers defaulted. The riskier lower levels were given relatively low ratings of BBB or below, but the upper floors, representing the vast majority of the debt, were given the highest AAA rating by the ratings agencies, even though they too were composed of shaky subprime mortgages.

Then the banks started combining the risky, hard-to-sell BBB tranches into a whole new tower of debt called a collateralized debt obligation, or CDO. The bankers convinced the ratings agencies that, because of the benefits of diversification, this collection of the riskiest slices of other collections of high-risk mortgages was now mostly risk-free. The BBB tranches were turned into new securities mostly rated AAA. Between 2003 and 2007, Wall Street issued almost $700 billion in such CDOs, and in the words of the FCIC, "The CDO became the engine that powered the mortgage supply chain." In time, the lower levels of the CDOs were themselves packaged into other CDOs, creating a product called CDOs-squared.

Another financial product played a huge role in creating the crisis: credit default swaps, or CDSs. These products—one type of a larger class of derivatives—are often compared to insurance policies. The seller of the CDS essentially promises to pay off a debt if the borrower defaults; the buyer of the CDS pays for that protection through premium-like payments. Investors in CDOs could buy this insurance, making the CDOs seem virtually risk-free. One big difference between a CDS and insurance, though, is that by law you can only insure something you actually own. I cannot take out an insurance policy on my neighbor's house. However, someone who did not own a particular CDO but who predicted it would be defaulted on could buy a swap insuring it (called a naked credit default swap); if this CDO failed, the buyer would rake in a windfall.

And then Wall Street started collecting many swaps from those selling them and packaged them in a new product called a synthetic CDO. Unlike other CDOs, synthetic ones did not help finance any home purchases because they contained no actual mortgages; this was handy because after a while Wall Street had a hard time acquiring as many subprime loans to securitize as it wanted. In essence, Wall Street had created a gigantic unregulated casino, where those who expected the collapse of the sub-prime-mortgage-backed house of cards could place enormous bets against those who thought the house of cards would keep growing. The billions that went into these side bets meant that when the inevitable defaults began, the losses were multiplied, triggering the shock wave that would bring the financial system to its knees.

Who was betting the market would collapse? In some cases, it was hedge funds that could see what was about to happen. In two notorious cases, hedge funds betting against CDOs were allowed by investment banks to play a behind-the-scenes role in building the CDOs, without the knowledge of those buying them; these hedge funds profited hugely when the CDOs failed. (Goldman and Merrill Lynch would both later pay fines to settle SEC charges for their role in these deals.) But some investment banks also started betting that the housing market would drop, meaning the financial products they were still selling to their clients would fail. A congressional investigation would find that Goldman, for instance, saw evidence that subprime defaults were accelerating in December 2006, and then it "quietly and abruptly reversed course," betting against the market while continuing to create and sell subprime products to clients. Goldman took some mortgage losses in 2007, but thanks to these bets its losses were overwhelmed by its gains.

What did the bankers themselves think of their complex products? There is evidence that they did not really understand them and knew they did not, and that even though they considered the products somewhat monstrous, they were still having fun creating them. Fabrice Tourre was a young Goldman trader involved in selling synthetic CDOs, including the hedge fund–influenced CDO that brought SEC's civil fraud charges against Goldman (and him personally). Goldman would settle for $550 million, while Tourre would face trial, lose, and be fined $825,000. Tourre is a rare example of an individual actually found liable for these products and is sometimes seen a scapegoat, given his low status at the bank.

Due to the controversy surrounding that deal, some of Tourre's intimate emails would become public. An odd blend of sweet nothings and financial prognostications, the emails give a peek into the mind of someone at the center of the storm. In one email to a girlfriend in January 2007, as the mortgage market was starting to wobble, Tourre wrote lightheartedly about an article warning that the entire system might crumble at any moment, predicting that he (writing about himself in third person) might be the sole survivor, "standing in the middle of all these complex, highly levered, exotic trades he created without necessarily understanding all the implications of those monstruosities [*sic*]!!!"

A few days later Tourre wrote, "When I think that I had some input into the creation of this product (which by the way is a product of pure intellectual masturbation, the type of thing which you invent telling yourself: 'Well, what if we created a "thing," which has no purpose, which is absolutely conceptual and highly theoretical and which nobody knows how to price?') it sickens the heart to see it shot down in mid-flight. . . . It's a little like Frankenstein turning against his own inventor ;)." The winky-face emoticon in his email, as much as his words, reveals a disturbing lack of seriousness in someone manufacturing the type of risky products that would be at the center of the global crisis to come.

Tourre was writing in 2007, after years of frenzied Wall Street selling had mutated innovations that were once the subject of high, even apparently idealistic, hopes. Gillian Tett, journalist for the *Financial Times* and author of the 2009 book *Fool's Gold: How Unrestrained Greed Corrupted a Dream, Shattered Global Markets, and Unleashed a Catastrophe*, describes how bankers at JPMorgan pioneered the development of a new type of derivative.* Derivatives were already being used to manage financial risks like shifting interest rates and currency values, but what if they were used to manage the risk of a borrower defaulting on a debt—in Tett's words, "the risk most central to the traditional craft of banking"?

In 1994, the JPMorgan team believed this new derivative—the credit default swap (CDS) discussed above—would transform banking and release a great wave of capital into the economy. Mark Brickell, a JPMorgan banker who would play a major role in keeping derivatives

---

* Derivatives are defined by the FCIC as "financial contracts whose prices are determined by, or 'derived' from, the value of some underlying asset, rate, index, or event. They are not used for capital formation or investment, as are securities; rather, they are instruments for hedging business risk or for speculating on changes in prices, interest rates, and the like."

unregulated, later said, "I've known people who worked on the Manhattan Project—for those of us on that trip, there was the same kind of feeling of being present at the creation of something incredibly important." Veteran investors would also compare derivatives in general to nuclear bombs—however, not with excitement but with alarm. In 1993, Felix Rohatyn warned that derivatives were financial hydrogen bombs, built on personal computers by twenty-six-year-olds with MBAs. A decade later, investor Warren Buffet would call derivatives "financial weapons of mass destruction."

One might also compare these financial innovations to another radio-active milestone, the discovery of radium. The financial industry's attitude toward its potent and mysterious new financial products echoed the attitude a century earlier toward that potent and mysterious new element. In both cases, an aura of wizardry surrounded the creators: the Wall Street "quants" (quantitative analysts) tapping into the power of computer modeling and the earlier era's scientists and doctors tapping into the power of radioactivity. In both cases, idealism about the innovations was soon supplanted by self-serving commercial claims about the products' benefits and self-serving denials about their risks. The products' inherent risks—the potential to be badly burned by concentrations of either radium or financial risk—were obvious, but in both cases people diluted that risk enough that it was no longer easily detectable. That let them claim that these products were safe enough to market to the world, and they did so aggressively, ultimately causing great public harm.

Did Wall Street really believe that the vast default risks accumulating in the subprime realm had been transformed into safe investments? Many on Wall Street apparently never understood the risk, lost sight of it in the face of all that money, or at least miscalculated when the bubble would burst. Many banks kept enough of this toxic debt on their own books to cause them crippling losses. In the parlance of the industry, they "ate their own cooking." It was a little like Joe Flannery spreading his company's radioactive waste on his own garden, except where Flannery soon died, possibly due to radiation-induced illness, most of the Wall Street leaders escaped with large personal fortunes earned during the bubble years.

As for hurting their clients, that was relatively easy to ignore since the future investment losses would largely fall on a distant group of strangers;

people have been shown to have less empathy when victims are unidentifiable, when there are multiple victims, and when they are far away. The abstract nature of finance, especially global finance, makes it easier to see it as just a big game and ignore or casually dismiss the human consequences. For example, months after acknowledging that the market for his monstrous products could soon collapse, Goldman's Tourre emailed about having just sold more of them to Belgian "widows and orphans."

Tourre and his Wall Street colleagues could never have sold these investment products to conservative investors like pension funds without the seal of approval of the ratings agencies. Moody's alone gave nearly 45,000 mortgage-related securities a triple-A rating between 2000 and 2007. How could sophisticated organizations that exist for the purpose of calculating investment risk not have seen the subprime risk? They too had a powerful financial incentive to be blind. The agencies are paid by bankers, who can shop for the ratings they want. One former Moody's managing director was asked if the investment banks threatened to withdraw their business if a rating was too low. He answered, "Oh God, are you kidding? All the time. I mean, that's routine. I mean, they would threaten you all of the time. . . . It's like, 'Well, next time, we're just going to go with Fitch and S&P.'"

Ratings analysts knew they were not providing a sound measure of risk. That was partly because they did not have the underlying loan-level data they needed and were not allowed by their market-share-focused managers to demand it. In late 2006, one Standard and Poor's analyst wrote in an email chain, "Ratings agencies continue to create [an] even bigger monster—the CDO market. Let's hope we are all wealthy and retired by the time this house of cards falters." The IBGYBG philosophy that had infected Wall Street banks had spread to the ratings agencies.

Meanwhile, Wall Street figured out how to exploit loopholes and blind spots in the computer models that the agencies used to rate risk. For example, it learned that it could get a higher rating if recent immigrants were included in the borrower pool; as noted above, they had high credit scores because they had so little credit history and the models did not factor that in. And some on Wall Street clearly held the lower-paid staff of the ratings agencies in intellectual contempt; a quantitative analyst who engineered mortgage bonds for Morgan Stanley told Michael Lewis that the agency staff who rated subprime mortgage bonds were "basically like brain-dead."

In 2010, Lloyd Blankfein, Goldman's chair and CEO, appeared before the Financial Crisis Inquiry Commission to offer his insights into why the crisis happened. Among the factors he listed was a "systematic lack of skepticism . . . with respect to credit ratings. Rather than undertake their own analysis, too many financial institutions relied on the rating agencies to do the central work of risk analysis." He also blamed people's failure to use their own judgment when it came to risk, relying instead on "risk models."

In other words, investors were fools to trust the agencies' ratings of the unsafe products Wall Street was selling. They should have known, perhaps, that Wall Street would corrupt the ratings process by threatening to withhold its business and skillfully exploiting computer model defects.

TRUSTING MARKETS TO SELF-REGULATE: "A FLAW IN THE MODEL"

Among the things that the financial industry denied in the precrisis years was that subprime lending or derivatives needed to be regulated. Countrywide's Angelo Mozilo told a lobbyist, "No regulator is going to tell me what kind of products I can offer." Some investment bankers held the regulators themselves in contempt. Luyendijk quotes a trader explaining that "the trouble is, regulators are idiots. I am sorry to put it so bluntly but you can't expect it any other way. Why would a smart, aggressive, competitive 22-year old decide to work for the regulators?"

More broadly, many on Wall Street believed as a matter of ideology that financial markets were so smart, self-disciplined, and risk-aware that they did not need government oversight to behave responsibly. Even before the rise of credit default swaps, there was a push to regulate derivatives because of their complexity and inherently high leverage. A 1994 cover story in *Fortune* began, "Like alligators in a swamp, derivatives lurk in the global economy. Even the CEOs of companies that use them don't understand them." The article warned that derivatives could ten years into the future become "a villain, or even the villain, in some financial crisis that sweeps the world." It would take fourteen years, not ten, for the prophecy to come true.

The General Accounting Office similarly warned that derivatives threatened the entire financial system and called for regulation. Four bills on derivatives were introduced in Congress that summer, and Wall Street unleashed a fierce lobbying campaign to stop them.

The campaign was led by JPMorgan's Mark Brickell, who headed a derivatives trade group. Tett describes Brickell as a passionate libertarian who often said, "I am a great believer in the self-healing power of markets. . . . Markets can correct excess far better than any government. Market discipline is the best form of discipline there is." For Brickell, Tett writes, "the battle in Washington was not about mere business, it was an ideological fight of the highest order." A congressional aide who favored the legislation said that the derivatives dealers' attitude during this campaign was basically "How dare anybody question the functioning of this market! How presumptuous!" But the campaign worked. All four of the bills were killed, in what Tett calls "one of the most startling triumphs for a Wall Street lobbying campaign in the twentieth century."

Wall Street's efforts were helped enormously by the chairman of the Federal Reserve, Alan Greenspan, who shared Brickell's ideological faith in markets. Greenspan opposed the derivatives legislation, telling Congress that the risks "in financial markets, including derivatives markets, are being regulated by private parties. . . . There is nothing involved in federal regulation per se which makes it superior to market regulation."

Greenspan's position had deep ideological roots. Greenspan was not merely a fan of libertarian guru and novelist Ayn Rand but actually part of her cultlike* inner circle since the 1950s. Rand's philosophy celebrated selfishness as a virtue, held that an individual's "only moral purpose" was his or her own happiness, embraced an extreme form of laissez-faire capitalism, and rejected economic regulation as immoral. Greenspan's antiregulatory ideology did not stop him from rising to the pinnacle of economic

---

*Was it really cultlike? Well, Greenspan and others in Rand's group signed in 1968 a decree essentially excommunicating two other members, one of whom had a long-term affair with Rand but then cheated on her. The decree said that because the two "have betrayed fundamental principles of Objectivism [the name Rand gave her philosophy], we condemn and repudiate these two persons irrevocably."

regulatory power, but it surely disinclined him from using that power. Another effort to regulate derivatives in 1998 was blocked by Greenspan and the industry, and in 2000 Congress passed a law explicitly *preventing* regulation of derivatives. The FCIC would call this "a key turning point in the march toward the financial crisis."

Congress had already removed a pillar of post-Depression banking regulation when in 1999 it repealed a law known as Glass-Steagall, which had kept commercial banks from taking on the riskier activities of investment banks, like trading in securities. Glass-Steagall had been greatly eroded over the years by the Federal Reserve's loosening interpretations, but it was finally eliminated after hundreds of lobbyists descended on Congress. Citicorp, the nation's largest financial firm, led the charge because Citi would otherwise have had to undo its recent megamerger with Traveler's Insurance, which owned investment bank Salomon Smith Barney (the repealing legislation was known as the "Citi-Travelers Act" on Capitol Hill). The repeal of Glass-Steagall was a milestone in the commercial banking industry's cultural shift toward aggressive risk taking. It would let Citigroup (as it became post-merger) and other commercial banks plunge even more deeply into subprime lending and securities, helping inflate the bubble. When the bubble burst, Citigroup would suffer such huge losses that Treasury officials started calling it "the Death Star"; it needed a bigger federal bailout than any other bank.

Meanwhile, mortgage lending standards were plummeting and mortgage fraud was skyrocketing. The FBI held a press conference in 2004 warning that mortgage fraud "has the potential to become an epidemic." Many states tried to clamp down on predatory lending, winning legal judgments against FAMCO, Ameriquest, and others, and passing stricter lending laws. However federal bank supervisors (at the Office of the Comptroller of the Currency and the Office of Thrift Supervision) actively preempted many of these state actions and urged more banks to pursue a national charter, which would give them immunity from many state laws.

The one federal agency that had clear authority to stop subprime predatory lending by both banks and nonbanks was the Federal Reserve. Consumer advocates appealed to the Fed repeatedly over the years to use that authority and were infuriated by its failure to act. Greenspan was even urged to tighten supervision of subprime lending by another member of the Federal Reserve's Board of Governors, but Greenspan was opposed. The FCIC would find that the Federal Reserve had "neglected its mission 'to ensure the safety and soundness of the nation's banking and financial system and to protect the credit rights of consumers.'"

Sheila Bair, appointed head of the Federal Deposit Insurance Corporation (FDIC) by President Bush in 2006, spoke the next year to a group of young Wall Street deal makers, encouraging them to support restructuring the tidal wave of subprime mortgages then heading for default. One member of her audience explained to her that it was not possible to help "these people," the subprime borrowers, because if they are given a break, "they will just go out and buy a flat-screen TV." When she asked why, if he felt that way, they were lending to them, he answered, "Bad regulation." Bair concluded, "So much for the self-regulating market."

In October 23, 2008, as the financial markets were seizing up and the economy was plummeting, Greenspan admitted to the House Oversight Committee that "those of us who have looked to the self-interest of lending institutions to protect shareholder's equity, myself especially, are in a state of shocked disbelief."

Chairman Henry Waxman pressed him about his failure to regulate subprime lending and his years of fighting regulation of derivatives. He asked if Greenspan's antiregulatory, free-market ideology had pushed him to make decisions that he wished he had not made. Greenspan answered, "Yes, I found a flaw, I don't know how significant or permanent it is, but I have been very distressed by that fact. . . . I found a flaw in the model that I perceived is the critical functioning structure that defines how the world works, so to speak." The flaw in the model that shocked Greenspan was the failure of the banks' pursuit of self-interest to protect the banks' shareholders, but the more consequential flaw from the perspective of humanity was the failure of the bankers to resist the opportunity to exploit others and gravely damage the global economy in their pursuit of short-term profits.

AN INDUSTRY ON DEFENSE: JUST "DOING GOD'S WORK"

For the industry, the financial crisis really became terrifying with the bankruptcy of Lehman Brothers, in September 2008. Its CEO, Dick ("rip their heart out and eat it") Fuld, was unable to get other banks to save his firm, and the federal government also refused to save it. Investors started to panic, partly because they did not know where this toxic debt—so thoroughly distributed and concealed by derivatives—was currently positioned. Some bankers thought society itself was on the brink of chaos, recalling to Luyendijk that they called their families and told them to hoard food and cash and get ready to "evacuate the kids to the countryside." Some bankers were reportedly stocking up on guns, "ready to bed down in bunkers if civil society collapsed."

Civil society did not collapse, partly because the United States and other governments stepped in to prop up the financial system. But the damages were still profound and lasting, including severe damage to people's faith in markets, governments, and other institutional pillars of society.

In the face of such widespread human suffering, shame flooded throughout the industry. Most on Wall Street became deeply introspective, examining their own role in causing the wreckage. Bankers saw they had created workplaces that inflamed people's innate greed and competitiveness while dampening their empathy, making deception and exploitation inevitable. They conceded that they had long been overpaid, that the heavy flow of money impaired their judgment about risk and morality, and that the financial system would function far better if people were paid less and pressured less to make short-term profits. They admitted that they had created products that were inherently dangerous because they hid systemic risk, and other products that were nothing but speculative side bets that amplified the risk without providing any social benefits. They acknowledged that they had corrupted the private sector system put in place to protect investors (the ratings agencies) and had used their power to undo or block the public laws that might have prevented the crisis. Most industry leaders not only resigned but donated much of their fortunes to funds to help defrauded borrowers and investors. The industry has in the years since its bailout fully supported creation of a robust regulatory system, recognizing the need for government oversight.

Okay, no. As you probably realized by the first sentence, the previous paragraph is a bit of social fiction, imagining how the industry might have responded if it had very different social norms. Most of us would have been stunned if the industry had responded with so much honest remorse and responsibility, which shows how low our expectations are under current social norms.

In fact, although there were a few expressions of contrition, the dominant tone from the industry after the crisis was one of blame-evasion, defensiveness, and before long, grievance. Andrew Ross Sorkin, author of *Too Big to Fail: The Inside Story of How Wall Street and Washington Fought to Save the Financial System—and Themselves,* interviewed more than two hundred sources, including many at the front lines of managing the crisis. He reported in 2010 that while the bankers have some sense of remorse, "they see this as a crisis with many fathers so they consider themselves to be almost blameless" and many "feel vilified now." This many-fathers defense is an example of the kind of diffusion of responsibility that psychologist Albert Bandura identified as enabling moral disengagement.

Among the other fathers the industry has pointed to were the historically low interest rates that inflated the bubble, lots of foreign savings looking for high-yield investments, federal housing policies encouraging home ownership, and the role of Fannie Mae and Freddie Mac.* While some of these factors did set the stage for what happened and contributed to the crisis, the dangerous mortgage-securitization frenzy that followed was hardly an inevitable response. The compulsion driving the predatory subprime mortgage lenders and the bankers selling overrated mortgage-backed securities was not a compulsion to comply with federal housing laws.

Some industry leaders argued that the crisis was a rare and unforeseeable confluence of factors comparable to a natural disaster. Goldman CEO Lloyd Blankfein compared it to an extraordinary series of hurricanes. The FCIC rejected this argument. While the timing and scale of the crisis was hard to predict, there had been clear warning signs, including the unprecedented housing bubble and the historically low lending standards.

Others cast blame widely and away from Wall Street. After the crisis, Robert Benmosche was brought in to run AIG, a company that sold billions

---

*Fannie Mae and Freddie Mac are private corporations, but they enjoy the implied guarantee of the federal government and have a mission to support home ownership as well as to earn profits for shareholders. They followed Wall Street's lead in expanding into subprime securities, helping inflate the bubble, but the majority of FCIC members found that they were not central to the crisis. However, a minority of FCIC members issued a dissenting statement that put more blame on Fannie and Freddie.

of dollars' worth of credit default swaps and needed a massive bailout, attracting particular public scorn. Benmosche told the *Wall Street Journal* that everyone just wants a villain for the crisis; "The problem is that there isn't a villain. There are villains. And they are everybody. They are the speculators in real estate. The people who flipped houses. People who lied and cheated [on mortgage applications]. Nobody did the income appraisals."

Benmosche, who was not involved in causing the crisis, voiced the industry's growing defensiveness over its compensation. He said the public uproar over bonuses paid to AIG employees was intended to "get everybody out there with their pitch forks and their hangman nooses, and all that—sort of like what we did in the Deep South [decades ago]. And I think it was just as bad and just as wrong." He was echoing the references to lynching and witch hunts that had been used by the leaded gas, CFC, and tobacco industries.

A Citigroup executive emailed a colleague saying, "No offense to Middle America, but if someone went to Columbia or Wharton, [even if] their company is a fumbling, mismanaged bank, why should they all of a sudden be paid the same as the guy down the block who delivers restaurant supplies for Sysco out of a huge, shiny truck?" Believing you deserve your very high salary because of your intelligence and credentials, regardless of your social impact, along with being steeped in a culture where pay is seen as the measure of human worth and status, will surely incline you to hold those who make less money in some contempt. You might look down on the guy who drives a truck, on your own clients ("muppets"), on the staff of the ratings agencies ("brain dead"), and on regulators ("idiots").

Even those bankers who know they are overpaid compared to most people are not embarrassed, because that isn't who they compare themselves to when rationalizing their compensation. A former Bear Stearns managing director told Gabriel Sherman of *New York Magazine* that he knew that a relative of his, a hardworking doctor, did far more for humanity than "anything that went on in the Bear Stearns building," but added, "We're in a hypercapitalistic society. No one complains when Julia Roberts pulls down $25 million per movie or A-Rod has a $300 million guarantee. . . . I don't think it's fair to say Wall Street is paid too much."

And of course they justified their pay by stressing the social value of their work, though they sometimes did this with a wink and a smile, suggesting a certain lack of sincerity. Goldman trader Fabrice Tourre, in the jaunty 2007 email he wrote to a girlfriend about the impending collapse of the entire financial system, added: "Anyway, not feeling too guilty about this, the real purpose of my job is to make capital markets more efficient and ultimately provide the US consumer with more efficient ways to leverage and finance himself, so there is a humble, noble and ethical reason for my job ;) amazing how good I am in convincing myself !!!"

Similarly, his boss, Goldman CEO Lloyd Blankfein, explained to the *Times of London* in 2009, after the house of cards had collapsed, that "we're very important. . . . We help companies to grow by helping them to raise capital. Companies that grow create wealth. This, in turn, allows people to have jobs that create more growth and more wealth. It's a virtuous cycle. . . . We have a social purpose." (Alas, this is not all they do; as Tourre put it, the product he helped create was a thing "which has no purpose.") So, Blankfein was asked, does Goldman just go on raking it in, getting richer than God? Blankfein, who personally earned $68 million in 2007 alone, said, with what the paper described an "impish grin," that he was just a banker "doing God's work."

Goldman had been working in particularly mysterious ways, though. The SEC soon brought against it the fraud charges mentioned above, for selling to investors a synthetic CDO that another investor, betting it would fail, was allowed to help design. Blankfein told clients the charges would ultimately "hurt America." One client said Blankfein "was very aggressive. . . . He feels that the government is out to kill them, that they are under attack and the whole thing is totally political." Even in late 2017, when Goldman's chief financial officer looked back on people's hatred of his firm, he would shrug it off: "When times are rough there seems to be a human tendency—I'm sure you read 'The Scarlet Letter' as a kid, right?—that if we find someone to name and shame and blame then we're good."

The crisis, the bailouts, the high pay on Wall Street even during the crisis, and the paucity of criminal prosecutions did indeed fuel a generalized public backlash against bankers, and that backlash often failed to note that not all bank employees did bad things and not all banks were equally liable for the runaway train. Admittedly, this chapter often fails to make those distinctions too, so let me state that while the banking culture I describe was widespread, many thousands of people working for the investment banks and megabanks played no role in the reckless securitization that caused the crisis (though they may have benefited from it), nor did many of the small community banks and credit unions.

Jamie Dimon, the head of JPMorgan Chase, was the most vocal defender of bankers against their critics after the crisis. While his commercial bank did some subprime lending and securitization, it did less than its competitors on Wall Street, leaving him with a reputation as a savvy risk manager. After the crisis, Dimon was dubbed "America's least-hated banker" by the *New York Times* and, for his defense of his industry, the "Martin Luther King Jr. of the overdog" by *Vanity Fair*. Asked by *New York Magazine*'s Jessica Pressler whether he regretted his outspoken defense of bankers, he said, "I'm an outspoken defender of the truth. . . . Everyone is afraid of retaliation and retribution. We recently had an event with a hundred small bankers here, and 85 percent of them said they can't challenge the regulation because of the potential retribution. That's a terrible thing. Okay? This is not the Soviet Union. This is the United States of America. . . . It's a free. Fucking. Country."

Dimon tends to deploy the classic bad-apple defense that has been used by criticized industries for centuries. Arguing against what he considered overregulation of banking in 2011, Dimon noted that "most of the bad actors are gone." The next year, though, a headline-making scandal at his own bank proved that some bad apples remained and just one could cause enormous damage. One of his London-based traders made a series of derivatives deals that went bad, costing the firm billions. The type of trade that caused the loss, called a portfolio hedge, was in fact a type that JPMorgan Chase had pressed Congress to exclude from a statutory ban on trading by banks like Dimon's with insured deposits. The event illustrated that the question society must ask when deciding whether to regulate an industry is not "What are the best actors doing?" but "What are the worst actors doing, and how dangerous is it?"

Consistent with his preference to focus on just a few bad apples rather than the barrels they work within, Dimon said to Jessica Pressler, "Everyone is talking about the culture, the culture, and all that, and it's just not true. . . . Most bankers are decent, honorable people. We're wrapped up in all this crap right now. We made a mistake. We're sorry. It doesn't detract from all the good things we've done. I am not responsible for the financial crisis."

There is evidence, though, that the culture of banking does indeed corrupt. Years after the crisis, the economist Alain Cohn and two colleagues at the University of Zurich tested the frequent claims that the financial sector's business culture was behind its fraud scandals. They recruited 128 employees from a large international bank and had them take a coin-tossing test where they won about $20 per toss depending on whether they reported heads or tails. The tests were unobserved, making it easy to cheat without detection. Before the test, half the bankers were asked questions to remind them of their professional identity as bankers, such as "What is your function at the bank?" The control group, bankers *not* reminded of their profession, reported close to the 50 percent of successful flips that chance would predict. The bankers who were reminded they were bankers reported 58.2 percent successful flips—significantly above chance and the control group. These results, in the authors' words, "suggest that the prevailing business culture in the banking industry weakens and undermines the honesty norm."

Moreover, many on Wall Street believe their colleagues are cheaters. A survey of over 1,200 US and UK financial service professionals published in 2015 found that 47 percent thought their competitors probably engaged in unethical or illegal behavior to gain a market edge; for those making over $500,000 annually, the figure was 51 percent. A third of respondents felt that the industry had not changed for the better in the seven years since the financial crisis. This is particularly troubling given evidence suggesting that people are more likely to comply with a social norm if they think others are doing so and are more likely to cheat when they think others are cheating.

JUSTICE, REGULATION, AND CULTURE CHANGE: TRYING TO REFORM AN INDUSTRY

After the savings and loan scandals of the 1980s, over one thousand bankers were convicted of felonies. By contrast, the 2008 crisis—about seventy times larger—resulted in only one criminal conviction among the large

Wall Street banks, of a former mid-level executive at Credit Suisse. The judge who sentenced him to thirty months in prison acknowledged that his crime was "a small piece of an overall evil climate within the bank and with many other banks."

Jesse Eisinger, a Pulitzer Prize–winning financial reporter for *ProPublica*, traces the lack of postcrisis convictions to the timidity of Justice Department prosecutors. Eisinger blames, among other things, prosecutors' reluctance to bring hard-to-win cases and a fear that criminally prosecuting large firms could hurt the economy—a too-big-to-indict mentality. An obscure federal agency set up during the bailout has managed to send to prison at least thirty-six bankers, but only from smaller community and regional banks. The head of that agency, Christine Goldsmith Romero, has said that the leaders of the big Wall Street banks are hard to prosecute because they are insulated by a culture that keeps them in the dark about potential fraud. One might say that the psychological mechanisms of denial that keep individuals from feeling responsible for causing harm were successfully institutionalized by the big banks, keeping their leaders from being held criminally liable for the banks' wrongdoing.

Regulators have brought civil actions, leading to payment of a record-breaking couple hundred billion dollars in fines by various financial firms. This would be more impressive if the crisis had not cost the economy a record-breaking trillions of dollars. Moreover, fines paid by individuals have been virtually absent; Goldman trader Fabrice Tourre, found liable for civil fraud, is a rare exception. In other cases, when individuals were named, their fines were ultimately paid by their companies and insurers. Phil Angelides, head of the Financial Crisis Inquiry Commission, said that "the people who are responsible for the financial crisis have still not been called to account."

Ameriquest was dissolved in 2007; its founder, billionaire Roland Arnall, died the next year. Countrywide, collapsing in 2007, was bought by Bank of America. Countrywide's founder, Angelo Mozilo (who still claimed in 2010 his company was "one of the greatest companies in the history of this country") settled SEC charges with a fine that was mostly covered by Countrywide and Bank of America. A handful of top bank executives were driven out of their leadership positions in disgrace, but like Arnall and Mozilo, most took large fortunes with them. Lehman Brothers' Dick Fuld, for example, walked away with the hundreds of millions he took in compensation before his firm collapsed into the biggest bankruptcy in history.

The debate over how to regulate the financial industry in the wake of the crisis was robust. A letter accompanying an August 2008 industry report, written by people from several top Wall Street banks, had claimed that "the sobering reality" of emotion-driven financial excesses "for centuries, has given rise to the universal recognition that finance and financial institutions must be subject to a higher degree of official oversight than is necessary for virtually all other forms of commercial enterprise."

However, this claim ignored the decades of antiregulatory ideology that allowed the excesses, and the crisis certainly did not yield universal recognition of the need for regulations. On the contrary, the crisis and bailout sparked the angry antiregulatory Tea Party movement; deepened political divisions (not just in the United States); and eroded social trust in government (especially on the right), in business (especially on the left), and in US institutions generally. The political impact of the financial crisis may prove to be its most lasting legacy.

In 2010, Congress managed to enact Dodd-Frank, the most sweeping financial regulations since the Great Depression (though, given the polarized era, it did so with virtually no Republican support). Among other things, the law regulated mortgage lending, required banks to reduce their leverage, regulated derivatives, and steered banks toward traditional banking and away from trading and speculation. Bank industry leaders expressed some support for the law but worked to weaken it and the many regulations that followed. Still, Dennis Kelleher, head of the Wall Street watchdog group Better Markets, said that a decade after the crisis, "the evidence is overwhelming that financial reform is working, that finance is more stable, that the risk of a crash or economic catastrophe is greatly reduced, that banks are highly profitable and increasing their lending, that the economy is steadily growing, and that investor confidence has been restored."

Despite this success—and the fact that Wall Street did not support his candidacy—President Trump has called Dodd-Frank a "disaster" and pledged his administration would be "doing a big number on Dodd-Frank." Some of its statutory provisions have already been weakened, and the administration is dismantling many regulations considered key to preventing another financial crisis.

As for Wall Street's exploitative culture, years after the crisis, calls for change are still coming from both outside and within the industry. Some banks have made changes, but it is too soon to tell if they will significantly reduce short-term greed, rampant risk-taking, and the willingness to exploit others, especially as the attention of regulators and the public wanes. Meanwhile, there is evidence that Wall Street's appetite for risk is rising, as it tries to stretch the regulatory limits put in place after the crisis.

Changing the culture and reckless behavior of entrenched and powerful corporations is hard, even after an undeniable global crisis has so vividly illustrated the need to do so. It is even harder when the global crisis in question is just starting to unfold and is still denied by some, as in the climate crisis discussed next, and when the corporations' core operations are so intimately tied to that crisis that it is hard to imagine how they can survive in the future without fueling a global catastrophe.

8 A "Deceitful, Hysterical, Out-of-Control Rampage"

FOSSIL FUELS, CLIMATE DENIAL, AND DISTRUST BUILDING

"Our world is deficient in carbon dioxide, and a doubling of atmospheric CO_2 is very beneficial."

—1992 video funded by coal producer Western Fuels Association

In 1995, I was surprised to find myself litigating the science of climate change. Although I was an environmental lawyer, I had no background in climate issues. I was a Minnesota assistant attorney general, advising my client agency on day-to-day implementation of clean air laws, none of which focused on climate. I was not expecting to plunge into one of the most daunting—and soon, polarizing—issues of our time.

State law required Minnesota energy regulators to quantify the environmental harms caused by power plants, launching a proceeding that would consider global warming costs. My client agency joined in, presenting the same alarming mainstream science that had already spurred the first global climate treaty. Coal interests intervened, bringing in a handful of scientists to testify that there was nothing to worry about: more carbon dioxide (CO_2) in the air from burning coal was actually a good thing; any warming would be mild and pleasant; and those scientists claiming otherwise were politically or financially biased.

When I first heard the industry witnesses' arguments, I wanted to believe them. Most people want to believe that we and future generations can live our lives on a stable, catastrophe-free planet. Climate change threatens that belief, triggering denial—perhaps the same primal denial mechanisms that let us avoid fixating on our mortality. For those most deeply invested in fossil fuels or most tribally or ideologically opposed to government regulation, that denial reflex will surely be even stronger.

As I was forced by this litigation to confront the evidence and dire predictions of the global scientific community, I saw how starkly it contrasted with the rosy alternate reality presented by the industry witnesses I was cross-examining. I was astonished by how casually these witnesses could wave away such a grave threat and how, with no evidence, they could attribute the warnings of thousands of mainstream scientists to bias.

In the years since, though, I have seen that the claims and denials the industry made in that hearing room were downright tame compared to what was to follow. Over the years, climate denial would become increasingly tribal, ideological, toxic, and detached from both empirical reality and prior norms of civility. And it would help usher in the very same disturbing changes in the nation's broader political norms.

AN EARLY CONSENSUS: "GLOBALLY CATASTROPHIC EFFECTS"

On February 29, 1980, five members of the US oil industry gathered in a conference room at New York's LaGuardia Airport for what must have been a very strange meeting. They were part of a special task force formed by the American Petroleum Institute to focus on the issue of climate change. They had invited Stanford's Dr. J. A. Laurman, described in the minutes as a "recognized expert in the field of CO_2 and climate," to speak. One of the bullet points in Dr. Laurman's slides was the "scientific consensus on the potential for large future climatic response to increased CO_2 levels." The likely impacts, he explained, would build from 2005 ("barely noticeable") to 2038 ("major economic consequences, strong regional dependence"), to 2067 ("globally catastrophic effects").

It was a sobering warning, but even then, not a new one. The scientific basics of climate change had been known since the nineteenth century. When you burn coal, oil, or gas, the carbon in these hydrocarbons transforms into airborne CO_2. While CO_2 is just a tiny fraction of the natural atmosphere, it plays a key role in warming the planet by keeping heat from radiating out to space (like the glass of a greenhouse, hence the term "greenhouse effect"). If global concentrations of this crucial gas were to change dramatically, so would the climate. Moreover, once CO_2 concentrations build up, it can take thousands of years for nature to bring them back down.

By the 1950s, measurements showed atmospheric CO_2 concentrations climbing yearly, mostly due to burning fossil fuels. Scientists began sounding the alarm. A 1965 report issued by President Johnson's science advisory committee warned that humanity was conducting a "vast geophysical experiment" that could lead to "perhaps marked changes in climate" by 2000. In 1979, the White House asked the National Academy of Sciences to weigh in. A blue-ribbon panel of scientists tried to identify any physical effects that might limit the expected warming to negligible proportions. They found none.

Dr. Laurman, talking to the oil task force in 1980, stressed how long it would take to replace fossil fuels. His presentation said, "Time for action? Market penetration time theory says there is *no* leeway." In essence, the oil industry's little task force was being told by their handpicked climate expert that, while there were uncertainties, it appeared that the world needed to immediately commence the long process of replacing fossil fuels to avoid global catastrophe later. The science strongly suggested that either the oil industry was doomed or the world was. After this presentation, as the minutes dryly note, the task force went on to discuss the implications of "introducing a new energy source into world wide use."

Given what we have seen from other industries, it is surprising that the oil industry did not respond more immediately with denial. The lack of reflexive defensiveness may have had to do with how secure the industry felt, at the very apex of corporate power even after the oil shocks of the 1970s. At the time, of the top ten Fortune 500 companies, seven were oil companies, with Exxon perched at the top, and two more were automakers. Oil prices were still high thanks to the 1979 oil crisis, and policy makers and the public were far more worried about near-term energy supplies than about the twenty-first century climate.

Exxon had done enough of its own research, in coordination with government and other scientists, to know the gravity of the climate threat, both to the world and to the oil industry. The company continued with its own research into the early 1980s, reaching conclusions described in internal documents as "in accord with the scientific consensus" and acknowledging that "catastrophic" effects for a substantial fraction of the earth's population were "distinctly possible." (These internal documents became news in 2015 when reporters from *InsideClimate News* and the *Los Angeles Times* went through archived company documents and highlighted the contrast with the company's later public statements challenging the scientific consensus.) Still, so little attention was being paid to the problem that this sobering science did not prompt a denial campaign.

By the late 1980s, though, the regulatory threat to the fossil fuel industry became much more real. In 1988, the Intergovernmental Panel on Climate Change (IPCC) was established under UN auspices. It pulled together the world's leading climate scientists and gave them the daunting task of conducting ongoing assessments of the growing mountains of data and writing periodic reports to advise world policy makers on the climate threat. The IPCC process would dwarf all scientific review panels that came before, including the ozone assessment panels.

Moreover, the ozone-saving Montreal Protocol, negotiated in 1987, made the prospect of a similar global treaty to protect the climate suddenly plausible. And unlike the companies that made CFCs, which had merely faced losing one of their many products and might profitably sell substitutes, fossil fuel companies were facing the prospect of the world mobilizing against the product at the core of their corporate existence.

THE POLITICAL RESPONSE: CREEPING TOWARD GLOBAL DECARBONIZATION

Now and then I see a movie where a scientist discovers a dire threat to the planet, warns authorities, and triggers some dramatic action that averts catastrophe. The closest we've seen to that happening in real life is probably the ozone crisis, which still took years of uncinematic research and committee meetings to go from first warning to final action. In the case of climate change, the process is taking decades to unfold.

The first IPCC assessment, in 1990, was already so compelling that at the Earth Summit in Rio in 1992—then history's largest gathering of world leaders—nations reached a treaty agreeing to stabilize greenhouse gas concentrations at a level that would prevent dangerous interference with the climate. President George H. W. Bush signed it, the Senate ratified it, and decades of negotiations and data collection were launched.

The IPCC is working on its sixth assessment of the science, due in 2021. Hundreds of scientists work as authors and editors, and thousands are expert reviewers. These scientists volunteer their time to support the most rigorous, sustained, large-scale, transparent, and vitally necessary effort of collective scientific assessment in human history. (The IPCC was corecipient, with Al Gore, of a Nobel Peace Prize in 2007 for this work.) The IPCC's reports have grown ever more certain over the decades, based on multiple lines of evidence, that humans are changing the climate and that much worse lies ahead unless we dramatically cut our emissions.

The IPCC has concluded that the warming of the planet's climate is "unequivocal." The dominant cause is humanity's greenhouse gases,* mainly CO_2 from burning fossil fuels, and warming has been linked to changes already observed around the world: Extremely hot days and heavy downpours have grown more common. Plants and animals on land and under water are shifting their ranges. The oceans are acidifying as they absorb CO_2 from the air, threatening marine life. Arctic sea ice, glaciers around the world, and the massive ice sheets in both Greenland and Antarctica are all melting—and sea levels are rising—at an accelerating pace. These changes will continue, but how severely we destabilize the climate depends on how quickly we can shrink global emissions.

The consensus that human actions are causing dangerous climate change is shared by the dozens of major scientific academies, institutes, laboratories, and societies with relevant expertise around the world; many have issued statements explicitly highlighting the urgency of the threat. I am not aware of a single such organization that disputes the climate threat, nor am I aware of another global threat that has provoked such a sustained series of warnings from the scientific community.

---

*Other important anthropogenic greenhouse gases include methane (from fossil fuel production, agriculture, and landfills), nitrous oxides (from agriculture, industry, and fossil fuels), and fluorinated gases (including the CFCs banned by the Montreal Protocol and some of the substitute gases used in refrigeration and other industrial processes).

In 2015, after decades of climate negotiations constrained by, among other things, powerful opposition from climate deniers,[*] the nations of the world finally agreed in Paris that climate change is indeed an "urgent threat" warranting global action from all nations. The Paris Agreement set an extremely ambitious global goal of limiting warming to "well below 2°C above pre-industrial levels," and beyond that, of trying to keep warming below 1.5°C, which is far safer. Each nation pledged specific actions to work toward that goal; the Obama administration was planning to have the United States further cut emissions from coal plants, improve the fuel efficiency of cars, control leaks from natural gas extraction, and take other steps. (The Trump administration subsequently declared that the United States no longer supports the Paris Agreement and is trying to repeal or weaken these and other climate regulations; so far it appears the nearly 200 other nations remain on board.)

The planet has already warmed by about 1°C, with more warming locked into the system as the climate responds to past emissions. Even if the United States and other national governments keep the pledges they made in Paris, we are on track for a warming of about 3°C—less than was projected a few years ago, but still far beyond the global target. In short, we are still headed deep into the danger zone. Exceeding the 2°C target increases the risk that we will trigger powerful self-reinforcing feedbacks—like, say, releasing large quantities of the methane currently trapped in permafrost—that would catapult us into more catastrophic warming regardless of our emissions. Indeed, we could trigger such runaway feedbacks even below 2°C warming, hence the 1.5°C target.

Limiting warming to 1.5°C is still technically possible, but it will be staggeringly difficult. A sobering 2018 IPCC report estimated the world's still-rising CO_2 emissions would need to drop about 45 percent below 2010

---

[*] A note on terminology: I apply the terms *climate denier* and *climate denial* to those who reject the bottom-line finding of the scientific climate consensus—namely, that there is an urgent global threat that warrants deep emission cuts over the next few decades. The terms are disliked by most, but not all, of those to whom they are applied. I use the terms anyway, not to antagonize (and not to suggest a link to Holocaust denial, as some suggest the phrases are meant to do) but because this is, after all, a book about denial, and climate denial is a variant of the other types of denial described. I use the term *consensus* to mean agreement of an overwhelming majority.

levels by 2030 and then keep falling toward net zero around 2050 ("net zero" means we release no more CO_2 than we draw in from the atmosphere). Even to stay within 2°C requires cutting CO_2 emissions by about 25 percent by 2030, falling toward net zero by around 2070. (Other greenhouse gases would have to be reduced as well.) This essentially requires replacing the planet's vast fossil fuel-based energy infrastructure with a virtually carbon-free one in the next few decades. It is basically the same daunting task the oil industry task force meeting at LaGuardia in 1980 was warned was needed, except now time is nearly out. Also, because of the delay, we will have to achieve deep *negative* emissions in the second half of the century, requiring the creation of an entirely new industry using technologies that are not yet commercial to draw vast quantities of CO_2 out of the air and bury it, a challenge we have barely begun to discuss.

Fortunately, clean energy technologies have made tremendous strides over the years, making it easier to imagine replacing fossil fuels, but only with, at a minimum, truly aggressive action and sustained political will. However, nothing collapses political will faster than the perception of an ongoing scientific dispute, as industries facing regulation have long known. Social scientists have seen evidence that this is true in the climate context, too, and climate deniers have been attacking the scientific consensus for years. Myron Ebell, a nonscientist with the far right Competitive Enterprise Institute (recipient of large sums from fossil fuel interests and conservative foundations) and a veteran Washington, DC, climate denier, explained that "if you concede the science is settled and that there's a consensus, . . . the moral high ground has been ceded to the alarmists." (To climate deniers, "alarmists" include the IPCC and virtually the entire global scientific establishment.)

DIFFERENT INDUSTRIES, DIFFERENT DENIALS: FOSSIL FUELS AND THE GROUPS THEY FUND

One way climate deniers have attacked the scientific consensus is just by denying it exists. At the 2000 annual meeting of ExxonMobil, after shareholders voiced worries about climate change, CEO Lee Raymond rebuffed them, saying, "At least seventeen thousand scientists" didn't agree with their concerns, and the company was not going to "follow what is politically correct." He was citing a 1998 petition saying there was no convincing evidence of catastrophic global warming. The petition would be discredited on many grounds over the years: it had been distributed using misleading tactics,* and the names included ones from fiction and popular music (including one of the Spice Girls) added by critics to show the utter lack of verification. Moreover, anyone with a bachelor's degree in any aspect of science, engineering, or medicine was invited to sign it. The august-sounding Oregon Institute of Science and Medicine, which circulated the petition, proved to be a tiny operation that also distributed survivalist literature and a homeschooling curriculum to "take America back from the anti-Christian forces that currently control American public life."

For a few years, moderate Republicans in the states and in Congress were active in crafting climate protection policies, but then climate change become one of the most polarized issues of a polarized age, even more polarizing than abortion. US conservatives and Republicans are far less likely to accept that climate change is real and human-caused than other Americans and far less likely to support policy action to fight it.

Indeed, it has become politically dangerous for Republican candidates and elected officials to do other than dismiss the climate threat, and President Trump has repeatedly called climate change a "hoax." More broadly, in 2018 still only one in five Americans recognized that more than 90 percent of climate scientists have concluded that human-caused global warming is happening. (In fact, about 97 percent of studies in the peer-reviewed literature agree with the consensus view.) The overwhelming scientific consensus, accepted throughout the world, has been successfully obscured in the United States.

How did deniers create such doubt about such a broad scientific consensus? One way was by fostering distrust of the major societal institutions embracing that consensus: government, media, academia, leading scientific organizations, and "elites" generally. In their efforts to sow

---

*The petition was accompanied by a paper formatted to look like it had been published in the prestigious science journal *Proceedings of the National Academy of Sciences*. It created so much confusion that the National Academy issued a rare statement stressing that the article had not been published by it or any peer-reviewed journal, and it did not reflect the conclusions of expert reports of the academy.

doubt, climate deniers have fueled the political tribalism and vulnerability to partisan manipulation that characterizes the current "post-truth" era.

In his 1997 exposé *The Heat Is On: The High Stakes Battle over Earth's Threatened Climate,* investigative journalist and author Ross Gelbspan first described the stirrings of climate denial from what he called "the deepest-pocketed, biggest private interest in history." Before further exploring the parade of denials the fossil fuel interests have originated or sponsored, it's worth looking at some of its major players.

The most conspicuous are the publicly traded oil giants like ExxonMobil, powerful icons of the industrial establishment. (ExxonMobil, still one of the biggest corporations in the world, is also the successor of Standard Oil of New Jersey, an early maker of tetraethyl lead.) ExxonMobil played a prominent role in raising doubts about the climate science, particularly during the Clinton and George W. Bush administrations. Big oil companies have generally been more measured in the tone of their denials than other industry segments (or than the advocacy groups they have funded), perhaps because they are more exposed to consumer and shareholder pressures and securities laws. Today most oil companies, including ExxonMobil, publicly accept the need for policies to reduce carbon emissions, though many of the groups and people they funded over the years (and in some cases still fund) continue to dispute it.

Another major player is the privately owned Koch Industries, a conglomerate that is based in oil refining. For decades it had been co-owned and controlled by two brothers, the controversial libertarian billionaires Charles and David Koch. David died in August 2019, leaving Charles, the long-time CEO and chair of the company, to carry on their work of promoting a rigid libertarian agenda that would, among other things, eliminate virtually all environmental, consumer, and other regulation. (Charles has said that "my whole being is dedicated to changing the system.") This agenda has been advanced through the creation of a powerful network of political donors to elect right-wing candidates and a far-flung network of think tanks and front groups that deny the climate threat. Charles Koch himself has publicly acknowledged that people are in fact causing some global warming, but he still denies it is a problem that demands government action, while David Koch had stressed the benefits of a warmer world.

The growing natural gas industry has not historically been a major player in climate denial; it benefited from some of the early climate policies and is hurt by others. However, some in the gas industry are part of the Koch political network or trade groups hostile to climate protection, and there is substantial overlap with the oil industry (ExxonMobil being the top gas producer).

The coal industry is quite distinct from oil and gas, and competes with gas in the electricity markets. Coal advocates have always felt more threatened by climate policies (rightly so, because coal is the most carbon-polluting fossil fuel) and have been quicker to resort to aggressive tribal rhetoric. The industry includes large publicly traded international coal corporations like Peabody and privately owned ones like Murray Energy, run by the right-wing coal magnate Bob Murray. Many of the largest US coal companies, including Peabody, have been through bankruptcy as the United States has been shifting away from coal power to cleaner energy, creating a growing fury and sense of desperation within the coal industry.

Since almost all coal is sold to power plants, electric companies have over the years sometimes partnered with coal in climate denial. There have always been major regional and cultural differences, though, and many utilities have made serious progress in reducing emissions. (Today, even Southern Company—a utility with a long history of climate denial and whose CEO questioned climate change as recently as 2017—claims to be moving toward low- to no-carbon technologies by 2050.) And—proving that climate denial is not driven by profit motive alone—among the most passionate deniers have been nonprofit, consumer-owned electric cooperatives in the West and Midwest. These cooperatives are a vestige of the New Deal, largely serving rural customers; clean energy advocates joke about them as socialist organizations run by conservative Republicans. Western Fuels Association, a coal cooperative run by electric cooperatives, was at the cutting edge of climate denial in the 1990s (and brought climate-denying witnesses to our Minnesota proceeding in 1995[*]).

After 1990 or so, an array of right-wing, antiregulatory, "free market" groups took up the cause of climate denial, attracting funding not just

---

[*]Among the witnesses who testified were Frederick Seitz, Richard Lindzen, Robert Balling, Patrick Michaels, and Keith Idso, some of whom are quoted below.

from fossil fuel corporations but from right-wing foundations. Several such groups, along with a few outspoken members of the coal industry, have been the most unhinged in their attacks on the mainstream science and on those who accept it and want to respond. These groups have become a political force on their own, and under the Trump administration some of the more combative groups, along with the coal industry, are driving US climate and energy policy.*

LAYERED VEILS: THE DEEPENING OF CORPORATE ANONYMITY

In 2014, a room full of oil and gas executives in Colorado heard a sales pitch from Rick Berman, a veteran Washington, DC, strategist who gets paid by corporate clients in various industries to attack their critics. Berman told the executives, who were facing opposition from environmentalists, of the importance of playing hardball, of appealing to the public's "fear and anger," and of "taking away people's moral authority." Berman's response to clients who don't want to stoop to such personal attacks was blunt: "Well, you know, you can either win ugly or lose pretty." And he assured the executives they could make such attacks without exposure: "We run all of this stuff through nonprofit organizations that are insulated from having to disclose donors. There is total anonymity. People don't know who supports us."

One executive in the room taped Berman's presentation and leaked it (anonymously) to the *New York Times*, saying that it "just left a bad taste in my mouth." However, the presentation was warmly received by others in the room who rose to speak, and Berman said that some companies there had already employed him. Although Berman was talking at the time about fracking, not climate change, he had already published a full-page ad in national outlets comparing EPA's rules limiting carbon emis-

---

*This in no way represents the full spectrum of climate denial. Arguments originated by fossil fuel companies and people they fund have also been taken up by some on the religious right. For example, author Grant R. Jeffrey adds an apocalyptic spin to the science denials used by industry deniers, calling global warming claims "a major tactic being used by Satan to advance his evil agenda on earth," paving the way for the Antichrist.

sions from power plants to terrorism; the ad identified only a Berman-created front group as its source, keeping its funders hidden. When coal producer Peabody Energy went bankrupt, Berman and several other climate-denying groups were among the creditors listed in court filings.

Channeling an industry's arguments through fronts is, of course, a time-honored strategy, grounded in the recognition that the financial interests of the industry make it less credible than a seemingly more neutral party. Fronts were likely used by the slave trade in the eighteenth century and used repeatedly by the tobacco industry in the twentieth. And the fossil fuel industry had been using front groups to undermine climate concerns for years (though usually with less complete anonymity and deploying less blatant personal attacks on the industry's critics than Berman's company offered).

In 1991, Southern Company and other power and coal interests launched a front group called ICE, which stood either for "Informed Citizens for the Environment" or "Information Council for the Environment." (They ultimately picked the latter because test marketing found that technical-sounding sources were more trusted than activist or industry sources). An internal planning document said ICE's goal was to "reposition global warming as theory (not fact)." Test marketers also found that people were more comfortable assessing motives than science, and they advised targeting certain "older, less-educated males" because they would be "most receptive to messages describing the motivations and vested interests of people currently making pronouncements on global warming." The whole scheme was quickly leaked to the press, however, after which ICE quickly melted away.

Later in the nineties, Western Fuels launched a group called the Greening Earth Society dedicated to the proposition that coal emissions were good for the environment because CO_2 is a plant fertilizer; hence, the more the better. When in 2002 I asked a staffer about who funded this group, he told me that "there's a large segment of the coal industry . . . that really appreciates" the work it does, but "nobody wants to be associated with us," so the group described its funders only generically.

The corporate form already introduces a degree of anonymity into human transactions, letting those who own or run a corporation disappear behind the corporate veil, with both legal and psychological implications.

And we know that anonymity lets people feel less constrained by the social norms that normally inhibit them. Although the results are not always antisocial, they often are; just look at the Internet. The chance to post anonymous comments brings out a casual viciousness far less common when identities are known and people feel more personally accountable. When a corporation's actions are filtered through another organization—a trade group, advocacy group, think tank, or front group—it creates another layer of obscurity. Working through an ostensibly independent entity— even when that entity's members or funders are not completely masked— likely reduces the feeling of moral accountability (not to mention political and legal accountability).

By the late 1980s, Exxon had begun to publicly dispute the climate consensus it once accepted, including through a highly influential business group it helped found and lead called the Global Climate Coalition (GCC). By 2000 the company, now ExxonMobil, started to get heat for disputing the science, including from its own shareholders. By 2003, ExxonMobil was taking a softer public line on climate and was funding low-carbon energy research at Stanford, but it was also quietly ramping up its funding of groups disputing the climate science.

ExxonMobil did not need to create its own front groups to create doubts about climate science. There was already a growing crop of right-wing "think tanks" and advocacy groups opposing government regulation, largely funded by corporations and conservative or libertarian foundations. ExxonMobil's CEO Lee Raymond was already on the board of the American Enterprise Institute, the largest and oldest such group, but the company also funded many of the newer, smaller, and more combative groups too. And some of these groups and the individuals who worked for them also denied the dangers of tobacco, CFCs, and other harms, reflecting tobacco's apparent success in cloaking its own anti-EPA efforts behind a "larger mosaic" of EPA-bashing by other industries.

When the *New York Times* asked about this funding in 2003, ExxonMobil's spokesperson said, "We want to support organizations that are trying to broaden the debate on an issue that is so important to all of us." That year the Competitive Enterprise Institute, which would receive nearly two million dollars from ExxonMobil between 2000 and 2005, would try to "broaden the debate" by suing the federal government for the second time (unsuccessfully) to block the release of its landmark, statuto-rily mandated National Climate Assessment. ExxonMobil—a company actually commended by federal officials for its contribution to climate research a couple decades earlier—was by 2003 helping bankroll litiga-tion to keep from the American public an authoritative description of the dangers they faced.

By 2006 and 2007, ExxonMobil had been getting criticism for funding climate denial groups from Greenpeace, the British Royal Society, two US senators, and the Union of Concerned Scientists (a former employer of mine*). Moreover, public concern over climate change was rising with the release of Al Gore's *Inconvenient Truth* and the latest IPCC report. Steve Coll, in his book *Private Empire: ExxonMobil and American Power*, describes how the company's new CEO, Rex Tillerson, ordered a reevalu-ation of its climate policies, think tank funding, and public messaging. The company softened its climate denial without admitting it had ever been wrong and dialed back its funding of denial groups, or at least the most hardline ones.

Many climate-denying free market groups were also getting funding from the Koch brothers' foundations. In 2010, Greenpeace released a report calling Koch Industries a "financial kingpin of climate science denial," outspending ExxonMobil in that role. However, by this time, traceable donations from the Koch foundations to climate denial groups were already declining. Picking up the slack were dark money groups, especially Donors Trust. Founded by an ardent libertarian with ties to the Koch policy empire, Donors Trust (and the associated Donors Capital Fund) has allowed those funding climate denial to do so without leaving any fingerprints. The Donors Trust website stressed the value of anonym-ity, "especially gifts funding sensitive or controversial issues." Drexel University sociologist Robert Brulle, who has studied the funding sources of dozens of groups that are part of what he calls the "climate change counter-movement" has documented this dramatic shift toward untrace-able sources.

---

*I was consulting for the Union of Concerned Scientists at the time of the ExxonMobil report and would later work on its staff for a few years, on coal and climate policy. However, I had no role in the group's ExxonMobil report or on the other UCS reports exposing climate denial cited in this chapter.

The most provocative denier groups, like Heartland Institute and the Competitive Enterprise Institute, benefit greatly from donations rendered untraceable through Donors Trust and Donors Capital Fund. In 2012, Heartland sparked controversy for putting up a Chicago billboard comparing those who "still" believe in global warming to the Unabomber. According to its press release, the group planned to also feature Charles Manson, Fidel Castro, and Osama bin Laden, because "the most prominent advocates of global warming aren't scientists" but rather these people, and like them, the leaders of the global warming movement "are willing to use force and fraud to advance their fringe theory." They added that believing in man-made global warming in 2012 was "more than a little nutty" and those who still did "are mostly on the radical fringe of society." The resulting outcry did bring the billboard down, but the funding coming anonymously to Heartland through these dark money groups only rose the next year.

In late 2017, a rift appeared between Heartland and ExxonMobil, which had stopped funding it a decade earlier. Heartland wanted the EPA to revoke the "endangerment finding" (a finding made years ago that carbon emissions endanger health and welfare, creating the legal requirement for the EPA to regulate greenhouse gases under the Clean Air Act). ExxonMobil was opposed, prompting Tim Huelskamp, Heartland's new president, to dismiss ExxonMobil as yet another member of "the discredited and anti-energy global warming movement. They've put their profits and 'green' virtue signaling above sound science and the interests of their customers." One observer compared the conflict to "Robespierre beheading Danton," but climate journalist Neela Banerjee, covering the story in *InsideClimate News,* saw a more recent political parallel: "Just like the Republican upstarts that threaten the party establishment, Heartland is taking climate denial farther than many fossil fuel companies can support."

Under the Trump administration, groups like Heartland have played a key role in pushing the government to repeal EPA climate regulations and withdraw from the Paris climate deal (over the objections of former ExxonMobil CEO and Trump's first secretary of state, Rex Tillerson). Among the biggest Heartland donors willing to be named in the last few years has been the Mercer Family Foundation. The Mercer family—whose money comes not from fossil fuels but a hedge fund—is also a co-owner of Breitbart News, the far-right nationalist website that fosters various conspiracy theories, including ones about climate science. The Mercers also played a major role in funding and promoting Donald Trump's candidacy.

In short, the seeds of climate denial were planted by the fossil fuel companies years ago in rich ideological soil and watered with generous donations. That denial took root in the US political landscape and is now being nurtured—at least in part—by groups with their own tribal and ideological goals that go beyond just profit-seeking through the sale of fossil fuels. Still, the role of fossil fuel companies in supporting these groups over the years (and to some extent today, though often less traceably) means the groups must be included in any discussion of corporate climate denial.

DISTRUST BUILDING: BLAMING "LIBERAL ELITISTS WHO INHERITED THEIR WEALTH"

Solving climate change demands a critical mass of social unity—between nations and within nations. This is hard enough to achieve even when everyone is feeling warmly about our common humanity. It is even harder when opponents of action are fanning both international and domestic resentments.

The 1997 Kyoto Protocol was rejected in the United States partly thanks to an industry coalition stressing the unfairness of exempting poor nations from emissions cuts (even though the United States had already agreed in the 1992 Rio Treaty that rich nations would act first). The Global Climate Coalition (GCC), representing Exxon and other major fossil fuel producers and users, argued that the draft text "gives a UN body—dominated by developing countries" control over US economic growth. Mobil (soon to merge with Exxon) took out full-page ads arguing that "developing countries ... must participate in the solution." Meanwhile, Exxon's Lee Raymond, in a speech in Beijing, applauded the rising oil consumption of China and other developing nations and urged them to join with the oil industry to oppose the protocol.

Climate deniers also appealed to tribal divisions within the United States. Fred Palmer, then CEO of Western Fuels, said in a 1990 speech that environmentalists wanted to "insure that life on Earth becomes as miserable as it can be and lived at the lowest common denominator."

Why? Because they value the earth and other species over humans and want to make sure the "human species does not proliferate." Joseph Bast in 2004, then head of the Heartland Institute (at the time partly funded by ExxonMobil), told a legislative committee in Iowa that the "real goal of the global warming lobby is rather obvious." Environmentalists, he said, "believe fossil fuels make possible a life style that is too materialistic, or too much better than what is common in other countries. They feel guilty, and they want us to share their pain."

Claiming that climate protection advocates really just wanted to cause pain and misery was creative but not terribly convincing. Over the years, though, the rhetoric shifted. Although opponents were still cast as extremists, instead of implying they were hippies fighting materialism while riding the bus, they were more typically characterized as members of a powerful, self-interested, hypocritical "elite." The denial movement tapped with great success into growing populist resentments, especially after the financial crisis, and exploited cultural fault lines already separating Americans by income, politics, region, and the urban/rural divide. After decades of the left attacking the "establishment," now something similar was coming from the right.

The identity of the enemy elitists varied. Coal magnate Bob Murray charged in 2014 that President Obama adopted climate policies to appease his constituency of "Hollywood characters, radical unionists, liberal elitists who inherited their wealth or made it the easy way off of somebody else on Wall Street, and radical environmentalists." (Ironically, during this time Obama was also being criticized by Wall Street for being hostile to the financial industry.)

Don Blankenship in 2009—then the CEO of Massey Energy, later imprisoned for conspiring to violate mine safety laws, and in 2018 an unsuccessful candidate for the US Senate in West Virginia—had a slightly different take on the elitist enemy. At a West Virginia festival, he railed not only against environmental extremists and the US government but against the "warped" climate views of America's corporate leaders (who, he felt, were too accepting of the climate threat).

Myron Ebell of the Competitive Enterprise Institute spoke in 2012 of deniers' success reducing the public's belief in the climate threat. He said, "There are holdouts among the urban bicoastal elite, but I think we've won the debate with the American people in the heartland, the people who get their hands dirty, people who dig up stuff, grow stuff and make stuff for a living, people who have a closer relationship to tangible reality, to stuff." Ebell would later head Donald Trump's EPA transition team.

A commercial run in Virginia in 2009 by the advocacy group Americans for Prosperity would become a classic in the effort to stereotype those worried about climate change. An actor begins, "Hey there, I'm Carlton, the wealthy eco-hypocrite. I inherited my money and attended fancy schools." After Carlton mentions his three homes, five cars, and concern for the environment, he says he wants Congress to pass climate legislation even if it "digs people like you even deeper into the recession. Who knows? Maybe I'll even make money off of it!" The irony of this ad is particularly rich. Americans for Prosperity was founded by the late David Koch, for years the richest person in New York City, who actually did inherit great wealth, attend fancy schools, and own multiple homes and cars. Jane Mayer, in her compelling exposé *Dark Money: The Hidden History of the Billionaires Behind the Rise of the Radical Right*, describes how this group sprang into action when the Tea Party emerged after the financial crisis, holding training sessions, organizing rallies, and channeling the rising anger into the fight against climate protection.

PROJECTION: CHARACTERIZING THE "GLOBAL WARMING INDUSTRY"

A billionaire-founded group accusing climate policy advocates of being rich elitists is not the only example of projection to be found in climate denial. Just like the tobacco industry calling its opponents the "anti-smoking industry," climate deniers refer to those seeking to mitigate climate change as the "global warming industry," and onto this industry they project many of the faults climate deniers themselves are more legitimately accused of, including greed, deception, hysterical fear-mongering, persecution, and an extreme ideological agenda.

For the deniers, such projection may be both subconscious and intentional, and it has both psychological and strategic value. Psychologically, if deniers can convince themselves that their opponents have no moral superiority, they avoid the morale-lowering guilt that would otherwise inhibit them in the fight. In fact, by nursing their own resentments (like those in the tobacco industry bunker), they can build an energizing sense of righteousness and comradery. And (as discussed in chapter 7) if they believe everybody indulges in self-serving dishonesty, their own actions feel consistent with the social norm.

Strategically, the deniers benefit from creating a kind of cognitive vertigo in the public. Rather than trying to discern what is true, people might just see a dizzying, discomforting display of mutual attacks. Some will just shrug and wait for certainty, benefiting the deniers with their political inaction. For others, though, the resulting confusion and sense of threat will strengthen their attachment to their own tribe and ideology (a phenomenon discussed in chapter 5). This will make them even more vulnerable to future climate denials, further eroding social trust and society's sense of a shared reality. The public, or at least the tribe most receptive to climate denial, then also becomes more likely to accept the notion of "alternative facts" and to dismiss formerly trusted sources as "fake news."

Projecting Greed: Scientists Riding a "Gravy Train"

Climate deniers often claim that mainstream climate scientists—mostly working for universities but getting financial grants from the federal government, like other US scientists—have a financial incentive to exaggerate the risk. For example, Christopher Horner, senior fellow at the Competitive Enterprise Institute, would charge that scientists seeking federal funding make scary predictions to keep the "gravy train" of federal grants chugging. Fear that this funding would be cut off should the "doomsaying" be proven faulty, he once wrote, was driving "the alarmist industry as it scurries to protect its franchise."

Of course, all people are potentially subject to financial bias, but it is absurd to suggest that such bias is stronger among scientists getting federal funding than among people funded by fossil fuel companies or groups openly devoted to unregulated markets. Most people, including those within the federal government, would prefer to avoid global catastrophe and would welcome evidence that the threat was less than feared. Indeed, when charges against mainstream scientists became commonplace, the president was a former Texas oil man running an administration that was both very pro-oil and antiregulation. It is unlikely the US government—not to mention the other governments of the world struggling to decarbonize—would avoid funding scientists who could find data that legitimately reduced the need to so quickly replace fossil fuels.

By contrast, fossil fuel companies and groups that exist to reduce regulation have strong incentives to fund any research that could plausibly suggest ongoing pollution was safe. Moreover, the alternate gravy train available to scientists disputing the climate threat might offer even more gravy, given the deep pockets of the industries and ideological interests eager to disprove climate change. A blog edited by veteran climate denier Patrick Michaels (and funded by Western Fuels) once boasted that scientists who downplayed climate warnings were envied by other scientists and were good at "commanding hefty honoraria and rarely flying in coach, which is especially irritating to the rank and file, condemned to seat 13E on the way to the Biloxi Regional Assessment of Global Climate Change." (This statement deviated from Michaels's more typical claims disparaging money-chasing mainstream scientists, such as his claim that it was "profitable to scream apocalypse.")

Projecting Deception: The "Hoax"

Climate deniers have been flinging charges of deception at mainstream scientists and others for years, dismissing global warming as a hoax, scam, or fraud, invented by people who were "cooking the books." These claims came from the more extreme side of the denial landscape, mainly the coal industry and the more provocative front groups and think tanks.

Given the scope of the scientific consensus, such charges amount to an allegation that thousands of scientists must have conspired together for over three decades, across a multitude of nations and disciplines, including all the relevant scientific academies and societies, forging the data in thousands of studies to invent a frightening but fake global crisis and tricking every government in the world (except the Trump administration) into believing them. Moreover, they must have chosen to keep up the hoax even though it has thrust many of them into a white-hot public controversy (exposing not a few to death threats and other harassment),

driven an unnecessary scramble to transform the world's energy infrastructure, and forced them to devote their careers to concocting a pretend
problem rather than doing something useful with their hard-earned
training.

We saw unsuccessful efforts to discredit mainstream science in earlier
chapters. In 1986, the Tobacco Institute accused the surgeon general of
"censorship and abuse of science." By 1993, tobacco reached out to other
industries to jointly attack the EPA's scientific credibility, launching front
groups to attack purportedly "junk science." In 1995, S. Fred Singer told the
members of a House committee they had been "bamboozled" by federal
ozone scientists, even after the CFC industry itself had accepted the science
(Singer would also dispute tobacco and climate science). Since the nineties,
a chorus of climate deniers have brought such claims to a new level, crying
"hoax" so often that they have shattered the social norm of trust in the collective scientific assessments, at least on the political right.

A low point came in 2009, just before world leaders gathered in
Copenhagen to negotiate a climate treaty. Hackers stole thousands of
emails from prominent British climate scientists and posted them on a
Russian server. Climate deniers took a few innocent phrases out of context
to make it seem like the scientists were altering data and then declared it
a major scandal (dubbed "Climategate"). Patrick Michaels, a scientist with
deep ties to fossil fuels, said to the *New York Times*, "This is not a smoking
gun; this is a mushroom cloud." The Competitive Enterprise Institute's
Christopher Horner would write that the emails affirmed his earlier claims
about "the scams being run by the booming industry of Big Academia and
Big Science suckling at the teat of the 'global warming' panic they are also
fostering."

The climate scientists whose emails were stolen would later be exonerated by multiple independent investigations. But by then the Copenhagen
talks had failed, for which this contrived scandal surely deserves part of
the blame. The criminals who stole the scientists' emails have never been
found or prosecuted. The use of a Russian server does not necessarily
mean the hackers were Russian, and unlike the hacking during the 2016
presidential campaign, there have been no government investigations formally linking the crime to Russia. The parallels, though, between 2009
and 2016—including the release of stolen, mischaracterized emails just

weeks before a critical public event, amplified in an echo chamber of bloggers and right-wing media—raise obvious suspicions.

Projecting Hysteria and Fear-Mongering: "Seeking to Stir Up All Kinds of Fears"

Those drawing attention to the dangers of climate change and pushing to cut carbon pollution are continually accused of hysteria. Coal magnate Bob Murray in 2007 warned a House subcommittee that the push for climate policies was a "deceitful, hysterical, out-of-control rampage perpetrated by fear-mongers in our society."

Murray's claim encompasses both the charge of hysteria and the charge of selling fear to others. To be clear, the climate science consensus is frightening, and scientists (and others, like me) are indeed alarmed about what lies ahead. But *hysteria* suggests fear with no basis, driven by an irrational emotionalism; the same charge, with its not-so-subtle sexist overtones, was brought against the extremely rational scientists pointing to the dangers of lead and CFCs. As with ozone, the Chicken Little metaphor would prove irresistible; the short-lived ICE front group would create a print ad in 1991 asking, "Who told you the earth was warming . . . Chicken Little?" The group also wrote a radio ad for Rush Limbaugh to read, that included the command, "Stop panicking!" (Right-wing media outlets have long amplified climate denial.)

The charge of fear-mongering, though, suggests that the mongers themselves are not actually afraid but are just trying to induce fear in others in order to manipulate them. Lee Raymond, CEO of Exxon (later ExxonMobil), warned an audience in 1996 that energy activists were "seeking to stir up all kinds of fears" in order to "force wrenching changes in our lifestyles and in the economies of the world's industrialized nations, with their real objectives often obscure."

As someone who worked for years in coalitions with various environmental groups, I can say that those charging fear-mongering have it largely backwards. Rather than cranking up the alarm, we were frequently warned by communications specialists that if we were too blunt about climate risks, people would just get scared and refuse to listen. Journalists covering climate change have also written about the challenge of responsibly conveying the outlines of the threat, including worst-case scenarios, without leaving people despairing and hopeless, or provoking charges of fear-mongering. Surely, some activists and media do exaggerate the risk, but mainstream activists, media, and scientists are subject to some very real pressures to understate it.

As for climate scientists being alarmists, science historian Keynyn Brysse and her coauthors make a compelling case that the culture of science—cautious, skeptical, and dispassionate—actually inclines scientists to err on "the side of least drama." Fear of being accused of alarmism by climate deniers likely enhances this inclination. As for the IPCC, the summaries it prepares for policy makers must get line-by-line acceptance from over one hundred world governments, making its reports something like the least common denominator of agreed-upon risk. Indeed, the IPCC reports have a history of underestimating many planetary changes, including the astounding speed at which Arctic sea ice has melted, with disruptive impacts for weather patterns around the world.

Meanwhile, many climate deniers are anything but reticent in warning about the risks of climate-protection policies. Western Fuels' former CEO Fred Palmer once warned a gathering of rural electric cooperatives that climate change policies meant "your future is at stake, the future of rural people is at stake. . . . Your communities, your way of life, the whole thing. They are after us, they want to change America." When the Obama EPA proposed rules limiting carbon emissions from the power sector in 2014, Joseph Bast, president of the Heartland Institute, said that by the time the EPA was finished, "millions of Americans will be freezing in the dark."

Obviously, those who claim not to fear climate change are not fearless; they simply fear something else (unless they are just fear-mongering). Dan Kahan, a professor of law and psychology at Yale, studies how culture and identity influence perception of public risk. He dug into what other social scientists have called the "white male effect"—the reported tendency of white men to be less concerned than women or minority men about public risks. Kahan and his colleagues found that it was only a subset of white men—those with a hierarchical and individualist world view—who were more "risk dismissive" than other segments of the population, and among them the effect was dramatic.

Importantly, these men are not dismissive of all risks. Whereas they see far *less* risk to society from global warming than others do, they see far *more* risk to society from environmental regulation.

In the case of climate deniers, the threat that clearly terrifies them most is the threat posed by government policies. Of course, worrying about bad government policies is not unreasonable; making sure governments do not abuse their tremendous power is a core function of any society. But believing that the only thing we have to fear is government itself blinds people to the dangers we need government to help us confront.

Projecting Persecution: "Stop Politicizing Science!"

Each of the industries profiled in this book complained of unfair persecution by its critics, with many referring to witch hunts or lynchings. In the case of climate denial, the complaints are coming not just from the corporations but from the scientists they have funded. They claim they are badly treated by mainstream climate scientists, and the resentment seems genuine. Of course, it would be surprising in such a high-stakes context if everyone, even the tiny minority whose views were rejected, felt fairly treated. The process of scientific peer review, which we count on to protect society from bad science, demands that scientists screen each other's work. When your peers judge your work as subpar, that might feel an awful lot like persecution. Put a few such rejected scientists together, mix in some ideological provocateurs affirming the unfairness of the scientifically ruling tribe, and pretty soon people start muttering about Galileo and how he was badly treated too.

A case in point is Dr. Willie Soon, who claims to be the victim of a "shameless attempt to silence my scientific research and writings, and to make an example out of me as a warning to any other researcher who may dare question in the slightest their fervently held orthodoxy" on global warming. Soon works at the Harvard-Smithsonian Center for Astrophysics. He has a doctoral degree in aerospace engineering but has written papers far outside the field of his formal training, including ones on paleoclimatology, sea level rise, and even polar bear population forecasts (claiming the bears would actually do better with more warming and less ice).

A few years ago it was revealed that Soon's compensation came not from Harvard or the Smithsonian but solely from outside grants, and since 2006 the grants had entirely come from fossil fuel and antiregulatory interests, including Southern Company, ExxonMobil, and the Charles Koch Foundation. Moreover, Soon often failed to report this funding in his scientific papers, in violation of conflict-of-interest disclosure standards. Southern Company was even promised that its role as funder would not be revealed without permission. In response to the resulting controversy, the Heartland Institute's president wrote that Soon's "critics are all ethically challenged and mental midgets by comparison."

This was by no means Soon's first controversy. In 2003, a paper he co-wrote about temperature trends over the past millennium was deemed so flawed that five of the ten editors of the small journal that published it resigned in protest. Soon had argued that the twentieth century was not particularly unusual, in contrast to widely accepted evidence that it was in fact dramatically warmer. He was quickly invited to testify before a Senate hearing held by Oklahoma senator James Inhofe, who would cite Soon as he declared global warming a "hoax" on the Senate floor.

Soon's study—a reinterpretation of other research—was partly funded by the American Petroleum Institute (disclosed, in this case). A former lobbyist for that group, Philip Cooney, had become chief of staff of the Bush White House's Council on Environmental Quality. Cooney, who had no scientific training, saw the Soon report as a "counterbalance" to the "dogmatic" views of the IPCC and National Academy of Sciences, according to a later-revealed memo. Cooney tried to force the EPA to cite the Soon paper in an agency report and delete references to the twentieth century's unusual warmth. The EPA decided to delete the entire climate chapter rather than so misrepresent the science. Two years later Cooney left the White House to work for ExxonMobil.

In short, Soon's views were rejected by scientific experts but elevated by industry-aligned, scientifically untrained politicians and appointees, who then used his rejected views to censor and attack the mainstream scientists. Despite his success depending entirely on this warm political embrace, Soon would go on to demand, before an audience at a right-wing think tank, that the scientific mainstream "stop politicizing science! . . . just stop!"

Meanwhile, Dr. Michael Mann—the prominent climate scientist and coauthor of the study about twentieth-century warming that Soon claimed to refute—would be subject to years of truly aggressive legal and political harassment by deniers (including conservative politicians). Antiregulatory groups launched a sustained campaign using public-records laws to get scientists' email communications with colleagues, along with other records normally part of private scientific deliberations. Although Mann was targeted most, the campaign continues to be waged against other scientists around the country. The most aggressive group, Energy and Environmental Legal Institute, pursues these records in the name of transparency while keeping its own funding secret, though some coal company funding has come to light through industry bankruptcy filings.

Some climate deniers have themselves been subject to public-records requests; the documents about Soon's funding were obtained from the Smithsonian by Greenpeace and the Climate Investigations Center using the Freedom of Information Act. As the Union of Concerned Scientists (UCS) has pointed out, though, there is a line between seeking funding agreements using narrow requests to "ferret out special interest influence on public institutions" and "intrusive requests for documents that were part of the research process." UCS has defended that line by publicly opposing requests that crossed into the intrusive, even when they were directed to climate deniers.

Projecting a Political Agenda: "Green Is the New Red"

Climate deniers often blame climate activism on that old standby, the Communist plot. Christopher Monckton, an eccentric British right-wing political activist, told a Tea Party rally that "the scientists who are pushing this scam have a political agenda. It's a Marxist agenda. Of course, they wouldn't call themselves that. They call themselves environmentalists. Green is the new red, if you like." Monckton has no obvious ties to industry but is a policy advisor to the Heartland Institute and frequently speaks at events hosted by industry-funded groups. (He has also carefully calculated that the odds that President Obama's birth certificate is genuine are "just 1 in 75 sextillion.")

Others allege different political agendas behind the push to preserve the climate. Western Fuels' Fred Palmer called the climate warnings part of a "jihad against industrial activity." Joseph Bast, former head of the Heartland Institute, called global warming part of progressives' "war on capitalism." Another Heartland statement would call climate lawsuits part of a strategy "attacking fossil fuels, progress, and modernity." (The antimodernity charge is particularly inaccurate since climate protection advocates are desperately pushing for the deployment of new, high-tech substitutes for old-fashioned fossil fuels.) Claims that an industry's critics are zealots of some sort go back at least as far as the slave trade and appear in almost every denial campaign. They can take various forms, evolving until they find one that works for the audience and moment at hand.

In the 1990s, charges of a political agenda were more vague, letting the public fill in whatever shadowy political motives they wished. One high-profile dispute erupted in 1996 when the Global Climate Coalition (GCC) and Frederick Seitz accused Benjamin Santer, a highly respected climate scientist and lead author of an important chapter of a recent IPCC report, of editing the chapter to downplay uncertainties with what the GCC called an "obvious political purpose." Dozens of IPCC scientists came to Santer's defense, making it clear the edits were entirely proper. Seitz himself, meanwhile, was hardly apolitical. A truly prominent physicist during the Cold War, his ardent anti-Communism inspired him after retirement to cofound a think tank to defend President Reagan's controversial nuclear missile defense plans. He also had worked for the R.J. Reynolds tobacco company for years, and he and his think tank—which would attract substantial funding from ExxonMobil and Koch foundations—would challenge the science around tobacco and ozone as well as climate.

Charges that those pushing for climate policies are actually driven by a political agenda other than climate protection never made much sense given the wide range of people involved. Within the United States, they have included not just Democrats and the left, but some prominent Republicans prior to about 2009, when climate denial took over the party. Most were moderate Republicans, but one conservative—former congressman Bob Inglis of South Carolina—lost a primary after admitting he believed people were changing the climate. Inglis dates the shift in his party's mood to the financial crisis, telling *Frontline* that the crisis "made it possible for some well-spent money to blow doubt into the science because, you know, the bankers failed us, the federal government is failing us, it's spending too much money, and these scientists who are funded by that federal government, they're probably in it, too. And besides, they're godless liberals."

Globally, the goal of limiting global warming is supported by people of virtually every political stripe in the world outside of American conservatism/libertarianism. Indeed, it is remarkable that all the nations of the world (except now the United States) were able to overcome their ideological differences to adopt the Paris Agreement in 2015. Climate protection may be the most nonideological—or at least ideologically inclusive—effort in history. It currently excludes only those who enshrine unfettered market activity as the centerpiece of their political beliefs, as the most vocal climate deniers have done.

THE HUBRIS OF DENIAL: RISK, DOUBT, AND THE BURDEN OF PROOF

There are many reasons why the risks of climate change would not fully register in the human mind. In addition to the denial-provoking gravity of the threat, climate change is not the type of risk our minds evolved to detect. It is gradual, and it derives largely from the familiar and widespread practice of burning fossil fuels. It is something we all contribute to and cannot just blame on enemy evildoers. And it manifests as natural phenomena like heat waves, droughts, fires, storms, and floods; we need experts, assessing global data and long-term trends, to tell us if what is happening is truly unusual. As such, climate change just does not provoke the sense of threat we would get from a stalking tiger, a hostile attacker, or an eerie and unrecognizably novel situation. All these factors surely make it easier for climate deniers to internally deny the risk and to convince others to do the same.

But what exactly are they still denying? The Heartland Institute has for years hosted conferences where climate deniers talk to each other and the media (events known to critics as "denial-paloozas"). At one such event in 2014, speaker Christopher Monckton surveyed the room and declared that everyone there agreed that humanity's "emissions of CO_2 and other greenhouse gases have contributed to the measured global warming since 1950." His point was to make it clear that "we are not climate change deniers." Monckton also predicted additional CO_2-emission-driven warming in the decades ahead, though less than the consensus predictions. (He undermined his bid to appear reasonable, though, when he went on to berate the media for ignoring facts that "go against the climate Communist party line.")

What continues to define these people as "deniers" in my book is their unshaken belief that climate change is simply no big deal and there is no reason to go out of our way to prevent more of it.[*] "There is no need to reduce carbon dioxide emissions and no point in attempting to do so," as one recent Heartland document succinctly put it.

One reason people might be confused about how much climate deniers actually accept about the science is the vitriolic rhetoric of so many of them. Only two years before this conference, Heartland had issued its press release saying that manmade global warming was a "fringe" view (held by mass murderers, etc.) and that still believing in it was "more than a little nutty." After this conference, in 2016, Heartland's science director gave a speech entitled "Man-Caused Global Warming: The Greatest Scam in World History" (rather than one called, say, "Man-Caused Global Warming: We Agree We're Causing It But Predict Less Warming Than Others Do.")

Charles Koch is among the deniers who accept that our CO_2 emissions are causing global warming, but he is confident the climate is "changing in a mild and manageable way." It is worth noting here that evidence from psychological studies suggests that the experience of power promotes "illusory control"—that is, a belief among power holders that they can control outcomes that are actually beyond their influence.

Contrast Charles Koch's view with that of one of the pioneers of climate science, Columbia's Dr. Wallace Broecker. He is winner of the President's National Medal of Science for, among other things, shedding light on the abrupt climate changes of earth's distant past. The "paleoclimate," he says, shows that the "Earth tends to over-respond. . . . The Earth system has amplifiers and feedbacks that mushroom small impacts into large responses." He does not view climate change as mild and manageable. On the contrary, he says, "The climate system is an angry beast and we are poking it with sticks."

---

[*] By this definition, ExxonMobil and most other major oil companies no longer qualify as deniers; they publicly accept the need for a carbon tax or other policies to cut emissions. However, their continued search for and investment in new oil supplies are not consistent with the deep and rapid emission cuts we need to stay well below 2°C warming, and ExxonMobil does still fund some groups that qualify as climate deniers.

It is worth pausing here to appreciate the breathtaking hubris of this now-dominant strain of climate denial. These deniers accept that humanity's pollution has disrupted a fundamental, complex, and awesomely powerful planetary system with a history of violent shifts, yet they express complete confidence that the global changes we are inadvertently unleashing will be harmless, even beneficial. It is a bit like a pregnant woman who, after learning that a drug she is consuming causes sometimes devastating chromosomal changes, especially as it accumulates in the body, continues to consume it in ever greater quantities, somehow confident her baby will only benefit from the resulting genetic mutations.

Maintaining such wholly unfounded confidence (and selling it to others) requires spinning every uncertainty your way by keeping the burden of proof perpetually on those pointing to a climate threat. Sometimes this spin is explicit, like when the Global Climate Coalition argued in 1996 that "the scientific community has not yet met the 'burden of proof' that greenhouse gas emissions are likely to cause serious climatic impacts." More often, it is implicitly built into the conversation, as it was in so many other public debates, like those over leaded gas, ozone, and tobacco. And because there is no discussion of who should initially bear the burden of proof, there is also no discussion of whether to revisit the question and shift that burden once the evidence reaches a certain point.

Whoever does not bear the burden of proof gets the benefit of the doubt and thus has an incentive to exaggerate or manufacture doubt. The tobacco industry responded to this incentive ("doubt is our product") as do climate deniers. A recent analysis of decades of ExxonMobil's climate change communications by Harvard science historians Geoffrey Supran and Naomi Oreskes found that while 80 percent or more of the company's internal documents and peer-reviewed papers acknowledged that climate change is real and human-caused, only 12 percent of its paid "advertorials" aimed at the general news-reading public did so. Instead, 81 percent of these ads raised doubts.

Oil and gas executives were recently reminded of the value of raising scientific doubt by Rick ("win ugly or lose pretty") Berman who explained in his secretly taped 2014 presentation that "people get overwhelmed by the science and [think] 'I don't know who to believe.' But, if you got enough on your side you get people into a position of paralysis about the issue. . . . You get in people's mind a tie. They don't know who is right. And you get all ties because the tie basically insures the status quo. . . . I'll take a tie any day if I'm trying to preserve the status quo."

Imagine how different the climate debate would be if—after decades of analysis and mountains of data pointing to extreme danger—we now finally shifted the burden of proof and started demanding that climate deniers prove the safety of continued pollution. Where is the proof that we can safely raise atmospheric CO_2 to levels not seen on earth for millions of years, since long before humans existed, when the earth was much warmer and seas far higher? What is your alternative explanation for the melting ice, shifting ecosystems, growing extremes, and other evidence of warming? Show us the sophisticated computer models that accurately simulate the climate system, that factor in ongoing pollution, and that still show a stable future climate with no significant risk of catastrophic changes. Demonstrate precisely how we can be confident that pushing CO_2 levels higher will not trigger the feedback systems that in Earth's past have repeatedly amplified small changes into extreme planetary transformations.

Those urging us to heedlessly continue down our current polluting path would need to show evidence of virtually complete scientific consensus, including assurances from all the major scientific academies and relevant scientific societies throughout the world, that pushing CO_2 concentrations ever higher was safe. (We would not, however, insist on agreement from all scientists, even those who were the most financially and ideologically invested in the opposite conclusion, because that would be ridiculous.) And wherever there was a gap in our knowledge—about exactly how our complex climate and life on earth would react to these unprecedented changes—that uncertainty would not make us feel safer. We would understand that it increases risk because what we don't know can hurt us.

IT ISN'T POLLUTION: "OUR WORLD IS DEFICIENT IN CARBON DIOXIDE"

Climate deniers have tried to raise doubts about the science in more ways that I can list, but a few arguments warrant mention here. One approach has been to trivialize humanity's impact on the natural world. A 1998

Exxon pamphlet has a pie chart showing that only a small amount of CO_2 emissions come from fossil fuels compared to natural sources, and it asks, "Does the tiny portion of greenhouse gases caused by burning fossil fuels have a measurable effect on worldwide climate? No one knows for sure." As Exxon well knew, there is a big difference between natural CO_2, which is emitted and absorbed as part of a balanced natural cycle, and fossil CO_2 which disrupts that balance by building up in the atmosphere over the decades. Exxon's argument here was similar to the arguments of those who minimized the threat of humanity's CFC emissions by pointing to nature's greater chlorine emissions.

Deniers have often questioned whether the world is really warming. Exxon CEO Lee Raymond claimed in 1997, for example, that "the Earth is cooler today than it was twenty years ago." He was ignoring ground level temperature readings, which clearly showed warming, in favor of records derived from satellites which, for a time, seemed to show cooling. But inferring temperatures indirectly via satellite is a complex process. Various errors in that process have been discovered, and once corrected, the satellite records have shown warming.

More recently, many deniers claimed that warming has not progressed in the twenty-first century. This claim depended on starting with 1998, a particularly high spike in the annual surface temperature record, rather than looking at the multidecade trend. In fact, the warming trend was continuing, just at a slower pace. Then after 2014 the speed of warming accelerated again, returning to the fast pace of the late twentieth century. As of this writing, the years from 2014 through 2018 were the five warmest years on Earth since records began in 1880.

A more dramatic means of creating doubt about the climate risk has been to try to radically reframe rising CO_2 levels not as a threat but as a global blessing. Western Fuels' CEO Fred Palmer was an early evangelist of the idea that the world needs us to emit more CO_2, not less. Plants need CO_2 to carry out photosynthesis, so, the argument goes, more CO_2 makes plants happier, the world greener, and life better. Western Fuels even funded a video released in 1992 in which a narrator explains that "our world is deficient in carbon dioxide, and a doubling of atmospheric CO_2 is very beneficial." Western Fuels later launched the Greening Earth Society to spread the message.

Palmer has called adding CO_2 to the air "doing the work of the Lord," not unlike Goldman Sachs CEO Lloyd Blankfein claiming bankers were doing "God's work." However, Blankfein reportedly said it with an impish grin, while Palmer describes CO_2 pollution as literally part of a divine plan. And he thinks calling a warmer, high-CO_2 world a bad thing is "preposterous. Warm is good, cold is bad."

A witness for coal giant Peabody Energy (for which Palmer worked after Western Fuels) testified in a Minnesota proceeding in 2015 that the benefits of CO_2 exceed its harms by "orders of magnitude" and "there is no limit for the foreseeable future to these benefits as CO_2 emissions increase." Craig Idso, a researcher whose work has long attracted industry support, has even stressed the danger of *not* emitting CO_2, claiming that it will be "next to impossible to meet the challenge of feeding Earth's population without a rise in the Earth's temperature," adding, "CO_2 is not a pollutant. It is the very elixir of life."

All this is not quite as insane as it sounds, but close. CO_2 is indeed a plant fertilizer. Net plant growth appears to have increased with rising CO_2 levels. However, the fact that CO_2 levels directly affect plant growth and physiology does not make it wise to haphazardly crank up global CO_2 concentrations, any more than it's wise to crank up global levels of rainfall, solar radiation, or heat. In fact, the CO_2 fertilizer effect just means we are destabilizing the world's ecosystems in yet another way, triggering another chain of unintended planetary consequences we cannot predict or control. Higher CO_2 advantages some plants over others, including several fast-growing weeds, threatening agricultural production and altering natural landscapes; poison ivy, for example, seems to really love the extra CO_2 and grows extra big and toxic.

Moreover, while higher CO_2 stimulates plant growth and carbohydrate production, it actually lowers the nutritional value of most food crops, reducing protein and minerals levels, with frightening implications for a rising population. By burning fossil fuels we are turning yesterday's hydrocarbons into tomorrow's carbohydrates, effectively putting the whole planet onto a higher-carb diet. And even if all the impacts of higher CO_2 on plant life were somehow positive, those benefits would come hand in hand with the more severe heat, droughts, storms, and floods and the more acidified ocean of a high-CO_2 world—a combination that truly threatens food security.

The strongest advocates for more CO_2 pollution have long displayed not just a financial stake in the issue but a passionate ideological streak. Botanist Keith Idso (part of a father-and-two-sons team devoted to singing the praises of CO_2) once ended an article describing the benefits of CO_2 with this less-than-scientific observation: "This good news is not what those intent on destroying our freedoms and imposing their will on the nations of the earth want us to hear, and they skillfully promote alternative voices to confuse the issue. The truth, however, will not be suppressed." The article was published in the magazine of the ultraconservative John Birch Society.

THE FUTILITY DEFENSE: MOTIVATED TECHNO-HELPLESSNESS

There are many psychological barriers to feeling truly responsible for climate change, including the fact that everybody contributes to it and there is not much a single person, business, or even nation can do to slow it. Among the arguments that deniers have successfully used to block efforts to reduce our carbon emissions is claiming that such efforts were simply futile: small steps will have a trivial climate impact, and major strides will be impossible because humanity is tied to rising fossil fuel use and emissions for the foreseeable future.

This is an easy argument for the deniers themselves to believe, and it likely reduces any sense of guilt for stopping action on carbon emissions. Steve Coll, in his history of ExxonMobil, describes how CEO Lee Raymond did not believe there were any cost-effective steps yet available to ease the climate change problem. ExxonMobil's long-term energy modeling kept projecting rising fossil fuel use and rising emissions, and after 2004 the company presented its projections to various audiences as a "reality check." Coll quotes a UK environmental activist writing in 2005 that Raymond was no longer questioning the science; he "simply predicts an endless rise in the demand for the fossil fuels his company sells, and maintains that there is nothing that can be done to alter that."

Coal advocate Fred Palmer stated in 2000 that "the current batch of renewables (the solar and wind) I really do not believe, long-term, are going to be viable," adding that "we're not going to reduce coal or gasoline consumption in the United States." He called those worried about climate change the "ultimate pessimists," while claiming for himself the mantle of technological optimism, which he associated with keeping the existing coal plants running while working on a "new generation of clean coal technologies." The technology he was referring to was carbon capture and storage (CCS), a costly and still developing technology that collects carbon emissions from a power plant and sequesters it in geologic formations underground (though Palmer's preference for a world with more rather than less CO_2 surely undermined his enthusiasm for carbon capture).

In the years since, solar and wind have delivered far more cause for optimism than carbon capture technology (and US coal consumption has fallen significantly). Solar and wind power costs have plummeted and installations have skyrocketed, in no small part due to government policies around the world that stimulated innovation by guaranteeing a market or providing a direct subsidy. These policies have drawn wind and solar into the marketplace, creating the critical opportunity to "learn by doing"—gaining the efficiency lessons available only from real-world deployment—and to achieve economies of scale. Meanwhile, despite government support, carbon capture technology progress has been slow at best.

Kenneth P. Green, of the free market American Enterprise Institute (AEI), argued before a House committee in 2010 that we should basically stop even trying to reduce carbon emissions. Even if you think there is a looming disaster, he said, "there is no rational argument for continuing to focus on mitigating greenhouse gas emissions in the near and even mid-term. It is time policy makers recognize that despite the claims of renewable energy and efficiency hucksters, we do not have the technologies needed to significantly curb greenhouse gas emissions without causing massive economic disruption." He was urging, in essence, that we give up trying to reduce emissions, not unlike the writer secretly funded by the tobacco industry, who told smokers to give up trying to quit. In claiming the futility of policies to reduce carbon emissions, Green was deviating from the position of one of AEI's funders, ExxonMobil, which since 2009 has publicly supported a carbon tax. ExxonMobil stopped funding some denier groups around 2006, but it has continued to fund other denier groups like AEI that work against carbon taxes.

Also unlike some of the groups it supports, ExxonMobil did not support abandoning the Paris Agreement. In fact, the company actually joined the Oil and Gas Climate Initiative, a group of oil companies that support the Paris Agreement's "agenda for global action and the need for urgency." And yet the company's latest annual long-term global energy projection, on which it bases its investment decisions, still shows carbon emissions continuing to rise until 2035, staying at a high plateau until 2040, the outer edge of the forecast. This projection is alarming because the latest IPCC analysis finds that even by 2030 global emissions need to fall by about a quarter just to give us a decent chance at limiting warming to 2°C, and by roughly half for a chance at achieving the much safer 1.5°C limit. So despite ostensibly supporting the Paris Agreement, the company is planning on a world that utterly fails to meet the Paris goals. And despite the climate turmoil that would result from this failure, ExxonMobil's forecast blithely assumes a doubling global GDP. The company still effectively denies the essential conflict between a thriving world and high carbon emissions, decades after that conflict became apparent.[*]

ExxonMobil has apparently little confidence in humanity's ability to find ways to live without fossil fuels, but it has expressed in the past complete confidence in society's ability to adapt to the irreversible harms associated with a destabilized climate. As then-CEO Rex Tillerson put it in 2012, "We [humans] have spent our entire existence adapting, OK? So we will adapt to this. Changes in weather patterns that move crop production areas around—we'll adapt to that. It's an engineering problem, and it has engineering solutions. . . . It's not a problem that we can't solve."

This self-serving blend of techno-pessimism and techno-optimism is similar to what we saw in chapter 3. GM executives claimed little

---

[*] A Trump administration EPA document has similarly projected warming of about 4°C in the twenty-first century, which is surprising given that administration officials have not embraced this prospect in more public statements. However, rather than using such catastrophic warming to justify more aggressive pollution controls, the administration has used it to justify dismantling Obama-era fuel efficiency standards for cars.

confidence in engineers' ability to design more crashworthy cars but had lots of ideas about how society could reengineer the nation's millions of miles of roadways, even imagining roads built upon city rooftops. In the same way, it is much easier for those in the fossil fuel industry and the deniers they support to imagine the world reengineering itself around a dangerously destabilized climate than to imagine engineering a world without carbon-emitting fossil fuels.

A BLINDING IDEOLOGY: "THIS IS WHO I AM"

Climate denial is clearly fueled by both profit-seeking and tribalism. It is also fueled by ideology—especially the passionate libertarianism of the sort embraced by Charles and David Koch. Over the decades the brothers built a political infrastructure to promote the idea that virtually all of society should be governed by unfettered market forces.

The Koch brothers were steeped in the politics of the paranoid right from an early age. Their father, Fred Koch, had built refineries in the Soviet Union during Stalin's rule. According to Daniel Schulman's book *Sons of Wichita: How the Koch Brothers Became America's Most Powerful and Private Dynasty*, Fred's "firsthand experiences witnessing a society fully under the boot heel of government was regular table talk for the Koch boys." Fred would become a founding member of the ultraconservative John Birch Society, a group whose leader suspected Eisenhower of being a secret Communist. According to one person who attended Birch Society meetings in his youth, the group used phony front groups, ironically modeling itself on the subterfuge of the Communist Party.

Charles and David would join the Birchers in the early 1960s, but by the mid-1960s, Charles had embraced an extreme libertarianism, declaring that the government's role in a capitalist system should be "only to keep a check on those who might attempt to interfere with the laws of supply and demand." (Charles would reportedly consider both Alan Greenspan and Milton Friedman sellouts for trying to make government more efficient rather than trying to tear it out at the root.) Charles set out in the 1970s to build a movement that would bring about wholesale social and political change, founding and funding a host of libertarian groups, projects, and publications. Charles was so contemptuous of government that a fellow libertarian said he "seemed to me to be an anarchist."

David Koch became the Libertarian Party candidate for vice president in 1980 in a largely Koch-funded campaign. The Libertarian platform that year advocated, among other things, abolishing virtually all regulations (environmental, consumer, worker safety, nuclear safety, antitrust, food and drug), dismantling the social safety net (Social Security, Medicare, Medicaid, all aid to the poor), privatizing virtually all traditional government functions (schools, roads, mail, water systems, even the issuance of money), and eventually eliminating all taxation. In its ideological rigidity and utopianism, it was a movement reminiscent of Communism, except instead of destroying the private sector, it wanted to virtually destroy the public one.

Over the next three decades the Koch brothers contributed over $100 million to dozens of groups advancing their views. As *New Yorker* writer Jane Mayer put it in her book *Dark Money: The Hidden History of the Billionaires behind the Rise of the Radical Right,* their "front groups demonized the American government, casting it as the enemy rather than the democratic representatives of its citizens. . . . Cumulatively, the many-tentacled ideological machine they built came to be known as the Kochtopus." The Kochs and their foundations gave more to climate-denying groups than ExxonMobil. The Kochs would also acquire tremendous political power as the hub of a network of like-minded wealthy political donors capable of doling out hundreds of millions of dollars per major election. The head of the most powerful Koch-affiliated group, Americans for Prosperity, would take credit for driving out of office the remaining Republicans who took the climate threat seriously and for a significant role in defeating climate legislation early in the Obama administration.

Charles Koch has said that "market principles have changed my life and guide everything I do." This view is not incompatible with fighting climate change; however, markets are essentially blind to the problem as long as greenhouse gases can be emitted for free. Companies that pollute more will outcompete those that use newer, cleaner but costlier technology. The point of a cap-and-trade law or a carbon tax is to correct this glaring market failure by creating a price signal that markets will respond to by innovating cleaner technologies and practices.* Some libertarians recognize this, which is why a branch of the movement (including refugees from the Koch's Cato Institute) supports a carbon tax.

Charles Koch does not. When pressed by *Fortune* magazine to explain how markets can solve climate change without any financial incentive, he said that there *is* an incentive because customers worried about climate change will pressure companies to act, like Walmart has apparently been pressuring Koch Industries. But of course, customer pressure depends on sophisticated and powerful customers who understand the urgency of the threat, which would require utterly rejecting everything the Kochs and the groups they fund say about the climate science. The nation's loudest evangelists for the miraculous power of markets are inhibiting those markets from helping solve climate change both by blocking a market price signal and muting customer pressure.

Charles Koch adamantly insists his political agenda is in no way driven by a profit motive—on the contrary, he says, his company benefits from today's corporate welfare and even by regulations, and it will lose out by eliminating them (a view that glosses over his company's deep involvement in refining and distributing oil). He fights for libertarianism, he says, because "I'd rather die for something than live for nothing. So there's no alternative for me. This is who I am."

An ideology that defines who you are could blind you to many things, like the fact that government bestows some "special favors" through inaction rather than action, such as letting the fossil fuel industry keep shifting the costs of pollution onto the world rather than building it into the cost of its products. An ideology you would die for could let you believe you are fighting corporate "cronyism" and "special interests" and trying to fix a system rigged by the wealthy, as Charles Koch claims he is doing, even while building a political operation that gives unprecedented power to a handful of rich donors. Such unshakeable ideology could even give

---

* For the record, I support putting a price on carbon through a tax or cap-and-trade, but given the urgency of the crisis we face and the well-documented inefficiencies in the energy markets, I think it would be a mistake to rely solely on a market signal to drive the necessary technological changes. Even with a strong price signal in place, other government policies that have proven highly effective—like energy efficiency standards, renewable energy standards, and aggressive public investment in cleaner infrastructure—would still be needed to drive the transformation as quickly as possible with the least human cost and social disruption.

you the confidence that humans can disrupt the planet's climate and somehow keep that climate change "mild and manageable."

NEW FRONTS IN THE BATTLE: FIGHTING CLIMATE CHANGE WITHOUT FEDERAL SUPPORT

One could conclude that climate change is a problem humans lack the psychological ability to address. The long-term risk is too hard to perceive, the diffused responsibility is too hard to accept, and our innate tribalism makes it too hard to build the needed trust and cooperation. At the very least, these factors help explain why climate deniers have been so successful in stalling progress.

Another way to look at it is to recognize just how much humanity has achieved despite these psychological barriers and the decades of well-funded climate denial. The climate threat has been acknowledged by people around the world who have indeed taken action in both the public and private sectors to advance new carbon-free or low-carbon technologies. Globally, hundreds of billions of dollars are being invested in renewable energy every year. The clean energy revolution is finally underway; it just needs to grow at a *much* faster pace given how little time we have left to make the needed emission cuts.

Unquestionably, climate denial has slowed humanity's progress in this race against time. US CO_2 emissions from fossil fuels kept rising for more than a quarter century after the oil industry's sobering meeting at LaGuardia in 1980, not peaking until 2007. Without the industry's denial campaign, US emissions might well have peaked in the early 1990s, as they did in some other advanced nations where denial never took root. In that case, today's US emissions would be far lower and clean energy even more widely deployed and technologically advanced. The United States could have pushed more ambitious targets in global climate talks, rather than so often weakening them, meaning global emissions would be lower; global concentrations of greenhouse gases would be lower; and we would have a better chance of avoiding catastrophic future warming.

In the United States, today's climate policies are being set by yesterday's most-hardline deniers, especially from the coal industry. (Andrew Wheeler, the current head of the EPA, was until recently a lobbyist representing coal magnate Bob Murray.) The Trump administration is working to dismantle the Obama-era regulations driving pollution cuts, and US energy-related carbon emissions rose in 2018. Indeed, the administration has even tried to force the purchase of power from uncompetitive old coal plants. It tried to justify this unprecedented market interference using national security arguments, even though those who oversee power grid reliability see no need to keep those polluting old plants running. At the same time it is trying to slash critically important federal research and development funding into renewables and energy efficiency technologies.

Fortunately, a rising tide of US states and cities are stepping up to drive climate action using their own authority. State and local standards have been pushing emissions down for years, but now they are getting far more aggressive. As of this writing, five states have new laws requiring 100 percent carbon-free electricity by 2045 or 2050, led by California (the world's fifth largest economy), and many other states are moving toward such a commitment. Locally, over one hundred cities have made similar or more aggressive pledges. One major American electric utility, Xcel Energy, has voluntarily committed itself to 100 percent carbon-free electricity by 2050.

Some states and cities are also turning to the courts, challenging the dismantling of federal regulations or suing big oil companies for compensation for climate damages. The New York and Massachusetts attorneys general have been investigating ExxonMobil to see if its years of downplaying climate risks amounted to fraud upon investors, and New York sued in 2018 alleging "a long-standing fraudulent scheme." ExxonMobil—represented by a lawyer that earlier defended the tobacco industry against government claims—responded aggressively even by litigation standards, seeking court authority to question the attorneys general for evidence of "bad faith." ExxonMobil has complained—with no apparent sense of irony—that it is the victim of a "campaign of misinformation," of "fake journalism," and of politically motivated foundations "funding a conspiracy against us."

While trying to avoid responsibility for its past denials, ExxonMobil stepped up its claimed support for climate action. ExxonMobil (and many other major corporations) have endorsed a carbon tax plan, authored by elder statesmen of the Republican Party from earlier administrations, with significant bipartisan backing. The plan would eliminate EPA climate regulations, block litigation of the sort oil companies are facing, impose a gradually rising tax on carbon emissions, and give revenues back to taxpayers. ExxonMobil has even contributed money to promote the plan, though at the same time it and other oil companies spent heavily to defeat a 2018 Washington ballot initiative establishing a carbon fee.

Even if the oil industry truly supports this federal carbon tax plan (and the litigation immunity is a substantial incentive), it has virtually no chance of passage until there is a dramatic shift of political power. The alternate reality created by decades of corporate-sponsored climate denial is now entwined with the larger US political polarization. Meanwhile, those racing to prevent global catastrophe must do so over the opposition of the world's most powerful national government. It is the most vivid example yet of how industrial-strength denial can put blinders on enough people to endanger the entire world and why efforts to overcome such denial are so important.

Conclusion

SHIFTING THE SOCIAL NORM TOWARD THE PUBLIC INTEREST

Let's begin by looking at what went right. This book recounts eight case studies where people stepped forward and drew attention to a grave social harm caused by profit-seeking commercial enterprises. These problem solvers confronted ignorance, falsehoods, and powerful interests, bringing evidence forward in the enlightened belief that public opinion and policy could be shaped by facts and reason. They urged people to work toward solutions in the name of the greater good, and they often kept at it for decades.

These scientists, journalists, activists, doctors, lawyers, judges, legislators, regulators, diplomats, and others rallied society toward change by appealing to the better angels of our nature: our reason and our concern for others and the future. Their efforts, in many cases still underway, made the world safer, healthier, less cruel, and more sustainable.

The people confronting corporate denial in the past built on social norms that elevate the pursuit of truth and the public good. These norms were developed over centuries and manifested, if only imperfectly, in society's support of science, a free press, civic activism, the rule of law, representative democracy, and international cooperation. As we consider the norms and incentives that promote corporate denial and touch on some ways to confront it, remember the countervailing forces that have already helped us overcome it in the past and will help us in the future. We are not starting from scratch.

IF YOU WERE A SUPERVILLAIN: A SYSTEM DESIGNED TO EVADE MORAL ALARMS AND TRIGGER COGNITIVE BIASES

As I mentioned in the introduction, my interest in this topic derives from confronting climate denial and wondering with some astonishment what was wrong with the people doing the denying. And while my frustration was directed at the individuals involved, my curiosity was drawn to the larger social context that seemed to promote the denial. My subsequent research confirmed my suspicion that corporate denial is a powerful and dangerous social phenomenon that can be understood and overcome only with social forces in mind.

It is hard to see past the individual deniers and focus on the social context, perhaps due in part to the fundamental attribution error discussed in the auto safety chapter. We seem naturally inclined to overattribute the causation of an event to a person's choices or disposition, rather than to situational factors, whether we are discussing an auto accident or an instance of corporate denial. In America, this tendency may be strengthened by our enhanced cultural emphasis on individualism and a lurking suspicion that looking at the role of social forces on personal behavior represents a dangerous collectivism. And of course our instinct to morally judge each other discourages the consideration of social context; looking at factors contributing to people's bad behavior feels too much like we are excusing them from personal blame. This is especially difficult when the wrongdoers are powerful people.

When a dangerous behavior appears again and again through history, though, manifested in similar ways by so many people, it is critical to look past the individual if you actually want to break the cycle. To do so does not mean exoneration or abandoning the push for accountability, but it might require stepping outside a judgmental framework and recognizing that people's innate moral instincts evolved to resolve very different

challenges. These instincts are insufficient to prevent many ordinary people from causing and denying the kind of inadvertent systemic harms so
often resulting from competitive group economic activity, at least when
other social incentives and messages discourage them from worrying
about such harms.

In fact, if you were trying to design a society that would encourage people to impose grave risks on each other and the planet—because, say, you
were a supervillain hoping to get our civilization to destroy itself—you
would look for ways to evade people's moral instincts and trigger their
cognitive biases. The society you would design would look a lot like the
modern, corporation-dominated global economy.

You would have people work in groups, the larger the better, because
that would promote moral disengagement, but that is just the starting
point. You would divide their labor into many narrow roles, encouraging
people to feel responsible for just their role (to mind their own business).
You would create a steep hierarchy. The people not at the top would feel
powerless, prompting them to mentally yield responsibility for the group's
actions to those above. The power of those at the top, meanwhile, would
tighten their focus on their own and the group's goals, leaving less brain
space to consider the risks their goal pursuit may impose on society.

Then—and this is particularly creative—you would encourage all the
humans to pretend that this group is actually a distinct person, morally
separate from each of them, with its own name, rights and responsibilities, as if it had its own body, or *corpus*. You would call it a corporation.
This imaginary person could own property, enter into debts, hire people,
sell goods, and take all other economically relevant actions in its own
name.

Even better, you would divide official control of the corporation into
tiny shares so that an entirely different and distant group of humans could
own little pieces of it. The existence of these "shareholders" would reduce
managers' sense of moral responsibility for the corporation's social impact,
since they would feel a stronger duty to the shareholders than to society.
The shareholders, meanwhile, would not feel morally responsible for the
corporation's social impact either, given their ignorance of its activities
and the abstract, anonymous, transactional, and often temporary nature
of their connection to it. For good measure, your laws would say that

shareholders could not be held liable for whatever damage the corporation does.

You would make the corporations legally immortal with no limit on size, letting some of them accumulate tremendous wealth and power. Those profiting from the corporation would naturally come to feel that their enterprise has a right to exist in perpetuity and would fight to ensure its survival. Even though they are socially created pretend persons (which were once formed solely for specific purposes), modern corporations would not need to pursue a socially beneficial goal. They could pursue any legal purpose, and you would give them great influence over society's process of deciding what remained legal.

You would have the corporations compete with other corporations. In fact, this formation would echo the tribes-in-conflict-with-other-tribes setting within which our social and moral instincts first evolved, making it easier to trigger tribal loyalties, animosities, and biases. Competition would occur in far-flung market environments that emphasize short-term anonymous transactions rather than sustained human relationships. As global markets became more entwined and as supply chains became longer and more obscure, the humans working for the corporations would feel ever more distant from the other humans affected by their activities. Each link in the economic chain would reduce their awareness of and sense of responsibility for what happened elsewhere in the chain.

You would reward corporations for innovation, and with their accumulating wealth they would often operate at the cutting edge of technology, inadvertently creating new and unknown risks from new products or pollutants. The competitive setting would mean that if they spent more on safer practices, they would lose out to competitors employing cheaper, more dangerous practices, creating a constant downward pressure toward socially costly behavior. And each corporation would know that even if it stopped the risky behavior, its competitors would just pick up more market share with no net change in harm. This sense of the futility of trying to reduce social costs would further drain any sense of responsibility for those costs.

You would set up corporate systems that kept humans tightly focused on money. Shareholders would come to expect a continuous flow of short-term profits, and managers would feel pressured to deliver. In fact, you would tell managers they had a legal obligation to maximize shareholder profit. The time pressure and fixation on the bottom line would keep everyone in a transactional mindset that discourages awareness of the human impact of their actions. Corporate profits would be frequently and publicly announced, widely celebrated by society at large when high and bemoaned when low. Money would be treated within some corporations as the sole measure of social status, competence, worth, and dominance. In a way, money would become a substitute for the social relationships around which their moral instincts first evolved.

You would still need to help many humans reframe their behavior to avoid moral qualms when harms caused by their corporate activity came to light. So you would immerse them in an ideology that assured them that their corporation's pursuit of profit would automatically, as if through an invisible hand, result in the public good. This ideology would exonerate and amplify their natural greed while muting their natural concern for others and help reduce the fear that society might condemn them for their actions. If society got too comfortable with the idea of a government check on corporate activities, you would promote a more extreme ideology that had an almost religious faith in the power of markets to solve any problem and condemned government interference in those markets as immoral. This sort of market fundamentalism would be particularly popular with people who had financially benefited from markets, and they would use that wealth to further promote this ideology.

Your courts would give corporations key constitutional rights originally put in place to protect the most vulnerable individual humans. These rights would ensure corporations could use some of their accumulated wealth to influence the democracy and to delay societal efforts to reduce corporate-caused harms. This would further help the humans associated with your harm-causing corporations to avoid feeling immoral because they would remain comfortably within the social norm. The flow of information through your society would also be given mostly to media corporations with their own profit motives, and most would be heavily dependent on advertising revenues from other corporations, making it hard for them to criticize corporate activity.

With these features in place, it is easy to imagine what would happen when a corporation was charged by outsiders with causing harm. Those who run or own it will not *feel* morally responsible, and because their moral alarms are not ringing, their minds will find ways to explain why the charges must be wrong. They will experience a jolt of tribalism, intensifying their defensive confirmation bias. They will exalt their own tribe's character and contributions, attack critics' motives, convince themselves they are defenders of freedom and the victims of unfairness, and nurse a sense of injured entitlement if society's judgment rises against them. This cultivated resentment will help them rationalize the use of front groups and other deceptions to, in their minds, level the playing field. They will deny causal links between their actions and the harm in question, express baseless confidence in their future exoneration, exaggerate any shred of doubt to maintain the status quo, minimize the alleged harm, shift blame for it to other causes, and/or find ways to justify the harm by viewing it as unavoidable or surely better than the alternatives.

And these approaches will succeed in perpetuating the harm in question for decades, even to the point of endangering the entire world.

But corporations were not created by a supervillain hoping to see the world destroy itself. They were created by us, or rather our governments, hoping among other things to help the world build itself. They were formed to stimulate collective economic action outside the confines of government by harnessing the personal profit motive and reducing personal financial risk, and their success has brought astounding wealth and social benefits. The question is how to reduce the social costs that also come from corporate activity while hanging on to as many of the benefits as possible or even enhancing them. We can't change human nature, but we don't need to. We can change the social structures and norms that we, by nature, are so profoundly influenced by.

This book recounts several dramatic shifts in the social norms. Societies were persuaded that the slave trade was a respectable industry, and then that it was evil. They were persuaded that consuming radium was healthful, and then that it was deadly. They were persuaded that smoking could be harmlessly integrated into public life, and then to socially discourage this deadly addiction. And so they can be persuaded that despite all the wealth created by corporations, their activities pose particular threats that we must address.

TACKLING CLIMATE DENIAL FIRST

I first conceived of this book years before I actually began to write it. Climate denial was on the rise in the United States, but so was climate awareness and action. I remember naïvely assuming this denial fever would soon break, if only because it was so obviously and dangerously delusional. Once our reason was restored, I imagined the nation would quickly launch an aggressive drive to protect the climate and replace fossil fuels. This book would then contribute to climate denial's postmortem, as people asked, "How did that happen?" and "How do we make sure it never happens again?" You might say I was in denial about the strength and persistence of denial.

Instead, this book is emerging into an America still dangerously hindered by climate denial, with federal climate policies being dismantled when they need to be strengthened. This crisis cannot wait for us to figure out long-term social changes that will reduce the risk of future rounds of dangerous corporate denial. We must use all the tools now at our disposal across all segments of society to rebuild our energy infrastructure and reduce emissions, just as an earlier generation of Americans, after some delay, finally threw everything it had at transforming the economy to fight World War II.

What lessons do past sagas of corporate denial offer in the fight against climate change and its denial? One is that there is little reason to believe that presenting the fossil fuel corporations with more scientific proof of the urgency of the threat will help. The one time when science played an apparently direct role in overcoming denial and prompting a corporate decision to stop making the dangerous product was when DuPont and other chemical companies finally accepted the threat to ozone and agreed to phase out CFCs. But that is not a good historical analogy for climate denial, because the stakes for the industry were so much lower. CFCs were a small share of the chemical industry's profits, and its makers could also profit from selling substitutes; admitting causality and walking away from their product posed a relatively small threat to the industry.

A closer analogy for the fossil fuel industry would be tobacco, where an entire global industry revolves around the dangerous product and where laws restricting that product threaten the industry's long-term existence.* Both tobacco and big oil companies have abandoned their most blatant denials—likely due more to external pressure than new evidence—and it has made little direct difference to the size of the threat. The troubling lesson from tobacco is that an industry's begrudging admission of its product's dangers after decades of denial does not necessarily diminish the industry's eagerness and ability to sell it; you can strip away the cognitive denial about causation but the moral denial about responsibility persists. Tobacco companies may now admit they kill half of their most loyal customers, but they still market cigarettes as aggressively as the law allows. Oil companies may now admit their product causes irreversible warming, but they still pursue long-term investments to extract and sell as much of it as they can.

Moreover, such admissions do not remove the social and political obstacles to a policy response that have been nourished by decades of corporate denial and have taken root in the body politic. Hence the need to focus on the social norm. History shows that changing social norms is arduous but possible using the many tools our pluralistic society provides—including social activism informed by an attentive media and catalyzed by effective advocacy groups; litigation bringing evidence to light and focusing attention on corporate-caused harm; state action to drive technology improvements and build momentum for federal action; congressional hearings to build awareness; and international diplomatic efforts to push global solutions.

Electing people who respect science and are willing to regulate industry in the name of the greater good is obviously critical. And so is supporting and respecting science itself—from the individual researchers pursuing evidence and confronting powerful industries, to the agencies that fund and organize independent research, to the panels of scientists brought in to assess the evidence and inform the world of the threats it faces. Most of the preceding chapters also tell of sweeping federal

---

* Tobacco companies may find a way to survive through new technology, promoting still-addictive but presumably safer e-cigarettes. It is harder to imagine fossil fuel companies surviving by embracing new technologies given how deeply invested they remain in fossil fuels. Certainly, their long-term survival would be less threatened if they had not kept making such huge long-term investments in high-carbon resources and infrastructure in the decades since they could first foresee the coming climate crisis.

legislation or rules, and those are absolutely needed to fight climate change too. Meanwhile, much can be done through these other avenues until we have a Congress willing to pass strong laws and a president willing to sign and enforce them.

In the fight to protect the climate, people are already pushing all these levers of change and the social norm is indeed shifting as the public increasingly recognizes the urgency of the threat. Author and long-time climate activist Bill McKibben sees this as a "remarkable moment, when, after years of languishing, climate concern is suddenly and explosively rising to the top of the political agenda." Democratic voters are starting to list climate change as their top political concern for the 2020 presidential election, and many of the Democratic presidential candidates are offering aggressive climate protection plans that would truly herald a new era if implemented. The proposed Green New Deal, which brought a new level of ambition and urgency to the issue, has not only proven remarkably popular in concept among Democrats but also among the more moderate Republicans, though the latter's views are not reflected by their party's elected officials.

History suggests we will eventually reach a tipping point when climate denial will no longer have enough political support to delay action; hardline climate deniers will still exist but they will be outvoted. This tipping point may or may not be reached in time to keep climate change from spinning utterly out of our control, but larger trends are bringing it closer, including high-profile climate-related disasters, a younger generation more alarmed than the older ones, expanding clean-energy technologies, and the rising power of clean energy corporations. Climate change may be an epic disaster for some corporations, but it is an epic opportunity for others. This book stresses the dark side of the profit motive, but that motive is also a force we can harness to help us rebuild our global energy infrastructure as fast as possible.

The new industries developing new low-carbon technologies may, of course, also pose new societal and environmental dangers (though likely much less dire threats than climate change, given the inherently cleaner technologies gaining momentum). The people running and owning the corporations in question will be subject to the same denial-promoting corporate structure, incentives, and norms as in other industries, though other cultural changes may mitigate that denial. Some of these changes may even unfold voluntarily within corporations.

REDUCING DENIAL BY CHANGING CORPORATE CULTURE AND STRUCTURE

Power corrupts. Studies suggest it can make people more egocentric, more tightly focused on their own goals, less risk aware, and less aware of others. But other research finds that power can promote prosocial action in the right context, especially among those with a more communal mindset and a stronger moral identity. This suggests the corrupting influence of power can at least sometimes be countered by culture, and if culture can influence the powerful—who are generally *less* susceptible to outside influence—it can surely influence the powerless too.

The corporate power structure is already paying attention to cognitive bias, thanks to so many research findings drawing attention to it, and there is a corresponding interest in "debiasing" business decisions. A 2014 survey of eight hundred corporate board members and chairpersons by the consulting firm McKinsey found they ranked "reducing decision biases" as their top aspiration for improving performance. Of course, they likely meant overcoming biases that threaten the corporation's financial performance, not biases that threaten their ability to recognize the harms they inflict on society, but awareness of bias is a good step.

Business school educators and others are also trying to draw attention to the role of unconscious bias in undermining corporate ethics. Max Bazerman and Ann Tenbrunsel, business school professors at Harvard and Notre Dame, have written about how business ethics are undermined by biases and propose tactics to reduce those biases. Business writer Margaret Heffernan has similarly tried to raise awareness of psychological bias and how it can lead to business disasters. One multidisciplinary effort by psychologists and others, most of whom are on the faculties of America's business schools, is called Ethical Systems. It focuses on training businesses in strategies to confront the ethical risks posed by motivated reasoning, among other things. Some of the strategies are as simple as setting up formal devil's-advocate processes to identify what the group is inclined to believe and then deliberately trying to believe the opposite. I do not know if such processes can significantly reduce or prevent the kind of denial this book describes, but I consider it a worthy part of any corporate effort to improve its social responsibility.

The exact nature of a corporation's social responsibility will always be hard to define, but it surely helps if executives at least accept that they have some responsibility beyond increasing profits. This was once uncontroversial, at least in theory; no less of a corporate icon than GM's Alfred P. Sloan Jr. argued in the early 1940s that corporate leaders needed to expand their horizon of responsibility to consider the welfare of the economy and community broadly (though as we saw earlier, GM fell far short when it came to designing more crashworthy cars). Later the very notion of corporate social responsibility was contested, as free market advocates defined as immoral any corporate motive other than chasing profits. Whether maximizing shareholder profits is indeed a corporation's only legitimate goal is very much debated—Lynn Stout, a corporate law professor at UCLA, argues that this narrow view of the law is in fact a myth—but it remains a widely held view.

Clearly, though, many shareholders themselves want the corporations they invest in to factor social concerns into their operations. Socially responsible investing as a movement has been around for a long time, motivated by an array of issues including concern over apartheid, tobacco, firearms, worker rights, and the environment. Today over thirty trillion dollars' worth of the world's professionally managed investment assets are managed using some form of social responsibility criteria, and of course many major corporations claim to pursue social responsibility goals. One driver of the field's remarkable growth recently has been the rising understanding of climate change and of humanity's overriding need to replace its existing fossil-fuel based energy infrastructure with a clean and modern one as soon as possible.

The fact that serious investment dollars are pushing corporate social responsibility provides some counterpressure to the notorious push for short-term profits. It surely gives those individuals within a corporation who want to implement antidenial social-responsibility strategies more room to do so.

What would be a more socially responsible corporate reaction to evidence that it is causing harm? Some things are obvious. Corporate representatives would stick to debating the facts they dispute without attacking their critics' motives, and they would resist the temptation to glorify their own motives or believe themselves victims of a witch hunt. They would not deceptively channel their views through front groups. They would recognize that their corporate interests inevitably create bias, so they would try to find and support truly independent expert assessments of the issue. They would not exaggerate doubts about the threat or expect to be able to continue the suspect behavior until all doubts are resolved, recognizing that at some point they should cease the behavior unless they can prove it is safe. And they would respect the legitimacy of efforts by other segments of society—like scientists, activists, media, and government—to investigate the threat and take steps to reduce it. Accepting the legitimate role of others will require a conscious effort to see beyond the corporation's interests to consider what is good for society, and we should recognize that this broader perspective will be hard to achieve given the financial incentives, tribal instincts, and other denial-promoting factors at play.

Some people are trying to create businesses that have a built-in social perspective using what are called "benefit corporations." These are corporations formed under laws already on the books in most US states allowing corporations to explicitly embrace not just the pursuit of profit but the pursuit of a general public benefit. Benefit corporations also have higher transparency standards and must publicly report on their social impacts with reference to third-party standards. Still other corporations around the world call themselves B Corporations because they have amended their corporate charters to incorporate broader social goals and have been certified by the nonprofit B Lab as creating value for stakeholders other than shareholders. These are all encouraging experiments in how the corporate form might be used in more publicly beneficial ways, reflecting an important threshold recognition that corporations are human constructs that could be creatively altered to enshrine a different social norm. However, these altered forms are voluntary, and those most prone to causing harm and denying it will not adopt them.

What about mandatory changes in the corporate structure? We might be seeing the beginning of a long-overdue reimagining of the corporation, revisiting the terms of the social contract that creates them. For example, Germany requires large corporate employers to have on their boards members elected by the workers rather than just by the shareholders, and legislation promoting something similar has been introduced in the US Congress. This particular reform would not necessarily reduce corporate denial about social and environmental impacts—in my experience, coal miners deny climate change just as reliably as coal mine owners—but it is an example of how corporate law might be altered to promote not just shareholder interests but something broader in exchange for the benefits of incorporation. Future generations may look back at today and wonder why we accepted so uncritically for so long a basic institutional structure devised for an earlier century, despite profound changes in our values, our technologies, and the challenges we face.

Deep reform of the corporate structure, if it happens, will likely unfold slowly. To reduce the damage of corporate denial in the meantime, we will need pressure from forces outside the corporate world—the countervailing social norms, institutions, and laws that have long confronted corporate denial. History shows that these forces assert themselves in waves, which then ebb until problems reach a level that prompts the next wave.

THE NEXT WAVE: CHANGING THE BALANCE OF POWER

Every few decades, America grows alarmed at the accumulation and abuse of corporate power and pushes back. The abuses of the Gilded Age, for example, prompted the Progressive Movement and Theodore Roosevelt's trust-busting campaigns. Roosevelt warned in 1910 that "one of the most sinister manifestations of great corporate wealth during recent years has been its tendency to interfere and dominate in politics." He also reminded Americans that "the corporation is the creature of government, and the people have the right to handle it as they desire; all they need pay attention to is the expediency of realizing this right in some way that shall be productive of good and not harm."

Later, the Great Depression led to New Deal laws governing securities, banking, and labor. And the post–World War II economic boom created new industrial threats that eventually led to the environmental and consumer laws of the 1960s and 1970s. Critics in all these eras labelled these limits on corporate power socialism or communism and warned of the demise of capitalism. As both fans and critics of capitalism have long argued, though, these reforms more likely preserved capitalism by reducing the public harms and increasing the public benefits of corporate activity.

Unlike these earlier eras, the recent financial crisis has not yet led to a reduction in corporate power, except somewhat within the financial industry. On the contrary, corporations have continued to concentrate their economic and political power, thanks largely to the constitutional rights courts have granted them over more than a century and especially in the last decade. Until recently, states could regulate corporate political spending to curb what the Supreme Court recognized as "the corrosive and distorting effects of immense aggregations of wealth that are accumulated with the help of the corporate form and that have little or no correlation to the public's support for the corporation's political ideas." But that view was rejected in the Court's 2010 *Citizens United* decision granting protection to corporate campaign-related spending under the First Amendment.

The *Citizens United* decision has proven strikingly unpopular. A 2015 poll showed nearly eight in ten Americans opposed it (proving that the social norm alone does not automatically determine policy), and nineteen states have called for a constitutional amendment to overturn it. More significantly, capitalism itself is becoming increasingly unpopular, especially among young people. A 2018 Gallup poll found that only 45 percent of Americans between eighteen and twenty-nine have a positive view of capitalism, compared to 68 percent in 2010. Among respondents over age fifty, 60 percent had a positive view of capitalism in 2018, a still surprisingly low endorsement of this pillar of American life and mainstay of political rhetoric. As with so many other things, there is a partisan divide: among US Democrats in 2018, Gallup found 47 percent had a positive view of capitalism, compared to 71 percent of Republicans.

This poll found that Americans under age thirty were actually more positive about socialism (51 percent) than they were about capitalism, though given how the term socialism has been splashed around over the years, it is hard to know precisely what this means. Still, although the sustained effort by libertarians to delegitimize government regulation of market activity has been remarkably successful in influencing policy, it has clearly not led to a widespread public embrace of unfettered markets.

The growing dissatisfaction with capitalism might be traced to growing income inequality, demographic changes in employment due to globalization and information technologies, the decline of unions, and the trauma of the financial crisis. For many, it also reflects alarm over climate change and our inability to address it. The need to both slash emissions and cope with a rising toll of climate-related disasters is driving calls for a broader shift away from the values of the marketplace and toward, in the words of author and social activist Naomi Klein, "an alternative worldview to rival the one at the heart of the ecological crisis—embedded in interdependence rather than hyper-individualism, reciprocity rather than dominance, and cooperation rather than hierarchy."

The shrinking support for capitalism and the growing popularity of political candidates embracing the socialist label suggest that another wave of reforms reducing corporate political power may be on its way. Truly limiting that power in the United States may have to wait for major changes on the Supreme Court or even a constitutional amendment, but laws in the meantime could reduce the political influence of corporate money through greater public funding for elections. Laws could also require corporations to reveal just how much they are spending to influence public policy, or otherwise shine a light on the influence of dark money.

Reducing corporations' power over our democracy will not necessarily reduce the incidence of corporate denial, but it will reduce the likelihood such denial can succeed in perpetuating the harm in question. It would surely mean more restrictions on harmful activities like pollution, and it could lead to more systematic oversight and reform of industries found to pose particularly grave threats. Reducing corporate political power might also result in corporations playing a smaller role in our economy, with more human needs met by other organizations. The role of nonprofits could grow, especially in education and health care, and we may decide that some services are better delivered by the public sector. People working in nonprofits or the public sector will not be immune to pressures to deny any harms they may cause, but that denial will not be amplified by the fiercely competitive mindset, the tight focus on profit, and the justifying market ideology that give corporate denial such force and momentum.

The current political divisions in the United States make it hard to imagine truly sweeping political changes, and we are in political waters so uncharted that predictions are particularly speculative. But clearly, social norms are in flux, and we should try to imagine how they might be shifted to advance the greater good.

·   ·   ·   ·   ·

One pattern illustrated in this book is the rise of social harms caused by corporate denial, followed much later by a social response to reduce those harms. If that pattern holds, social efforts will eventually repair some of the damage corporate denial has done to the public's faith in science and government. Society will find ways to overcome the political polarization to which corporate denial has contributed, including by slowly rebuilding trust in a more broadly shared, evidence-based reality. We will reduce the threat posed by corporate denial by striking a better balance of power between corporations and other social forces, and we may even reduce the frequency of corporate denial by reforming corporate culture and structure.

I hope that efforts to reduce corporate denial and its impacts will benefit from growing insights about human nature and how the world we build can bring out the best in us or the worst. The history of corporate denial shows that people can be morally and cognitively blinded by the social norms they collectively embrace, but it also shows that people can change those norms in a collective push toward enlightenment.

Acknowledgments

In writing this book, I have tiptoed through the work of many other people, harvesting bits and pieces of it to combine into something new. I must begin by thanking all those who have written the articles and books, conducted the interviews, undertaken the studies, created and maintained the archives, and otherwise built the broad landscape of information upon which I've been able to draw. They are listed in the bibliography and endnotes, and I hope readers seeking more information will plunge into this valuable literature. I also wish to thank the University of Minnesota library system for access to their vast print and online resources.

My thanks to those who reviewed all or parts of the manuscript and provided helpful insights, including Prentiss Cox, Jean Sternlight, and Gerald Markowitz, and to those I corresponded with over the years in search of relevant studies and stories.

I am tremendously grateful to my agent, Susan Rabiner, who understood what this book could be even before I did and who greatly improved it with her enthusiasm, candor, and guidance. And I thank Naomi Schneider, my editor at the University of California Press, for seeing the book's potential and making it a reality. Thanks, too, to Benjy Malings, Summer Farah, Jessica Moll, and the rest of the team at the University of

California Press for all their work, and to Barbara Armentrout for her skillful edits.

I owe a great deal of thanks to the many friends and family members who discussed this book with me over the years, read parts of it, or just provided the encouragement a project like this demands, including Leslie Freese, Ginny Freese, Andie Rosener, Nick Rosener, Lynn James, Rich James, Sherry Coben, Pat McMahon, Betsy Sansby, Al Dworsky, John Whitmore, Ann Cohen, Tom Coben, Ella Swanson-Hysell, and Ben Swanson-Hysell. And I want to acknowledge Hallie, whose birth helped strengthen my determination to work toward a safer future.

Finally, my deepest thanks go to my husband, Jim Coben. Jim read multiple versions of every chapter, helped me sharpen my thesis with his insightful feedback, and cheered this project forward for years. My gratitude for his unflagging support goes beyond words.

Notes

INTRODUCTION

Page 1: **"Do I feel badly about selling cigarettes?"**: Geoffrey Bible, quoted in Goldberg. **told a newspaper that he had quit:** Brian Hale, "Big Mo's Snack Attack Cuts Tobacco Drag," *Sydney Morning Herald*, June 28, 2000.

Page 2: **about seven of every ten members:** my estimate based on Bureau of Labor Statistics (BLS) data drawn from *Household Data*, Table A-8, Employed persons by class of worker and part-time status, seasonally adjusted (last modified February 1, 2019); and BLS, "Nonprofits Account for 12.3 Million Jobs, 10.2 Percent of Private Sector Employment, in 2016" (August 31, 2018). These numbers suggest that about 73 percent of the US civilian workforce work in for-profit organizations, 8 percent in the nonprofit sector, 13 percent in government, and 6 percent are unincorporated self-employed. **in businesses of over five hundred employees:** U.S. Small Business Administration, *2018 Small Business Profile.*

Page 4: **"need for urgent action":** "G8+5 Academies' Joint Statement: Climate Change and the Transformation of Energy Technologies for a Low Carbon Future," May 2009, https://sites. nationalacademies.org/cs/groups/internationalsite/documents/webpage/international_080856 .pdf. **daunting challenge:** IPCC Special Report, *Global Warming of 1.5°C,* 2018, Summary for Policymakers, 14.

Page 5: **nineteenth-century coal dealer:** Stradling, 208.

Page 7: **focused on climate science denial:** Gelbspan. **focused on . . . public relations industry:** Rampton and Stauber. **scientists who . . . promoted unfounded doubts:** Michaels. See also Freudenberg; McGarity and Wagner.

Page 8: **"somehow, somewhere, defending America":** Oreskes and Conway, 164.

Page 9: **"a legally-designated 'person'":** Bakan, 28. **"half-believe realities" . . . Other managers . . . "Our society is the way it is":** Jackall, 188, 170, 199.

Page 10: **Babies get distressed:** Liddle, Bradley, and Mcgrath. **If a researcher drops something:** Warneken and Tomasello. **documented displays of empathy:** De Waal. **"dumber, nicer,**

and weaker": R. H. Thaler, "Doing Economics without Homo Economicus," in Medema and Samuels, 227.

Page 11: **Critics have pointed out:** Open Science Collaboration.

Page 13: **"deceit and self-deception":** Trivers, 3. **Others argue that we evolved:** Varki and Brower. Varki and Brower take the argument even further, suggesting that the human ability to deny reality was critical to our species' unique evolutionary success. **people usually start with a moral feeling:** Haidt, ch. 2. **Side effects appear less likely:** Greene, 224. **power they hold could have narrowed their mental focus:** see chs. 2 and 3.

Page 14: **"affinity groups central to their personal well-being":** Kahan, 418. **our brains are highly tribal:** Cikara and Van Bavel; Molenberghs.

Page 15: **displacement and diffusion of responsibility:** Bandura, Caprara, and Zsolnai, 58–59. **less empathy for . . . unidentified group of victims:** Small and Loewenstein; Konis, Haran, Saporta, and Ayal.

Page 16: **growing list of constitutional rights:** Winkler.

Page 17: **"preaching pure . . . socialism":** Milton Friedman, "The Social Responsibility of Business Is to Increase Its Profits," *New York Times Magazine,* September 13, 1970.

CHAPTER 1. A "MORE PLEASING REPRESENTATION"

Page 20: **"Nine out of Ten":** Richard Miles, quoted in Board of Trade, part 1, hearings. **"would be detestable":** Thomas, 156.

Page 21: **in the United States . . . rationalization of slavery:** In fact, almost half the proslavery tracts in the United States were written by ministers: Tise, xvii. **earliest English slaving voyages . . . early form of corporations:** Pollitt, 31. **Royal African Company:** Thomas, 202. **"clandestine or piratical business":** Thompson, 11. **those who owned shares:** Thomas, 201, 239, 241.

Page 22: **potential profits . . . Liverpool's slave ships:** Wallace, 229–30. **slave lobby argued:** Norris, 161. **six million were brought to sugar plantations:** Thomas, 805. **one physician:** Slare, 3–7. **work on sugar plantations:** Hochschild, 63. **One plantation owner:** Newton, *Thoughts,* 38.

Page 23: **defender of the slave trade:** Estwick, 30–31. **Slave ships did not even record:** Walvin, 44. **"buried a girl slave":** Newton, *Journal,* June 28, 1751, log entry. **brutally literal example:** Thomas, 14. **Psychologists trying to understand:** Bandura, 195, 200. **experimental evidence:** Gwinn, Judd, and Park. **prominent slaveholder wrote:** Swaminathan, 53. **"unenlightened Hordes":** Anonymous, *Slavery,* 12.

Page 24: **"something never seen before" . . . many of the strategies:** Hochschild, 5–6. **"narration of miseries":** Thomas Cooper, 1787, quoted in Rediker, 309. **Some of the stories . . . Olaudah Equiano:** for a biography of Equiano, see Walvin. **minister James Ramsay:** for a biography of Ramsay, see Shyllon. **minister Thomas Clarkson . . . :** Hochschild, 237.

Page 25: **government hearings:** Hochschild, 152–63. **400,000 names . . . 300,000 would join a boycott:** Hochschild, 230, 7. **committee of plantation owners . . . "abolitionists were the prototype":** Hochschild, 159–60.

Page 26: **conditions below deck:** Parliament, House of Commons, *Abstract,* ch. 3; Newton, *Thoughts,* 15. **diagram of slave ship:** Rediker, 308–42. **"horrid and fictitious picture":** Turnbull, 21. **theory of system justification:** Jost. **Africans wanted to be enslaved:** Richard Miles, quoted in Board of Trade, part 1.

Page 27: **"when from kind treatment":** William Craig Harborne, quoted in Francklyn, *Substance,* Appendix. **"lodging on board":** Renwick Sergent, 14. **"Slave on Board":** Robert Heatley, quoted in Board of Trade, part 2. **"If the weather is sultry," . . . "their little Humours":** James Penny, quoted in Board of Trade, part 2. **To exercise them . . . would "dance the Men":** James Arnold, quoted in Board of Trade, part 2; see also William Wilberforce, May 12, 1789, in Parliament, *Parliamentary History,* vol. 28, col. 47.

Page 28: **Pregnant women "cherished":** Francklyn, *Observations*, 38–39 (Francklyn is not listed as author of 1788 edition, but he is listed as author in the 1789 London reprint; page numbers refer to 1788 edition.) **"comfortable and commodious":** Norris, 176–77. **"instantly exempted"** . . . **"a richer man":** Norris, 178–79. **Francklyn similarly assured readers:** Francklyn, *Observations*, 38. **"old age, in this state":** Norris, 179. **"appearance of those of a relation":** Francklyn, *Observations*, 43. **hunger so prevalent** . . . **Work in the sugar-cane fields:** Parliament, House of Commons, *Abstract*, ch. 4.

Page 29: **"so intolerably** . . . **inconsiderate":** Anonymous West-Indian planter, quoted in Swaminathan, 54. **"infesting the public streets"** . . . **"giving them free":** Parliament, House of Commons, *Abstract*, 3, 74. **slave lobby often focused:** Swaminathan.

Page 30: **"Morality"** . . . **"wired for tribalism":** Greene, 23, 54. **line between us and them** . . . **is fluid:** Greene, 53. **"the Liberty of Negroes":** quoted in Swaminathan, 51. **"Are we not men?":** Francklyn, *Observations*, 43.

Page 31: **"not tyrants":** Turnbull, 58. **"men of better education":** Francklyn, *Observations*, 57. **"Britons' abiding need":** Brown, 48. **"one of the greatest evils":** abolitionist literature, quoted by Rediker, 314. **"poor peasant":** Turnbull, 62–63. **"to be envied":** Francklyn, *Observations*, 12. **"infinitely better":** Turnbull, 61–62, footnote.

Page 32: **"life of the poor victim":** Francklyn, *Observations*, 19. **"vulgar landlords"** . . . **"happy as a human being can be":** Fitzhugh, 234, 245–46. **whippings, mutilations, and other punishments:** Parliament, House of Commons, *Abstract*, ch. 4. **"such thefts":** Martin, 5. **"all these flagellations":** Francklyn, *Observations*, 42. **"are previously strangled":** James Tobin, quoted in Hochschild, 162, footnote. **Advantageous comparison:** Bandura, 195. **the "dishonesty germ":** Ariely, 191.

Page 33: **printed by the slave lobby:** Hochschild, 230. **"little snug houses":** A Plain Man, 4. **"begin at home":** Turnbull, 64. **killed as prisoners of war:** Norris, 160; Thompson, 21; Renwick Sergent, 11; Turnbull, 10. **form of slavery in Africa:** Martin, 5. **human sacrifice:** Turnbull, 10. **cannibalism:** Martin, 3; Anonymous, *Slavery*, 14–15. **idolatry** . . . **tyrannical leader:** Martin, 5. **"refuse of her population":** Anonymous, *Slavery*, 14.

Page 34: **"really a redemption":** Martin, 5. **"house of bondage":** Norris, 160. **"instruments of the massacres"** . . . **"thousands of people":** Francklyn, *Substance*, Appendix. **"sake of humanity,"** . . . **"milk of human kindness":** Duke of Clarence, 19, 31. **"Be it so":** quoted in Hochschild, 124. **"extreme cruelty"** . . . **"gates of mercy":** Thomas, 478.

Page 35: **"suits their characters":** Innis, 10–13. **"love of rational freedom":** Norris, 159. **"cram liberty down the throats":** Francklyn, *Observations*, viii. **captives were brought:** Francklyn, *Substance*, 8–10. **they were criminals:** Francklyn, *Substance*, 24.

Page 36: **"crimes" like witchcraft** . . . **family to be enslaved:** Parliament, House of Commons, *Abstract*, ch.1. **industry repeatedly denied:** Francklyn, *Substance*, Appendix; Innis, 47. **abolitionists, however, brought forth:** Parliament, House of Commons, *Abstract*, ch. 1. **"No foreign nation":** Renwick Sergent, 12; see also Norris, 166.

Page 37: **1.8 percent of its annual income:** Hochschild, 5. **"Britain itself":** Martin, 11. **"overturn our resources":** Renwick Sergent, 31–32. **"national importance":** Norris, 183. **"What calamities":** Anonymous, *Slavery*, 23. **"the people of England":** Francklyn, *Observations*, ix.

Page 38: **"left to starve"** . . . **saved many:** Innis, 8–10, 15. **"vegetable substance":** Anonymous, *Vindication*, 20.

Page 39: **alternative to emancipation:** Hochschild, 344. **ships from Liverpool:** Walvin, 40. **"interest can draw a film":** William Wilberforce, May 12, 1789, in Parliament, *Parliamentary History*, vol. 28, col. 46. **above-average religiosity** . . . **"divine communion":** Hochschild, 19, 28–29. **spiritual awakening:** Walvin, 59. **habit of swearing** . . . **invested in slave ships:** Hochschild, 19, 77.

Page 40: **failed to condemn slavery:** Hochschild, 77. **Wilberforce:** Walvin, 86–88. **"I never had a scruple"** . . . **"inattention and interest":** Newton, *Thoughts*, 4, 7.

CHAPTER 2. "A WONDERFUL STIMULANT"

Abbreviations

House Radium Hearing.   *Radium: Hearing before the House Committee on Mines and Mining,*
    63rd Cong., 2nd sess., January 19–28, 1914
ORAU.   Oak Ridge Associated Universities' online collection of articles and images about
    the radium industry's history and radioactive quack cures, searchable from https://www
    .orau.org/

Page 41: "**Radium for several years**": Field, 393. "**potato shed**" . . . **a heavy iron rod:** Froman. "**feebly luminous silhouettes**": Froman. **burns that appeared:** Mould, 77.
    Page 42: **most expensive** . . . **substance:** Landa, "Brief History," 504. **Edison** . . . **urged:**
Mullner, 16–17. "**afraid of radium**": Harvie, 148. **he launched** . . . **sold vanadium:** "A Sketch of
the Life and Work of Joseph M. Flannery," *Radium* 14, no. 6 (March 1920). "**stimulation of cell
activity**" . . . **no evidence:** Council on Pharmacy and Chemistry.
    Page 43: "**greatest tonic**": Joseph Flannery, House Radium Hearing, 135. "**actuated by a
motive**": Flannery, House Radium Hearing, 54. **Flannery was familiar:** Clark, 46–47. **priced at
$120,000:** Flannery, House Radium Hearing, 54. **Flannery once told a newspaper:** "A $25,000
Sneeze," *Pittsburgh Press,* June 22, 1914. **significant industrial enterprise:** Joel O. Lubenau, "A
Brief History of Standard Chemical Company," ORAU. **largest radium producer:** Harvie, 83.
Curies did not even patent: Mullner, 21. **European governments** . . . **scientists** . . . **philanthropic groups:** Rentetzi; see also Slaughter, 169. **Bureau of Mines** . . . **breakthrough:** US
National Park Service, *U.S. Radium Corporation: Photographs, Written Historical and Descrip-
tive Data,* Historic American Buildings Survey (HAER No. NJ-121), n.d., 16. **public-private
partnership:** Rentetzi, 443; Mullner, 28. **radium monopoly:** Franklin Lane, House Radium
Hearing, 175–76. "**hands of quacks**": Rep. James Byrnes, House Radium Hearing, 125.
    Page 44: "**if the Government wants**": "Against Radium Monopoly," *New York Times,* Janu-
ary 12, 1914. **Congress yielded:** Rentetzi, 446. **radium near a patient's tumor:** Robert Abbe,
House Radium Hearing, 25.
    Page 45: **treat arthritis, gout** . . . "**body ferments**": Clark, 47; William H. Cameron,
"Mechanical and Physical Agents, Special Reference to Radium," *Pennsylvania Medical Jour-
nal,* December 1913; Field, 391–92. *Radium,* **which it sent** . . . "**25 times more people**": Flan-
nery, House Radium Hearing, 71–72, 58–59. **epilepsy** . . . **insanity and tuberculosis:** Flannery,
Radium: Hearing before the Senate Committee on Mines and Mining, 63rd Cong., 2nd sess.,
February 10–24, 1914, 27–28. **When pressed** . . . "**I feel this way**": William Cameron, House
Radium Hearing, 208–9. "**going to kill the people**": Rep. James Byrnes, House Radium Hear-
ing, 210. "**To Joe Flannery**": Clark, 52.
    Page 46: **Field** . . . **administered radium:** Rowland, 5. "**intensely stimulating effect**": W.
Engelmann, "Radium Emanation Therapy," *Lancet,* May 3, 1913: 1225–28. "**enhancing the sec-
ondary symptoms**": Engelmann, "Radium Emanation Therapy." **French and British research:**
Clark, 57. **Radium rays** . . . **Proescher** . . . **different spin:** Clark, 57–58.
    Page 47: "**render the organism**": Frederick Proescher, "The Intravenous Injection of Solu-
ble Radium Salts," *Radium* 2, no. 4 (January 1914). **AMA began including:** Clark, 56. "**nearly
all vegetables** . . . **improved**" . . . **most crops:** H. H. Rusby, "Radium a Wonderful Stimulant of
Farmers' Crops," *New York Times,* October 25, 1914. **A few weeks later:** Cyril G. Hopkins and
Ward H. Sachs, *Radium as a Fertilizer,* bulletin no. 177, University of Illinois Agricultural
Experiment Station, January. 1915.
    Page 48: **death certificate:** Flannery's 1920 death certificate obtained from Pennsylvania
Bureau of Vital Statistics. **company promoted radium** . . . **anemia:** "Standard Radium Solu-
tion for Drinking (ca. 1915–1925)," ORAU. "**what was denied others**": "Joseph M. Flannery,"
Pittsburgh Leader, February 19, 1920. "**gates of opportunity**": "He Sought Ways to Serve,"

Pittsburgh Sun, February 19, 1920. Both articles reprinted in *Radium* 14, no. 6 (March 1920). **Flannery's life:** "A Sketch of the Life and Work of Joseph M. Flannery," *Radium* 14, no. 6 (March 1920): 106; see also Mullner, 21–29.

Page 49: **"optimism is highly valued":** Kahneman, 262. **two brain systems:** Amodio, Master, Yee, and Taylor. **approach/inhibition theory:** Keltner, Gruenfeld, and Anderson; Galinsky, Gruenfeld, and Magee. **diminished risk perception:** Anderson and Galinsky.

Page 50: **von Sochocky . . . Radium Luminous Materials Corporation:** Mullner, 41–42. **Demand for his paint:** Mullner, 43. **radium paint . . . glowed green:** Paul Frame, "Radioluminescent Paint," ORAU. **doorbells . . . fishing lures:** Mullner, 43–44. **crucifixes:** Lang, 54. **toy animals and dolls:** Mullner, 43–44.

Page 51: **New Jersey . . . Illinois . . . Connecticut:** Clark, 7. **enough to make them glow:** Moore, 87. **"neighborhood kids" . . . painted her teeth:** Lang, 85, 88. **government investigator . . . supervisor . . . "glow in our cheeks":** Clark, 100.

Page 52: **"most hygienic" and "more beneficial":** Clark, 17. **red blood cells:** Martland, Conlon, and Knef. **transient stimulation:** Lang, 57–59. **blood-forming processes:** Martland, Conlon, and Knef. **"gelatinous liquefaction":** Flinn, 2078. **Mollie Maggia:** Clark, 34–35; Mullner, 48; Moore, 35–41. **phossy-jaw:** Mullner, 49–50.

Page 53: **State and local officials . . . culprit was radium:** Clark, 35–36. **Consumers' League:** Clark, 66. **mental strain . . . "agitation":** Clark, 105–6. **"tainted with Socialism":** Clark, 68 (quoting Hamilton's autobiography).

Page 54: **Drinker team . . . radium was the cause:** Mullner, 56–59. **The company concluded . . . threatened to sue:** Clark, 90–92; Moore, 92, 139. **Roeder found Frederick Flinn:** Mullner, 69. **unbiased opinion . . . not really sick:** Clark, 107–8; Deville and Steiner, 292–93. **stunned to later learn:** Moore, 188, 194. **"industrial hazard":** Flinn, 2081. **US Radium employees . . . "not baneful effect":** "Begin Wide Inquiry into Radium Deaths," *New York Times*, June 20, 1925.

Page 55: **"a number who were unfit":** "Begin Wide Inquiry into Radium Deaths," *NYT*. **exhaling radon . . . bones emitted radiation:** Martland, Conlon, and Knef. **In 1927, even Flinn:** Clark, 110. **"persons similarly incapacitated":** Rowland, 13. **bone necrosis and anemia . . . rare cancers:** Clark, 8.

Page 56: **developed these cancers:** Clark, 8. **Over 60 percent:** Milgram, 35.

Page 57: **more than 90 percent:** Milgram, 11. **displacement and diffusion of responsibility:** Bandura, 196–98. **von Sochocky . . . not his responsibility:** Moore, 218–19; Clark, 127. **"unknown to us" . . . Roeder would even testify:** Moore, 216, 219. **federal court concluded:** LaPorte v. US Radium Corp., 13 F. Supp. 263, 268 (D. N.J. 1935). **reckless in handling radium:** Harvie, 175. **part of a finger:** Mullner, 45–46.

Page 58: **denied he had been poisoned:** "Radium Paint Takes Its Inventor's Life," *New York Times*, November 15, 1928. *Time* **magazine:** "Radium Women," *Time*, August 11, 1930. **"no industry is in existence":** "To Begin Two Suits against Radium Co.," *New York Times*, June 24, 1925. **"is *blind to the harmful side effects*"** (emphasis in original): Greene, 224.

Page 59: **"ingenious device":** Bierce. **"humanitarian considerations":** "Radium Victims Win $50,000 and Pensions in Suit Settlement," *New York Times*, June 5, 1928. **Radium Dial Company:** Clark, 100. **close-to-empty shell . . . corporate officers:** Clark, 191–92.

Page 60: **Internal use of radium:** Landa, "Buried Treasure," 34–35; "Radio X Tablets (ca. 1920)," ORAU. **toothpaste, . . . "nose cups":** Paul Frame, "Radioactive Curative Devices and Spas," *Oak Ridger*, November 5, 1989, repr., ORAU. **eyewash, . . . bath salts:** Landa, "Buried Treasure," 36. **face-creams, powders, lipstick:** "Tho-radia Items (ca. 1950s)," ORAU. **"weak discouraged men":** "Vita Radium Suppositories (ca. 1930)," ORAU. **Radium suppositories:** Landa, "Buried Treasure," 36. **"light, the enemy":** "Radio X Tablets (ca. 1920)," ORAU. **chocolate and bread:** Harvie, 149; "Radium Bread (ca. 1920)," ORAU. **make radioactive water . . . "life element":** "Revigator (ca. 1924–1926)," ORAU. **"greatest remedy and cure":** Paul Frame, "R.W. Thomas and the Revigator," ORAU. **water that contained:** "Standard Radium Solution for Drinking (ca. 1915–1925)," ORAU.

Page 61: **"monkey gland" fad:** Hamilton. **"few minutes ionization":** "Says Gamma Rays Could Cure Thaw," *New York Times,* April 26, 1924. **"Science to Cure":** ad reproduced in Macklis, "Great Radium Scandal," 94–95. **including his denials:** "Doubts Death by Radium," *New York Times,* June 28, 1925. **Bailey's scientific credentials:** Macklis, "Great Radium Scandal." **worked at US Radium:** "Radium Drinks," *Time,* April 11, 1932. **convenient radium source:** Clark, 172. **Radiendocrinator:** "The Radiendocrinator (ca. 1924–1929)," ORAU; Mullner, 112.

Page 62: **flatulence . . . character and memory:** Bureau of Investigation, 1398. **collection maintained by the Oak Ridge Associated Universities:** Radioactive Quack Cures, ORAU, www.orau.org/ptp/collection/quackcures/quackcures.htm. **ailments . . . aphrodisiac:** Macklis, "Radithor," 618. **400,000 bottles:** Macklis, "Great Radium Scandal," 98. **book Bailey ghost-wrote:** Clark, 173. **"liberate their energy":** Morris, 143. **"recreational drug":** Macklis, "Radithor," 618.

Page 63: **"whole upper jaw":** Macklis, "Great Radium Scandal," 98. **"mouths will be equipped":** Morris, 158. **Byers's death:** "Death Stirs Action on Radium 'Cures,'" *New York Times,* April 2, 1932. **pamphlets . . . "fee-splitting quackery":** Macklis, "Radithor," 617. **95 percent:** Landa, "First Nuclear Industry," 191. **Radithor sales:** Clark, 175–76.

Page 64: **internal medicine:** Clark, 61. **health departments . . . new warnings:** Mullner, 117. **contraceptive jelly:** Landa, "Buried Treasure," 37. **trace the fate . . . cancer:** Rowland, 6–7, 11. **one of Byers's friends:** Mullner, 114. **prescribed Radithor:** "Death Stirs Action on Radium 'Cures,'" *NYT.* **radium-induced sarcoma:** Mullner, 114. **Madame Curie herself:** "Mme. Curie Is Dead; Martyr to Science," *New York Times,* July 5, 1934. **other radioactive products:** Bureau of Investigation, 1399. **died in 1949:** Macklis, "Radithor," 618.

Page 65: **appeared in workers:** Clark, 199. **safety standards:** Lang, 52. **body-burden limits:** Clark, 194. **cancer rate double:** Clark, 198. **Luminous Materials:** Clark, 198–99. **More lawsuits:** Clark, 198–201; Mullner, 141–42. **cleanup costs:** U.S. Environmental Protection Agency, "EPA Proposes to Remove Montclair/West Orange and Glen Ridge Radium Superfund Sites from Its Superfund List," news release, April 29, 2009. **Safer radioactive materials:** Landa, "First Nuclear Industry" 193.

CHAPTER 3. "THE NUT BEHIND THE WHEEL"

Abbreviations

House Seat Belt Hearings, 1957. *Automobile Seat Belts: Hearings Before a Subcommittee of the House Committee on Interstate and Foreign Commerce,* 85th Cong., 1st sess., April 30, August 5–8, 1957, https://catalog.hathitrust.org/Record/001620059

House Traffic Safety Hearings, 1956. *Traffic Safety: Hearings Before a Subcommittee of the House Committee on Interstate and Foreign Commerce,* 84th Cong., 2nd sess., July–September 1956, https://catalog.hathitrust.org/Record/000970775

Ribicoff Hearings, part 2, 1965. *Federal Role in Traffic Safety: Hearings Before Subcommittee on Executive Reorganization of Senate Committee on Government Operations,* 89th Cong., 1st sess., part 2, July 1965, https://catalog.hathitrust.org/Record/100666181

Ribicoff Hearings, part 3, 1966. *Federal Role in Traffic Safety: Hearings Before Subcommittee on Executive Reorganization of Senate Committee on Government Operations,* 89th Cong., 2nd sess., part 3, February 1966, https://catalog.hathitrust.org/Record/100666181

Ribicoff Hearings, part 4, 1966. *Federal Role in Traffic Safety: Hearings Before Subcommittee on Executive Reorganization of Senate Committee on Government Operations,* 89th Cong., 2nd sess., part 4, March 22, 1966, https://catalog.hathitrust.org/Record/100666181

Page 67: **"substantially more":** Nader, 117. **"crest of prosperity":** "Man of the Year: First among Equals," *Time,* January 2, 1956. **traffic accidents . . . "staggers the imagination":** Sen. Paul Douglas and Sen. Kenneth Roberts, House Traffic Safety Hearings, 1956, 3, 1.

Page 68: **research and development staff:** Francis Bello, "How Strong is G.M. Research?," *Fortune,* June 1956. **founding principles of GM:** Sloan, 205. **"sound philosophy":** Sloan, quoted by GM vice president Charles Chayne, House Traffic Safety Hearings, 1956, 326. **"I delight":** Nader, 116.

Page 69: **"accident which happens":** Eastman, 121. **"Pain and horror"** . . . **"lethal array":** J. C. Furnas, "—And Sudden Death," *Readers Digest,* August 1935. **public concern** . . . **"reckless drivers":** Eastman, 137-38. **victim blaming** . . . **world is just:** Rubin and Peplau.

Page 70: **"fundamental attribution error":** Ross. **neuroscientific evidence:** Kestemont et al. **safety management:** Holden. **"more continuous attention":** William L. Laurence, "Safety Belt Held Vital to Motorist," *New York Times,* June 16, 1956. **"safe driver":** Eastman, 141. **"caused by attitude":** Lemov, 55.

Page 71: **GM's chief engineer:** Lillian Bellison, "Expert Advises on Buying a Car," *New York Times,* January 19, 1956. **auto industry supported:** Eastman, 143. **"stop doing the things":** Ned Dearborn, quoted in National Safety Council statement, House Traffic Safety Hearings, 1956, 225. **President's Highway Safety Committee:** Eastman, 147. **"firm conclusion":** Harlow Curtice, House Traffic Safety Hearings, 1956, 385. **not made clear:** Daniel P. Moynihan, *Traffic Safety: Hearings Before House Committee on Interstate and Foreign Commerce,* 89th Cong., 2nd sess., March–May 1966, 1317-18.

Page 72: **"the safest":** Paul G. Hoffman, quoted in Eastman, 140-41. **wheels that snapped off:** Charles Chayne, House Traffic Safety Hearings, 1956, 326. **"at once charming":** Mehling, 42.

Page 73: **Gandelot's experiences:** Eastman, 210. **"a ceiling":** Mehling, 41. **"catastrophic nature":** Kenneth Stonex, GM's *Engineering Journal,* 1963, quoted in Nader, 175. **"over the buildings":** quoted in Nader, 179.

Page 74: **"save faces and maybe lives":** Mehling, 40. **"I made it"** . . . **"impossible":** Mehling, 40-41. **"General Motors hasn't said":** Mehling, 42. **Research at Cornell University:** 1952, 1954 reports described in Eastman, 217, 222.

Page 75: **injury from a seat belt:** Mehling, 43. **Cornell's research:** Eastman, 222. **"all this talk"** . . . **"people fall":** Mehling, 42. **"you will fold"** . . . **"factually known":** Mehling, 41.

Page 76: **auto stylists:** Katz, repr. in House Traffic Safety Hearings, 1956, 53. **"meat cleavers":** Eastman, 232.

Page 77: **Dr. Claire Straith:** Lemov, 19; Eastman, 182-84. **Straith and other doctors:** Woodward; Lemov, 18-20, 22-23; Gikas, 327. **"more like hogs"** . . . **crash tests found:** Col. John Stapp, House Seat Belt Hearings, 1957, 18-45.

Page 78: **"frightening demonstration":** quoted in Eastman, 212. **In 1938** . . . **Cornell Medical College:** Eastman, 213; Lemov, 17-18; John Moore, House Traffic Safety Hearings, 1956, 19. **caused no injury:** Eastman, 214-15. **"placement and design":** Eastman, 216. **Cornell's database:** John Moore, House Seat Belts Hearings, 1957, 16. **a crashing car:** Eastman, 217, 222. **87 percent** . . . **also found that cars:** John Moore, House Seat Belt Hearings, 1957, 5, 13.

Page 79: **medical groups** . . . **"some resistance":** Paul R. Hawley, House Traffic Safety Hearings, 1956, 258. **"degree of control"** . . . **lab studies:** Eastman, 218, 222-23. **energy-absorbing materials:** A. L. Haynes, House Traffic Safety Hearings, 1956, 440-41. **seat belts as an option:** Eastman, 227; GM Annual Report 1955, 18.

Page 80: **"exceedingly difficult":** Nader, 119-20. **Haynes and his boss** . . . **overcame resistance:** Eastman, 224-25. **Ford made some changes:** Cordtz, 207. **advertising campaign** . . . **enthusiastic response:** Eastman, 230-31. **"It isn't often ":** Cordtz, 207. **"Whenever I'm asked why":** Mehling, 45. **"dumbfounded":** Cordtz, 207.

Page 81: **saying at Ford:** Nader, xiii. **executives at Ford:** Eastman, 231-32; Cordtz, 207. **Ford and then Chrysler:** Eastman, 228-29. **"harsh refusal"** . . . **"hurting the business":** Cordtz, 207. **death toll predictions:** Eastman, 162. **"'Driving for Fun'":** Gartman, 125.

Page 82: **"don't like to be reminded":** quoted in David R. Jones, "Auto Makers Defend Safety Record Despite Criticism," *New York Times,* January 28, 1965. **McNamara would be fired:** Cordtz, 207-8. **Industry outsiders:** Nader, xii-xv; Cordtz, 208; Lemov, 7. **Industry insiders:** Iacocca, 313. **campaign's supporters:** Patrick J. Sloyan, "Auto Safety and Detroit," *Washington*

Post, April 24, 1966; Eastman, 232. **padded dash . . . extra-cost seat belts:** Ford Motor Co. press release, November 18, 1956, quoted in Nader, xiv. **could not keep up:** Robert McNamara, House Traffic Safety Hearings, 1956, 486. **Future historians:** Larry Ronan, *Seat Belts: 1949–1956* (Washington, DC: National Highway Traffic Safety Administration, US Department of Transportation, April 1979).

Page 83: **"We can't put that car out":** Eastman, 178; *The Reminiscences of Mr. E. G. Liebold*, part 2, interview (Dearborn, MI: Benson Ford Research Center, 1953) 846. **"thousands of accidents":** Eastman, 180. **"Accidents or no accidents" . . . "for our stockholders":** Mintz and Cohen, 319–21. **In the case of safety glass:** Eastman, 179–80.

Page 84: **"industrial management":** Sloan, 145. **Nazi Germany's politics:** Michael Dobbs, "Ford and GM Scrutinized for Alleged Nazi Collaboration," *Washington Post*, November 30, 1998. **"I cannot conceive of one":** Charles E. Wilson, *Nominations: Hearings Before the Senate Committee on Armed Services*, 83rd Cong., 1st sess., January 15–16, 1953, 26.

Page 85: **narrow their focus:** Ana Guinote, "How Power Affects People: Activating, Wanting, and Goal Seeking," *Annual Review of Psychology* 68 (2017): 353–81. **"self-focused":** Keltner, 102. **heightened sense of power:** Chen, Lee-Chai, and Bargh. **"personal warmth" . . . "long, loving hours":** Peter Drucker, introduction, Sloan, *My Years*, 1990 reprint, viii, x.

Page 86: **lawyers began arguing:** Katz, repr. in House Traffic Safety Hearings, 1956, 51. **"calls from Detroit" . . . "very nervous":** Irwin Bross, quoted in O'Connell and Myers, 105. **"never going to do anything":** O'Connell and Myers, 216. **"tired of hearing":** "Car Makers Blamed in Highway Deaths," *New York Times*, October 3, 1958. **push through a law:** Lemov, 43. **"good customer relations":** Joseph C. Ingraham, "Experts Hail Auto Industry on Use of Seat Belts," *New York Times*, August 25, 1963. **auto clubs:** Joseph C. Ingraham, "Auto Man Rebuts Safety Criticism," *New York Times*, September 23, 1964. **traffic safety polled:** Sen. Abraham Ribicoff, Ribicoff Hearings, part 2, 1965, 648.

Page 87: **"blue murder" . . . "safety sells cars":** "Ribicoff Presses for Auto Safety," *New York Times*, February 19, 1965. **"hostile Congressional reaction":** Dan Cordtz, "Auto Executives Hurt Own Cause," *Wall Street Journal*, July 20, 1965. **highway deaths had risen:** David R. Jones, "U.S. Agency Spurs Car Safety Drive," *New York Times*, January 28, 1965. **Nader would later explain:** Ralph Nader, Ribicoff Hearings, part 3, 1966, 1275.

Page 88: **"driver is most important":** Jones, "Auto Makers Defend Safety Record," *NYT*. **"driver is the most important factor":** "Text of Ford's Remarks on Automobile Safety," *New York Times*, April 16, 1966. **"chorus of criticism" . . . "number of accidents":** Jones, "Auto Makers Defend Safety Record," *NYT*. **"abandon hope":** "Head of G.M. Assails 'Experts' Asking 'Unrealistic' Car Safety," *New York Times*, October 18, 1961. **"seat-belt craze":** O'Connell and Myers, 146. **"makes them safer":** Charles Chayne, House Traffic Safety Hearings, 1956, 339.

Page 89: **major carmakers:** Eastman, 99. **Donner assured senators:** Frederic Donner, Ribicoff Hearings, part 2, 1965, 655. **"prodded a throttle":** Skylark Gran Sport ad, in Nader, 309. **"Look, we could build":** Herndon, *Ford*, 263. **"startling problems":** quoted in Nader, 119. **Donner assured:** Frederic Donner, Ribicoff Hearings, part 2, 1965, 653, 657.

Page 90: **costly styling features:** Nader, 308. **"anything that might be done" . . . "We can't afford":** "GM President Says Industry Must Refute Safety Critics by Better Public Relations," *Wall Street Journal*, January 13, 1966. **auto industry also warned:** Ford vice president John Bugas, 1966 Congressional testimony, quoted in Lemov, 96; Chrysler vice president Paul Ackerman, quoted in Joseph C. Ingraham, "G.M. Offers Plan for Safer Roads," *New York Times*, April 12, 1958. **"corporate inbreeding":** Cordtz, 119. **power itself:** Briñol et al.

Page 91: **mightiest industrial enterprise:** Cordtz, 117. **"making 18 percent":** Lemov, 10–11. **singled out:** John McDonnell, "G.M. President Assails Critics of Auto Safety," *Chicago Tribune*, February 19, 1966. **"attacked on all sides":** "Text of Ford's Remarks on Automobile Safety," *NYT*. **"we in the industry":** Jones, "Auto Makers Defend Safety Record," *NYT*. **"potentially popular rationale":** Bill Mulligan, "The 'Perfectly Safe' Vehicle Crowd," *Rubber World*, January 1965, quoted in O'Connell and Myers, 162–63. **"amateur engineers" and "self-styled experts":** "Head of G.M. Assails

'Experts' Asking 'Unrealistic' Car Safety," *New York Times*, October 18, 1961. **"amateur experts":** O'Connell and Myers, 15. **"full of crap":** Herndon, 262–63.

Page 92: **"based on facts":** John McDonnell, "G.M. President Assails Critics of Auto Safety," *Chicago Tribune*, February 19, 1966. **a "scapegoat":** James M. Roche, "G.M. Chief Urges Wide Approach to Improve Automotive Safety," *Chicago Tribune*, February 20, 1966. **"totally biased attack":** Gikas, 334. **classified as "engineering data":** quoted in Nader, 117. **"relied on facts"** . . . **bulk of accidents:** quoted by Ralph Nader, Ribicoff Hearings, part 3, 1966, 1282–83. **"best that can be said":** Ralph Nader, Ribicoff Hearings, part 3, 1966, 1284.

Page 93: **active on GM's board:** "Alfred P. Sloan Jr. Dead at 90," *New York Times*, February 18, 1966. **"archetypal corporation man":** "Alfred P. Sloan Jr.," *New York Times*, February 19, 1966. **Nader perceived** . . . **compromising situation:** Walter Rugaber, "Critic of Auto Industry's Safety Standards Says He Was Trailed and Harassed," *New York Times*, March 6, 1966. **"spokesmen"** . . . **"You can bet":** Rugaber, "Critic of Auto Industry's Safety Standards," *NYT*. **Ribicoff asked:** Walter Rugaber, "G.M. Acknowledges Investigating Critic," *New York Times*, March 10, 1966. **"routine investigation"** . . . **"limited only":** GM statement, repr. in Ribicoff Hearings, part 4, 1966, 1389.

Page 94: **Ribicoff pointed out** . . . **"smear a man":** Sen. Abraham Ribicoff, Ribicoff Hearings, part 4, 1966, 1396, 1444, 1449. **"harassment, intimidation":** Sen. Robert Kennedy, Ribicoff Hearings, part 4, 1966, 1398. **Roche apologized:** James Roche, Ribicoff Hearings, part 4, 1966, 1381–82, 1397. **GM's general counsel** . . . **"the other way":** Aloysius F. Power, Ribicoff Hearings, part 4, 1966, 1403, 1453. **"priority second to none":** James Roche, Ribicoff Hearings, part 4, 1966, 1384.

Page 95: **"senseless carnage":** quoted by Ralph Nader, Ribicoff Hearings, part 3, 1966, 1285. **"Everybody was so outraged":** Elizabeth Brenner Drew, "The Politics of Auto Safety," *Atlantic Monthly*, October 1966, 99. **"I get mad":** Cordtz, 210. **Motor Vehicle Safety Act of 1966:** Lemov, 102. **"good start"** . . . **"we can live with" it:** quoted in John D. Morris, "Auto Safety Bill Voted by Senate; Johnson Pleased," *New York Times*, June 25, 1966. **The first standards:** "Text of Simplified U.S. Safety Standards," *New York Times*, February 1, 1967. **factories would have to be closed:** Lemov, 116–17. **fight over airbags:** Lemov, chs. 9–10. **highway death toll** . . . **per 100 million:** National Highway Traffic Safety Administration (NHTSA), *Traffic Safety Facts 2015*, 18, https://crashstats.nhtsa.dot.gov/Api/Public/ViewPublication/812384; NHTSA, *2017 Fatal Motor Vehicle Crashes: Overview*, https://crashstats.nhtsa.dot.gov/Api/Public/ViewPublication/812603.

Page 96: **auto safety technologies:** NHTSA, *Lives Saved by Vehicle Safety Technologies and Associated Federal Motor Vehicle Safety Standards, 1960 to 2012: Passenger Cars and LTVs*, 2015, https://crashstats.nhtsa.dot.gov/Api/Public/ViewPublication/809833. **settled for $425,000** . . . **watchdog and consumer groups:** "Unsafe at Any Speed—Fiftieth Anniversary," Ralph Nader (website), November 30, 2015, https://blog.nader.org/2015/11/30/unsafe-at-any-speed-fiftieth-anniversary/.

CHAPTER 4. "HOW WRONG ONE CAN BE"

Abbreviations

Senate Air Pollution Hearings.   *Air Pollution—1966: Hearings Before the Subcommittee on Air and Water Pollution of the Senate Committee on Public Works*, 89th Cong., 2nd sess., June 8–15, 1966, https://hdl.handle.net/2027/umn.31951d035807529

Page 97: **"The whole proceeding":** Robert, *Ethyl*, 307. **convivial, whimsical:** McGrayne, 79. **each had its drawbacks:** Kettering, 369. **"mixture of garlic and onions":** Boyd, *Professional Amateur*, 145. **engine parts** . . . **most dramatic:** Boyd, *Professional Amateur*, 146. **"non-scientific jig":** Nriagu, "Rise and Fall," 14.

Page 98: "**lead makes the mind give way**": Landrigan, 156. **warnings from experts:** Kovarik, "Ethyl-Leaded Gasoline," 385. "**such frightening phrases**": Boyd, *Professional Amateur*, 151.

Page 99: "**malicious and creeping" poison:** Cagin and Dray, 37. "**lead poisoning in human beings**": Cagin and Dray, 36. "**serious consideration**" . . . "**average street**": Rosner and Markowitz, "A 'Gift of God?,'" 345. "**lead-lined lungs**": Cagin and Dray, 35. **his body temperature:** McGrayne, 90.

Page 100: "**but no one knows**": Cagin and Dray, 37. **leaded gas went on sale . . . as "Ethyl**": McGrayne, 90. **ten thousand filling stations:** Kovarik, "The Ethyl Controversy," 114. **in Dayton, Ohio:** Robert, 121. **dozens were hospitalized:** Kovarik, "Ethyl-Leaded Gasoline," 385. "**tremendously upset**". . . "**calmer approach**": Robert, 121. **Kettering was pushing:** Kovarik, "The Ethyl Controversy," 80. **Poisonings at the DuPont plant:** Silas Bent, "Tetraethyl Lead Fatal to Makers," *New York Times*, June 22, 1925. "**Odd Gas Kills One**": "Odd Gas Kills One, Makes Four Insane," *New York Times*, October 27, 1924; "Another Man Dies from Insanity Gas," *New York Times*, October 28, 1924; "Gas Madness" headline quoted in Kovarik, "The Ethyl Controversy," 109. "**if ever a company**": Robert, 120.

Page 101: "**violently insane**" . . . "**insanity gas**": "Another Man Dies from Insanity Gas," *NYT.* "**doing nicely**" . . . "**fits of insanity**": "Another Man Dies from Insanity Gas," *NYT.* **at least one of the survivors:** Kovarik, "Ethyl-Leaded Gasoline," 384. "**delirium tremens" or . . . rabies:** US Public Health Service, 50; Cohen, 40. "**this reason destroyer**": "No Peril to Public Seen in Ethyl Gas," *New York Times*, November 1, 1924. **Kettering was reported:** Hounshell and Smith, 154. "**nothing ought to be said**": "Odd Gas Kills One," *NYT.* "**little good tendency**": Galloway, 107–8.

Page 102: "**probably went insane**": "Odd Gas Kills One," *NYT.* "**probably made the statement**": Kovarik, "The Ethyl Controversy," 108. "**failed to appreciate**" . . . "**man's undertaking**": "Bar Ethyl Gasoline as 5th Victim Dies," *New York Times,* October 31, 1924. "**The minute a man**": Rosner and Markowitz, "A 'Gift of God?,'" 348. **benefit of the reporters:** Rosner and Markowitz, "A 'Gift of God?,'" 348. **safety precautions at the Bayway facility:** Hounshell and Smith, 154.

Page 103: **views of our in-group:** Pool, Wood, and Leck. **resist out-group efforts:** Mackie, Gastardo-Conaco, and Skelly. **used neuroimaging . . . identified neural processes:** Cikara and Van Bavel; Molenberghs. **typically more aggressive:** Cikara. **our own moral standards:** Cikara, Jenkins, Dufour, and Saxe.

Page 104: **Our brains . . . out-group members:** Cikara and Van Bavel; Van Bavel, Packer and Cunningham; Molenberghs. **experts GM had initially contacted:** "Foretold His Attack on Leaded Gasoline: Dr. Henderson Says Company Didn't Employ Him When He Indicated Adverse Finding," *New York Times*, April 24, 1925; Kovarik, "The Ethyl Controversy," 90. **close relationships with industry:** Cagin and Dray, 37. "**scare headlines**" . . . **bureau also agreed:** Rosner and Markowitz, "A 'Gift of God?,'" 345.

Page 105: **various subtle forms:** US Public Health Service, 76. "**seemingly remote**": "No Peril to Public Seen in Ethyl Gas," *NYT.* **independent experts:** Kovarik, "Ethyl-Leaded Gasoline," 387.

Page 106: "**conditions will grow worse**": "Sees Deadly Gas A Peril in Streets," *New York Times,* April 22, 1925.

Page 107: "**diametrically opposed conceptions**": US Public Health Service, 62. **decisions about TEL . . .** "**no question**": US Public Health Service, 69–70. **Kehoe Paradigm:** Nriagu, "Clair Patterson." **his company's morals:** "Ethyl Gas Official Denies Monopoly," *New York Times*, April 23, 1925. "**no one is more anxious**": Midgley. **average person believes:** Pronin, Gilovich and Ross.

Page 108: "**price of progress**": Boyd, "Charles F. Kettering," 255. **Kettering made the case:** US Public Health Service, 9. **genuine concern:** Kitman, 16. "**continued development**" . . . "**gift of God**": US Public Health Service, 106. "**human progress cannot go on**": For an analysis of the 1920s controversy, see Rosner and Markowitz, "A 'Gift of God?,'" 344, 350. **Reframing a harmful action:** Bandura, 194. **TEL plant:** Robert, 156–59. **TEL technology was shared:** *Sci-*

entific and Technical Mobilization: Hearings before a Subcommittee of the Senate Committee on Military Affairs, 78th Cong., 1st sess., part 6, 1943, 725, 939–40.

Page 109: **"present method of warfare":** *Elimination of German Resources for War: Hearings Before a Subcommittee of the Senate Committee on Military Affairs*, 79th Cong., 1st sess., part 7, 1945, 945. **blended with ethanol:** Kovarik, "Ethyl-Leaded Gasoline," 389. **successfully experimented . . . "knowingly overstated":** Kitman, 18–19, 12. **"not be allowed to lapse":** Rosner and Markowitz, "A 'Gift of God?,'" 350.

Page 110: **symbol of the intimate ties:** Graebner, 142. **one dollar per year:** Nriagu, "Clair Patterson," 72. **"You are God" . . . "the last word":** Denworth, 60. **Kehoe's data . . . important conclusions:** Warren, 130; Denworth, 59.

Page 111: **Patterson devised . . . 4.5 billion years ago:** Cohen. Denworth, ch. 1. **attention to the seas . . . source of this extra lead:** Cohen, 27; Denworth, ch. 3. **He knew his findings:** Cohen, 32. **try to buy him off:** Denworth, 56. **"Wham!":** Cohen, 32. **fired from his job at Caltech:** Denworth, 113.

Page 112: **concept of tenure:** Cohen, 58. **lead in their bodies:** Denworth, 65. **adjust this estimate:** Needleman, 22. **"impugns the life work":** Denworth, 66. **"let the man" . . . "swept under the rug":** Needleman, 22, 23. **"little or no obvious effort":** Warren, 214. **"remarkably naïve" . . . "so woefully ignorant":** Needleman, 22.

Page 113: **"without caution" . . . "astonishingly dogmatic":** Kehoe, 736, 739. **"incompetent and hysterical" . . . "misguided zealots":** "Demands Fair Play for Ethyl Gasoline," *New York Times*, May 7, 1925. **small but interesting study:** Branscombe and Wann.

Page 114: **US military base in Greenland . . . team to Antarctica:** Denworth, 69–73. **two articles:** Walter Sullivan, "Lead Pollution of Air 'Alarming,'" *New York Times*, September 8, 1965; Walter Sullivan, "Warning Is Issued on Lead Poisoning," *New York Times*, September 12, 1965. **"no evidence of danger" message:** Marjorie Hunter, "U.S. Study Hinted on Perils of Lead," *New York Times*, December 15, 1965; Denworth, 73–74.

Page 115: **"almost felt sorry":** Denworth, 74. **"a bit under the gun":** Warren, 217. **"naïve realism":** Pronin, Gilovich, and Ross.

Page 116: **something of a "kook" . . . wearing a gas mask:** Denworth, 16, 57. **"there is no way" . . . "more experience":** Robert Kehoe, Senate Air Pollution Hearings, 206, 217. **"chronic lead insult":** Clair Patterson, Senate Air Pollution Hearings, 312. **"rabble rousing" . . . "Rachel Carson":** Herbert Stockinger, quoted in Senate Air Pollution Hearings, 318–19.

Page 117: **"fanatic defender":** "'Silent Spring' Is Now Noisy Summer," *New York Times*, July 22, 1962. **"sinister parties" . . . "east-curtain":** Lear, 417. **one Ethyl executive:** Robert, 297.

Page 118: **actually increase smog . . . "lead is going to be":** "Ethyl Hits Altering Gasoline," *Washington Post*, January 16, 1970. **"no proof whatsoever":** John J. Abele, "Pollution Role of Lead Disputed," *New York Times*, February 3, 1970. **"proceed only on the basis:** "Ethyl Asserts Removal of Lead from Gasoline Wouldn't Be Beneficial," *Wall Street Journal*, February 2, 1970. **"Who kills the most". . . "interested in clean air":** "Ethyl Hits Altering Gasoline," *Washington Post*, January 16, 1970. **virtually unanimous support:** "Clean Air Bill Cleared with Auto Emission Deadline," *Congressional Quarterly Almanac*, 1970; the Senate version passed by 73–0, and a weaker House bill passed by 374–1. **newly formed environmental group . . . promptly sued:** Denworth, 95.

Page 119: **starting to link:** Carothers, 703–10. **"science does not":** Markowitz and Rosner, *Lead Wars*, 78–79, quoting Ethyl Corp. v. EPA, 541 F.2d 1 (D.C. Cir. 1976). **"deaths of innocent people":** "Court Says EPA Can Regulate Lead in Gasoline," *Wall Street Journal*, March 22, 1976. **essential micronutrient:** Needleman, 33. **"lead deficiency":** US Environmental Protection Agency, *Air Quality Criteria for Lead*, 12-3. **"ghetto children":** "Lead Balloon," *Wall Street Journal*, August 27, 1982; Markowitz and Rosner, *Lead Wars*, 90.

Page 120: **Reagan administration:** Needleman, 30–31. **Reagan's Office of Management and Budget:** Denworth, 155. **"juvenile and simplistic":** John M. Berry, "Leaded-Gas Analysis Praised," *Washington Post*, April 1, 1984. **"novelists" and "bastards":** Francine Schwadel, "Ethyl Corp. Still Defends Failing Product as It Hunts for Replacement Acquisitions," *Wall*

Street Journal, May 16, 1984. **"would abandon its effort":** Markowitz and Rosner, 95. **chief target:** Rosner and Markowitz, "Standing Up"; Denworth, 147–52, 179–97. **"took three years":** Denworth, 197. **children's blood:** Bohning, "Interview with Richard E. Heckert," 29; Markowitz and Rosner,77. **blaming leaded gasoline:** David Rosner, quoted in "Getting the Lead Out," *Think: The Online News Source for Case Western Reserve University,* Fall-Winter 2010. **Ethyl officials:** Robert, 295. **"sacrificial lamb":** Vasil Pappas, "Taking Knocks: Ethyl Corp., a High-flier until the 1970s, Keeps Reeling from Environmental Jabs," *Wall Street Journal,* October 2, 1979. **would be "crucified":** Kenneth B. Noble, "Lead Industry Digs in Its Heels on Gas Additives," *New York Times,* August 5, 1984. **"industry under siege":** Markowitz and Rosner, 88.

Page 121: **"rabid environmentalists":** Noble, "Lead Industry Digs in Its Heels," *NYT.* **TEL poisonings in the 1920s:** Cohen, 40. **almost in lockstep:** Centers for Disease Control and Prevention, 1991, *Preventing Lead Poisoning in Young Children,* Figure 2.5, Change in Blood Lead Level in Relation to a Decline in Use of Leaded Gasoline, 1976–1980, CDC Prevention Guidelines Database (archive), https://wonder.cdc.gov/wonder/prevguid /p0000029/p0000029.asp. **millions of tons:** It has been estimated that six million tons of lead was burned as a gas additive in the United States alone between 1926 and 1985; Nriagu, "Clair Patterson." **lead was associated:** Needleman et al.; US Environmental Protection Agency, *Integrated Science Assessment for Lead.*

Page 122: **childhood blood lead levels:** Raymond, Wheeler, and Brown. **American preschoolers . . . 10 μg/dL:** National Toxicology Program, *Health Effects of Low-Level Lead,* xvii. **Screenings of children:** Needleman, 26. **most of the lead exposure:** Robbins et al., 4125. **Flint, Michigan:** Hanna-Attisha et al., 285. **Separate analyses:** Nevin, "How Lead Exposure Relates to Temporal Changes"; Nevin, "Understanding International Crime Trends"; Reyes; see also Drum.

Page 123: **different series of crime statistics:** Lauritsen, Rezey, and Heimer. **international research effort:** Global Burden of Disease 2017 Risk Factor Collaborators. **2018 analysis . . . 400,000 deaths:** Lanphear et al. **480,000 early deaths:** Surgeon General, *Health Consequences of Smoking,* 1–2. **Ethyl diversified:** Francine Schwadel, "Ethyl Corp. Still Defends Failing Product as It Hunts for Replacement Acquisitions," *Wall Street Journal,* May 16, 1984. **"face the hysteria":** Agis Salpukas, "Ethyl Aides See Future for Leaded Fuels," *New York Times,* December 27, 1970. **only nation still using leaded gas:** UNEP and Partnership for Clean Fuels and Vehicles, "Leaded Petrol Phase-Out: Global Status," online maps, April 2014 and July 2018.

Page 124: **at the age of 73:** Denworth, 177. **He left unfinished:** Cohen, 50–51. **living legend:** Cagin and Dray, 89. **"human carcinogens":** National Toxicology Program, *Report on Carcinogens.* **award-winning chemists:** Leslie. **at the age of 51 . . . American Chemical Society:** Cagin and Dray, 81–83.

CHAPTER 5. "OUR FREE ENTERPRISE SYSTEM
IS AT STAKE"

Abbreviations

House EPA Rulemaking Hearings, 1981.   *EPA Proposed Rulemaking on Chlorofluorocarbons (CFCs) and its Impact on Small Business: Hearing Before the Subcommittee on Antitrust and Restraint of Trade Activities Affecting Small Business of the House Committee on Small Business,* 97th Cong., 1st sess., July 15, 1981, https://hdl.handle.net/2027/ purl.32754078074980

House Scientific Integrity Hearing, 1995.   *Scientific Integrity and Public Trust: The Science behind Federal Policies and Mandates: Case Study I—Stratospheric Ozone: Myths and Realities: Hearing Before the Subcommittee on Energy and Environment of the House*

Committee on Science, 104th Cong., 1st sess., September 20, 1995, https://archive.org/details
/scientificintegr00unit

Senate Ozone Hearings, 1975. *Stratospheric Ozone Depletion: Hearings Before the
Subcommittee on the Upper Atmosphere of the Senate Committee on Aeronautical and Space
Sciences*, 94th Cong., 1st sess., part 2, September 18–23, 1975, https://babel.hathitrust.org/
cgi/pt?id=mdp.39015078060137&view=1up&seq=1

Senate Ozone and Climate Hearings, 1987. *Ozone Depletion, the Greenhouse Effect, and Climate
Change: Joint Hearing Before the Subcommittees on Environmental Protection and Hazardous
Wastes and Toxic Substances of the Senate Committee on Environment and Public Works*,
100th Cong., 1st sess., part 2, January 28, 1987, https://babel.hathitrust.org/cgi/pt?id=
ucl.aa0006564165&view=1up&seq=1

Page 126: **"My theory is":** quoted in Michael L. SanGiovanni, "Keeping a High Profile," *Aerosol Age*, September 1977, 35. **mysterious recent deaths:** "Ice Machine Gas Kills 15 in Chicago,"
New York Times, July 2, 1929; "Cay Ice-Box Gas Killed Family of 3," *New York Times*, July 17,
1929. **"slight and rather pleasant odor":** "Move to Prevent Ice-Box Anxiety," *New York Times*,
August 1, 1929.

Page 127: **To demonstrate CFCs' safety . . . "desire to sing":** Cagin and Dray, 66. **Freon . . .
"outstanding scientific achievements":** Cagin and Dray, 66.

Page 128: **allow life to finally emerge . . . stratospheric ozone:** Dotto and Schiff, 27,
35–36.

Page 129: **"an armor plate":** Robert E. Martin, "Lonely Outposts of Science Study Cyclones
in the Sun," *Popular Science*, January 1934, 14. **death rays . . . "even terrifying":** "1/8 Inch of
Ozone Alone Saves Life," *New York Times*, October 30, 1933. **"Knowing how fine a thread":**
Cagin and Dray, 136. **Lovelock invented . . . "no conceivable hazard":** Dotto and Schiff, 8–12.
Rowland . . . Lovelock's CFC measurements: Dotto and Schiff, 12–13.

Page 130: **"casual thought" . . . funding:** Dotto and Schiff, 13. **destroy many thousands:**
Dotto and Schiff, 16. **alarming depletion:** Dotto and Schiff, 17. **"work is going well":** Roan, 2.
covered the story: Walter Sullivan, "Tests Show Aerosol Gases May Pose Threat to Earth," *New
York Times*, September 26, 1974; "Scientists Study Action on Aerosol Gas," *New York Times*,
September 27, 1974; Dotto and Schiff, 24.

Page 131: **"imaginability":** Tversky and Kahneman. **"'Wait a minute'":** Gabrielle Noone,
"Donald Trump Says Hair Spray Is 'Not Like It Used to Be,'" *New York Magazine*, May 9,
2016. **"we had a terrific responsibility":** Cagin and Dray, 207.

Page 132: **by over 20 percent:** "Fluorocarbons and Ozone: New Predictions Ominous," *Science News*, October 5, 1974. **In 1973, Americans bought:** "Aerosol Output Up, But What's
Ahead?" *Soap/Cosmetics/Chemical Specialties*, June 1974. **half of spray cans:** Brodeur, "Annals
of Chemistry: Inert," 47. **half of US aerosols:** Dotto and Schiff, 146. **hundreds of aerosol
sniffers:** Walter Rugaber, "Consumer Panel Will Open Hearings on Safety of Aerosol Sprays,"
New York Times, February 19, 1974. **on the defensive:** "Aerosol Output Up, But What's Ahead?"
Soap/Cosmetics/Chemical Specialties, June 1974. **"distorted and alarmist":** "CPSC Aerosol
Hearings," *Soap/Cosmetics/Chemical Specialties*, April 1974. **"humorless stridency":** Dotto and
Schiff, 150.

Page 133: **our kitchen knives:** Commentary, *Aerosol Age*, March 1974, 8. **"hundreds of thousands of people":** "'Regulatory Zealots' Lack of Perspective," *Soap/Cosmetics/Chemical Specialties*, January 1974. **NRDC's petition:** Walter Sullivan, "Federal Ban Urged on Spray-Can Propellants Suspected in Ozone Depletion and Possible Cancer Rise," *New York Times*, November 21,
1974. **vast array of changes:** Parson, 87; Cagin and Dray, 204, 222. **congressional hearings . . .
reviews of the science:** Dotto and Schiff, 176–205. **Half the CFCs used:** Senate Ozone Hearings, 1975, 549.

Page 134: **"parent-like":** Salvatore Noto, "Letters," *Aerosol Age*, July 1975, 7. **"unfeeling
monster types":** Montfort Johnsen, "Letters," *Aerosol Age*, May 1975, 16. **"atmosphere of**

objectivity": Ralph Engel, "The Ozone Issue—Who's in Control," *Aerosol Age*, July 1976, 26–27. *Aerosol Age* article: "Exploring Stratospheric Chemistry," *Aerosol Age*, November 1974, 14. As for regulators: Commentary, *Aerosol Age*, June 1975, 20. "stacked deck": "Fluorocarbons: Clearly Safe or Banned by '78?," *Aerosol Age*, Special Report, June 1975, 14b. "whipping boy": Commentary, *Aerosol Age*, June 1975, 18. "vendetta": "Aerosols' Latest Problem: Ozone," *Soap/Cosmetics/Chemical Specialties*, October 1974. "vigilantes": Ralph Engel, "The Ozone Issue—Who's in Control?," *Aerosol Age*, July 1976, 26. "lynching party": Walter Sullivan, "Studies are Cited to Show That Effects of Fluorocarbons on Ozone Layer May Be Cut 'Nearly to Zero,'" *New York Times*, May 13, 1976. "pious concern": "Fluorocarbons: Clearly Safe or Banned by '78?," *Aerosol Age*, 14b. "Everything and everybody in the U.S.A.": "Plaze Inc., Uses Advertising, Letter to Editor to Counteract Ozone Publicity," *Aerosol Age*, February 1975, 9. "group of crusaders": "Lights, Camera, Action!" *Aerosol Age*, January 1975, 11. Footnote: "S. C. Johnson Drops Fluorocarbons," *Soap/Cosmetics/Chemical Specialties*, July 1975, 12.

Page 135: He wrote in 1975: George Diamond, "Readers Speak Out," *Aerosol Age*, June 1975, 26. chief engineer for Boeing: John Swihart, "Cancer Charge Refuted," *Aviation Week and Space Technology*, April 12, 1971, 60. work of the KGB: Michael L. SanGiovanni, "Keeping a High Profile," *Aerosol Age*, September 1977, 35.

Page 136: most prominent member: Linda Greenhouse, "Robert Abplanalp, 81, Inventor and Nixon Confidant, Dies," *New York Times*, September 2, 2003. Abplanalp gave a speech: "Defends Aerosols as Life Savers," *Soap/Cosmetics/Chemical Specialties*, November 1974. His company would later: Precision Valve advertisement ("Don't Give Up on Fluorocarbon Aerosols . . . Yet !!!"), *Aerosol Age*, March 1976. Ralph Engel: quoted in "'Fight Back,' Aerosol Producers Urged," *Soap/Cosmetics/Chemical Specialties*, July 1975, 55.

Page 137: head of the Can Manufacturers Institute: quoted in Commentary, *Aerosol Age*, June 1975, 20. "uncanny enthusiasm": Jost and Amodio, 55. core psychological needs: Jost, Federico, and Napier. if subjects are made insecure: Jost, Federico, and Napier, 320–21. finding out that we disagree: Pool, Wood, and Leck.

Page 138: need for certainty: Jost, Federico, and Napier, 318. Scorer wrote: R. S. Scorer, "Freon in the Stratosphere," *New Scientist*, October 10, 1974. lacking in actual scientists: Dotto and Schiff, 155. "utter nonsense": Walter Sullivan, "Scientist Doubts Spray Cans Imperil Ozone Layer," *New York Times*, July 8, 1975. Scorer's powerful certainty: Dotto and Schiff, 157. aerosol industry hailed: "Aerosol Producers in Counterattack," *Soap/Cosmetics/Chemical Specialties*, August 1975, 12.

Page 139: disputing facts outside their field: Dotto and Schiff, 156; Cagin and Dray, 201. "legitimate cause for concern": Dotto and Schiff, 191. trumpeted Scorer's findings: "Scorer: Ozone Theory Is 'Utter Nonsense,'" *Aerosol Age*, August 1975, 23. Scorer argued: "Scorer: Ozone Theory Is 'Utter Nonsense,'" *Aerosol Age*, August 1975, 23.

Page 140: "people have the belief": Dotto and Schiff, 215. "I'm personally convinced": Roan, 67. Rowland-Molina theory was "nonsense": Steven Greenhouse, "Aerosol Feels the Ozone Effect," *New York Times*, June 22, 1975. "all the factors together": "A Stroke of Genius," *New Scientist*, October 2, 1975.

Page 141: "Papa Sweetie Pie": Senate Ozone Hearings, 1975, 611. "should reputable evidence": DuPont advertisement ("The ozone layer vs. the aerosol industry. DuPont wants to see them both survive"), *New York Times*, June 30, 1975, 30.

Page 142: "what US law holds": Precision Valve advertisement ("Don't Give Up on Fluorocarbon Aerosols . . . Yet !!!"), *Aerosol Age*, March 1976. "rule of witchcraft": Dotto and Schiff, 264.

Page 143: "just a hypothesis": "NAS Launches Study on Fluorocarbons," *Science News*, November 30, 1974. some "missing factor": Senate Ozone Hearings, 1975, 799. panel concluded . . . depleted by about 7 percent: National Research Council, *Halocarbons: Effects on Stratospheric Ozone* (Washington, DC: National Academies Press, 1976), 4. "almost certain to be necessary": National Research Council, *Halocarbons: Environmental Effects of Chlorofluoromethane Release* (Washington, DC: National Academies Press, 1976), 7–8. "we cannot afford to give chemicals": Brodeur, "In the Face," 74.

Page 144: **"simple case"**: Harold M. Schmeck, Jr., "FDA Urges a Curb on Fluorocarbons," *New York Times,* October 16, 1976. **swift regulatory action:** Roan, 84. **DuPont explained:** Gene Smith, "Outwitting the Aerosol Ban: New System Ready," *New York Times,* May 13, 1977. **"surprising upbeat feeling".** . . **"the aerosol situation":** Commentary, *Aerosol Age,* February 1977, 12. **a "hoax":** Nellie Blagden, "From Nixon's Buddy Bob Abplanalp Comes a New Safe Spray Valve: Aquasol," *People,* July 18, 1977. **amendments:** Clean Air Act Amendments of 1977, section 126 (42 USC section 7457, repealed in 1990).

Page 145: **EPA's regulatory plan:** Brodeur, 70, 77. **"free enterprise system":** Linda Kohler, House EPA Rulemaking Hearings, 1981, 28–29. **"the battleground":** Cagin and Dray, 237. **Nazi Germany and Communist Russia:** Philip Shabecoff, "Nearing Complete Renovation of Interior Department Rules," *New York Times,* January 23, 1983. **NAS reports:** National Research Council, *Stratospheric Ozone Depletion by Halocarbons: Chemistry and Transport* (Washington, DC: National Academies Press, 1979); National Research Council, *Causes and Effects of Stratospheric Ozone Reduction: An Update* (Washington, DC: National Academy Press, 1982).

Page 146: **move the goalposts:** Roan, 108. **"statistical technique":** "Comments of the Alliance for Responsible CFC Policy," House EPA Rulemaking Hearings, 1981, 76. **"an extreme stance":** Parson, 82. **"here were people":** Curtis Moore, quoted in Roan, 108. **confirmation bias:** Nickerson.

Page 147: **Pennwalt . . . DuPont:** Brodeur, "In the Face," 79, 87. **"monumental achievement":** Ronald Reagan, "Statement on Signing the Montreal Protocol on Ozone-Depleting Substances," April 5, 1988, www.reaganlibrary.gov/research/speeches/040588a. **British team published findings:** Cagin and Dray, 283. **NASA soon confirmed . . . NASA computers:** Cagin and Dray, 275, 285; Gribbin, 111.

Page 148: **"sheer speculation":** Brodeur, 84. **"continued releases of CFCs":** *Ozone Depletion, the Greenhouse Effect, and Climate Change: Hearings Before the Subcommittee on Environmental Pollution of the Senate Committee on Environment and Public Works,* 99th Cong., 2nd sess., June 10–11, 1986, 186, 271. **growth of CFC production:** Parson, 78–79, 124–25.

Page 149: **"available, acceptable alternatives":** House EPA Rulemaking Hearings, 1981, 78. **In 1981 the industry:** Parson, 123; Reinhardt and Vietor, (A)10. **suit brought by the NRDC:** Brodeur, "In the Face," 85; Doniger, 88. **DuPont representative:** Parson 123; DuPont had apparently made a similar announcement about alternatives in 1980, but in such a way that its announcement was widely misunderstood, and so its announcement in 1986 came as a major surprise to the workshop participants. **"development of alternatives":** "Response to Ozone Depletion," *Chemical and Engineering News,* 64, no. 47 (November 24, 1986): 49. **"Since the early 1970s":** Elwood P. Blanchard, *Stratospheric Ozone Depletion: Joint Hearing Before the Subcommittees on Hazardous Wastes and Toxic Substances and Environmental Protection of the Senate Committee on Environment and Public Works,* 100th Cong., 2nd sess. March 30, 1988, 41.

Page 150: **wait-and-see argument:** Brodeur, "In the Face," 86. **international assessment:** Parson, 124; Glas, 145–46. **skin cancer deaths:** U.S. Environmental Protection Agency, *Regulatory Impact Analysis,* ES-6. **cut by 85 percent:** Anderson and Sarma, 69. **pursue deep cuts:** Maxwell and Briscoe, 281. **"shill" . . . pressure from his own family:** Parson, 126–27; Brodeur, "In the Face," 86. **the Alliance and DuPont:** Parson, 126; Maxwell and Briscoe, 280. **the Alliance announced:** Richard Barnett, Senate Ozone and Climate Hearings, 1987, 178, 182. **DuPont announced its support:** Parson, 126. **NRDC hailed the shift:** Anderson and Sarma, 74. Footnote: **"Remember a few years back":** Cagin and Dray, 249.

Page 151: **shifted the burden of proof:** Senate Ozone and Climate Hearings, 1987, 172. **"not sufficiently developed":** Richard Barnett, Senate Ozone and Climate Hearings, 1987, 182. **expedition to Antarctica . . . "probably too timid":** Cagin and Dray, 314–17. **NASA scientists:** Parson, 153. **US delegation . . . opposed by the Alliance:** Parson, 129, 133–36. **"industry got exercised":** Cagin and Dray, 321. **a backlash:** Parson, 133–36. **"personal protection" plan:** Cagin and Dray, 332; Doniger, 90. **"stand out in the sun":** Robert E. Taylor, "Advice on Ozone May Be: 'Wear Hats And Stand in the Shade," *Washington Post,* May 29, 1987. **Senate passed . . .**

industry seemed to retreat: Parson, 135. **Montreal Protocol:** For the story of the negotiation of the Montreal Protocol, see Parson, 137–46; Anderson and Sarma, 81–94. **"borders on being catastrophic":** Jonathan P. Hicks, "Chemical Industry Sees Rush to Invent Safer Alternatives," *New York Times*, September 17, 1987. **opposed the protocol:** Parson, 249. **The Alliance thought:** Philip Shabecoff, "Dozens of Nations Reach Agreement to Protect Ozone," *New York Times*, September 17, 1987.

Page 152: **A DuPont representative:** Cagin and Dray, 337. **specially modified planes:** Shirley Christian, "Pilots Fly over the Pole into Heart of Ozone Mystery," *New York Times*, September 22, 1987. **"more dangerous"** . . . **their samples showed:** Cagin and Dray, 346, 352. **"more in the nature of":** Gribbin, 133. **whether enough evidence existed:** Reinhardt and Vietor, (A)13. **Ozone Trends Panel:** World Meteorological Association and National Aeronautics and Space Administration, *Report of the International Ozone Trends Panel 1988*, vols. 1 and 2, https://acd-ext.gsfc.nasa.gov/Documents/O3_Assessments/index.html. **In the winters . . . Over the mainland:** Parson, 155. **sworn to secrecy:** Maxwell and Briscoe, 14. **"not one time that week":** Reinhardt and Vietor, (B)1. **earned widespread praise:** Parson, 156. **"honorable and honest corporate scientists":** Anderson, 149.

Page 153: **Pennwalt:** Parson, 158. **sliver of the company's revenues:** Parson, 158. **high respect for science:** Reinhardt and Vietor, (A)8. **profits . . . replacement products:** Maxwell and Briscoe.

Page 154: **a stronger Montreal Protocol:** Cagin and Dray, 357. **"warranted by the scientific evidence":** Keith Schneider, "Bush Orders End to Ozone Destroyers by 1996," *New York Times*, February 12, 1992. **faster phaseout:** Cagin and Dray, 358. **cheaper and easier:** Cook, vi, 6–7. **clean electronic parts:** Andrew Pollack, "Moving Fast to Protect the Ozone Layer," *New York Times*, May 15, 1991. **Air conditioning and refrigeration manufacturers:** Cook, vi, 6–7. **support from industry:** Hiroko Tabuchi, and Danny Hakim, "How the Chemical Industry Joined the Fight against Climate Change," *New York Times*, October 16, 2016. **DuPont has captured:** Cook, 7. **Global *emissions* . . . global *concentrations* . . . Global ozone averages:** Hegglin et al., 53, 56, 46. **Ozone is on track:** World Meteorological Organization, ES-1. **ozone hole in Antarctica:** Hegglin et al., 38. **first evidence:** Solomon et al. **close to full recovery:** Samson Reiny, "NASA Study: First Direct Proof of Ozone Hole Recovery Due to Chemicals Ban," news release, NASA, January 4, 2018. **alarming ozone loss:** United Nations Environmental Programme, *Montreal Protocol and Human Health*, 2015, www.unep.fr/ozonaction/information/mmcfiles/7738-e-TheMontrealProtocolandHumanHealth.pdf, 20.

Page 155: **much-cited NASA model:** Newman; Michael Carlowicz, "The World We Avoided by Protecting the Ozone Layer," NASA Earth Observatory (website), May 13, 2009, https://earthobservatory.nasa.gov/features/WorldWithoutOzone. **EPA estimates that the Montreal Protocol:** US EPA, *Updating Ozone Calculations*, 20. **cut global agricultural production:** Andersen, 144. **Sherwood Rowland:** Lanie Jones, "Ozone Warning: He Sounded Alarm, Paid Heavy Price," *Los Angeles Times*, July 14, 1988. **new field of scientific research:** Felicity Barringer, "F. Sherwood Rowland, Cited Aerosols' Danger, Is Dead at 84," *New York Times*, March 12, 2012. **These reports were apparently critical:** Parson, 8. **helped slow global warming:** "Sherwood Rowland, CFCs, Ozone Depletion and the Public Role of Scientists," *Real Climate* (blog), March 13, 2012.

Page 156: **group connected to Lyndon LaRouche:** Parson, 337. **"green gestapo"** . . . **"neo-Satanic organization"** . . . **environmental leaders:** Maduro and Schauerhammer, 199, 259, 277, and chs. 9 through 11 for others listed in the coalition. Footnote: **du Pont Smith:** Maduro and Schauerhammer, 235–39. **his parents succeeded:** Michael de Courcy Hinds, "DuPont Millions at Issue in an Heir's Sanity Case," *New York Times*, January 29, 1990. **Lewis's father:** Associated Press, "Father Cleared in DuPont Kidnapping Case," *New York Times*, January 1, 1993.

Page 157: **what Singer would call:** Oreskes and Conway, 134. **conservative media:** Oreskes and Conway, 130 (citing S. Fred Singer and Candace Crandall, "Misled by Lukewarm Data," *Washington Times*, May 30, 1991); Fred S. Singer, "Ozone Scare Generates Much Heat, Little

Light," *Wall Street Journal,* April 16, 1987; Fred S. Singer, "My Adventures in the Ozone Layer," *National Review,* June 30, 1989; **Limbaugh's books and radio program:** Taubes. **Fred Singer told . . . Delay would state:** House Scientific Integrity Hearing, 1995, 50, 28–29. **defending the phaseout:** House Scientific Integrity Hearing, 1995, 203–4.

CHAPTER 6. "PSYCHOLOGICAL CRUTCHES"

Abbreviations

UCSF Archives.   Truth Tobacco Industry Documents, University of California San Francisco Library, https://www.industrydocuments.ucsf.edu/tobacco/docs

Page 159: **"company as a whole believed":** Wakeham, in "Death in the West," *This Week,* Thames Television, September 2, 1976, transcript, UCSF Archives, 5, www.industrydocuments .ucsf.edu/tobacco/docs/#id=pgbh0112. **"defraud smokers" . . . "survives, and profits":** US v. Philip Morris USA, Inc., 449 F. Supp. 2d 1, 28, 852 (D.D.C. 2006), aff'd in part and vacated in part, 566 F.3d 1095 (D.C. Cir. 2009)(per curiam), cert. denied, 130 S.Ct. 3501 (2010). **Wall Street saw it:** Philip Shenon, "New Limits Set over Marketing for Cigarettes," *New York Times,* August 18, 2006. **Polling that year showed:** Harris Poll, "Americans Less Likely to Say 18 of 19 Industries Are Honest and Trustworthy This Year," news release, December 12, 2013.

Page 160: **unheard of elsewhere:** Gately, 23. **Old World . . . passionate defenses:** Burns; Gately. **history of cigarettes:** Kluger; Brandt.

Page 161: **seven states . . . "addicted to this habit":** Brandt, 47. **"a small army" . . . key congressional committees:** Kluger, 40. **General Pershing:** Brandt, 51. **public was bombarded:** Stanford has posted a collection of old tobacco ads at http://tobacco.stanford.edu/ tobacco_main/index.php.

Page 162: **more healthful or less irritating:** Brandt, 93–95. **encouraged the film industry:** Brandt, 86. **nephew of Sigmund Freud:** Brandt, 80. **"the mental processes":** Pollay, 41. **"torches of freedom":** Brandt, 84–85. **80 percent of men:** David M. Burns et al., "Cigarette Smoking Behavior in the United States," 17, in *Changes in Cigarette-Related Disease Risks and Their Implications for Prevention and Control,* Monograph 8, ch. 2 (Rockville, MD: National Cancer Institute, 1997).

Page 163: **"liable to insanity":** Gunn, 605. **cancer of the nostrils:** Kluger, 15. **Freud's doctors:** Brecher et al., 91–93. **denture-like prosthesis:** Lewis Cohen, "How Sigmund Freud Wanted to Die," *Atlantic,* September 23, 2014. **he found it a "torture":** Brecher et al., 91–93. **studies linking cigarettes:** Cameron. **two major studies:** Wynder and Graham; Doll and Hill.

Page 164: **the British study's results:** Brandt, 138. *Reader's Digest* **. . . advertising:** Kluger, 152. **painting tar:** Wynder, Graham, and Croninger. **"But, naturally," he wrote:** E. Dakin. "Forwarding Memorandum, To Members of the Planning Committee," n.d. (probably December 1953), UCSF Archives. **full-page ad:** Tobacco Industry Research Council, "A Frank Statement to Cigarette Smokers," January 4, 1954, UCSF Archives; Kluger, 164. **newspapers around the country:** Brandt, 171.

Page 165: **"ultraconservative" . . . "You all know it":** "Press Conference of the Tobacco Industry Research Committee," June 15, 1954, UCSF Archives. **sterilization of "the misfit":** Brandt, 176. **American Cancer Society . . . retrospective studies:** Cameron, 73. **"no standards of proof":** Cameron, 75. **"retreated behind impossible":** Sidney J. Green, "Smoking, Associated Diseases and Causality," 1976, UCSF Archives; see also Glantz et al., 441–42.

Page 166: **"with one exception":** H.R. Bentley, D.G.I. Felton, and W.W. Reid, "Report on Visit to U.S.A. and Canada, 17th April–12th May 1958," UCSF Archives. **"within the business" . . . "Truth is our message":** Brown and Williamson, "Smoking and Health Proposal," 1969(?), UCSF Archives; emphasis in the original. **"Manhattan Project mentality":** Kluger, 258. **thousands of studies:** Surgeon General, *Health Consequences of Smoking—50 Years,* 5.

Page 167: **panel was carefully constituted . . . consensus report:** Brandt, 219–20; Kluger, 258–59. **It confidently linked smoking:** Surgeon General, *Smoking and Health.* **Future historians and judges:** Brandt, 229; *US v. Philip Morris USA, Inc.,* 449 F. Supp. 2d 1, 174. **One of the heaviest smokers:** Brandt, 229. **"one would suppose" . . . "odds are greatly against":** Addison Yeaman, "Implications of Battelle Hippo I & II and the Griffith Filter," July 17, 1963, UCSF Archives. **"propaganda blast" . . . "rationale":** George Weissman to Joseph F. Cullman III, "Surgeon General's Report," January 29, 1964, UCSF Archives. **"their own addiction":** Brandt, 157.

Page 168: **"doubt is our product":** Brown and Williamson, "Smoking and Health Proposal," UCSF Archives; Glantz et al., 189–91. **"Just What the Doctor Ordered!" . . . "harmless material":** Kluger, 151, 155. **"safer" cigarettes:** *US v. Philip Morris USA, Inc.,* 449 F. Supp. 2d 1, 456. **"constitutional" theory:** Tobacco Industry Research Committee, "Dr. Little Gives TIRC View," press release, October 11, 1954, UCSF Archives. **"ready-made credible alternatives":** Fred Panzer to Horace R. Kornegay, Tobacco Institute, "The Roper Proposal," memorandum, May 1, 1972, UCSF Archives. **"sex drives" . . . "a heavy smoker":** Stanley Frank, "To Smoke or Not to Smoke—That Is Still the Question," *True Magazine,* January 1968, UCSF Archives.

Page 169: **Tobacco Institute formed:** E. A. Darr to Paul M. Hahn, letter, July 30, 1957, UCSF Archives. **tobacco industry had secretly . . . subterfuge was revealed:** Glantz et al., 179–80. **expressing an opinion with confidence:** Pulford et al. **"we believe the products":** Tobacco Industry Research Council, "A Frank Statement to Cigarette Smokers," January 4, 1954, UCSF Archives. **"I just don't believe it":** "Tobacco: The Controversial Princess," *Time,* April 11, 1960. **"I think eventually cigarettes":** Kluger, 233. **"believed it in my heart" . . . "extremely clear conscience":** Gerald H. Long, quoted in Richard Mackenzie, "A Loyalist Views Tobacco's Fate," *Insight,* May 19, 1986.

Page 170: **Most said they "believed":** *Regulation of Tobacco Products: Hearings Before the Subcommittee on Health and the Environment of the House Committee on Energy and Commerce,* 103rd Cong., 2nd sess., part 1, March 25 and April 14, 1994, 628. **belief-based wording:** Brandt, 369. **"personal opinion" . . . "tirade against us":** Byrne. **"I just don't know" . . . "I am not":** testimony of Geoffrey C. Bible, March 2, 1998, State of Minnesota v. Philip Morris, transcript of proceedings, vol. 30, 5738–39, 5782, UCSF Archives. **baseless "propaganda":** American Tobacco, "Luncheon Meeting—November 5, 1953, Representatives of Industry, Yale Club," meeting minutes, UCSF Archives. **Scientists just seeking publicity:** Hill and Knowlton, "Background Material on the Cigarette Industry Client," December 15, 1953, UCSF Archives. **an industry "harassed":** Brown and Williamson, "Smoking and Health Proposal," UCSF Archives. **"lynching parties":** Hill and Knowlton, "Public Relations Report to the Tobacco Industry Research Committee," April 28, 1955, UCSF Archives. **"witch hunts":** Kerry Hall, "Former Lorillard CEO Dies of Cancer at 68," *Greensboro News and Record,* January 29, 2001. **"unfairly pilloried":** Kluger, 488. **"reckless campaign of propaganda":** Chip Jones, "Philip Morris Primed for 'War': CEO Predicts a Win over 'The Bad Guys,'" *Richmond Times-Dispatch,* April 25, 1996.

Page 171: **"Day of Judgment":** Byrne. **intuitive dog wags the rational tail:** Haidt, ch. 2. **Rosenblatt concluded:** Roger Rosenblatt, "How Do Tobacco Executives Live with Themselves?" *New York Times,* March 20, 1994. **"arrogance, bred by insularity":** Parrish, 111.

Page 172: **critics as prohibitionists:** Weissman to Cullman, "Surgeon General's Report," UCSF Archives. **"fanatically prejudiced":** Hill and Knowlton for the Tobacco Institute, untitled press release, July 1, 1958, UCSF Archives. **"do-gooders who want to attack":** Howard Cullman, quoted in Brecher et al., 131. **"joyless tribe":** "Smoking: Whose Rights," NPR Town Meeting, August 23, 1979, transcript, Radio TV Reports, UCSF Archives. **"liked being in a battle":** Kluger, 468. **"free market system":** Kluger, 467. **"In Germany, the Nazis":** Remarks of William Dwyer at the Annual Convention Banquet, National Association of Farm Broadcasters, November 16, 1975, UCSF Archives. **"Winston Churchill":** Chip Jones, "Philip Morris Primed for 'War,'" *Richmond Times-Dispatch.* **"truth is undermined":** Goldberg.

Page 173: **psychologists would call projection:** Schimel, Greenberg and Martens. **antitobacco . . . "industry":** Philip J. Hilts, "Tobacco Chiefs Say Cigarettes Aren't Addictive." *New*

York Times, April 15, 1994; Kluger, 468. **hypothesized that the "anti-smoking industry":** Clark C. Abt, "The Anti-Smoking Industry," 1983, UCSF Archives. **individuals who feel . . . unfairly treated:** John, Loewenstein, and Rick.

Page 174: **bombshell report:** Surgeon General, *Health Consequences of Involuntary Smoking.* **industry feared the issue:** Philip Morris, "Project Down Under Conference Notes," June 24–26, 1987, 8, UCSF Archives. **Tobacco Institute released a report:** Tobacco Institute, "Government Health Officials Involved in Efforts to Censor Dissenting Scientific Viewpoints," news release, December 11, 1986, UCSF Archives. **one in ten Americans:** Roper Organization, "A Study of Public Attitudes toward Cigarette Smoking and the Tobacco Industry in 1984," prepared for the Tobacco Institute, June 1984, UCSF Archives. **"slitting our throats":** Hilts, 40; "Smokescreen," episode 2, *Tobacco Wars,* TLC and BBC miniseries, 1999.

Page 175: **keep its scientific findings secret:** *US v. Philip Morris USA, Inc.,* 449 F. Supp. 2d 1, 801; Brandt, 236, 377; Barry Meier, "A Silent Witness in Cigarette Trials," *New York Times,* March 30, 1998. **Participants complained . . . group rant:** Philip Morris, "Project Down Under Conference Notes," UCSF Archives. **EPA declared . . . charged the EPA:** Brandt, 306. **pointed optimistically:** "ETS Media Strategy," February 1993, UCSF Archives. **played a substantial role:** Oreskes and Conway.

Page 176: **a "thug" and a "bully":** Jeffrey Goldberg, "Next Target: Nicotine," *New York Times,* August 4, 1996. **persuade the Supreme Court:** Brandt, 395.

Page 177: **"the guilty fear":** E. Dakin, "Forwarding Memorandum," UCSF Archives. **secretly written:** Hill and Knowlton to T. V. Hartnett, "Report of Activities through July 31, 1954," UCSF Archives. **"relax and enjoy it":** Donald G. Cooley, "Smoke without Fear," pamphlet (*True* editors, 1954), UCSF Archives. **scientist for British American Tobacco:** Charles Ellis, "The Smoking and Health Problem," comments at Research Conference, Southampton, 1962, UCSF Archives. **Later research:** Anahad O'Connor, "The Claim: Smoking Relieves Stress," *New York Times,* August 9, 2010. **1964 surgeon general's report:** Surgeon General, *Smoking and Health,* 355–56. **Philip Morris executives:** Weissman to Cullman, "Surgeon General's Report," UCSF Archives. **"the tobacco industry":** Claude Teague Jr., "Research Planning Memorandum on the Nature of the Tobacco Business and the Crucial Role of Nicotine Therein," April 14, 1972, UCSF Archives.

Page 178: **Philip Morris researcher:** William L. Dunn, Jr., "Motives and Incentives in Cigarette Smoking," 1972, UCSF Archives. **help our consumer rationalize":** Glantz et al. 1996, 375. **"we were performing":** Kluger, 488. **"nobody knows":** quoted in Goldberg. **"some women":** Joseph F. Cullman III, *Face the Nation,* transcript, January 3, 1971, UCSF Archives. **"people that like to cough":** Joseph F. Cullman III, *Cigarette Labeling and Advertising—1969: Hearings Before the House Committee on Interstate and Foreign Commerce,* 91st Cong., 1st sess., part 1, April and May, 1969, 577.

Page 179: **"bacterial content of a kiss":** Cooley, "Smoke without Fear," UCSF Archives. **"all kinds of things":** Wakeham, in "Death in the West," transcript, 3, 8, UCSF Archives. **"desire to die":** Kluger, 488. **"best way to avoid dying":** Wakeham, in "Death in the West," transcript, 3, UCSF Archives. **"abhorrent and horrendously":** State of Minnesota et al. v. Philip Morris Inc. et al., No. C1–94–8565, Slip Op. (Minn. Dist.Ct., Jan. 24, 1998). **"unacceptable disregard":** Gordon Fairclough, "Philip Morris Says It's Sorry for Death Report," *Wall Street Journal,* July 26, 2001.

Page 180: **"the way we won":** Hilts, 197. **"assumption of risk":** Kluger, 290. **"cave dweller":** "Smoking: Whose Rights," NPR Town Meeting, UCSF Archives. **"I really believed":** Kluger, 468. **"People think there's something":** Brandt, 341. **"take a step back":** Roger Rosenblatt, "How Do Tobacco Executives Live with Themselves?" *New York Times,* March 20, 1994. **"the commercial manifestation":** Patrick Muttart, interviewed by Sarah McVeigh, *How Do You Sleep at Night?,* Australian Broadcasting Corporation, September 11, 2017.

Page 181: **"we can't defend continued smoking":** Paul Knopick, Tobacco Institute, to William Kloepfer, memorandum, September 9, 1980, UCSF Archives. **"dangerous implications":** Patrick M. Sirridge to Fredric S. Newman, memo attached to letter, July 27, 1983, UCSF Archives. **new surgeon general's report:** Surgeon General, *Health Consequences of Smoking: Nicotine Addiction,* vi, 9. **memo by the Brown and Williamson general counsel:** Addison Yeaman,

"Implication of Battelle Hippo I & II and The Griffith Filter," July 17, 1963, UCSF Archives. **"carefully analyzed":** James W. Johnston, written statement to US House Subcommittee on Health and the Environment, Federal Document Clearing House, Congressional Testimony, April 14, 1994, UCSF Archives. **"gummi bears":** James Morgan, *60 Minutes* transcript, CBS-TV, May 4, 1997, UCSF Archives. **seven out of ten smokers:** Gallup, *Tobacco and Smoking*, online data series, accessed May 3, 2019, http://news.gallup.com/poll/1717/tobacco-smoking. aspx. **The industry would eventually:** *US v. Philip Morris USA, Inc.*, 449 F. Supp. 2d 1, 308.

Page 182: **"pediatric disease":** quoted in Goldberg. **"14 to 18 year old group":** "Planning Assumptions and Forecast for the Period 1977–1986 for R.J. Reynolds Tobacco Company," Research Department, March 15, 1976, UCSF Archives. **The federal court found:** *US v. Philip Morris USA, Inc.*, 449 F. Supp. 2d 1, 691. **"the 16–20 year old":** Dr. H. Wakeham, "R&D Presentation to the Board of Directors," November 26, 1969, UCSF Archives. **"psychosocial symbolism":** "First Draft of Annual Report to Philip Morris Board by V.P. for Research and Development," Fall 1969, UCSF Archives. **Brown and Williamson researcher:** Claude Teague Jr., "Research Planning Memorandum on Some Thoughts about New Brands of Cigarettes for the Youth Market," February 2, 1973, UCSF Archives. **"still mysterious":** describing its 1977 study, Kwechansky Marketing Research, *Project Plus/Minus, Report for Imperial Tobacco Limited*, May 7, 1982, UCSF Archives. **peer pressure:** Kwechansky Marketing Research, *Project 16, Report for Imperial Tobacco Company*, October 18, 1977, UCSF Archives.

Page 183: **"assume these risks":** Kwechansky Marketing Research, *Project Plus/Minus*, UCSF Archives. **Nine out of ten smokers:** Gallup, *Tobacco and Smoking*, online data series. **the company's past:** testimony of Geoffrey C. Bible, *State of Minnesota v. Philip Morris*, vol. 30, 5717–18, UCSF Archives. **moral alarm system:** Greene, 224. **"likely that some children":** Goldberg. **wrote an RJR researcher:** Teague, "Research Planning Memorandum on . . . Cigarettes for the Youth Market," UCSF Archives.

Page 184: **One tobacco CEO:** Steven F. Goldstone, CEO of RJR Nabisco, speech to National Press Club, April 8, 1998, UCSF Archives.**Company stock prices:** Goldberg. **could yank their license:** Joe Nocera, "If It's Good for Philip Morris, Can It Also Be Good for Public Health?" *New York Times*, June 18, 2006. **"new breed of CEOs":** Brandt, 421.

Page 185: **"we could not":** Goldberg. **"a legitimate right":** Goldstone, speech to National Press Club, UCSF Archives. **"deliberate mendacity":** Gingrich, quoted in Goldberg. **"vengeance" and "eradication":** Goldberg. **some psychological research:** Lammers et al.

Page 186: **an article describing:** Byrne. **if they believed smoking:** George Weissman, "Public Relations and Cigarette Marketing," speech to NATD Convention, Chicago, March 30, 1954; Thomas Whiteside, "A Cloud of Smoke," *New Yorker*, November 30, 1963; *Death in the West*, transcript, 1, 5, UCSF Archives; Richard Mackenzie, "A Loyalist Views Tobacco's Fate," *Insight*, May 19, 1986; Michael Janofsky, "On Cigarettes, Health and Lawyers," *New York Times*, December 6, 1993. **could openly admit:** Bennett S. LeBow, quoted in Janofsky, "On Cigarettes, Health and Lawyers," *NYT*. **"these guys love":** Goldberg. **Philip Morris finally stated:** Parrish, 114.

Page 187: **much denial:** *US v. Philip Morris USA, Inc.*, 449 F. Supp. 2d 1. **Steven Parrish:** Parrish, 114–15. **business columnist:** Nocera, "If It's Good for Philip Morris," *NYT*.

Page 188: **federal court agreed:** *R.J. Reynolds Tobacco Co., v. U.S. FDA*, 845 F. Supp.2d 266 (D. D.C. 2012). **a different federal court:** tobaccofreekids.org, "Federal Court Orders FDA to Quickly Implement Graphic Cigarette Warnings As Mandated By Law," press release, September 5, 2018. **In 1965:** Centers for Disease Control and Prevention, "Achievements in Public Health, 1900–1999: Tobacco Use—United Stated, 1900–1999," *MMWR Weekly*, November 5, 1999. **that rate had fallen:** Centers for Disease Control and Prevention, "Current Cigarette Smoking Among Adults—United States, 2017," fact sheet, February 4, 2019.

Page 189: **"for a lifetime smoker":** Dr. David O'Reilley, quoted in Peter Taylor, "If Cigarettes Kill, Why Do Tobacco Giants Still Wield So Much Power?," *Guardian*, May 28, 2014. **Wall Street Journal article:** Jennifer Maloney and Saabira Chaudhuri, "Against All Odds, the U.S. Tobacco Industry Is Rolling in Money," *Wall Street Journal*, April 23, 2017.

Page 190: **those below poverty line . . . those with schizophrenia:** Menaka Wilhelm, "How to Drive Down Smoking in Groups That Still Light Up," *Shots: Health News from NPR,* January 31, 2018. **Tobacco is blamed:** World Health Organization, *WHO Report on the Global Tobacco Epidemic, 2008: The MPOWER Package,* 2008. **seven million people:** World Health Organization, *WHO Report on the Global Tobacco Epidemic, 2017: Monitoring Tobacco Use and Prevention Policies,* 2017. **between 1964 and 2014:** Surgeon General, *Health Consequences of Smoking—50 Years,* "Executive Summary," 1-2. **accidents . . . suicides . . . murders:** figures are for 2017, Centers for Disease Control and Prevention, FastStats, accessed September 10, 2019. **billion people smoke:** Institute for Health Metrics and Evaluation, "Nearly 1 Billion People Still Smoke Daily," news release, April 5, 2017. **population that smokes:** Global Burden of Disease 2015 Tobacco Collaborators.

Page 191: **one study credits:** Levy et al. **Chinese pharmacist:** Sabrina Tavernise, "A Hot Debate over E-Cigarettes as a Path to Tobacco, or From It," *New York Times,* February 22, 2014. **American Medical Association:** Julie Steenhuysen, "U.S. Doctors' Group Says Just Stop Vaping as Deaths, Illnesses Rise," *Reuters,* September 9, 2019. **an "epidemic":** Surgeon General, "Advisory on E-Cigarette Use among Youth," 2018. **kid-appealing flavors:** Sheila Kaplan, "FDA Delays Rules That Would Have Limited E-Cigarettes on Market," *New York Times,* July 28, 2017. **public health community:** Tavernise, "A Hot Debate," *NYT.*

Page 192: **"make sure we can":** Stephanie Cordisco, quoted in Matt Ritchel, "A Bolder Effort by Big Tobacco on E-Cigarettes," *New York Times,* June 17, 2014. **Altria described the deal:** David Goldman, "The Biggest American Cigarette Company Buys a $13 Billion Stake in the Biggest E-Cigarette Startup," *CNN Business,* December 20, 2018. **"smoke-free alternatives":** Philip Morris International, website, accessed February 19, 2018, https://www.pmi.com/who-we-are/our-goal-and-strategies. **"much longer":** Saabira Chauduri, "Behind Philip Morris International's Smokeless Bet," *Wall Street Journal,* October 30, 2017. **working to oppose:** Aditya Kalra, Paritosh Bansal, Duff Wilson and Tom Lasseter, "Inside Philip Morris' Campaign to Subvert the Global Anti-Smoking Treaty," Reuters, July 13, 2017. **"non-addictive":** FDA, "FDA's Plan for Tobacco and Nicotine Regulation," announcement, July 28, 2017. **"loud objections":** Richard Craver, "Gottlieb's Resignation May Turn Down FDA Heat on Tobacco Industry," *Winston-Salem Journal,* March 10, 2019.

Page 193: **Vapor Technology Association accused:** Sheila Kaplan, "Trump Administration Plans to Ban Flavored E-Cigarettes," *New York Times,* September 11, 2019.

CHAPTER 7. "BOTTOM LINE. NOTHING ELSE MATTERS"

Abbreviations

FCIC Report.   Financial Crisis Inquiry Commission, *The Financial Crisis Inquiry Report: Final Report of the National Commission on the Causes of the Financial and Economic Crisis in the United States,* (Washington, DC: US GPO, January 2011), https://fcic.law.stanford.edu/

FCIC Supporting Materials.   transcripts and recordings of interviews and public hearings and other supporting materials collected by the Financial Crisis Inquiry Commission, https://fcic.law.stanford.edu/

Senate Financial Crisis Hearing Exhibits.   Additional Exhibits, *Wall Street and the Financial Crisis: The Role of Credit Rating Agencies: Hearing Before the Senate Permanent Subcommittee on Investigations,* April 23, 2010, posted online in *New York Times,* "Senate Subcommittee Investigating Financial Crisis Releases Documents on Role of Investment Banks," news release, April 24, 2010, https://int.nyt.com/data/int-shared/nytdocs/docs/322/322.pdf

Senate Financial Crisis Report. Senate Permanent Subcommittee on Investigations, *Wall Street and the Financial Crisis: Anatomy of a Financial Collapse: Majority and Minority Staff Report,* April 13, 2011, www.hsgac.senate.gov//imo/media/doc/Financial_Crisis /FinancialCrisisReport.pdf

Page 195: "**We are all here**": Hudson, 7.

Page 196: "**It's a high-risk**": *American Banker* article, cited in McLean and Nocera, 34. "**Every closing**": Hudson, 3. **relatively good credit:** Diana B. Henriques with Lowell Bergman, "Mortgaged Lives: Profiting from Fine Print with Wall Street's Help," *New York Times,* March 15, 2000.

Page 197: "**no clue**": Prentiss Cox, "FCIC Staff Audiotape of Interview with Prentiss Cox," October 15, 2010, FCIC Supporting Materials. **Ameriquest salespeople:** Hudson, 3. **Borrowers:** McLean and Nocera, 130. "**Whatever you had to do**": Mike Hudson and E. Scott Reckard, "Workers Say Lender Ran 'Boiler Rooms,'" *Los Angeles Times,* February 4, 2005. "**Art Department**": Hudson, 3. "**The reality was**": McLean and Nocera, 131–32. **the story of Carolyn:** Hudson, 6.

Page 198: **$30,000 to $40,000:** McLean and Nocera, 125. "**flipping burgers**" . . . **earn millions:** *FCIC Report,* 8. **an SUV or a Mercedes:** Hudson, 98. **the Big Spin:** Hudson, 98. "**I've already got one**": McLean and Nocera, 129. "**wanted to go to Maui**": Hudson, 98. "**I don't think there's a day**": Hudson and Reckard, "Workers Say," *LA Times.*

Page 199: "**chop shop**": McLean and Nocera, 129–30. **FAMCO loan officer:** Hudson, 112. "**absolutely**" **corrupt . . . previous criminal convictions:** *FCIC Report,* 14. **cocaine:** Hudson, 2. **brain scans:** Zweig, 66. "**we cheat**": Ariely, 23. **cheated more:** Ariely, 200. **feeling underpaid:** John, Loewenstein, and Rick.

Page 200: **Boiler Room** . . . "**the energy, the impact**": Hudson, 202. "**How soon**" . . . **Russ Jedinak:** Hudson, 14, 29.

Page 201: "**We are best**": Hudson, 107. "**gold rush**" . . . "**Housing prices**": *FCIC Report,* 5. **most subprime loans:** G. Amromin and A. L. Paulson, "Default Rates of Prime and Subprime Mortgages: Differences and Similarities," *Profitwise News and Views,* Federal Reserve Bank of Chicago, September 2010. **low-income immigrants:** Lewis, 97–100.

Page 202: "**liar's loans**" . . . "**invitations to fraud**": *FCIC Report,* 111. "**ninja loans**": *FCIC Report,* 6. "**That's insanity**": *FCIC Report,* 17. **full of "crooks**" . . . **waded into subprime:** McLean and Nocera, 36–37, 138. **banks and thrifts:** *FCIC Report,* 79. **WaMu dropped:** *Senate Financial Crisis Report,* part 3. "**regulatory no-man's-land**": *FCIC Report,* 88. **this poorly regulated system:** *FCIC Report,* 70.

Page 203: **memo to his colleagues:** Hibbert, quoted in Hudson, 77, 85. "**Lehman Brothers**" . . . **FAMCO's main financier:** Hudson, 85, 192. "**packaged, sliced**": *FCIC Report,* 7. "**believed they could off-load**": *FCIC Report,* xxiv.

Page 204: "**betting that home prices**" . . . "**in mortgage underwriting**": *FCIC Report,* 111. **The bankers asked** . . . "**don't need to worry**": McLean and Nocera, 135, 150.

Page 205: "**Don't forget**": Luyendijk, 72. **private partnerships** . . . "**petri dishes**": William D. Cohan, "When Bankers Started Playing with Other People's Money," *Atlantic,* February 28, 2017. "**It's only OPM**": Luyendijk, 72. "**being the managers**": Smith, vol. 2, 741.

Page 206: **Wall Street had been:** Gautam Mukunda, "The Price of Wall Street's Power," *Harvard Business Review,* June 2014. **IBGYBG:** *FCIC Report,* 8. **Princeton graduates:** Ho, 44. "**smartest and most ambitious**": Ho, 39. "**Show me the money!**" . . . **listed the money:** Ho, 75, 257.

Page 207: **in constant danger:** Ho, 223–28. "**the cull**" . . . "**you're getting closer**": Luyendijk, 82. "**you need to be thinking**": Ho, 233–34. "**deliberately recruits**": Ho, 89.

Page 208: "**shove each other**": Ho, 260. "**guy next to you**": Sam Polk, "For the Love of Money" *New York Times,* January 18, 2014. "**You think, wow**": Luyendijk, 180. "**completely money-obsessed**": Arlidge. **as the brain adapts:** Mateu, Monzani, and Muñoz Navarro.

research also suggests: DeVoe, Pfeffer, and Lee. **investment banker told:** Luyendijk, 143–44. **immediacy of the reward:** McClure et al.

Page 209: **"not from the benevolence":** Smith, vol. 1, 26–27. **former banker at Goldman Sachs:** Greg Smith, "Why I Am Leaving Goldman Sachs," *New York Times*, March 14, 2012. **objectify other people:** Wang and Krumhuber. **easier to harm:** Bandura, 200. **"in the fine print":** Luyendijk, 109. **Bankers told him:** Luyendijk, 98.

Page 210: **"I just ripped that":** Cohan, 267. **"I want to reach in":** "Dick Fuld Rip Out Your Heart," internal Lehman Brothers video, posted with introduction by former Lehman head of corporate communications, Andrew Gowers, YouTube, 2007. **John Coates:** Coates, 21, 28.

Page 211: **accept social inequality:** Caruso et al. **less prosocial . . . ask others for help:** Vohs, Mead, and Goode. **findings have been challenged:** Rohrer, Pashler, and Harris; but see Vohs. **controversy within psychology:** Open Science Collaboration; but see Gilbert et al. **heightened scrutiny:** Brian Resnick, "What Psychology's Crisis Means for the Future of Science," *Vox*, March 14, 2016. **"anything goes":** Luyendijk, 99.

Page 212: **Thousands of mortgages . . . living on the ground floor:** FCIC Report, 73; Lewis, 73. **riskiest slices . . . almost $700 billion . . . CDOs-squared:** FCIC Report, 127, 129, 132. **credit default swaps:** FCIC Report, 132. **naked credit default swap:** FCIC Report, 50. **synthetic CDO . . . did not help finance:** FCIC Report, 142.

Page 213: **losses were multiplied:** FCIC Report, 142. **two notorious cases:** "Goldman Settles with S.E.C. for $550 Million," *New York Times*, July 15, 2010; Jake Bernstein and Jesse Eisinger, "SEC Issues More Fines over Magnetar Deals—and Appears to Move On," *ProPublica*, December 12, 2013. **congressional investigation . . . losses were overwhelmed:** *Senate Financial Crisis Report*, 9. **Tourre would face trial:** Susanne Craig and Ben Protess, "Former Trader Is Found Liable in Fraud Case," *New York Times*, August 1, 2013. **fined $825,000:** Ben Protess, "Former Goldman Trader Tourre Says He Will Not Appeal," *New York Times*, May 27, 2014.

Page 214: **"standing in the middle":** email from Fabrice Tourre, January 23, 2007, Senate Financial Crisis Hearing Exhibits, 80. **"When I think":** email from Fabrice Tourre, January 29, 2007, Senate Financial Crisis Hearing Exhibits, 100. **"the risk most central":** Tett, 24. Footnote: **"Financial contracts":** FCIC Report, 45–46.

Page 215: **"I've known people":** Tett, 24. **financial hydrogen bombs:** Bailey Morris, "Jumping Blind into the Futures: Few Understand Financial Derivatives," *Independent*, October 10, 1993. **"financial weapons of mass destruction":** "What Worries Warren," *Fortune*, March 4, 2003.

Page 216: **less empathy:** Small and Loewenstein, "Helping a Victim"; Konis et al.; Greene, 260. **Belgian "widows and orphans":** email from Fabrice Tourre, June 13, 2007, Senate Financial Crisis Hearing Exhibits, 88, 90. **Moody's alone:** FCIC Report, xxv. **"Oh God, are you kidding?":** FCIC Report, 210. **market-share-focused managers:** Rep. Henry Waxman, *Credit Rating Agencies and the Financial Crisis: Hearing Before the House Committee on Oversight and Government Reform*, 110th Cong., 2nd sess., October 22, 2008, 11. **"Ratings agencies":** *Senate Financial Crisis Report*, 297. **IBGYBG philosophy:** Richard Michalek, *Wall Street and the Financial Crisis: The Role of Credit Rating Agencies: Hearing Before the Senate Permanent Subcommittee on Investigations*, 111th Cong., 2nd sess., vol. 3., April 23, 2010, 44. **Wall Street figured out:** Tett, 119. **a higher rating . . . "brain-dead":** Lewis, 98, 100.

Page 217: **"lack of skepticism":** Lloyd C. Blankfein, First Public Hearing of the Financial Crisis Inquiry Commission, January 13, 2010, official transcript, 7, FCIC Supporting Materials. **"No regulator":** McLean and Nocera, 149. **"regulators are idiots":** Luyendijk, 152. **"Like alligators" . . . "a villain":** Carol J. Loomis and Erick Schonfeld, "The Risk That Won't Go Away," *Fortune*, March 7, 1994.

Page 218: **similarly warned:** General Accounting Office, *Financial Derivatives: Actions Needed to Protect the Financial System* (Washington, DC: GAO, 1994). **Tett describes Brickell:** Tett, 36, 45–47. **risks "in financial markets":** Robert Lenzner, "The Confessions of Central Bankers," *Forbes*, September 7, 2010. **Rand's philosophy:** Rand, *Virtue of Selfishness*. **"only moral**

purpose": Rand, *Atlas Shrugged*, 934, 1075. Footnote: **"betrayed fundamental principles"**: Weiss, 218–19.

Page 219: **effort to regulate derivatives:** McLean and Nocera, 109. **"key turning point"**: *FCIC Report*, xxiv. **Glass-Steagall:** *FCIC Report*, 35. **"Citi-Travelers Act"**: interviews with Arthur Levitt and Charles Geisst, "The Wall Street Fix," *Frontline*, PBS, May 8, 2003. **"Death Star"**: Sorkin, 530. **bigger federal bailout:** Eamon Javers, "Citigroup Tops List of Banks Who Received Federal Aid," CNBC, March 3, 2011. **"to become an epidemic"**: Terry Frieden, "FBI Warns of Mortgage Fraud 'Epidemic,'" CNN.com, September 17, 2004. **states tried . . . immunity from many state laws:** *FCIC Report*, 96, 111. **Greenspan was even urged:** *FCIC Report*, 95.

Page 220: **"neglected its mission"**: *FCIC Report*, xxiii. **spoke the next year:** Bair, 66. **"those of us who" . . . "flaw in the model":** Alan Greenspan, *The Financial Crisis and the Role of Federal Regulators: Hearing Before the House Committee on Oversight and Government Reform*, 110th Cong., 2nd sess., October 23, 2008, 12, 46.

Page 221: **"evacuate the kids"**: Luyendijk, 28. **"bed down in bunkers"**: Luyendijk, 29, quoting Matthew Hancock and Nadhim Zahawi, *Masters of Nothing: How the Crash Will Happen Again Unless We Understand Human Nature*.

Page 222: **"see this as a crisis"**: Sorkin interviewed by Klaus Brinkbaumer and Thomas Schulz, "Wall Street Bankers Are Not Pure Evil," *Spiegel Online*, August 20, 2010. **Blankfein compared it:** Lloyd Blankfein, First Public Hearing of the Financial Crisis Inquiry Commission, January 13, 2010, official transcript, 36, FCIC Supporting Materials. **FCIC rejected this argument:** *FCIC Report*, 3. Footnote: **Fannie Mae and Freddie Mac:** *FCIC Report*, xxvi, 437.

Page 223: **Benmosche told:** Leslie Scism, "AIG's Benmosche and Miller on Villains, Turnarounds, and Those Bonuses," *Wall Street Journal*, September 23, 2013. **Citigroup executive . . . Bear Stearns managing director:** Gabriel Sherman, "The Wail of the 1%," *New York Magazine*, April 19, 2009.

Page 224: **"not feeling too guilty"**: email from Fabrice Tourre, January 23, 2007, Senate Financial Crisis Hearing Exhibits, 80. **Blankfein, explained to the *Times*:** Arlidge. **"hurt America" . . . "very aggressive"**: Henny Sender and Stephanie Kirchgaessner, "Blankfein Fights Back on SEC Case," *Financial Times*, April 22, 2010. **"When times are rough"**: William D. Cohan, "Marty Chavez Muses on Rocky Times and the Road Ahead," *New York Times*, November 14, 2017.

Page 225: **Dimon was dubbed:** Roger Lowenstein, "Jamie Dimon, America's Least-Hated Banker," *New York Times*, December 1, 2010. **"Martin Luther King Jr. of the overdog"**: Graydon Carter, "Dimon in the Rough," *Vanity Fair*, April 2011. **"outspoken defender of the truth"**: Jessica Pressler, "122 Minutes with Jamie Dimon," *New York Magazine*, August 12, 2012. **"most of the bad actors"**: Mark Gongloff, "Jamie Dimon Asks Ben Bernanke to Not Regulate Banks Too Much," *Wall Street Journal*, Marketbeat (blog), June 7, 2011. **JPMorgan Chase had pressed:** Edward Wyatt, "JPMorgan Sought Loophole on Risky Trading," *New York Times*, May 12, 2012. **Dimon said to Jessica Pressler:** Pressler, "122 Minutes with Jamie Dimon," *New York*.

Page 226: **128 employees . . . "prevailing business culture"**: Cohn, Fehr, and Marechal. **financial service professionals:** University of Notre Dame's Mendoza College of Business and Labaton Sucharow LLP, "The Street, The Bull, and the Crisis: A Survey of the US & UK Financial Services Industry," May 2015. **more likely to comply:** Cohn, Fehr, and Marechal. **more likely to cheat:** Ariely, 200. **bankers were convicted:** Joshua Holland, "Hundreds of Wall Street Execs Went to Prison during the Last Fraud-Fueled Bank Crisis." BillMoyers.com, September 17, 2013.

Page 227: **"overall evil climate"**: Jesse Eisinger, "The Rise of Corporate Impunity," *ProPublica*, April 30, 2014. **lack of postcrisis convictions:** Eisinger, "Rise of Corporate Impunity," *ProPublica*. **managed to send to prison:** Renae Merle, "This Obscure Government Agency Has a Plan to Put Wall Street CEOs in Prison," *Washington Post*, October 26, 2016. **couple hundred billion:** William D. Cohan, "A Clue to the Scarcity of Federal Prosecutions," *New York Times*, July 21, 2016. **trillions of dollars:** General Accounting Office, *Financial Regulatory Reform: Financial Crisis Losses and Potential Impacts of the Dodd-Frank Act* (Washington, DC: GAO, January 2013). **One**

individual, Fabrice Tourre: Peter J. Henning, "Prosecution of Financial Crisis Fraud Ends with a Whimper," *New York Times,* August 29, 2016. **Phil Angelides:** Stephen Gandel, "The Toxic Billion Dollar Goldman Sachs Bond Deal That the SEC Let Get Away," *Fortune,* April 29, 2016. **Angelo Mozilo:** Gretchen Morgenson, "Countrywide Mortgage Devastation Lingers as Ex-Chief Moves On," *New York Times,* June 24, 2016. **Dick Fuld:** William D. Cohan, "Wall Street Executives from the Financial Crisis of 2008: Where Are They Now?" *Vanity Fair,* April 2015.

Page 228: **A letter accompanying:** E. Gerald Corrigan and Douglas J. Flint, transmittal letter, *Containing Systemic Risk: The Road to Reform*, report of the Counterparty Risk Management Policy Group III, August 6, 2008, iii–v. **"evidence is overwhelming":** Dennis M. Kelleher, "Deregulation Unleashes Wall Street to Prey on Investors, Consumer and All Hard-Working Americans," Bettermarkets.com, December 4, 2017. **President Trump:** Glenn Thrush, "Trump Vows to Dismantle Dodd-Frank 'Disaster,'" *New York Times,* January 30, 2017. **statutory provisions:** Alan Rappeport and Emily Flitter, "Congress Approves First Big Dodd-Frank Rollback," *New York Times,* May 22, 2018.

Page 229: **Wall Street's exploitative culture:** Group of Thirty, *Banking Conduct and Culture: A Call for Sustained and Comprehensive Reform*, July 2015; William C. Dudley, "Opening Remarks at Reforming Culture and Behavior in the Financial Services Industry: Workshop on Progress and Challenges," Federal Reserve Bank of New York, November 5, 2015. **banks have made changes:** William D. Cohan, "Can Bankers Behave?" *Atlantic,* May 2015. **Wall Street's appetite:** Sridhar Natarajan, Sally Bakewell, and Kiel Porter, "Wall Street Is Taking on More Risk Again," Bloomberg.com, February 2, 2018.

CHAPTER 8. A "DECEITFUL, HYSTERICAL, OUT-OF-CONTROL RAMPAGE"

Page 230: **"deficient in carbon dioxide":** Institute for Biospheric Research, *The Greening of Planet Earth,* 1992, video (distr. Western Fuels Association).

Page 231: **Dr. J.A. Laurman:** Dr. J.A. Laurman, "The CO_2 Problem: Addressing Research Agenda Development," presentation outline attached to American Petroleum Institute, CO_2 and Climate Task Force (AQ-9), Minutes of Meeting, February 29, 1980, posted at ClimateFiles.com. (ClimateFiles.com is an archival database maintained by the Climate Investigations Center, a group that monitors corporations, front groups, and others working to delay efforts to respond to the climate crisis.)

Page 232: **"vast geophysical experiment":** Environmental Pollution Panel, President's Science Advisory Committee, *Restoring the Quality of Our Environment* (Washington, DC: White House, 1965), https://catalog.hathitrust.org/Record/001515388, App. Y4, 126. **blue-ribbon panel of scientists:** National Research Council, *Carbon Dioxide and Climate: A Scientific Assessment*, Consensus Study Report (Washington, DC: National Academies Press, 1979). **top ten Fortune 500 companies:** "Fortune 500: A Database of 50 Years of *Fortune's* List of America's Largest Corporations," 1980, https://archive.fortune.com/. **Exxon had done:** Neela Banerjee, Lisa Song, and David Hasemyer, "Exxon Believed Deep Dive into Climate Research Would Protect Its Business," *InsideClimate News,* September 17, 2015.

Page 233: **conclusions described in internal documents:** Roger W. Cohen, letter to Mr. A.M. Natkin, September 2, 1982, posted at ClimateFiles.com; R.W. Cohen, Exxon interoffice memo to W. Glass, August 18, 1981, posted at ClimateFiles.com. **internal documents became news:** Neela Banerjee, Lisa Song, and David Hasemyer, "Exxon: The Road Not Taken," articles beginning September 16, 2015, *Inside Climate News;* and Katie Jennings, Dino Grandoni, and Susanne Rust, "How Exxon Went from Leader to Skeptic on Climate Change Research," *Los Angeles Times,* October 23, 2015.

Page 234: **nations reached a treaty:** United Nations Framework Convention on Climate Change, 1992, https://unfccc.int/resource/docs/convkp/conveng.pdf, Article 2. **IPCC has**

concluded: Intergovernmental Panel on Climate Change (IPCC), *Climate Change 2013: The Physical Science Basis*, Summary for Policymakers; IPCC, *Climate Change 2014: Synthesis Report*, Summary for Policymakers. **major scientific academies:** NASA, "Scientific Consensus: Earth's Climate Is Warming," accessed August 2, 2018, https://climate.nasa.gov /scientific-consensus/; Ginger Pinholster, "Thirty-One Top Scientific Societies Speak with One Voice on Global Climate Change," press release, AAAS, June 28, 2016.

Page 235: **finally agreed in Paris:** Paris Agreement, adopted December 2015 by the parties to the UN Framework on Climate Change, https://unfccc.int/resource/docs/2015/cop21/eng /l09r01.pdf. **the other 195 nations:** Andrew Light, "The World Is Moving On since Trump Announced Intent to Withdraw from the Paris Agreement on Climate Change," World Resources Institute, blog, May 30, 2018. **already warmed 1°C:** *Climate Science Special Report: Fourth National Climate Assessment*, vol. 1 (Washington, DC: US Global Change Research Program, 2017). **warming of about 3°C:** UN Environment Programme, 2018, *The Emissions Gap Report 2018*, November 27, 2018. **feedbacks even below 2°C:** Steffen et al. **2018 IPCC report:** *IPCC Special Report, Global Warming of 1.5°C*, 2018, Summary for Policymakers, 14.

Page 236: **negative emissions:** David Roberts, "It's Time to Start Talking about 'Negative' Carbon Dioxide Emissions," *Vox*, August 18, 2017. **Social scientists:** McCright, Dunlap, and Xiao. **"if you concede":** Myron Ebell, in "Climate of Doubt," *Frontline*, PBS, October 23, 2012 (transcript online). **Lee Raymond rebuffed them:** quoted in Coll, 89.

Page 237: **included ones from fiction:** Lahsen, "Technocracy, Democracy, and U.S. Climate Politics." **bachelor's degree:** Global Warming Petition Project, "Qualifications of Signers," petitionproject.org, accessed September 5, 2018. **"take America back":** "Homeschooling Problems/ Needs," The Robinson Self-Teaching Curriculum, robinsoncurriculum.com, accessed September 5, 2018. **more polarizing than abortion:** Seth Borenstein, "Temperatures Rise, US Splits," Associated Press, August 15, 2016. **US conservatives and Republicans:** Anthony Leiserowitz et al., *Politics and Global Warming*, December 2018, Yale University and George Mason University. **Trump has repeatedly:** John Schwartz, "Trump's Climate Views: Combative, Conflicting and Confusing," *New York Times*, March 10, 2017. **one in five Americans:** Anthony Leiserowitz et al., *Climate Change in the American Mind*, December 2018, Yale University and George Mason University. **97 percent of studies:** J. Cook et al. Footnote: **National Academy issued:** "Statement by the Council of the National Academy of Sciences Regarding Global Change Petition," April 20, 1998.

Page 238: **"the deepest-pocketed":** Gelbspan, 13. **"my whole being":** Charles Koch, interviewed by Stephen J. Dubner, "Why Hate the Koch Brothers?" (part 2), *Freakonomics* radio broadcast, June 22, 2017. **David Koch had stressed:** Andrew Goldman, "The Billionaire's Party," *New York Magazine*, July 25, 2010.

Page 239: **CEO questioned climate change:** David Anderson, Matt Kasper, and David Pomerantz, *Utilities Knew: Documenting Electric Utilities' Early Knowledge and Ongoing Deception on Climate Change from 1968–2017*, Energy and Policy Institute, July 2017. **claims to be moving:** Gavin Bade, "Southern Co. To Be 'Low to No Carbon' by 2050, CEO Says," *Utility Dive*, April 9, 2018.

Page 240: **Berman told:** Richard Berman, presentation to the Western Energy Alliance Annual Meeting, June 25, 2014, link to transcript in Eric Lipton, "Hard-Nosed Advice from Veteran Lobbyist: 'Win Ugly or Lose Pretty,'" *New York Times*, October 30, 2014. **"bad taste in my mouth":** Lipton, "Hard-Nosed Advice," *NYT*. **full-page ad:** Suzanne Goldenberg, "Lobbyist Dubbed Dr. Evil behind Front Groups Attacking Obama Power Rules," *Guardian*, February 23, 2015. Footnote: **"being used by Satan":** Jeffrey, 15.

Page 241: **Berman and several other:** Suzanne Goldenberg and Helena Bengtsson, "Biggest US Coal Company Funded Dozens of Groups Questioning Climate Change," *Guardian*, June 13, 2016. **internal planning document:** Kathy Mulvey and Seth Shulman, *The Climate Deception Dossiers: Internal Fossil Fuel Industry Memos Reveal Decades of Corporate Disinformation*, Union of Concerned Scientists, 2015; see also accompanying materials at UCS website. **was quickly leaked:** Matthew L. Wald, "Pro-Coal Ad Campaign Disputes Warming Idea," *New York*

Times, July 8, 1991. **"large segment of the coal industry":** author's telephone interview with Ned Leonard, February 8, 2002.

Page 242: **anonymity:** Hirsh, Galinsky, and Zhong. **Global Climate Coalition:** Neela Banerjee, Lisa Song, and David Hasemyer, "Exxon's Own Research Confirmed Fossil Fuel's Role in Global Warming Decades Ago," *InsideClimate News*, September 16, 2015. **dangers of tobacco:** Oreskes and Conway. **"support organizations":** Jennifer Lee, "Exxon Backs Groups That Question Global Warming," *New York Times*, May 28, 2003. **Competitive Enterprise Institute:** Greenpeace, "ExxonSecrets Factsheet: Competitive Enterprise Institute," ExxonSecrets.org; the factsheet links to tax forms and giving reports. **"broaden the debate":** Chris Mooney, "Earth Last," *Prospect*, April 16, 2004.

Page 243: **commended by federal officials:** Banerjee, Song, and Hasemyer, "Exxon Believed Deep Dive," *InsideClimate News*. **getting criticism:** Seth Shulman, *Smoke, Mirrors & Hot Air: How ExxonMobil Uses Big Tobacco's Tactics to Manufacture Uncertainty on Climate Science* (Union of Concerned Scientists, 2007); "2006 Letter to ExxonMobil CEO Rex Tillerson from Senators Snowe and Rockefeller," posted at ClimateFiles.com; David Adam, "Royal Society Tells Exxon: Stop Funding Climate Change Denial," *Guardian*, September 20, 2006. **Steve Coll:** Coll, 87, 336–37. **"financial kingpin":** Greenpeace, *Koch Industries Secretly Funding the Climate Denial Machine*, March 2010. **dark money groups:** Mayer, 253. **Drexel University sociologist:** Robert J. Brulle, "Institutionalizing Delay: Foundation Funding and the Creation of U.S. Climate Change Counter-movement Organizations," *Climatic Change* 122, no. 4 (February 2014): 682–94.

Page 244: **benefit greatly from donations:** IRS Form 990s, filed by Donors Trust and Donors Capital Fund, available at ProPublica Nonprofit Explorer, https://projects.propublica .org/nonprofits/. **its press release:** Jim Lakely, Heartland Institute, "'Do You Still Believe in Global Warming?' Billboards Hit Chicago," press release, May 3, 2012 (deleted from Heartland's website, but a copy is preserved on UCS website). **resulting outcry:** Dean Kuipers, "Unabomber Billboard Continues to Hurt Heartland Institute," *Los Angeles Times*, May 9, 2012. **"discredited and anti-energy":** quoted in H. Sterling Burnett, "Endangerment Finding Resolution Withdrawn during ALEC Meeting," Heartland Institute, January 25, 2018, heartland.org. **"Republican upstarts":** Neela Banerjee, "How Big Oil Lost Control of Its Climate Misinformation Machine," *Inside Climate News,* December 22, 2017. **Mercer Family Foundation:** Kert Davies, "Who Is Paying for Heartland Institute Climate Denial-Palooza?" Climate Investigations Center, March 24, 2017, climateinvestigations.org; Kyla Mandel, "Here's How the Mercer Family's Climate Denial Funding Influenced Trump," Thinkprogress.org, January 26, 2018. **co-owner of Breitbart News:** Hadas Gold, "Breitbart Reveals Owners: CEO Larry Solov, the Mercer Family and Susie Breitbart," *Politico*, February 25, 2017.

Page 245: **Donald Trump's candidacy:** Matea Gold and Chris Mooney, "The Mercers, Trump Mega-donors, Back Group That Casts Doubt on Climate Science," *Washington Post*, March 27, 2017. **the draft text:** Greenpeace, *Denial and Deception: A Chronicle of ExxonMobil's Efforts to Corrupt the Debate on Global Warming*, May 2002, 18. **full-page ads:** "Reset the Alarm," advertorial by Mobil, October 30, 1997, posted by Polluterwatch.org. **speech in Beijing:** Lee R. Raymond, "Energy—Key to Growth and a Better Environment for Asia-Pacific Nations," speech to World Petroleum Congress, Beijing, China, October 13, 1997, posted at ClimateFiles.com. **1990 speech:** Fredrick D. Palmer, "The Main Event: H.R. 5996," speech to Intermountain Power Agency, November 27, 1990 (all cited Palmer speeches in author's possession).

Page 246: **Heartland Institute:** Greenpeace, "ExxonSecrets Factsheet: Heartland Institute," ExxonSecrets.org (with links to tax forms and giving reports). **Joseph Bast:** "Testimony by Joseph L. Bast, to the Environment Committee of the Iowa House," February 9, 2004, posted at heartland.org. **"Hollywood characters":** Robert Murray, "Murray: My Goal to Be the Last Man Standing," *Coal News*, July 2014. **Don Blankenship:** Carolyn Kormann, "The Hazard of Don Blankenship's Senate Campaign in West Virginia," *New Yorker*, May 7, 2018. **West Virginia festival:** Don Blankenship, speech to Friends of America Labor Day Festival, at mountaintop mine site near Logan, West Virginia, September 9, 2009, video posted by Fluxview.com. **"There are holdouts"**: Myron Ebell in "Climate of Doubt," *Frontline*.

Page 247: **Ebell would later:** Brady Dennis, "Trump Taps Climate-Change Skeptic to Oversee EPA Transition," *Washington Post,* November 11, 2016. **A commercial:** Mayer, 264. **richest person in New York City:** Dan Alexander, "Meet the Richest Person in America's 50 Largest Cities," *Forbes,* January 19, 2016. **Jane Mayer:** Mayer, 221, 265. **"global warming industry"**: Chris Horner, "The Global Warming Industry's RICO Gambit," *Washington Times,* March 29, 2016.

Page 248: **Christopher Horner:** Horner, 257–59.

Page 249: **veteran climate denier:** Gelbspan, 41. **"hefty honoraria"**: *"Nature* Nets 2001 Lump-O-Coal Award," *World Climate Report* 7, no. 8 (December 24, 2001). **"scream apocalypse"**: "NASA Climbs Aboard," *World Climate Report* 7, no. 10 (January 28, 2002). **global warming as a hoax:** Bob Murray, quoted in Andrew Breiner, "Watch: Energy CEO Says Carbon Regulations Are 'Evil,'" *ClimateProgress,* June 27, 2014. **scam:** Joseph Bast, "Eight Reasons Why 'Global Warming' Is a Scam," Heartland Institute, February 1, 2003, heartland.org. **fraud:** Christopher Horner, quoted in "Climate of Doubt," *Frontline.* **"cooking the books"**: Fred Palmer in "Global Warming Debate," Minnesota Rural Electric Association annual meeting, February 23, 2000 (transcript in author's possession). **Death threats:** Katherine Bagley and Naveena Sadasivam, "Climate Denial's Ugly Side: Hate Mail to Scientists," *InsideClimate News,* December 11, 2015.

Page 250: **tobacco reached out:** Oreskes and Conway, 150. **(Singer would also dispute)**: "Top Five Environmental Policy 'Myths' of 1995," press release, Science and Environmental Policy Project, January 10, 1996. **Patrick Michaels:** quoted in Andrew C. Revkin, "Hacked E-mail Is New Fodder for Climate Dispute," *New York Times,* November 20, 2009. **Christopher Horner:** Christopher Horner, "Media Missing the Plot on 'Climate Gate': It's the Fraud, Stupid!" *Breitbart,* November 23, 2009. **Exonerated:** Alex Knapp, "'Climategate' Scientists Cleared of Wrongdoing—Again," *Forbes,* August 24, 2011. **part of the blame:** Kevin Grandia, "Debunked Conspiracy Climategate Five Years Later," *DeSmogBlog,* November 19, 2014.

Page 251: **Murray in 2007:** Robert E. Murray, *Toward a Clean Energy Future: Energy Policy and Climate Change on Public Lands: Oversight Hearing Before the Subcommittee on Energy and Mineral Resources of the House Committee on Natural Resources,* 110th Cong., 1st sess., March 20, 2007, 41. **ICE front group:** Mulvey and Shulman, *Climate Deception Dossiers,* Union of Concerned Scientists, 19. **warned an audience:** Lee Raymond, "Energy, the Economy, and the Environment: Moving Forward Together," remarks to the Economic Club of Detroit, May 6, 1996, posted at ClimateFiles.com. **Journalists covering climate change:** David Roberts, "Did That New York Magazine Climate Story Freak You Out? Good." *Vox,* July 11, 2017.

Page 252: **culture of science:** Brysse et al. **As for the IPCC:** Glenn Scherer, "Climate Science Predictions Prove Too Conservative," *Scientific American,* December 6, 2012. **Fred Palmer once warned:** Palmer in "Global Warming Debate." **in 2014, Joseph Bast:** Peter Kelly-Detwiler, "Will Proposed EPA Coal Regulations Really Have Us Freezing in the Dark?," *Forbes,* June 3, 2014. **professor of law and psychology:** Dan Kahan, "What Are Fearless White Hierarchical Individualist Males Afraid Of? Lots of Stuff!," June 10, 2013; Dan Kahan, "Checking In on the 'White Male Effect' for Risk Perception," October 7, 2012, posted on Cultural Cognition Project website.

Page 253: **"shameless attempt"**: Justin Gillis, "Climate Change Researcher Offers a Defense of His Practices," *New York Times,* March 2, 2015. **degree in aerospace engineering:** Justin Gillis and John Schwartz, "Deeper Ties to Corporate Cash for Doubtful Climate Research," *New York Times,* February 21, 2015. **polar bear population forecasts:** Sabrina Shankman, "Willie Soon: 'Too Much Ice is Really Bad for Polar Bears,'" *Inside Climate News,* February 24, 2015.

Page 254: **since 2006 the grants:** Christopher Rowland, "Researcher Helps Sow Climate-Change Doubt," *Boston Globe,* November 5, 2013. **Soon often failed:** Lisa Song, "A Guide to Willie Soon's Climate Research Funded by Fossil Fuel Companies," *Inside Climate News,* February 23, 2015. **Southern Company:** David Hasemyer, "Documents Reveal Fossil Fuel Fingerprints on Contrarian Climate Research," *Inside Climate News,* February 21, 2015. **"ethically

challenged": Justin Gillis, "Climate Change Researcher Offers a Defense of His Practices," *New York Times*, March 2, 2015. **five of the ten editors:** Clare Goodess, "Stormy Times for Climate Research," *Scientists for Global Responsibility Newsletter*, November 2003. **invited to testify:** Andrew C. Revkin, "Politics Reasserts Itself in the Debate over Climate Change and Its Hazards," *New York Times*, August 5, 2003. **Inhofe, who would cite Soon:** *Congressional Record* 149, no. 113 (July 28, 2003), S10020. **Cooney tried:** *Political Interference with Climate Change Science under the Bush Administration*, House Committee on Oversight and Government Reform, December 2007. **Cooney left the White House:** Andrew C. Revkin, "Former Bush Aide Who Edited Reports is Hired by Exxon," *New York Times*, June 15, 2005. **Soon would go on:** Rowland, "Researcher Helps Sow," *Boston Globe*. **legal and political harassment:** Neela Banerjee, "The Most Hated Climate Scientist in the US Fights Back," *Yale Alumni Magazine*, March-April 2013.

Page 255: **Antiregulatory groups:** Michael Halpern, *Freedom to Bully: How Laws Intended to Free Information are Used to Harass Researchers*, Union of Concerned Scientists, 2015. **coal company funding:** Nick Surgey, "Bankruptcy Filing Show Arch Coal Funding for Climate Denial Legal Group, *PRWatch*, February 24, 2016. **UCS has pointed out:** Michael Halpern, "What Kinds of Scrutiny of Scientists Are Legitimate?" Union of Concerned Scientists, blog, February 24, 2015. **Tea Party rally:** "Climate of Doubt," *Frontline*. **"1 in 75 sextillion":** Lord Monckton, "Win or Lose, Obama Was Not and Is Not the President," online post, WND.com, November 6, 2012, and linked affidavit. **called the climate warnings:** Palmer in "Global Warming Debate." **"war on capitalism":** Joseph Bast, "Winning the Global Warming War," Heartland Institute, February 17, 2017, heartland.org. **Another Heartland statement:** H. Sterling Burnett, "Federal Judge Tosses Out Bogus Climate Lawsuit," Heartland Institute, June 29, 2018, heartland.org.

Page 256: **"obvious political purpose":** Leggett, 243. **Dozens of IPCC scientists:** Oreskes and Conway, 208. **Seitz . . . was hardly apolitical:** Oreskes and Conway, 56, 134–35, 142. **ExxonMobil and Koch foundations:** Greenpeace, "Factsheet: George C. Marshall Institute," Exxonsecrets.org; Greenpeace USA, "Grants to Koch-Funded Climate Denial Front-Groups," Greenpeace.org. **"made it possible":** Inglis, in "Climate of Doubt," *Frontline*.

Page 257: **event in 2014:** Christopher Monckton, keynote speech, 9th International Conference on Climate Change, July 10, 2014.

Page 258: **"There is no need":** "The Global Warming Crisis Is Over," Heartland Institute, May 19, 2015, heartland.org. **Heartland had issued:** Lakely, "'Do You Still Believe in Global Warming?,'" Heartland Institute, press release. **Heartland's science director:** Jay Lehr, "Man-Caused Global Warming: The Greatest Scam in World History," speech to Freedom Summit, October 29, 2016. **"mild and manageable way":** Charles Koch interview, *Powerhouse Politics* (podcast), ABC Radio, April 28, 2016; Rebecca Leber, "Charles Koch Finds a Lot of Things Scary—Except Climate Change," *Grist*, May 2, 2016. **power promotes "illusory control":** Fast et al. **The "paleoclimate":** Eve Savory, "Wallace Broecker: How to Calm an Angry Beast," CBS News, November 19, 2008. **"an angry beast":** Broecker, quoted in William K. Stevens, "If Climate Changes, It May Change Quickly," *New York Times*, January 27, 1998.

Page 259: **argued in 1996:** "Global Climate Coalition: An Overview," Global Climate Coalition, November 1996, posted at ClimateFiles.com. **A recent analysis:** Supran and Oreskes. **secretly taped 2014 presentation:** transcript linked to Eric Lipton, "Hard-Nosed Advice from Veteran Lobbyist: 'Win Ugly or Lose Pretty,'" *New York Times*, October 30, 2014.

Page 261: **Exxon pamphlet:** Exxon, "Global Climate Change: Everyone's Debate," pamphlet, 1998, posted at ClimateFiles.com. **Raymond claimed:** Lee Raymond, "Energy—Key to Growth and a Better Environment for Asia-Pacific Nations," speech to World Petroleum Congress, Beijing, October 13, 1997, posted at ClimateFiles.com. **Various errors:** US Climate Change Science Program, *Temperature Trends in the Lower Atmosphere: Steps for Understanding and Reconciling Differences*, Synthesis and Assessment Product 1.1, 2006, ch. 2; CarbonBrief, "Major Correction to Satellite Data Shows 140% Faster Warming since 1998," June 30, 2017, carbonbrief.org. **many deniers claimed:** Jennifer Jett, "Last Man Standing: Bob Murray and the War on

Coal," *West Virginia Executive*, May 30, 2014. **This claim depended:** UK Met Office, "A Pacific Flip Triggers the End of the Recent Slowdown," September 18, 2017. **five warmest years:** NOAA National Centers for Environmental Information, *Global Climate Report—Annual 2018*, "State of the Climate," published online January 2019. **funded a video:** Institute for Biospheric Research, *The Greening of Planet Earth*.

Page 262: **"work of the Lord":** Graham Readfearn, "'God Bless Trump': 25 Years Ago This Man Kick Started the First Fossil Fuel-Funded Campaigns to Attack Climate Science," January 29, 2017, *DeSmogBlog*, quoting a 1997 Dutch documentary. **CO2 pollution:** Fred Palmer, "Fossil Fuels or the Rio Treaty: Competing Visions for the Future," speech to COALTRANS 96, Madrid, Spain, October 21, 1996. **"Warm is good":** Palmer in "Global Warming Debate." **Peabody Energy:** Dr. Roger H. Bezdek, direct testimony, June 1, 2015, *In the Matter of the Further Investigation into Environmental and Socioeconomic Costs*, Docket No. E-999-CI-14-643, before MN Public Utilities Commission. **Craig Idso:** quoted in Gold and Mooney, "The Mercers," *Washington Post*. **Net plant growth:** Keenan et al. **Higher CO2 advantages:** *Climate Change Impacts in the United States: The Third National Climate Assessment* (Washington, DC: US Global Change Research Program, 2014), 157. **poison ivy:** *Global Climate Change Impacts in the United States* (Washington, DC: US Global Change Research Program, 2009), 76. **nutritional value:** *The Impacts of Climate Change on Human Health in the United States: A Scientific Assessment* (Washington, DC: US Global Change Research Program, 2016), ch. 7.

Page 263: **ended an article:** Idso, quoted in Gelbspan, 43. **history of ExxonMobil:** Coll, 180, 309.

Page 264: **Palmer stated in 2000:** Interview with Fred Palmer, "What's Up with the Weather: The Debate," *Nova* and *Frontline*, PBS, 2000. **"ultimate pessimists" . . . "new generation":** Statement of Fredrick D. Palmer, *Hearing on Solutions to Climate Change Before the Senate Committee on Commerce, Science and Transportation*, 106th Cong., 2nd sess., September 21, 2000, 27. **Solar and wind power costs:** International Renewable Energy Agency, *Renewable Power Generation Costs in 2017*, 2018. **installations have skyrocketed:** Bloomberg NEF, "World Reaches 1000GW of Wind and Solar, Keeps Going," August 2, 2018, BNEF website. **carbon capture technology progress:** International Energy Agency, *20 Years of Carbon Capture and Storage: Accelerating Future Deployment*, 2016. **Kenneth P. Green:** Kenneth P. Green, *Not Going Away: America's Energy Security, Jobs and Climate Challenges: Hearing Before the House Select Committee on Energy Independence and Global Warming*, 111th Cong., 2nd sess., December 1, 2010.

Page 265: **publicly supported a carbon tax:** Rex Tillerson, "Strengthening Global Energy Security," speech to Woodrow Wilson International Center for Scholars, January 8, 2009. **stopped funding some denier groups:** Elliot Negin, "Why Is ExxonMobil Still Funding Climate Science Denier Groups?" UCS Blog, August 31, 2018. **company actually joined:** "ExxonMobil to Join Oil and Gas Climate Initiative," ExxonMobil news release, September 20, 2018. **oil companies that support:** "About OGCI: A Catalyst for Change," http://oilandgasclimateinitiative.com/policy-and-strategy/, accessed September 29, 2018. **global energy projection:** ExxonMobil, *2019 Outlook for Energy: A View to 2040*, 38, 6. **latest IPCC analysis:** *IPCC Special Report, Global Warming of 1.5°C*, 14. **Tillerson put it:** Council on Foreign Relations CEO Speaker Series: A Conversation with Rex W. Tillerson, June 27, 2012. Footnote: **EPA document:** Juliet Eilperin, Brady Dennis, and Chris Mooney, "Trump Administration Sees a 7-Degree Rise in Global Temperatures by 2100," *Washington Post*, September 28, 2018.

Page 266: **Their father:** Schulman, 41, 49. **suspected Eisenhower:** Welch, 249. **phony front groups:** Mayer, 48. **extreme libertarianism:** Schulman, 94, 99, 103, 106. **sellouts:** Doherty, 443.

Page 267: **Libertarian platform:** Union of Concerned Scientists, "Who's Backing Scott Pruitt to Head the EPA? The Koch Brothers," February 2017 (links to platform). **Jane Mayer:** Mayer, 71. **Kochs and their foundations:** "Koch Industries Secretly Funding the Climate Denial Machine," *Greenpeace*, March 2010. **tremendous political power:** Matea Gold, "Koch-Backed Political Network, Built to Shield Donors, Raised $400 Million in 2012 Elections," *Washington*

Post, January 5, 2014. **Americans for Prosperity:** Coral Davenport and Eric Lipton, "How G.O.P. Leaders Came to View Climate Change as Fake Science," *New York Times,* June 3, 2017. **significant role:** Jason M. Breslow, "Tim Phillips: The Case against Climate Legislation" on website for "Climate of Doubt," *Frontline.* **"market principles":** Koch, quoted in Mayer, 57.

Page 268: **Some libertarians:** David Roberts, "The Arguments That Convinced a Libertarian to Support Aggressive Action on Climate," *Vox,* May 12, 2015. **When pressed by *Fortune*:** "Full Transcript of Charles Koch's Interview with Fortune," *Fortune,* July 12, 2016. **Charles Koch adamantly insists:** Interview by Jonathan Karl, "Charles Koch: Political System 'Rigged,' But Not by Me," ABC News, April 24, 2016. **"I'd rather die":** "Full Transcript of Charles Koch's Interview," *Fortune.* **fighting corporate "cronyism":** "Why Hate the Koch Brothers?" (part 1), *Freakonomics,* June 21, 2017. **system rigged by the wealthy:** Interview by Jonathan Karl, "Charles Koch," ABC News.

Page 269: **hundreds of billions of dollars:** International Renewable Energy Agency, *Global Landscape of Renewable Energy Finance 2018.* **US CO2 emissions:** U.S. Energy Information Administration, *U.S. Energy-Related Carbon Dioxide Emissions, 2016,* 2017. **other advanced nations:** Kelly Levin and David Rich, *Turning Points: Trends in Countries' Reaching Peak Greenhouse Gas Emissions over Time,* World Resources Institute, 2017. **Wheeler:** Lisa Friedman, "Andrew Wheeler, New E.P.A. Chief, Details His Energy Lobbying Past," *New York Times,* August 1, 2018.

Page 270: **Obama-era regulations:** the three most important regulations being dismantled are the Clean Power Plan (benefiting the coal industry), standards for more fuel efficient cars (benefiting the oil industry), and rules limiting methane leakage (benefiting the natural gas industry); Lisa Friedman, "Trump Administration Formally Rolls Back Rule Aimed at Limiting Methane Pollution," *New York Times,* September 18, 2018. **US energy-related carbon emissions:** U.S. Energy Information Administration, *Short-Term Energy Outlook,* May 2019. **market interference . . . those who oversee:** John H. Cushman Jr., "There's No Power Grid Emergency Requiring a Coal Bailout, Regulators Say," *InsideClimate News,* June 12, 2018. **critically important federal research:** Dan Gearino, "Trump's Budget Could Have a Chilling Effect on U.S. Clean Energy Leadership," *InsideClimate News,* April 2, 2019. **five states . . . one hundred cities:** David Roberts, "A Close Look at Washington's Superb New 100% Clean Electricity Bill," *Vox,* April 18, 2019. **Xcel Energy:** Paul Huttner, "Xcel Energy Going Carbon-Free by 2050," *MPR News,* December 4, 2018. **New York sued:** David Hasemyer, "New York AG Sues Exxon, Says Oil Giant Defrauded Investors over Climate Change," *InsideClimate News,* October 24, 2018. **seeking court authority:** David Hasemyer, "With Bare Knuckles and Big Dollars, Exxon Fights Climate Probe to a Legal Stalemate," *InsideClimate News,* June 5, 2017. **"campaign of misinformation":** Suzanne McCarron, "The Coordinated Attack on ExxonMobil," Perspectives, blog, ExxonMobil, April 20, 2016, energyfactor.exxonmobil.com. **"fake journalism":** Brendan DeMelle and Kevin Grandia, "'There Is No Doubt': Exxon Knew CO_2 Pollution Was a Global Threat By Late 1970s," *DeSmogBlog,* April 26, 2016. **"conspiracy against us":** David Kaiser and Lee Wasserman, "The Rockefeller Family Fund vs. Exxon," *New York Review of Books,* December 8, 2016. **carbon tax plan:** John Schwartz, "ExxonMobil Lends Its Support to a Carbon Tax Proposal," *New York Times,* June 20, 2017.

Page 271: **Washington ballot initiative:** Bill McKibben, "Big Oil Is Sloshing a Crude Tsunami across the Country," *Washington Post,* October 30, 2018.

CONCLUSION

Page 280: **Bill McKibben:** Bill McKibben, "Notes From a Remarkable Political Moment for Climate Change," *New Yorker,* May 1, 2019. **Democratic voters are starting:** Miranda Green, "Poll: Climate Change Is Top Issue for Registered Democrats," *Hill,* April 30, 2019. **proposed Green New Deal:** A. Gustafson et al., *Changes in Awareness of and Support for the Green New*

Deal: December 2018 to April 2019 (New Haven, CT, and Fairfax, VA: Yale University and George Mason University, 2019).

Page 281: **Power corrupts:** Keltner. **power can promote prosocial action:** Galinsky, Gruenfeld, and Magee; Chen, Lee-Chai, and Bargh; DeCelles et al. **generally *less* susceptible:** Briñol et al. **consulting firm McKinsey found:** Tobias Baer, Sven Heiligtag, and Hamid Smandari, "The Business Logic in Debiasing," McKinsey&Company, website, May 2017. **Max Bazerman and Ann Tenbrunsel:** Bazerman and Tenbrunsel. **Margaret Heffernan:** Heffernan. **One multidisciplinary effort:** the website EthicalSystems.org provides articles, videos, training materials, and other resources.

Page 282: **defined as immoral:** Milton Friedman, "The Social Responsibility of Business Is to Increase Its Profits," *New York Times,* September 13, 1970. **Lynn Stout:** Stout. **thirty trillion dollars' worth:** Global Sustainable Investment Alliance, *2018 Global Sustainable Investment Review.*

Page 283: **"benefits corporations":** Doug Bend and Alex King, "Why Consider a Benefit Corporation," *Forbes,* May 30, 2014. **B Corporations:** Suntae Kim et al., "Why Companies Are Becoming B Corporations," *Harvard Business Review,* June 17, 2016.

Page 284: **legislation promoting:** Matthew Yglesias, "Elizabeth Warren Has a Plan to Save Capitalism," *Vox,* August 15, 2018. **Roosevelt warned:** Theodore Roosevelt, "The Progressives, Past and Present," *The Outlook* 98, no. 1 (1910).

Page 285: **constitutional rights courts:** Winkler. **"corrosive and distorting effects":** Austin v. Michigan Chamber of Commerce, 494 U.S. 652, 660 (1990). **view was rejected:** Citizens United v. Federal Election Commission, 558 U.S. 310 (2010). **A 2015 poll:** Greg Stohr, "Bloomberg Poll: Americans Want Supreme Court to Turn Off Political Spending Spigot," *Bloomberg,* September 28, 2015. **nineteen states:** "Nevada Is 19th State to Call for a Constitutional Amendment to Overturn Citizens United; Half the States Needed Are Onboard," *Public Citizen,* May 25, 2017. **A 2018 Gallup poll:** Frank Newport, "Democrats More Positive about Socialism than Capitalism," Gallup, August 13, 2018.

Page 286: **Naomi Klein:** Klein, 462.

Major Works Cited in Notes

Amodio, David M., Sarah L. Master, Cindy M. Yee, and Shelley E. Taylor. "Neurocognitive Components of the Behavioral Inhibition and Activation Systems: Implications for Theories of Self-Regulation." *Psychophysiology* 45, no. 1 (2008): 11–19.

Anderson, Cameron, and Adam D. Galinsky. "Power, Optimism, and Risk-Taking." *European Journal of Social Psychology* 36, no. 4 (2006): 511–36.

Anderson, Stephen O. "Lessons from Stratospheric Ozone Layer Protection for Climate." *Journal of Environmental Studies and Sciences* 5 (2015): 143–62.

Anderson, Stephen O., and K. Madhava Sarma. *Protecting the Ozone Layer: The United Nations History.* Sterling, VA: United Nations Environment Programme, Earthscan Publications, 2002.

Anonymous. *Slavery No Oppression, or, Some New Arguments and Opinions against the Idea of African Liberty.* London: Lowndes and Christie, [1799?].

———. *A Vindication of the Use of Sugar, the Produce of the West-India Islands.* 2nd ed. London: T. Boosey, 1792.

A Plain Man. *The True State of the Question, Addressed to the Petitioners for Abolition of the Slave Trade.* London, 1792. https://archive.org/details/ASPC0002375700.

Ariely, Dan. *The (Honest) Truth about Dishonesty: How We Lie to Everyone—Especially Ourselves.* New York: Harper, 2012.

Arlidge, John. "I'm Doing 'God's Work': Meet Mr. Goldman Sachs." *Sunday Times of London,* November 8, 2009.

Bair, Sheila. *Bull by the Horns: Fighting to Save Main Street from Wall Street and Wall Street from Itself.* New York: Free Press, 2012.

Bakan, Joel. *The Corporation: The Pathological Pursuit of Profit and Power.* New York: Free Press, 2005.

Bandura, A. "Moral Disengagement in the Perpetration of Inhumanities." *Personality and Social Psychology Review* 3, no. 3 (1999): 193–209.

Bandura, A., G. Caprara, and L. Zsolnai. "Corporate Transgressions through Moral Disengagement." *Journal of Human Values* 6, no. 1 (2000): 57–64.

Bazerman, Max H., and Ann E. Tenbrunsel. *Blind Spots: Why We Fail to Do What's Right and What to Do about It.* Princeton, NJ: Princeton University Press, 2011.

Bierce, Ambrose. *The Devil's Dictionary.* Mineola, NY: Dover, 2019.

Board of Trade. *Report of the Lords of the Committee of Council Appointed for the Consideration of All Matters Relating to Trade and Foreign Plantations.* London, 1789. https://catalog.hathitrust.org/Record/001742015

Bohning, James J. "Oral History Interview with Richard E. Heckert." Philadelphia: Chemical Heritage Foundation Oral History Program, 1994. https://digital.sciencehistory.org/works/3x816n660.

Boyd, T.A. "Charles F. Kettering, Prophet of Progress." *Science* 129, no. 3344 (1959): 255–56.

————. *Professional Amateur: The Biography of Charles Franklin Kettering.* New York: E.P. Dutton, 1957.

Brandt, Allan M. *The Cigarette Century: The Rise, Fall, and Deadly Persistence of the Product That Defined America.* New York: Basic Books, 2007.

Branscombe, N.R., and D.L. Wann. "Collective Self-Esteem Consequences of Outgroup Derogation When a Valued Social Identity Is on Trial." *European Journal of Psychology* 24, no. 6 (1994): 641–57.

Brecher, Ruth, et al. *The Consumers Union Report on Smoking and the Public Interest.* Mount Vernon, NY: Consumers Union, 1963.

Briñol, Pablo, et al. "The Effects of Message Recipients' Power before and after Persuasion: A Self-Validation Analysis." *Journal of Personality and Social Psychology* 93, no. 6 (2007): 1040–53.

Brodeur, Paul. "Annals of Chemistry: Inert." *New Yorker,* April 7, 1975.

————. "In the Face of Doubt." *New Yorker,* June 9, 1986.

Brown, Christopher L. *Moral Capital: Foundations of British Abolitionism.* Chapel Hill: University of North Carolina Press, 2006.

Brulle, Robert J. "Institutionalizing Delay: Foundation Funding and the Creation of U.S. Climate Change Counter-movement Organizations." *Climatic Change* 122, no. 4 (2014): 682–94.

Brysse, Keynyn, Naomi Oreskes, Jessica O'Reilly, and Michael Oppenheimer. "Climate Change Prediction: Erring on the Side of Least Drama?" *Global Environmental Change* 23, no. 1 (2013): 327–37.

Bureau of Investigation. "Radium as a 'Patent Medicine': The Methods and Activities of William J.A. Bailey in the Field of Radioactivity." *JAMA* 98, no. 16 (1932): 1397–99.

Burns, Eric. *The Smoke of the Gods: A Social History of Tobacco.* Philadelphia: Temple University Press, 2007.

Byrne, John A. "Philip Morris: Inside America's Most Reviled Company." *Bloomberg Businessweek Archive,* November 28, 1999.

Cagin, Seth, and Philip Dray. *Between Earth and Sky: How CFCs Changed Our World and Endangered the Ozone Layer.* New York: Pantheon, 1993.

Cameron, Charles S. "Lung Cancer and Smoking: What We Really Know." *Atlantic,* January 1956.

Carothers, Leslie. "Upholding EPA Regulation of Greenhouse Gases: The Precautionary Principle Redux." *Ecology Law Quarterly* 41, no. 3 (2014): 683–749.

Caruso, Eugene M., Kathleen D. Vohs, Brittani Baxter, and Adam Waytz. "Mere Exposure to Money Increases Endorsement of Free-Market Systems and Social Inequality." *Journal of Experimental Psychology: General* 142, no. 2 (2013): 301–6.

Chen, Serena, Annette Y. Lee-Chai, and John A. Bargh. "Relationship Orientation as a Moderator of the Effects of Social Power." *Journal of Personality and Social Psychology* 80, no. 2 (2001): 173–87.

Cikara, M. "Intergroup Schadenfreude: Motivating Participation in Collective Violence." *Current Opinion in Behavioral Sciences* 3 (2015): 12–17.

Cikara, M., A.C. Jenkins, N. Dufour, and R. Saxe. "Reduced Self-Referential Neural Response during Intergroup Competition Predicts Competitor Harm." *NeuroImage* 96 (2014): 36–43.

Cikara, M., and J.J. Van Bavel. "The Neuroscience of Intergroup Relations: An Integrative Review." *Perspectives on Psychological Science* 9, no. 3 (2014): 245–74.

Clark, Claudia. *Radium Girls: Women and Industrial Health Reform, 1910-1935.* Chapel Hill: University of North Carolina Press, 1997.

Coates, John. *The Hour between Dog and Wolf: How Risk Taking Transforms Us, Body and Mind.* New York: Penguin, 2013.

Cohan, William D. *House of Cards: A Tale of Hubris and Wretched Excess on Wall Street.* New York: Doubleday, 2009.

Cohen, Shirley K. "Interview with Clair C. Patterson." Oral History Project, Pasadena: California Institute of Technology Archives. 1995. http://oralhistories.library.caltech.edu/32/1/OH_Patterson.pdf.

Cohn, Alain, Ernst Fehr, and Michel Andre Marechal. "Business Culture and Dishonesty in the Banking Industry." *Nature* 516, no. 729 (2014): 86–89.

Coll, Steve. *Private Empire: ExxonMobil and American Power.* New York: Penguin, 2013.

Cook, Elizabeth. *Ozone Protection in the United States: Elements of Success.* Washington, DC: World Resources Institute, 1996.

Cook, J., et al. "Quantifying the Consensus on Anthropogenic Global Warming in the Scientific Literature." *Environmental Research Letters* 8, no. 2 (2013).

Cordtz, Dan. "The Face in the Mirror at General Motors." *Fortune,* August 1966, 117.

Council on Pharmacy and Chemistry. "Proprietary Vanadium Preparations." *JAMA* 60, no. 3 (1913): 225.

DeCelles, Katherine A., D. Scott DeRue, Joshua D. Margolis, and Tara L. Ceranic. "Does Power Corrupt or Enable? When and Why Power Facilitates Self-Interested Behavior." *Journal of Applied Psychology* 97, no. 3 (2012): 681–89.

Denworth, Lydia. *Toxic Truth: A Scientist, A Doctor, and the Battle over Lead.* Boston: Beacon Press, 2008.

Deville, Kenneth A., and Mark E. Steiner. "New Jersey Radium Dial Workers and the Dynamics of Occupational Disease Litigation in the Early Twentieth Century." *Missouri Law Review* 62, no. 2 (1997): 281–314.

DeVoe, Sanford E., Jeffrey Pfeffer, and Byron Y. Lee. "When Does Money Make Money More Important? Survey and Experimental Evidence." *Industrial and Labor Relations Review* 66, no. 5 (2013): 1078–96.

De Waal, Frans. *The Age of Empathy: Nature's Lessons for a Kinder Society.* New York: Three Rivers Press, 2009.

Doherty, Brian. *Radicals for Capitalism: A Freewheeling History of the Modern American Libertarian Movement.* New York: Public Affairs, 2007.

Doll, Richard, and A. Bradford Hill. "Smoking and Carcinoma of the Lung." *BMJ* 2 (1950): 739–48.

Doniger, David. "Politics of the Ozone Layer." *Issues in Science and Technology* 4, no. 3 (1988): 86–92.

Dotto, Lydia, and Harold Schiff. *The Ozone War.* Garden City, NY: Doubleday, 1978.

Drum, Kevin. "America's Real Criminal Element: Lead." *Mother Jones,* January-February 2013.

Duke of Clarence. *Substance of the Speech of His Royal Highness The Duke of Clarence, in the House of Lords, on the Motion for the Recommitment of the Slave Trade Limitation Bill.* London: C. Whittingham, 1799.

Eastman, Joel W. *Styling vs. Safety: The American Automobile Industry and the Development of Automotive Safety, 1900-1966.* Lanham, MD: University Press of America, 1984.

Estwick, Samuel. *Considerations on the Negroe Cause Commonly So Called.* 2nd ed. London: J. Dodsley, 1773.

Fast, Nathanael J., D. H. Gruenfeld, N. Sivanathan, and Adam D. Galinsky. "Illusory Control," *Psychological Science* 20, no. 4 (2009): 502.

Field, C. E. "The Efficiency of Radioactive Waters for the Control of Faulty Elimination." *Medical Record* 87, no. 10 (1915): 390–94.

Financial Crisis Inquiry Commission (FCIC). *Financial Crisis Inquiry Commission Report.* Washington, DC: U.S. GPO, 2011. https://www.govinfo.gov/content/pkg/GPO-FCIC/pdf /GPO-FCIC.pdf.

Fitzhugh, George. *Sociology for the South: Or, The Failure of Free Society.* Richmond, VA: A. Morris, 1854.

Flinn, Frederick B. "Radioactive Material: An Industrial Hazard?" *JAMA* 87, no. 25 (1926): 2078–81.

Francklyn, Gilbert. *Observations Occasioned by the Attempts Made in England to Effect the Abolition of the Slave Trade.* Kingston, Jamaica, and Liverpool: A. Smith's Navigation Shop, 1788.

———. *Substance of a Speech Intended to Have Been Made on Mr. Wilberforce's Motion for the Abolition of the Slave Trade.* London: J. Owen, 1792.

Freudenberg, Nicholas. *Lethal but Legal: Corporations, Consumption, and Protecting Public Health.* New York: Oxford University Press, 2014.

Froman, Nanny. "Marie and Pierre Curie and the Discovery of Polonium and Radium." Lecture delivered to the Royal Swedish Academy of Sciences, Stockholm, February 28, 1996.

Furnas, J. C. "'—And Sudden Death.'" *Reader's Digest,* August 1935.

Galinsky, Adam D., Deborah H. Gruenfeld, and Joe C. Magee. "From Power to Action." *Journal of Personality and Social Psychology* 85, no. 3 (2003): 453–66.

Galloway, Robert. *A History of Coal Mining in Great Britain.* 1882. Reprint, Newton Abbot, Devon, UK: David and Charles, 1969.

Gartman, David. *Auto Opium: A Social History of American Automobile Design.* London: Routledge, 1994.

Gately, Iain. *Tobacco: A Cultural History of How an Exotic Plant Seduced Civilization.* New York: Grove Press, 2001.

Gelbspan, Ross. *The Heat Is On: The High Stakes Battle Over Earth's Threatened Climate.* Reading, MA: Addison-Wesley, 1997.

Gikas, Paul W. "Crashworthiness as a Cultural Ideal." In *The Automobile and American Culture,* edited by David L. Lewis and Laurence Goldstein, 327–39. Ann Arbor: University of Michigan Press, 1980.

Gilbert, Daniel T., Gary King, Stephen Pettigrew, and Timothy D. Wilson. "Comment on 'Estimating the Reproducibility of Psychological Science.'" *Science* 351, no. 6277 (2016): 1037.

Glantz, Stanton A., John Slade, Lisa A. Bero, Peter Hanauer, and Deborah E. Barnes. *The Cigarette Papers.* Berkeley: University of California Press, 1996.

Glas, Joseph P. "Protecting the Ozone Layer: A Perspective from Industry." In *Technology and Environment,* edited by J. H. Ausubel and H. E. Sladovich. Washington DC: National Academy Press, 1989.

Global Burden of Disease 2015 Tobacco Collaborators. "Smoking Prevalence and Attributable Disease Burden in 195 Countries and Territories, 1990–2015: A Systematic Analysis from the Global Burden of Disease Study 2015." *Lancet* 389 (2017): 1885–1906.

Global Burden of Disease 2017 Risk Factor Collaborators. "Global, Regional, and National Comparative Risk Assessment of 84 Behavioural, Environmental, and Occupational, and Metabolic Risks or Clusters of Risks for 195 Countries and Territories, 1990–2017: A Systematic Analysis for the Global Burden of Disease Study 2017." *Lancet* 392 (2018): 1923–94.

Goldberg, Jeffrey. "Big Tobacco's Endgame." *New York Times Magazine,* June 21, 1998.

Graebner, William. "Hegemony through Science: Information Engineering and Lead Toxicology, 1925–1965." In *Dying for Work: Workers' Safety and Health in Twentieth-

Century America, edited by David Rosner and Gerald Markowitz, 140–59. Bloomington: Indiana University Press, 1987.

Greene, Joshua. *Moral Tribes: Emotion, Reason, and the Gap between Us and Them.* New York: Penguin, 2013.

Gribbin, John. *The Hole in the Sky: Man's Threat to the Ozone Layer.* New York: Bantam Books, 1988.

Guinote, Ana. "How Power Affects People: Activating, Wanting, and Goal Seeking." *Annual Review of Psychology* 68 (2017): 353–81.

Gunn, John C. *Gunn's New Family Physician or Home Book of Health.* 210th ed. Chicago: A. B. Kuhlman, 1901.

Gwinn, J. D., C. M. Judd, and B. Park. "Less Power = Less Human? Effects of Power Differentials on Dehumanization." *Journal of Experimental Social Psychology* 49, no. 3 (2013): 464–70.

Haidt, Jonathan. *The Righteous Mind: Why Good People Are Divided by Politics and Religion.* New York: Pantheon, 2012.

Hamilton, David. *The Monkey Gland Affair.* London: Chatto and Windus, 1986.

Hanna-Attisha, Mona, Jenny LaChance, R. Casey Sadler, and Allison Champney Schnepp. "Elevated Blood Lead Levels in Children Associated with the Flint Drinking Water Crisis: A Spatial Analysis of Risk and Public Health Response." *American Journal of Public Health* 106, no. 2 (2016): 283–290.

Harvie, David I. *Deadly Sunshine: The History and Fatal Legacy of Radium.* Stroud, Gloucestershire, UK: Tempus, 2005.

Heffernan, Margaret. *Willful Blindness: Why We Ignore the Obvious at Our Peril.* New York: Walker, 2011.

Hegglin, Michaela I., et al. *Twenty Questions and Answers about the Ozone Layer: 2014 Update, Scientific Assessment of Ozone Depletion.* Geneva, Switz.: World Meteorological Organization, 2014.

Herndon, Booton. *Ford: An Unconventional Biography of the Men and Their Times.* New York: Weybright and Talley, 1969.

Hilts, Philip J. *Smoke Screen: The Truth Behind the Tobacco Industry Cover-Up.* Reading, MA: Addison-Wesley, 1996.

Hirsh, Jacob B., Adam D. Galinsky, and Chen-Bo Zhong. "Drunk, Powerful, and in the Dark." *Perspectives on Psychological Science* 6, no. 5 (2011): 415–27.

Ho, Karen. *Liquidated: An Ethnography of Wall Street.* Durham, NC: Duke University Press, 2009.

Hochschild, Adam. *Bury the Chains: Prophets and Rebels in the Fight to Free an Empire's Slaves.* Boston: Mariner Books, 2005.

Holden, Richard J. "People or Systems? To Blame Is Human. To Fix Is to Engineer." *Professional Safety* 54, no. 12 (2009): 34–41.

Horner, Christopher C. *Red Hot Lies: How Global Warming Alarmists Use Threats, Fraud, and Deception to Keep You Misinformed.* Washington, DC: Regnery, 2008.

Hounshell, David A., and John Kenly Smith Jr. *Science and Corporate Strategy: DuPont R&D, 1902–1980: Studies in Economic History and Policy.* New York: Cambridge University Press, 1988.

Hudson, Michael W. *The Monster: How a Gang of Predatory Lenders and Wall Street Bankers Fleeced America—And Spawned a Global Crisis.* New York: Times Books/Henry Holt, 2010.

Iacocca, Lee. *Iacocca: An Autobiography.* New York: Bantam Books, 1984.

Innis, William. *The Slave Trade Indispensable: In Answer to the Speech of William Wilberforce, Esq.* London: W. Richardson, 1790.

Jackall, Robert. *Moral Mazes: The World of Corporate Managers.* 20th anniv. ed. New York: Oxford University Press, 2010.

Jeffrey, Grant R. *The Global Warming Deception: How a Secret Elite Plans to Bankrupt America and Steal Your Freedom.* Colorado Springs: WaterBrook, 2011.

John, Leslie K., George Loewenstein, and Scott I. Rick. "Cheating More for Less: Upward Social Comparisons Motivate the Poorly Compensated to Cheat." *Organizational Behavior and Human Decision Processes* 123, no. 2 (2014): 101–9.

Jost, John T. "A Theory of System Justification." *Psychological Science Agenda*, June 2017.

Jost, John T., and David M. Amodio. "Political Ideology as Motivated Social Cognition: Behavioral and Neuroscientific Evidence." *Motivation and Emotion* 36, no. 1 (2012): 55–64.

Jost, J. T., C. M. Federico, and J. L. Napier. "Political Ideology: Its Structure, Functions, and Elective Affinities." *Annual Review of Psychology* 60 (2009): 307–37.

Kahan, Dan M. "Ideology, Motivated Reasoning, and Cognitive Reflection: An Experimental Study." *Judgment and Decision Making* 8 (2013): 407–24.

Kahneman, Daniel. *Thinking, Fast and Slow*. New York: Farrar, Straus and Giroux, 2011.

Katz, Harold. "The Liability in Tort or Warranty of Automobile Manufacturers for the Inherently Dangerous Design of Passenger Automobiles." *Chicago Bar Record,* May 1956.

Keenan, T. F., et al. "Recent Pause in the Growth Rate of Atmospheric CO_2 due to Enhanced Terrestrial Carbon Uptake." *Nature Communications* 7, no. 13428 (2016).

Kehoe, R. A. "Contaminated and Natural Lead Environments of Man." *Archives of Environmental Health* 11 (1965): 736–39.

Keltner, Dacher. *The Power Paradox: How We Gain and Lose Influence*. New York: Penguin, 2017.

Keltner, Dacher, Deborah H. Gruenfeld, and Cameron Anderson. "Power, Approach, and Inhibition." *Psychological Review* 110, no. 2 (2003): 265–84.

Kestemont, Jenny, et al. "Situation and Person Attributions under Spontaneous and Intentional Instructions: An fMRI Study." *Social Cognitive and Affective Neuroscience* 8 (2013): 481–93.

Kettering, Charles F. "Biographical Memoir of Thomas Midgley, Jr. 1889–1944." *National Academy of Sciences Biographical Memoirs*, vol. 24, Eleventh Memoir. Presented to the NAS at the annual meeting, 1947. www.nasonline.org/publications/biographical-memoirs /memoir-pdfs/midgley-thomas.pdf.

Kitman, Jamie Lincoln. "The Secret History of Lead." *Nation*, March 20, 2000.

Klein, Naomi. *This Changes Everything: Capitalism vs. the Climate*. New York: Simon and Schuster, 2014.

Kluger, Richard. *Ashes to Ashes: America's Hundred-Year Cigarette War, the Public Health, and the Unabashed Triumph of Philip Morris*. New York: Vintage Books, 1997.

Konis, D., U. Haran, K. Saporta, and S. Ayal. "A Sorrow Shared Is a Sorrow Halved: Moral Judgments of Harm to Single versus Multiple Victims." *Frontiers in Psychology* 7 (2016): 1142.

Kovarik, William. "The Ethyl Controversy: How the News Media Set the Agenda for a Public Health Controversy over Leaded Gasoline, 1924–1926." PhD diss., University of Maryland, 1993.

———. "Ethyl-Leaded Gasoline: How a Classic Occupational Disease Became an International Public Health Disaster." *International Journal of Occupational and Environmental Health* 11, no. 4 (2005): 384–97.

Lahsen, Myanna. "Technocracy, Democracy, and U.S. Climate Politics: The Need for Demarcations." *Science, Technology and Human Values* 30, no. 1 (2005): 137–69.

Lammers, J., A. D. Galinsky, E. H. Gordijn, and S. Otten. "Illegitimacy Moderates the Effects of Power on Approach." *Psychological Science* 19, no. 6 (2008): 558–64.

Landa, Edward R. "A Brief History of the American Radium Industry and Its Ties to the Scientific Community of Its Early Twentieth Century." *Environment International* 19, no. 5 (1993): 503–8.

———. "Buried Treasure to Buried Waste: The Rise and Fall of the Radium Industry." *Colorado School of Mines Quarterly* 82, no. 2 (1987): 1–77.

———. "The First Nuclear Industry." *Scientific American* 247, no. 5 (1982): 180–93.

Landrigan, Philip J. "Comment: Lead and the Heart: An Ancient Metal's Contribution to Modern Disease." *Lancet Public Health* 3, no. 4 (2018): e156–57.

Lang, Daniel. "A Most Valuable Accident." *New Yorker,* May 2, 1959.

Lanphear, Bruce P., et al. "Low-Level Lead Exposure and Mortality in US Adults: A Population-Based Cohort Study." *Lancet Public Health* 3, no. 4 (2018): e177–84.

Lauritsen, Janet L., Maribeth L. Rezey, and Karen Heimer. "When Choice of Data Matters: Analyses of U.S. Crime Trends, 1973–2012." *Journal of Quantitative Criminology* 32, no. 3 (2016): 335–55.

Lear, Linda J. *Rachel Carson: Witness for Nature.* New York: H. Holt, 1997.

Leggett, Jeremy. *The Carbon War: Global Warming and the End of the Oil Era.* New York: Routledge, 2001.

Lemov, Michael R. *Car Safety Wars: One Hundred Years of Technology, Politics and Death.* Madison, NJ: Fairleigh Dickinson University Press, 2015.

Leslie, Stuart W. "Thomas Midgley and the Politics of Industrial Research." *Business History Review* 54, no. 4 (1980): 480–503.

Levy, David T., Zhe Yuan, Yuying Luo, Darren Mays. "Seven Years of Progress in Tobacco Control: An Evaluation of the Effect of Nations Meeting the Highest Level MPOWER Measures between 2007 and 2014." *Tobacco Control* 27 (2018): 50–57.

Lewis, Michael. *The Big Short: Inside the Doomsday Machine.* New York: W.W. Norton, 2011.

Liddle, Mitzi-Jane E., Ben S. Bradley, and Andrew Mcgrath. "Baby Empathy: Infant Distress and Peer Prosocial Responses." *Infant Mental Health Journal* 36 (2015): 446–58.

Luyendijk, Joris. *Among the Bankers: A Journey into the Heart of Finance.* Brooklyn: Melville House, 2015.

Mackie, D. M., M. C. Gastardo-Conaco, and J. J. Skelly. "Knowledge of the Advocated Position and the Processing of In-Group and Out-Group Persuasive Messages." *Personality and Social Psychology Bulletin* 18, no. 2 (1992): 145–51.

Macklis, R. M. "The Great Radium Scandal." *Scientific American* 269 (August 1993): 94–99.

———. "Radithor and the Era of Mild Radium Therapy." *JAMA* 264, no. 5 (1990): 614–18.

Maduro, Rogelio A., and Ralf Schauerhammer. *The Holes in the Ozone Scare: The Scientific Evidence That the Sky Isn't Falling.* Washington, DC: 21st Century Science Associates, 1992.

Markowitz, Gerald, and David Rosner. *Lead Wars: The Politics of Science and the Fate of America's Children.* Berkeley: University of California Press, 2013.

Martin, Samuel. *A Short Treatise on the Slavery of Negroes in the British Colonies.* Antigua: Robert Mearns, 1775.

Martland, Harrison S., P. Conlon, and J. P. Knef. "Some Unrecognized Dangers in the Use and Handling of Radioactive Substances." *JAMA* 85, no. 23 (1925): 1769–76.

Mateu, Guillermo, Lucas Monzani, and Roger Muñoz Navarro. "The Role of the Brain in Financial Decisions: A Viewpoint on Neuroeconomics." *Mètode Science Studies Journal* no. 8 (2017): 6–15.

Maxwell, James, and Forrest Briscoe. "There's Money in the Air: The CFC Ban and DuPont's Regulatory Strategy." *Business Strategy and the Environment* 6 (1997): 276–86.

Mayer, Jane. *Dark Money: The Hidden History of the Billionaires behind the Rise of the Radical Right.* New York: Anchor, 2017.

McClure, S. M., D. I. Laibson, G. Loewenstein, and J. D. Cohen. "Separate Neural Systems Value Immediate and Delayed Monetary Rewards." *Science* 306, no. 5695 (2004): 503–7.

McCright, A. M., R. E. Dunlap, and C. Xiao. "Perceived Scientific Agreement and Support for Government Action on Climate Change in the USA." *Climatic Change* 119, no. 2 (2013): 511–18.

McGarity, Thomas O., and Wendy E. Wagner. *Bending Science: How Special Interests Corrupt Public Health Research.* Cambridge, MA: Harvard University Press, 2008.

McGrayne, Sharon Bertsch. *Prometheans in the Lab: Chemistry and the Making of the Modern World*. New York: McGraw-Hill, 2001.

McLean, Bethany, and Joe Nocera. *All the Devils Are Here: The Hidden History of the Financial Crisis*. New York: Portfolio/Penguin, 2011.

Medema, S. G., and W. G. Samuels. *Foundations of Research in Economics: How Do Economists Do Economics?* Brookfield, VT: Edward Elgar, 1996.

Mehling, Harold. "Big Three Fight over How Safe to Make Your Car." *Bluebook Magazine*, October 1955. Reprinted in *Traffic Safety: Hearings Before a Subcommittee of the House Committee on Interstate and Foreign Commerce*, 84th Cong., 2nd sess., July–September 1956, 40–47). Page references are to the 1956 reprint.

Michaels, David. *Doubt Is Their Product: How Industry's Assault on Science Threatens Your Health*. New York: Oxford University Press, 2008.

Midgley, Thomas, Jr. "Tetraethyl Lead Poison Hazards." *Industrial and Engineering Chemistry* 17, no. 8 (1925): 827–28.

Milgram, Stanley. *Obedience to Authority: The Unique Experiment That Challenged Human Nature*. New York: Perennial Classics, 2004.

Mintz, Morton, and Jerry S. Cohen. *America, Inc.: Who Owns and Operates the United States*. New York: Dell, 1971.

Molenberghs, Pascal. "The Neuroscience of In-Group Bias." *Neuroscience and Biobehavioral Reviews* 37, no. 8 (2013): 1530–36.

Moore, Kate. *The Radium Girls: They Paid with Their Lives, Their Final Fight Was for Justice*. London: Simon and Schuster, 2016.

Morris, Charles Evans. *Modern Rejuvenation Methods*. New York: Scientific Medical Publishing, 1926.

Mould, Richard F. "Pierre Curie, 1859–1906." *Current Oncology* 14, no. 2 (2007): 74–82.

Mullner, Ross. *Deadly Glow: The Radium Dial Worker Tragedy*. Washington DC: American Public Health Association, 1999.

Nader, Ralph. *Unsafe at Any Speed: The Designed-In Dangers of the American Automobile*, 2nd ed. updated. New York: Grossman, 1972. First published 1965.

National Toxicology Program. *Health Effects of Low-Level Lead*. NTP Monograph. June 2012. https://ntp.niehs.nih.gov/ntp/ohat/lead/final/monographhealtheffectslowlevellead_newissn_508.pdf.

———. *Report on Carcinogens*, 13th ed. Research Triangle Park, NC: U.S. Department of Health and Human Services, Public Health Service, 2014.

Needleman, H. L. "The Removal of Lead from Gasoline: Historical and Personal Reflections." *Environmental Research* 84 (2000): 20–35.

Needleman, H. L., C. Gunnoe, A. Leviton, R. Reed, H. Peresie, C. Maher, and P. Barrett. "Deficits in Psychologic and Classroom Performance of Children with Elevated Dentine Lead Levels." *New England Journal of Medicine* 300, no. 13 (1979): 689–95.

Nevin, R. "How Lead Exposure Relates to Temporal Changes in IQ, Violent Crime, and Unwed Pregnancy." *Environmental Research* 83 (2000): 1–22.

———. "Understanding International Crime Trends: The Legacy of Preschool Lead Exposure." *Environmental Research* 104, no. 3 (2007): 315–36.

Newman, P. A., et al. "What Would Have Happened to the Ozone Layer If Chlorofluorocarbons (CFCs) Had Not Been Regulated?" *Atmospheric Chemistry and Physics* 9 (2009): 2113–28.

Newton, John. *The Journal of a Slave Trader (John Newton) 1750-1754*. Edited by Bernard Martin and Mark Spurrell. London: Epworth Press, 1962.

———. *Thoughts upon the African Slave Trade*. London: J. Buckland, 1788. https://archive.org/details/thoughtsuponafri00newt/page/n4

Nickerson, Raymond S. "Confirmation Bias: A Ubiquitous Phenomenon in Many Guises." *Review of General Psychology* 2, no. 2 (1998): 175–220.

Norris, Robert. *Memoirs of the Reign of Bossa Ahadee, King of Dahomy . . . and a Short Account of the African Slave Trade*. London: W. Lowndes, 1789.

Nriagu, Jerome. "Clair Patterson and Robert Kehoe's Paradigm of 'Show Me the Data' on Environmental Lead Poisoning." *Environmental Research* 78, no. 2(1998): 71–78.

———. "The Rise and Fall of Leaded Gasoline." *Science of the Total Environment* 92 (1990): 13–28.

O'Connell, Jeffrey, and Arthur Myers. *Safety Last: An Indictment of the Auto Industry.* New York: Random House, 1966.

Open Science Collaboration. "Estimating the Reproducibility of Psychological Science," *Science* 349, no. 6251 (2015): 943.

Oreskes, Naomi, and Erik Conway. *Merchants of Doubt: How a Handful of Scientists Obscured the Truth on Issues from Tobacco Smoke to Global Warming.* New York: Bloomsbury Press, 2010.

Parliament. *Parliamentary History of England from the Earliest Period to the Year 1803,* vol. 28. London: Hansard, 1789. https://catalog.hathitrust.org/Record/100884619.

Parliament, House of Commons. *An Abstract of the Evidence Delivered before a Select Committee of the House of Commons, in the Years 1790 and 1791, on the Part of the Petitioners for the Abolition of the Slave Trade.* Edinburgh, 1791. https://archive.org/details /abstractofeviden00grea.

Parrish, Steven C. "Bridging the Divide: A Shared Interest in a Coherent National Tobacco Policy." *Yale Journal of Health Policy, Law, and Ethics* 3, no. 1 (2003): 109–17.

Parson, Edward A. *Protecting the Ozone Layer: Science and Strategy.* New York: Oxford University Press, 2003.

Pollay, Richard W. "Propaganda, Puffing, and the Public Interest: The Scientific Smoke Screen for Cigarettes." *Public Relations Review* 16, no. 3(1990): 39–54.

Pollitt, Ronald. "John Hawkins's Troublesome Voyages: Merchants, Bureaucrats, and the Origin of the Slave Trade." *Journal of British Studies* 12, no. 2 (1973): 26–40.

Pool, G.J., W. Wood, and K. Leck. "The Self-Esteem Motive in Social Influence: Agreement with Valued Majorities and Disagreement with Derogated Minorities." *Journal of Personality and Social Psychology* 75, no. 4 (1998): 967–75.

Pronin, Emily, Thomas Gilovich, and Lee Ross. "Objectivity in the Eye of the Beholder: Divergent Perceptions of Bias in Self Versus Others." *Psychological Review* 111, no. 3 (2004): 781–99.

Pulford, B.D., A.M. Colman, E.K. Buabang, and E.V. Krockow. "The Persuasive Power of Knowledge: Testing the Confidence Heuristic." *Journal of Experimental Psychology: General* 147, no. 10 (2018): 1431–44.

Rampton, Sheldon, and John Stauber. *Trust Us, We're Experts: How Industry Manipulates Science and Gambles with Your Future.* New York: Penguin Putnam, 2002.

Rand, Ayn. *Atlas Shrugged.* New York: Penguin, 1996. First published 1957.

———. *The Virtue of Selfishness: A New Concept of Egoism.* New York: Signet, 1964.

Raymond, Jaime, Will Wheeler, and Mary Jean Brown. "Lead Screening and Prevalence of Blood Lead Levels in Children Aged 1–2 Years." *Morbidity and Mortality Weekly Report* 63, no. 2 (2014): 36–42.

Rediker, Marcus. *The Slave Ship: A Human History.* New York: Penguin, 2007.

Reinhardt, Forest L. and Richard H.K. Vietor. "Du Pont Freon Products Division (A) and (B)." Harvard Business School Teaching Note, September 1993.

Rentetzi, Maria. "The U.S. Radium Industry: Industrial In-House Research and the Commercialization of Science" *Minerva* 46, no. 4 (2008): 437–62.

Renwick Sergent, Michael. *An Address to the Inhabitants in General of Great Britain, and Ireland; Relating to a Few of the Consequences Which Must Naturally Result from the Abolition of the Slave Trade.* Liverpool: Mrs. Egerton Smith, 1788. www.recoveredhistories .org/index.php.

Reyes, Jessica Wolpaw. *Environmental Policy as Social Policy? The Impact of Childhood Lead Exposure on Crime.* NBER Working Paper, no. 13097, (2007).

Roan, Sharon. *Ozone Crisis: The 15-Year Evolution of a Sudden Global Emergency.* New York: John Wiley and Sons, 1989.

Robbins, Norman, et al. "Childhood Lead Exposure and Uptake in Teeth in the Cleveland Area during the Era of Leaded Gasoline." *Science of the Total Environment* 408, no. 19 (2010): 4118–27.

Robert, Joseph. *Ethyl: A History of the Corporation and the People Who Made It.* Charlottesville: University Press of Virginia, 1983.

Rohrer, Doug, Harold Pashler, and Christine R. Harris. "Do Subtle Reminders of Money Change People's Political Views?" *Journal of Experimental Psychology: General* 144, no. 4 (2015): e73–85.

Rosner, David, and Gerald Markowitz. "A 'Gift of God'?: The Public Health Controversy over Leaded Gasoline during the 1920s." *American Journal of Public Health* 75, no. 4 (1985): 344–52.

———. "Standing Up to the Lead Industry: An Interview with Herbert Needleman." *Public Health Reports* 120 (June 2005): 330–37.

Ross, Lee. "The Intuitive Psychologist and His Shortcomings: Distortions in the Attribution Process." *Advances in Experimental Social Psychology* 10 (1977): 173–220.

Rowland, R. E. *Radium in Humans: A Review of U.S. Studies.* Argonne, IL: Argonne National Laboratory, 1994. https://publications.anl.gov/anlpubs/1994/11/16311.pdf.

Rubin, Zick, and Letitia Anne Peplau. "Who Believes in a Just World?" *Journal of Social Issues* 31, no. 3 (1975): 65–89.

Schimel, J., J. Greenberg, and A. Martens. "Evidence That Projection of a Feared Trait Can Serve a Defensive Function." *Personality and Social Psychology Bulletin* 29, no. 8 (2003): 969–79.

Schulman, Daniel. *Sons of Wichita: How the Koch Brothers Became America's Most Powerful and Private Dynasty.* New York: Grand Central, 2014.

Shyllon, Folarin. *James Ramsay: The Unknown Abolitionist.* Edinburgh: Canongate, 1977.

Slare, Frederick. *Experiments and Observations upon Oriental and Other Bezoar-Stones, . . . To Which Is Annexed a Vindication of Sugars against the Charge of Dr. Willis, Other Physicians, and Common Prejudices.* London: Tim Goodwin, 1715. https://archive.org /details/b30543733_0001/page/n5.

Slaughter, Aimee C. E. "Harnessing the Modern Miracle: Physicists, Physicians, and the Making of American Radium Therapy." PhD diss., University of Minnesota Digital Conservancy, 2013.

Sloan, Alfred P. Jr. *Adventures of a White-Collar Man.* New York: Doubleday, Doran, 1941.

———. *My Years with General Motors.* New York: Doubleday, 1963. Reprint, edited by John McDonald, with a new introduction by Peter Drucker. New York: Bantam Doubleday, 1990. Page references are to the 1990 edition.

Small, Deborah A., and George Loewenstein. "Helping a Victim or Helping the Victim: Altruism and Identifiability." *Journal of Risk and Uncertainty* 26, no. 1 (2003): 5–16.

Smith, Adam. *An Inquiry into the Nature and Causes of the Wealth of Nations.* 1776. Edited by R. H. Campbell and A. S. Skinner. New York: Oxford University Press, 1976. Reprint, Indianapolis: Liberty Fund, 1981. http://files.libertyfund.org/files/220/0141-02_Bk.pdf.

Solomon, Susan, et al. "Emergence of Healing in the Antarctic Ozone Layer." *Science* 353, no. 6296 (2016): 269–74.

Sorkin, Andrew Ross. *Too Big To Fail: The Inside Story of How Wall Street and Washington Fought to Save the Financial System—and Themselves.* New York: Penguin, 2009.

Steffen, W., et al. "Trajectories of the Earth System in the Anthropocene." *PNAS* 115, no. 33 (2018) 8252–59.

Stout, Lynn. *The Shareholder Value Myth: How Putting Shareholders First Harms Investors, Corporations, and the Public.* San Francisco: Berrett-Koehler, 2012.

Stradling, David. *Smokestacks and Progressives: Environmentalists, Engineers, and Air Quality in America, 1881–1951.* Baltimore: Johns Hopkins University Press, 1999.

Supran, Geoffrey and Naomi Oreskes. "Assessing ExxonMobil's Climate Change Communications (1977-2014)." *Environmental Research Letters* 12, no. 8 (2017).

Surgeon General. *The Health Consequences of Involuntary Smoking.* Washington, DC: US GPO, 1986. https://profiles.nlm.nih.gov/nn/b/c/p/m/.

———. *The Health Consequences of Smoking—50 Years of Progress.* Atlanta, GA: Centers for Disease Control and Prevention, 2014. www.ncbi.nlm.nih.gov/books/NBK179276/pdf/Bookshelf_NBK179276.pdf.

———. *The Health Consequences of Smoking: Nicotine Addiction.* Washington, DC: US GPO, 1988. https://profiles.nlm.nih.gov/NN/B/B/Z/D/.

———. *Smoking and Health: Report of the Advisory Committee to the Surgeon General of the Public Health Service.* Public Health Service Publication no. 1103. Washington, DC: US GPO, 1964. https://profiles.nlm.nih.gov/NN/B/B/M/Q/_/nnbbmq.pdf.

Swaminathan, Srividhya. "Developing the West Indian Proslavery Position After the Somerset Decision." *Slavery and Abolition* 24:3 (2003): 40-60.

Taubes, Gary. "The Ozone Backlash." *Science* 260, no. 5114 (1993): 1580-83.

Tett, Gillian. *Fool's Gold: How Unrestrained Greed Corrupted a Dream, Shattered Global Markets, and Unleashed a Catastrophe.* London: Little, Brown, 2009.

Thomas, Hugh. *The Slave Trade: The Story of the Atlantic Slave Trade: 1440-1870.* New York: Touchstone, 1997.

Thompson, Thomas. *The African Trade for Negro Slaves, Consistent with Humanity and Revealed Religion.* Canterbury: Simmons and Kirkby, 1772.

Tise, Larry E. *Proslavery: A History of the Defense of Slavery in America, 1701-1840.* Athens: University of Georgia Press, 1987.

Trivers, Robert. *The Folly of Fools: The Logic of Deceit and Self-Deception in Human Life.* New York: Basic Books, 2011.

Turnbull, Gordon. *An Apology for Negro Slavery: Or, the West-India Planters Vindicated from the Charge of Inhumanity.* London: Stuart and Stevenson, 1786.

Tversky, Amos, and Daniel Kahneman. "Judgment under Uncertainty: Heuristics and Biases." *Science* 185, no. 4157 (1974): 1124-31.

US Environmental Protection Agency (EPA). *Air Quality Criteria for Lead,* vol. 4. Washington, DC: EPA, 1986.

———. *Integrated Science Assessment for Lead.* Washington, DC: EPA, 2013.

———. *Regulatory Impact Analysis: Protection of Stratospheric Ozone,* vol. 1. No. 440R88003. Washington, DC: EPA, 1988.

———. *Updating Ozone Calculations and Emissions Profiles for Use in the Atmospheric and Health Effects Framework Model.* Washington, DC: EPA, 2015.

US Public Health Service. *Proceedings of a Conference to Determine Whether or Not There Is a Public Health Question in the Manufacture, Distribution, or Use of Tetraethyl Lead Gasoline.* Public Health Bulletin, no. 158. Washington, DC: US GPO, 1925.

Van Bavel, Jay, Dominic J. Packer, and William A. Cunningham. "The Neural Substrates of In-Group Bias: A Functional Magnetic Resonance Imaging Investigation." *Psychological Science* 19, no. 11 (2008): 1131-39.

Varki, Ajit, and Danny Brower. *Denial: Self-Deception, False Beliefs, and the Origins of the Human Mind.* New York: Hachette, 2013.

Vohs, Kathleen D. "Money Priming Can Change People's Thoughts, Feelings, Motivations, and Behaviors: An Update on 10 Years of Experiments." *Journal of Experimental Psychology: General* 144, no. 4 (2015): 86-93.

Vohs, Kathleen D., Nicole L. Mead, and Miranda R. Goode. "The Psychological Consequences of Money." *Science* 314, no. 5802 (2006): 1154-56.

Wallace, James. *A General and Descriptive History of the Ancient and Present State, of the Town of Liverpool.* Liverpool: R. Phillips, 1795. https://archive.org/details/generaldescripti00walliala/page/n5.

Walvin, James. *The Trader, the Owner, the Slave: Parallel Lives in the Age of Slavery*. London: Vintage Books, 2008.

Wang, Xijing, and Eva G. Krumhuber. "The Love of Money Results in Objectification." *British Journal of Social Psychology* 56, no. 2 (2017): 354–72.

Warneken, Felix, and Michael Tomasello. "The Roots of Human Altruism." *British Journal of Psychology* 100 (2009): 455–71.

Warren, Christian. *Brush with Death: A Social History of Lead Poisoning*. Baltimore: Johns Hopkins University Press, 2000.

Weiss, Gary. *Ayn Rand Nation*. New York: St. Martin's Press, 2012.

Welch, Robert. *The Politician: A Look at the Political Forces That Propelled Dwight David Eisenhower into the Presidency*. Appleton, WI: Robert Welch University Press, 2002.

Winkler, Adam. *We the Corporations: How American Businesses Won Their Civil Rights*. New York: Liveright, 2018.

Woodward, Fletcher D. "Medical Criticism of Modern Automotive Engineering." *JAMA* 138, no. 9 (1948): 627–31.

World Meteorological Organization Global Ozone Research and Monitoring. *Assessment for Decision-Makers: Scientific Assessment of Ozone Depletion: 2014*. Geneva: WMO, 2014.

Wynder, Ernest L., and Evarts A. Graham. "Tobacco Smoking as a Possible Etiologic Factor in Bronchiogenic Carcinoma." *JAMA* 143, no. 4 (1950): 329.

Wynder, Ernest L., Evarts A. Graham, and Adele B. Croninger. "Experimental Production of Carcinoma with Cigarette Tar." *Cancer Research* no. 36 (1953): 855–64.

Zweig, Jason. *Your Money and Your Brain: How the New Science of Neuroeconomics Can Help Make You Rich*. New York: Simon and Schuster, 2007.

Index